Microservices Communication in .NET Using gRPC

A practical guide for .NET developers to build efficient communication mechanism for distributed apps

Fiodar Sazanavets

Packt>

BIRMINGHAM—MUMBAI

Microservices Communication in .NET Using gRPC

Copyright © 2022 Packt Publishing

All rights reserved. No part of this book may be reproduced, stored in a retrieval system, or transmitted in any form or by any means, without the prior written permission of the publisher, except in the case of brief quotations embedded in critical articles or reviews.

Every effort has been made in the preparation of this book to ensure the accuracy of the information presented. However, the information contained in this book is sold without warranty, either express or implied. Neither the author(s), nor Packt Publishing or its dealers and distributors, will be held liable for any damages caused or alleged to have been caused directly or indirectly by this book.

Packt Publishing has endeavored to provide trademark information about all of the companies and products mentioned in this book by the appropriate use of capitals. However, Packt Publishing cannot guarantee the accuracy of this information.

Group Product Manager: Richa Tripathi
Publishing Product Manager: Sathya Mohan
Senior Editor: Rohit Singh
Content Development Editor: Kinnari Chohan
Technical Editor: Maran Fernandes
Copy Editor: Safis Editing
Project Coordinator: Deeksha Thakkar
Proofreader: Safis Editing
Indexer: Sejal Dsilva
Production Designer: Prashant Ghare
Marketing Coordinator: Sonakshi Bubbar

First published: January 2022
Production reference: 1050122

Published by Packt Publishing Ltd.
Livery Place
35 Livery Street
Birmingham
B3 2PB, UK.

ISBN 978-1-80323-643-8

www.packt.com

To my mother, Liliya Sazanavets, and to the memory of my father, Dzmirty Sazanavets, who sadly isn't with us anymore, for their sacrifices and for making me the person I am today. To my wife, Olga Sazanavets, who has always inspired and supported me in all of my endeavors.

– Fiodar Sazanavets

Contributors

About the author

Fiodar Sazanavets is an experienced lead software developer. His main areas of expertise are ASP.NET, SQL Server, Azure, Docker, Internet of Things, microservices architecture, and various frontend technologies.

Fiodar built his software engineering experience while working in a variety of industries, including water engineering, financial, railway, and defense. He has played a leading role in various projects and, as well as writing software, his duties have included performing architectural tasks.

Fiodar is passionate about teaching other people programming skills. He has published a number of programming courses on various online platforms. Fiodar regularly writes about software development on his personal website, `scientificprogrammer.net`.

I want to thank all the people who have supported and mentored me throughout my career, including Dikaios Papadogkonas, Vache Chek, Ian Turner, Paul Eccleston, Frank Lawrence, and all the other people I have worked or collaborated with.

About the reviewer

James Carter is a self-taught software developer located in the Midlands, UK. He is especially passionate about microservice-driven architectures and building large-scale cloud-based platforms. He is currently working at CSL Group doing just that – building a scalable IoT platform that will be capable of handling millions of devices.

In just 5 years of being a developer, James has developed a large range of skills in this area, from gRPC to Docker, building on solid expertise in Linux and Windows systems.

Besides developing software, James enjoys running and maintaining his home lab, comprising many servers and pieces of networking equipment, as well as spending time with his family and two cats, Oreo and Kitkat.

Table of Contents

Preface

Section 1: Basics of gRPC on .NET

1
Creating a Basic gRPC Application on ASP.NET Core

Technical requirements	4	Adding gRPC client components to the application	24
Introduction to gRPC	4	Applying gRPC client components to the code	27
gRPC on ASP.NET Core	6		
Using gRPC in your own distributed ASP.NET Core application	6	Understanding how proto files generate C# code	29
Preparing your system	6	Where is auto-generated code stored?	30
Setting up your environment on Windows	7	Modifying Protobuf namespaces	31
Setting up your environment on Mac	9	Sharing a proto file between the client and the server	34
Setting up your environment on Linux	10	Creating a shared class library	34
Downloading the .NET SDK (all operating systems)	11	Adding shared gRPC components to the class library	35
Setting up a gRPC server	11	Sharing gRPC dependencies between different projects	37
Initializing an ASP.NET Core project via an IDE	12	Running a gRPC service on Mac	39
Adding gRPC server components to an ASP.NET Core project	16	Configuring server-side components	39
Adding some code to use gRPC components	20	Modifying the client-side configuration	39
Setting up a gRPC client	22	Summary	40
Initializing the project for the client application	23	Questions	40
		Further reading	42

2
When gRPC Is the Best Tool and When It Isn't

Technical requirements	44	Testing asynchronous gRPC endpoints	72
Why gRPC is a great tool for microservices	44	Why gRPC is not the best tool for browsers	74
Setting up a solution and shared dependencies	45	Setting up a Blazor WebAssembly gRPC client	74
Setting up the status manager microservice	49	Modifying the gRPC server to enable gRPC-Web	79
Setting up a REST API gateway service	55	Launching the gRPC-Web application	80
Launching the distributed application	62	Where SignalR would beat gRPC	81
How gRPC can be a good tool for asynchronous communication	64	Setting up a SignalR application	81
		Adding a SignalR client and launching the application	83
Adding client-streaming and server-streaming gRPC endpoints	64	Summary	88
Configuring the gRPC client for asynchronous communication	68	Questions	89
		Further reading	90

3
Protobuf – the Communication Protocol of gRPC

Technical requirements	92	Using collections in Protobuf	109
The RPC types supported by gRPC	92	Repeated fields	109
		Map fields	111
The RPC types that Protobuf supports	93	Using special keywords in Protobuf	113
Making comments in Protobuf	95		
Reviewing the native Protobuf data types	95	How the oneof keyword can make communication more efficient	114
Integer data types	97	Customizing the behavior with the option keyword	117
Non-integer numeric types	101		
Non-numeric data types	102	Referencing other proto files	121
Enums	104	Importing external proto packages	121
Nested messages	106	Referencing internal proto files	122
		Using proto files as relays	124

Summary	125	Further reading	127
Questions	126		

Section 2: Best Practices of Using gRPC

4
Performance Best Practices for Using gRPC on .NET

Technical requirements	132	When streaming is better than individual calls	154
Why you need to reuse a gRPC channel	132	Setting up a bi-directional streaming RPC	155
Setting up the server application	133	Monitoring the performance of the bi-directional streaming call	158
Setting up the client application	137		
Comparing the performance of different client types	146	Using binary payloads to decrease the data's size	160
How to not get held up by a concurrent stream limit	149	Adding binary fields to Protobuf	160
Configuring connection concurrency on the gRPC client	149	Summary	164
Comparing the performance between a single connection and multiple connections	152	Questions	164
		Further reading	165
Ensuring that your connection remains alive	153		
Setting up keep-alive pings on the gRPC client	153		

5
Applying Versioning to the gRPC API

Technical requirements	168	Implementing the gRPC client logic	173
Why an API versioning strategy is important	168	Verifying that the client can talk to the server	174
Creating a server application	169	What the sequence numbers in the proto file represent	176
Implementing the server-side gRPC components	170	Modifying the Protobuf definition in the server application	177
Creating the gRPC client application	172		

Modifying the Protobuf definition in the client application	178	How to factor in API versioning at the design stage	190
Launching modified applications	179	Adding multiple Protobuf versions to the server application	191
Why you must not modify existing fields in future Protobuf versions	**181**	Allowing the server application to use multiple Protobuf versions	192
Modifying Protobuf definitions on the client side	183	Making the gRPC client implementation version-specific	194
Launching the applications	183	Making a gRPC call to a versioned endpoint	195
Making further changes to the client application	185	**Summary**	**196**
Re-launching the applications	186	**Questions**	**197**
How to deprecate old, unused fields in gRPC	**187**	**Further reading**	**198**
Applying the reserved keyword to the server-side Protobuf interface	187		
Testing the application	189		

6
Scaling a gRPC Application

Technical requirements	**200**	Enabling a DNS resolver for the load balancer	219
Introduction to load balancing	**200**	Using a static resolver for the load balancer	221
Adding shared gRPC dependencies	201	Creating custom load balancers and resolvers	224
Creating a shared library for server-side application instances	202		
Creating multiple instances of the server-side application	204	**Proxy load balancing with gRPC**	**230**
Creating a client application	205	Building a web application to act as a proxy	230
Running a load-balanced application	214	Launching the HTTP/2 proxy	233
Client-side load balancing with gRPC	**216**	**Summary**	**235**
Updating the NuGet package	216	**Questions**	**235**
Enabling client-side load balancing components	217	**Further reading**	**236**

Section 3: In-Depth Look at gRPC on .NET

7
Using Different Call Types Supported by gRPC

Technical requirements	242	server	269
Making unary calls on gRPC	242	Adding a server-streaming RPC to Protobuf	269
Setting up shared gRPC dependencies	243	Setting up a server-streaming call on the server side	270
Creating server-side implementations of the Protobuf definitions	245	Making a server-streaming call from a gRPC client	273
Building the gRPC client	251		
Applying different types of client-side call implementations	255	Enabling bi-directional streaming	274
Using gRPC dependencies in the client application	260	Enabling server-side components for bi-directional streaming	275
Testing different types of unary call endpoints	262	Adding a client-side implementation of a bi-directional streaming call	276
Streaming data from the client	265	Testing how to stream gRPC calls	278
Adding a client-streaming call to the server application	266	Summary	280
Adding client logic for a client-streaming gRPC call	267	Questions	281
		Further reading	282
Reading streams from the			

8
Using Well-Known Types to Make Protobuf More Handy

Technical requirements	284	Using dates and times in Protobuf	299
Using nullable types in Protobuf	285		
Setting up a gRPC server application	286	Adding timestamp and duration to the server	300
Examining auto-generated code for wrapper fields	287	Applying changes to the gRPC client and launching the app	301
Adding logic to gRPC server application	292		
Setting up shared dependencies	294	Exchanging empty messages	303
Setting up the gRPC client	296	Adding the Empty data type to the server-side application	303
Running the application	298	Applying an Empty object on the client	305

Using loosely typed fields in a Protobuf message	308	Summary	317
		Questions	317
Adding Any and Value data types to the gRPC server	308	Further reading	319
Populating the Any and Value fields from the gRPC client	313		

9
Securing gRPC Endpoints in Your ASP.NET Core Application with SSL/TLS

Technical requirements	322	Windows using PowerShell	341
Configuring the gRPC client and server for unencrypted communication	323	Creating a self-signed certificate on Unix using OpenSSL	344
		Applying a certificate on ASP.NET Core	345
The role of TLS certificates	323	Testing custom certificates and HTTPS redirection	348
Setting up a gRPC service application	325		
Removing TLS on both HTTP/1.1 and HTTP/2	329	Applying certificate authentication on the gRPC client and server	351
Exposing Protobuf definitions to clients	330		
Building the client for gRPC communication	333	Configuring the gRPC server for certificate authentication	352
Adding the remaining client logic	336	Enabling certificate authentication on the gRPC client	355
Creating and trusting a self-signed certificate	339	Testing certificate authentication	356
The basics of a TLS certificate	339	Summary	358
Trusting a default development certificate	340	Questions	358
Creating a self-signed certificate on		Further reading	359

10
Applying Authentication and Authorization to gRPC Endpoints

Technical requirements	362	Configuring IdentityServer4	366
Setting up the authentication backend	363	Adding SSO users, roles, and clients	369
		Forcing login redirect on a web application	372
OpenID Connect and OAuth flow	364		

Restricting gRPC endpoints to authenticated users	378	Applying different authorization rules to different gRPC endpoints	395
Setting up shared gRPC dependencies	378	Applying gRPC client changes	397
Setting up the gRPC server	380	Summary	401
Enabling gRPC client functionality	386	Questions	401
Restricting endpoints to authorized users only	391	Further reading	403
Configuring SSO provider to insert role claim into the JWT	392		

11

Using Logging, Metrics, and Debugging in gRPC on .NET

Technical requirements	406	Applying logs to gRPC	429
Debugging gRPC client components inside a .NET application	407	Configuring a logger on the gRPC client	430
		Applying a logger on the gRPC server	433
		Testing our log output	435
Setting up shared gRPC dependencies	407	Applying metrics to gRPC	438
Adding a gRPC service application and getting it to display detailed errors	409	Configuring metrics on the gRPC server	439
Adding a gRPC client with additional debugging capabilities	413	Enabling metric collection on the gRPC client	440
Viewing gRPC error information on the client	421	Viewing gRPC metrics	442
Debugging gRPC server components inside a .NET application	423	Summary	444
		Questions	445
		Further reading	446
Viewing the debug output on the gRPC server console	427		

Assessments

Index

Other Books You May Enjoy

Preface

This book explains how to use all the fundamental components of gRPC on .NET. As well as covering the core technical functionality of gRPC, this book also explains the best practices of using it.

gRPC is an efficient mechanism of communication over the web that was originally developed by Google. It has now been accepted as one of the web standards. As it runs over HTTP/2, it is much faster than the standard HTTP communication. gRPC is especially suitable for facilitating direct communication between microservices inside a distributed application.

RPC stands for **remote procedure call**, so applying it in the code to call endpoints on a remote server is just as easy as calling functions and methods inside an application. gRPC is standardized, so it's possible to find a suitable implementation of it in any modern programming language. Your distributed application does not have to have every component written in the same language. All services will still work together, regardless of which language they are written in.

Developers working with .NET will be able to put their knowledge to work with this practical guide to using gRPC. This book provides a hands-on approach to the implementation and the associated methodologies and will have you up and running and productive in no time. You'll start with the fundamentals of gRPC and how to use it inside .NET apps. Along with learning technical details, you'll explore best practices for performance and more. Next, you'll focus on scaling a gRPC app. Finally, you'll use different call types that gRPC supports and apply authentication and authorization to gRPC endpoints.

By the end of this book, you will be able to use gRPC in .NET applications to enable direct communication between microservices.

Who this book is for

.NET developers who work with microservices and are looking for efficient solutions to facilitate communication between the services will find this book useful. Anyone who knows the fundamentals of .NET Core, is somewhat familiar with the microservices architecture, but doesn't necessarily know anything about gRPC should be able to consume the content of the book.

What this book covers

Chapter 1, Creating a Basic gRPC Application on ASP.NET Core, explains how to build a basic ASP.NET Core server application that uses gRPC. We will also build a basic console application that will act as a gRPC client.

Chapter 2, When gRPC Is the Best Tool and When It Isn't, outlines use cases where gRPC is the best tool for the job. It will also cover some scenarios where other tools would be more suitable than gRPC.

Chapter 3, Protobuf – the Communication Protocol of gRPC, takes you through the structure of Protobuf – the communication protocol that gRPC uses. You will be shown the basic structure of a proto file – a file that defines the interface that both the client and the server use to communicate with each other. All native data types available with Protobuf will be covered, along with other structural components of the protocol.

Chapter 4, Performance Best Practices of Using gRPC on .NET, explains how to apply gRPC inside the code in the most efficient way possible. You will learn a few ways to make your gRPC communication as fast as it can be.

Chapter 5, How to Apply Versioning to the gRPC API, emphasizes the importance of applying a good versioning strategy to your server-side gRPC endpoints, also known as **application programming interfaces** (**APIs**). You will also learn some techniques for making API versioning easy.

Chapter 6, Scaling a gRPC Application, explains how microservices are supposed to be designed in such a way that they can easily be scaled. An assumption of microservices architecture is that it should be possible to add new instances of any given microservices when needed, especially when they are stateless. As gRPC has been primarily designed to enable communication between microservices, it needs to be scalable too.

Chapter 7, Using All Different Call Types That gRPC Supports, covers the four different types of calls – unary, client-streaming, server-streaming, and bi-directional streaming – that gRPC supports.

Chapter 8, *Using Well-Known Types to Make Protobuf More Handy*, explains that since native Protobuf data types don't perfectly map to data types commonly used in programming languages, Google has created a library of so-called well-known types to make this process easier. This enables developers to send requests without payloads, use nullable fields, work with dates, and exchange loosely-typed payloads.

Chapter 9, *Securing gRPC Endpoints in Your ASP.NET Core Application with SSL/TLS*, explains that just like any standard HTTP endpoint, gRPC endpoints can be secured with SSL or TLS encryption and made accessible via the HTTPS protocol. This chapter will show you how to enable this encryption and protocol.

Chapter 10, *Applying Authentication and Authorization to gRPC Endpoints*, explains that, if needed, gRPC endpoints can be made accessible only to authenticated users or users with specific permissions. This chapter shows how to enable this functionality for gRPC endpoints on .NET.

Chapter 11, *Using Logging, Metrics, and Debugging in gRPC on .NET*, explains that it's important to be able to identify problems with an application while it is being developed. It's also important to monitor what the application is doing once it's been deployed. This chapter shows how to do all of these things. You will learn how to debug an application that's under development and how to use logging and metrics inside an application that has already been deployed.

To get the most out of this book

You need to be somewhat familiar with C#, the .NET platform, ASP.NET Core, and web development in general. You need to have a suitable IDE or code editor installed on your machine. However, if you don't have one installed, instructions on how to do so will be provided in the first chapter.

Software/hardware covered in the book	Operating system requirements
gRPC	Windows, macOS, or Linux
gRPC client and server functionality on .NET 5 and 6	Windows, macOS, or Linux
TLS/SSL	Windows, macOS, or Linux
OpenID Connect and OAuth	Windows, macOS, or Linux

If you are using the digital version of this book, we advise you to type the code yourself or access the code from the book's GitHub repository (a link is available in the next section). Doing so will help you avoid any potential errors related to the copying and pasting of code.

Please note that there will be some differences between .NET 5 and .NET 6 implementations. However, where they are present, the text will mention it.

Also, some of the functionality described in the book will not work on macOS due to the absence of some fundamental features on the OS. However, when such cases occur, clear workaround instructions will be provided.

The book assumes that the reader is already somewhat familiar with ASP.NET Core and C#. These concepts are outside the scope of the book.

Download the example code files

You can download the example code files for this book from GitHub at `https://github.com/PacktPublishing/Microservices-Communication-in-.NET-Using-gRPC`. If there's an update to the code, it will be updated in the GitHub repository.

We also have other code bundles from our rich catalog of books and videos available at `https://github.com/PacktPublishing/`. Check them out!

Code in Action

The Code in Action videos for this book can be viewed at `https://bit.ly/31XSruD`.

Download the color images

We also provide a PDF file that has color images of the screenshots and diagrams used in this book. You can download it here: `https://static.packt-cdn.com/downloads/9781803236438_ColorImages.pdf`.

Conventions used

There are a number of text conventions used throughout this book.

`Code in text`: Indicates code words in text, database table names, folder names, filenames, file extensions, pathnames, dummy URLs, user input, and Twitter handles. Here is an example: "This class library project will be called `GrpcDependencies`."

A block of code is set as follows:

```
enum ClientStatus {
  OFFLINE = 0;
  ONLINE = 1;
  BUSY = 2;
}
```

Any command-line input or output is written as follows:

```
dotnet add GrpcBlazorClient.csproj package Grpc.Net.Client
dotnet add GrpcBlazorClient.csproj package Google.Protobuf
dotnet add GrpcBlazorClient.csproj package Grpc.Tools
dotnet add GrpcBlazorClient.csproj package Grpc.Net.Client.Web
```

> **Tips or Important Notes**
> Appear like this.

Get in touch

Feedback from our readers is always welcome.

General feedback: If you have questions about any aspect of this book, email us at customercare@packtpub.com and mention the book title in the subject of your message.

Errata: Although we have taken every care to ensure the accuracy of our content, mistakes do happen. If you have found a mistake in this book, we would be grateful if you would report this to us. Please visit www.packtpub.com/support/errata and fill in the form.

Piracy: If you come across any illegal copies of our works in any form on the internet, we would be grateful if you would provide us with the location address or website name. Please contact us at copyright@packt.com with a link to the material.

If you are interested in becoming an author: If there is a topic that you have expertise in and you are interested in either writing or contributing to a book, please visit authors.packtpub.com.

Share Your Thoughts

Once you've read *Microservices Communication in .NET Using gRPC*, we'd love to hear your thoughts! Scan the QR code below to go straight to the Amazon review page for this book and share your feedback.

https://packt.link/r/1-803-23643-4

Your review is important to us and the tech community and will help us make sure we're delivering excellent quality content.

Section 1: Basics of gRPC on .NET

This part teaches how to build a basic .NET application that uses gRPC. The chapters cover the most fundamental parts of gRPC functionality. After completing this part, you will know how to enable gRPC inside an ASP.NET Core application and how to connect to it from external applications. This part contains the following chapters:

- *Chapter 1, Creating a Basic gRPC Application on ASP.NET Core*
- *Chapter 2, When gRPC Is the Best Tool and When It Isn't*
- *Chapter 3, Protobuf – the Communication Protocol of gRPC*

1
Creating a Basic gRPC Application on ASP.NET Core

In this chapter, we will learn how to build a basic ASP.NET Core server application that uses gRPC. We will also build a basic console application that will act as a gRPC client.

The main objectives of this chapter are to introduce you to gRPC and to show you how easy it is to set up and use as a communication mechanism between separate services inside a distributed application. This would especially be relevant in a microservice architecture, where many different services act as one application with many moving components. You will see that using gRPC for communication between separate applications is almost as easy as calling methods inside the same application.

In this chapter, we will cover the following topics:

- Introduction to gRPC
- Preparing your system
- Setting up a gRPC server
- Setting up a gRPC client

- Understanding how Proto files generate C# code
- Sharing a Proto file between the client and the server
- Running a gRPC service on Mac

By the end of this chapter, you will have learned how to set up all the fundamental gRPC components on .NET and how to use them on both the client and server side. You will have also learned how to efficiently share protocol definitions between the client and the server.

Technical requirements

To follow the instructions in this chapter, you will need the following:

- A computer with either Windows, Mac, or Linux installed
- A supported IDE or code editor (Visual Studio, Visual Studio Code, or JetBrains Rider)
- .NET 5 SDK

The instructions for how to set up an SDK and IDE/code editor will be provided later in this chapter for all the supported operating systems. The code files for this chapter are available on GitHub at `https://github.com/PacktPublishing/Microservices-Communication-in-.NET-Using-gRPC/tree/main/Chapter-01`.

Please visit the following link to check the CiA videos: `https://bit.ly/3dQ78eM`

Introduction to gRPC

gRPC is a communication mechanism that was first introduced by Google, primarily to enable self-contained components within a distributed application, such as microservices, to communicate with each other easily. It was first made publicly available in 2016. Since then, it has been widely adopted by developers. Official libraries for it were written in the most popular programming languages.

gRPC stands for **Google Remote Procedure Call**. And, as the name suggests, its primary intention is to enable separate applications to call procedures inside each other's code remotely via the network.

Inside a single application, you would define your callable components (procedures, functions, or methods, depending on the language). By doing that, you can call them from any place within the same application. This means that you call the components of third-party libraries that you import into your application as they become part of your application once imported. But with an RPC mechanism in place, the code that calls your callable components doesn't have to be inside the same application as those components. So long as separate applications are hosted on the same network, they can be set up to call each other's endpoints in the code.

gRPC just happens to be the most widely adopted RPC mechanism. As well as being easy to set up compared to the alternatives, it's also very fast. Its communication protocol, known as **Protocol Buffer**, or **Protobuf**, enables very efficient message serialization while messages are in transit.

On top of this, gRPC runs on HTTP/2, which has many performance benefits over its predecessor, HTTP/1.1. Some of those benefits include multiplexing (working with multiple streams of data in a single request), header compression (which reduces message size), and server push (which enables messages to be sent from the server to a connected client without an explicit response from the client). gRPC utilizes these features, but it requires HTTP/2 protocol to be enabled on the network it's running on.

The key benefits of gRPC include the following:

- Highly performant due to the utilization of HTTP/2 features and a lightweight messaging mechanism.
- Multiple connection options instead of just a standard request/response mechanism available with bare HTTP.
- Easy and intuitive to set up with built-in code generators.
- Easy to write code against due to it having a strongly typed API schema that was designed to be highly readable.
- Widely adopted by developers with many existing libraries and code samples available.
- It is the de facto standard mechanism for direct communication between microservices.
- Official implementations are available on most of the popular programming languages and frameworks.
- Can enable communication between applications written in different languages.
- Has an in-built mechanism for hassle-free API versioning.

gRPC on ASP.NET Core

While gRPC has been publicly available since 2016, until 2019, it was only available on ASP.NET Core via third-party libraries, such as the Grpc.Core NuGet package. But with the release of ASP.NET Core 3.0, it was made available as one of the core components of the framework itself.

This has significantly simplified the process of setting up gRPC inside ASP.NET Core applications. As well as there being less boilerplate code to write, there is now better integration between gRPC and the .NET runtime, which improves the stability of the application.

On top of this, there are now pre-defined project templates available in Visual Studio IDE and the dotnet CLI (command-line interface) environment to allow you to initialize your projects with gRPC components that have already been enabled.

gRPC, along with existing features of ASP.NET Core, made it incredibly easy to build distributed applications by using a microservice architecture. The standard gRPC components are very easy to add to your application and the standard .NET build process will auto-generate all the relevant code for you.

As well as this, proto files, which, in gRPC, are used to define communication contracts, can be shared between the client and the server applications by using the standard library referencing mechanism of .NET, so the same proto file doesn't have to be duplicated in a separate project. Proto files can be stored in a reference library that both the client and the server applications use. Then, both of them can be updated simultaneously with the same copy of the communication contract so that no mismatches or incompatibility will accidentally be introduced.

Using gRPC in your own distributed ASP.NET Core application

We will start with the most fundamental part – step-by-step instructions on how to set up an ASP.NET Core application as a gRPC server and how to set up a .NET client that can talk to it.

Preparing your system

To be able to use gRPC on ASP.NET Core, you will need an **integrated development environment** (**IDE**) or a code editor that has full .NET support. You will also need the latest **software development kit** (**SDK**) version of .NET, which, at the time of writing, is .NET 5.

Other than these components, you don't need anything else to start developing a gRPC application for .NET. It's already included in the framework. And whenever you need an add-on library, you will be instructed on how to obtain it.

Because .NET is an OS-independent framework, you can write applications for it on either Windows, Mac, or Linux. However, your setup steps will be slightly different, so please follow the section that is relevant to your system.

Setting up your environment on Windows

On Windows, you have three main options regarding an IDE for .NET. They are listed here in order of preference, based on how many features they have and how easy they are to use:

- JetBrains Rider
- Microsoft Visual Studio
- Visual Studio Code

Rider is a fully functioning IDE. Compared to the other options, it has many additional tools. It's also easier to optimize and configure.

The downside of Rider is that it's only available as a paid-for premium, although a 30-day free trial is available for new users.

To download Rider, navigate to `https://www.jetbrains.com/rider/download/` and follow the setup instructions provided:

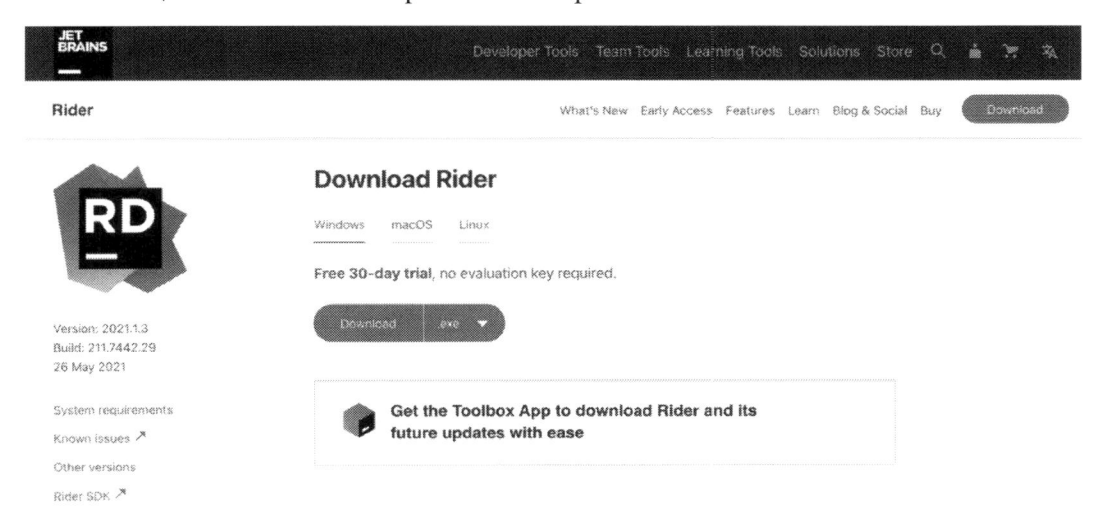

Figure 1.1 – JetBrains Rider download page

Alternatively, you can download Visual Studio. It's the official IDE for .NET from Microsoft. And, unlike Rider, it has a free tier version known as Community Edition.

To download the latest version of Visual Studio (Visual Studio 2019, at the time of writing), go to `https://visualstudio.microsoft.com/downloads/`:

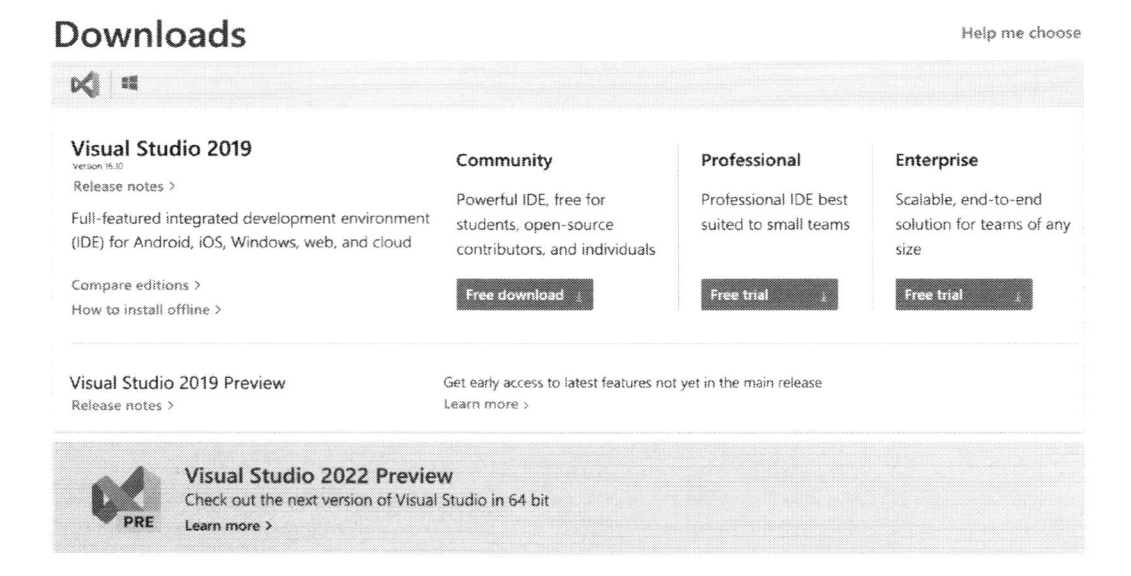

Figure 1.2 – Microsoft Visual Studio download page

Lastly, there is Visual Studio Code, which, despite sounding similar to Visual Studio, is a completely different product. While Visual Studio is a fully-fledged IDE, Visual Studio Code is merely a code editor.

However, despite being just a code editor, it's still a powerful tool that you can develop your code in. And it's highly configurable, so you will be able to use it to write code in many different languages, not just the ones that are specific to .NET.

The advantage of Visual Studio Code over either Visual Studio or Rider is that it's lightning-fast. Because it's just an editor that lacks many tools that IDEs have, it has far fewer things to load and run in the background.

The disadvantage of using Visual Studio Code over either Visual Studio or Rider is that, as a code editor, it lacks some basic features that are typically embedded into an IDE. For example, you will not be able to compile your project without integrating the editor with some add-on tool or using the CLI.

Visual Studio Code can be obtained via `https://code.visualstudio.com/download`:

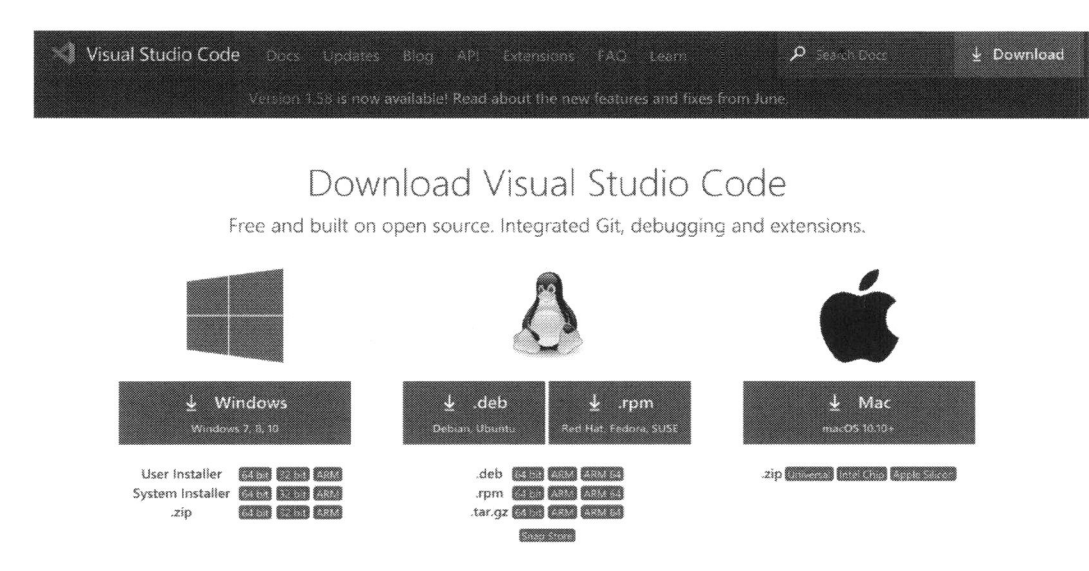

Figure 1.3 – Visual Studio Code download page

Once you have downloaded your preferred IDE, you can proceed with its installation.

Setting up your environment on Mac

On Mac, you have three main options regarding an IDE for .NET. They are listed here in their order of preference, based on how many features they have and how easy they are to use:

- JetBrains Rider
- Microsoft Visual Studio for Mac
- Visual Studio Code

Rider is a fully functioning IDE. Compared to the alternative options, it has many additional tools. It's also easier to optimize and configure.

The downside of Rider is that it's only available as a paid-for premium, although a 30-day free trial is available for new users.

To download Rider, navigate to `https://www.jetbrains.com/rider/download/` and follow the setup instructions provided.

Alternatively, you can download Visual Studio for Mac. It's the official IDE for .NET from Microsoft. And, unlike Rider, it can be downloaded for free.

To download the latest version of Visual Studio for Mac, go to `https://visualstudio.microsoft.com/vs/mac`.

Lastly, there is Visual Studio Code, which, despite sounding similar to Visual Studio for Mac, is a completely different product. While Visual Studio for Mac is a fully-fledged IDE, Visual Studio Code is merely a code editor.

However, despite being just a code editor, it's still a powerful tool for developing your code. And it's highly configurable, so you will be able to use it to write code in many different languages, not just the ones that are specific to .NET.

The advantage of Visual Studio Code over either Visual Studio for Mac or Rider is that it's lightning-fast. Because it's just an editor that lacks many tools that IDEs have, it has far fewer things to load and run in the background.

The disadvantage of using Visual Studio Code over either Visual Studio for Mac or Rider is that, as a code editor, it lacks some basic features that are embedded into an IDE. For example, you will not be able to compile your project without integrating the editor with some add-on tool or using the CLI.

Visual Studio Code can be obtained via `https://code.visualstudio.com/download`.

Setting up your environment on Linux

On Linux, you have two main options regarding an IDE for .NET. They are listed here in their order of preference, based on how many features they have and how easy they are to use:

- JetBrains Rider
- Visual Studio Code

Rider is a fully functioning IDE. Compared to the alternative options, it has many additional tools. It's also easier to optimize and configure.

The downside of Rider is that it's only available as a paid-for premium, although a 30-day free trial is available for new users.

To download Rider, navigate to `https://www.jetbrains.com/rider/download/` and follow the setup instructions provided.

Lastly, there is Visual Studio Code, which is a highly configurable code editor, so you will be able to use it to write code in many different languages, not just the ones that are specific to .NET.

The advantage of Visual Studio Code over Rider is that it's lightning-fast. Because it's just an editor that lacks many tools that IDEs have, it has far fewer things to load and run in the background.

The disadvantage of using Visual Studio Code over Rider is that, as a code editor, it lacks some basic features that are embedded into an IDE. For example, you will not be able to compile your project without integrating the editor without some add-on tool or using the CLI.

Visual Studio Code can be obtained via `https://code.visualstudio.com/download`.

With this, our IDE setup is complete.

Downloading the .NET SDK (all operating systems)

Lastly, to write .NET applications, you will need to download the .NET platform.

There are two versions of it: runtime and SDK. As a developer, you will need the SDK. The runtime is only suitable for running .NET applications that have already been compiled; it cannot be used to write application code and compile applications.

The .NET SDK can be obtained via the following link. Please use the latest full release version. Further instructions are available at `https://dotnet.microsoft.com/download/dotnet`.

Now that your environment has been set up, you can start building an ASP.NET Core application with basic gRPC capabilities.

Setting up a gRPC server

Now that your environment has been set up, you are ready to create your gRPC server application.

There are several ways to proceed. Regardless of whether you've chosen to use the IDE or CLI, you will be able to use the gRPC project template to initialize your application code, with all the gRPC capabilities already pre-defined. However, in real-life scenarios, you may want to add gRPC capabilities to an existing hosted web service. Therefore, we will go through the process of creating a bare-bones ASP.NET Core application and then add gRPC capabilities to it.

Initializing an ASP.NET Core project via an IDE

If you are using an IDE (Rider, Visual Studio, or Visual Studio for Mac), the process of initializing a new ASP.NET Core project is the same. When you launch the IDE, you will be presented with the option to create a new project. Click on this option and, from the list of templates, choose **Web App**.

This template will be called slightly differently, depending on what IDE you are using. For example, on Visual Studio for Windows, multiple templates represent an ASP.NET Core web application. For this project, any of them would be suitable. However, since you will only be using basic ASP.NET Core features, you should choose the most basic template. On the Windows version of Visual Studio, it is called **ASP.NET Core Web App**:

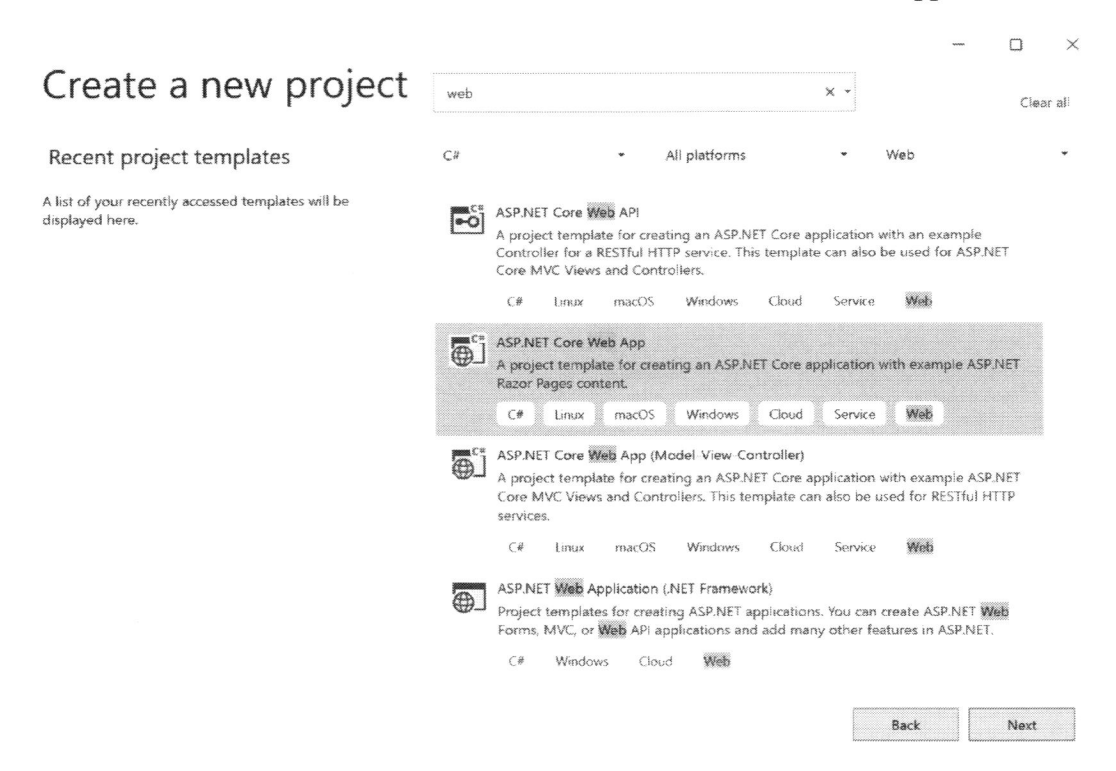

Figure 1.4 – Web App project template in Visual Studio 2019

JetBrains Rider will have a similar project template name with some variations, depending on the version. However, if you are using Visual Studio for Mac, the project template that you need will be called **Web Application**:

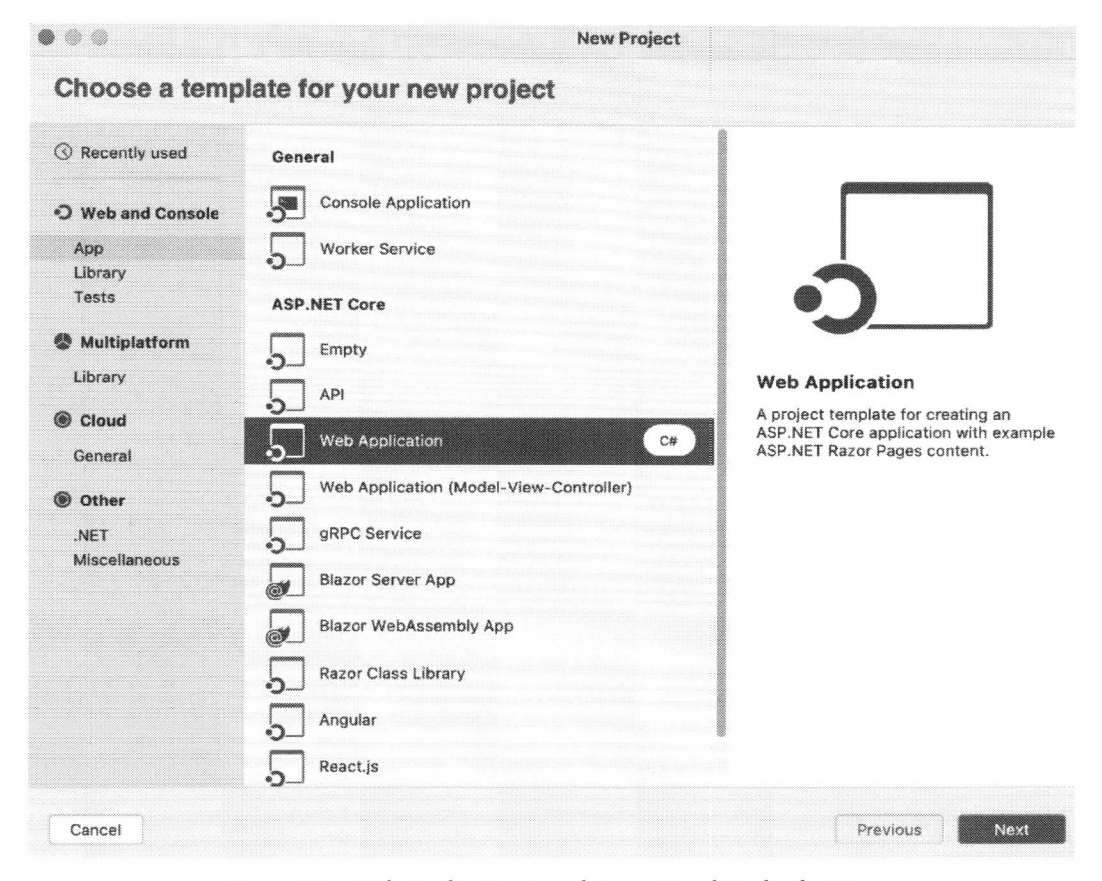

Figure 1.5 – Web Application template on Visual Studio for Mac

Once you select the template, you will be asked for the project's name. I have called mine `BasicGrpcService`. You can give yours any name, but for the convenience of following the instructions, you should give your project the same name:

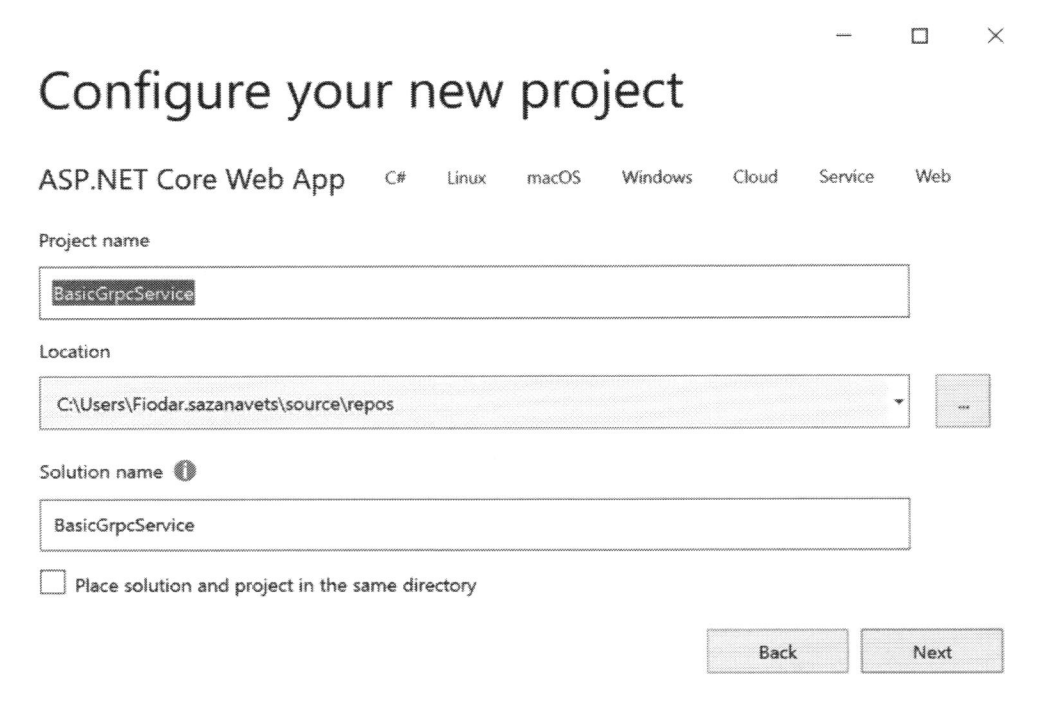

Figure 1.6 – Naming your project

When you're asked which framework version you would like to use, select the latest one, which, at the time of writing, is .NET 5.

Also, if you are asked for the authentication type, select **None**. If you have the **Configure for HTTPS** option, make sure that it's selected. Leave the remaining settings as-is and click on **Create**:

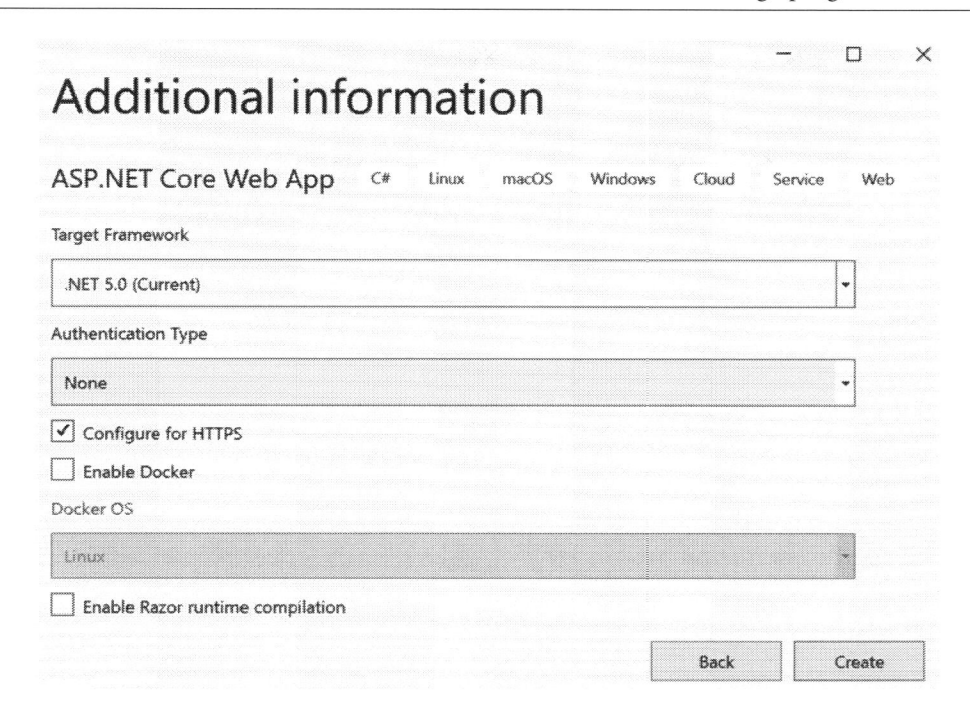

Figure 1.7 – Runtime selection and ensuring HTTPS is enabled

At this point, a solution should have been created with an ASP.NET Core project inside it.

Initializing an ASP.NET Core project via the dotnet CLI

If you don't have access to an IDE or if you prefer to work with the command line, you can create the project via the dotnet CLI, which will be available on any system that has the .NET 5 SDK installed. To do so, navigate to the folder that you want to place your project in and execute the following command:

```
dotnet new webapp -o BasicGrpcService
```

Finally, since you have selected to enable HTTPS (which is recommended for gRPC), you will need to install and trust the development HTTPS certificate for .NET.

If you are using a Mac, then you will not be able to configure the HTTPS on gRPC endpoints, so you will need to enable HTTP too. The instructions on how to do so are available in the *Running a gRPC service on Mac* section.

If you are using an IDE, such as Visual Studio or Rider, the process of installing and trusting the development certificate will happen automatically. You will receive a prompt when you launch your application via the IDE for the first time. Otherwise, you can configure the certificate via a CLI command.

To do so on Windows or Mac, you can execute the following command inside your project folder:

```
dotnet dev-certs https --trust
```

On Linux, this command may not work, as different Linux distributions have completely different mechanisms for trusting self-signed HTTPS certificates. If you are using Linux, you will need to obtain this information from the documentation that's specific to the distribution you are using.

Congratulations! You now have a functioning ASP.NET Core application that you can start adding gRPC server components to.

Adding gRPC server components to an ASP.NET Core project

Because you have initially chosen a basic ASP.NET Core application template, your project file (`BasicGrpcService.csproj`) should only contain the most basic markup, such as this:

```xml
<Project Sdk="Microsoft.NET.Sdk.Web">
    <PropertyGroup>
        <TargetFramework>net5.0</TargetFramework>
    </PropertyGroup>
</Project>
```

Now, we will need to modify it to add gRPC components. First, we will run the following command from the project folder to install the required NuGet package:

```
dotnet add BasicGrpcService.csproj package Grpc.AspNetCore
```

Here, we have added a NuGet package reference to the `Grpc.AspNetCore` library. This library adds all the necessary components to enable gRPC inside an ASP.NET Core application.

There is also another element that you may not be familiar with if you haven't used gRPC inside an ASP.NET Core application before. It's called `Protobuf` and its role is to tell the application which protocol buffer files are available for writing code against. This element will ensure that the right code snippets are generated inside your application.

You will need to add the following markup snippet to the `BasicGrpcService.csproj` file to enable this:

```xml
<ItemGroup>
  <Protobuf Include="Protos\greeter.proto"
    GrpcServices="Server" />
</ItemGroup>
```

Your file will look similar to this:

```xml
<Project Sdk="Microsoft.NET.Sdk.Web">
  <PropertyGroup>
    <TargetFramework>net5.0</TargetFramework>
  </PropertyGroup>
  <ItemGroup>
    <Protobuf Include="Protos\greeter.proto"
      GrpcServices="Server" />
  </ItemGroup>
  <ItemGroup>
    <PackageReference Include="Grpc.AspNetCore"
      Version="2.34.0" />
  </ItemGroup>
</Project>
```

Please note that the `Protobuf` element has the `GrpcServices` attribute set to `Server`. We've done this to tell our compiler that we only expect our application to act as a server while using the `greeter.proto` file from inside the `Protos` folder. This will ensure that only server-related classes will be generated by the compiler.

You can choose the `Client` role as well. In this case, it's only the client-side components that will be generated from our proto file. But since we are building the server-side application right now, it's certainly not the right role to choose.

Also, you can choose to omit the `GrpcServices` attribute completely. In this case, you will be able to generate both server-side and client-side components for your code.

Next, we will need to add a proto file that defines the communication mechanism between the client and the server. To do so, create a `Protos` folder inside your project folder and place the `greeter.proto` file inside it with the following content:

```
syntax = "proto3";

option csharp_namespace = "BasicGrpcService";

 package greeter;

// The greetings manager service definition.
service GreetingsManager {
  // Request the service to generate a greeting message.
  rpc GenerateGreeting (GreetingRequest) returns
    (GreetingResponse);
}

// The request message definition containing the name to be
   addressed in the greeting message.
message GreetingRequest {
  string name = 1;
}

// The response message definition containing the greeting
   text.
message GreetingResponse {
  string greetingMessage = 1;
}
```

This is a very bare-bones proto file. It's the equivalent of a *Hello World* application as it's only there to demonstrate the very basic functionality to a complete beginner.

We will cover the format of the proto file in more detail later. For now, let's go through the basics by using this example.

The first element is `syntax`. In our case, its value is set to `proto3`. There were several iterations of the gRPC communication protocol and the current one is the third iteration. Due to this, we have explicitly specified it here, as some applications may otherwise assume that this file represents an older version of the protocol.

Then, we have the `csharp_namespace` option. This option is specific to the C# language as it's the language that we will be working with. It tells our compiler what namespace it should use while generating classes based on these proto definitions. So, the server and client classes that are based on the `service` elements of the proto file will be under the namespace defined here.

Next, we have the `package` element. `package` in Protobuf is conceptually similar to C# namespaces, but it's intended for Protobuf rather than the code that gets generated from it. `package` allows one proto definition to reference other definitions, just like the C# class can reference external libraries by using namespaces.

Next, we have the `service` definition. A single proto file can have lots of these. But essentially, a single proto service represents a single client or server class in the code.

Inside the server, `rpc` definitions represent remotely called procedures, which are equivalent to C# methods. Each of those definitions has a unique name, a single message definition as its parameter (the request message), and a single message definition as its return object (the response message).

The RPC definition must always have a single request and a single response. You cannot have RPC without putting anything into the parameters or its return statement. Nor can you specify multiple message definitions in either of those places.

However, there are ways of sending or returning empty messages in gRPC calls. Even though a message definition must be specified, it doesn't need to have any fields.

Likewise, there are multiple ways of sending or receiving multiple messages. First, both the client and the server can stream messages, which will enable the system to send or receive multiple messages of the same schema rather than one. Also, each message can have other messages as data types in its fields. It can also use collections, which allows it to put multiple messages of the same kind into a single field.

Messages are defined by the `message` keyword in a proto file. The closest equivalent in C# is basic classes or structs that are used for data transfer.

Each message can have zero or any number of data fields. Each data field is defined by its data type (which we will cover in more detail in *Chapter 3, Protobuf – the Communication Protocol of gRPC*), unique name, and unique sequence number. For example, this is the only data field that we will use inside `GreetingRequest`:

```
string name = 1;
```

The sequence number at the end must start with 1 and be unique for each field. These sequence numbers simplify the process of API versioning in gRPC, which we will cover in more detail in *Chapter 3, Protobuf – the Communication Protocol of gRPC*.

Finally, our example contains multiple comments, which, just like in C#, start with //. They are completely ignored by the compiler.

Adding some code to use gRPC components

Now, we are ready to start modifying our application so that it can use the gRPC components that we have added.

First, you will need to create a `Services` folder inside your project folder. Then, we must add a file to it and name it `GreetingsManagerService.cs`. Then, we must put the following content into this file:

```
using System.Threading.Tasks;
using Grpc.Core;

namespace BasicGrpcService
{
    public class GreetingsManagerService :
        GreetingsManager.GreetingsManagerBase
    {
        public override Task<GreetingResponse>
            GenerateGreeting(GreetingRequest request,
            ServerCallContext context)
        {
            return Task.FromResult(new GreetingResponse
            {
                GreetingMessage = "Hello " + request.Name
            });
        }
    }
}
```

Please note that, at this stage, you may receive a compiler error. If you do, it will persist until you build the application. But don't worry about it for now.

This class represents the server-side logic that is defined by the `GreetingsManager` service, which we specified in the `greeter.proto` file. The basic code placeholders are auto-generated from the proto file and, in our case, are placed in the `GreetingsManager.GreetingsManagerBase` class, which our class extends. Then, we just need to override the methods from this class to apply our custom logic.

The override of the `GenerateGreeting` task is the representation of the `GenerateGreeting` RPC, which is defined inside the `GreetingsManagerer` service in the `greeter.proto` file. However, you may have noticed that it doesn't match the definition. Yes – as the proto file has specified, it accepts a parameter of the `GreetingRequest` type and returns an object of the `GreetingResponse` type. However, it also has an additional input parameter of the `ServerCallContext` type.

Well, this parameter is nothing but a collection of metadata that was populated by the client sending the request. It contains information such as the username and connection state. It plays a similar role to `HttpContext`, which is used by the HTTP endpoints (MVC, REST API, and so on) of ASP.NET Core.

This code is very simple. When a client calls this method, the `Name` property of the `GreetingRequest` input parameter is read. This value is inserted at the end of the `Hello` text. So, for example, if the name is John, the output would be `Hello John`. Then, this value is inserted into the `GreetingMessage` property of a newly initialized instance of the `GreetingResponse` object, which is returned to the calling client.

Next, we will need to modify our `Startup` class to register the `GreetingsManagererService` class as a valid gRPC endpoint. To do so, first, add the following line inside the `ConfigureServices` method. If you are using .NET 6 project template, there will be no `Startup` class. And neither will there be `ConfigureServices` method. So, you will just need to apply the following code to the main body of `Program.cs` class, replacing `services` with `builder.Services`. And it will need to be placed before the `Build` event:

```
services.AddGrpc();
```

Next, add the following code inside the call to `app.UseEndpoints`, inside the `Configure` method:

```
endpoints.MapGrpcService<GreetingsManagerService>();
```

Finally, inside your `Properties` folder in the root of your project folder, locate the `profiles` element and replace its content with the following:

```
"profiles": {
    "BasicGrpcService": {
        "commandName": "Project",
        "dotnetRunMessages": "true",
        "launchBrowser": false,
        "applicationUrl":
```

```
            "http://localhost:5000;https://localhost:5001",
        "environmentVariables": {
            "ASPNETCORE_ENVIRONMENT": "Development"
        }
    }
}
```

That's it – our gRPC server has been fully configured. Now, you can launch your application and see if it works correctly. If it does, you should see some console output, and the application shouldn't throw any visible errors:

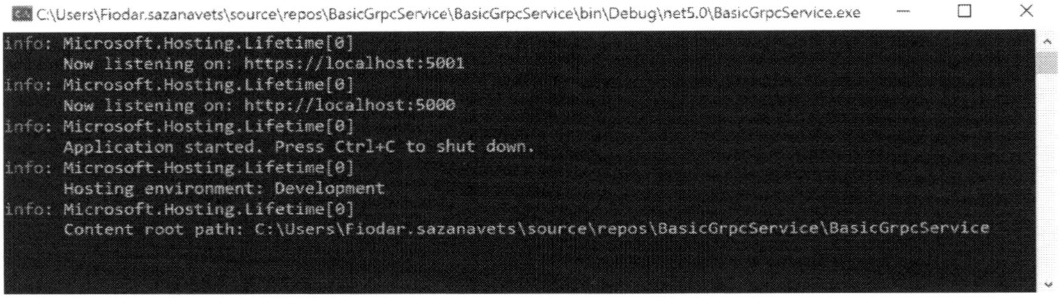

Figure 1.8 – Console output from the gRPC server

With this, we have set up our gRPC server. Now, let's move on to the next step and set up a gRPC client that can talk to it.

Setting up a gRPC client

Now, we will add a basic gRPC client that will be able to communicate with our service via gRPC. This will be a basic console application. The process will consist of the following steps:

1. Initialize the console application project.
2. Add some gRPC client dependencies to the project.
3. Add some code to connect to the gRPC client.

Once you've followed these steps, your basic console application will be able to send requests to the gRPC server and receive responses from it.

Initializing the project for the client application

If you are using an IDE, you can add a new project to your solution. The template that you will need is called **Console Application** or **Console Project**, depending on which IDE you're using. However, you need to make sure that you don't choose the .NET Framework version of the template, which will be clearly labeled. Likewise, make sure that you select the C# template as the IDE may present you with options for other languages too:

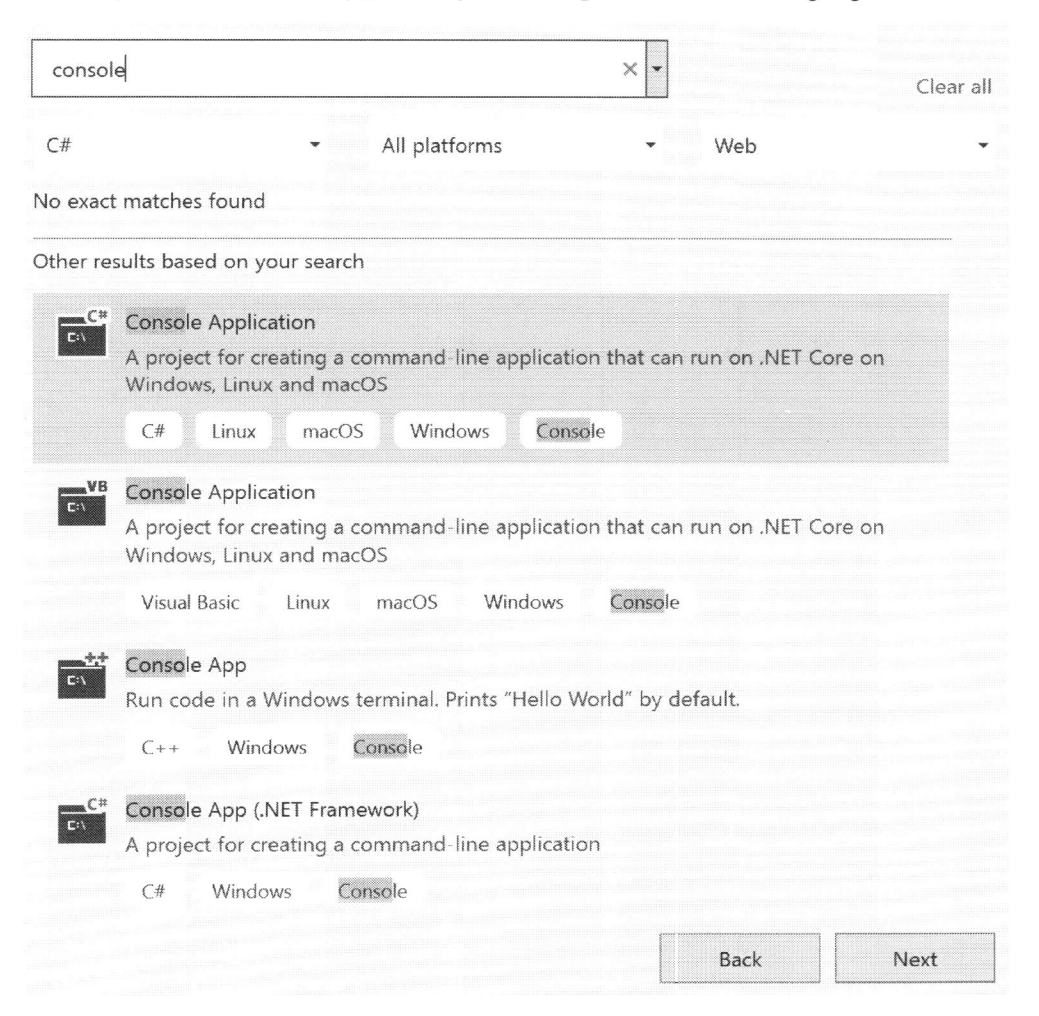

Figure 1.9 – Console Application template on Visual Studio 2019

As console application is a very basic application type; there won't be any complex setup options to select while creating the project. You can leave all the default options selected. Let's call our new project `BasicGrpcClient`.

If you are using a code editor and CLI instead of a fully-fledged IDE, you can create the project by executing a dotnet CLI command. Please ensure that you execute this command from the folder where the `BasicGrpcService` project folder is located. It will create the new project folder at the same level inside of your filesystem that your original project folder is located at. The command will be as follows:

```
dotnet new console -o BasicGrpcClient
```

Adding gRPC client components to the application

Now, to make your console application act as a gRPC client, you will need to add some NuGet references to your project. You can do so by executing the following commands inside your `BasicGrpcClient` project folder:

```
dotnet add BasicGrpcClient.csproj package Grpc.Net.Client
dotnet add BasicGrpcClient.csproj package Google.Protobuf
dotnet add BasicGrpcClient.csproj package Grpc.Tools
```

Once the packages have been installed, the content of your `BasicGrpcClient.csproj` file should be similar to this:

```xml
<Project Sdk="Microsoft.NET.Sdk">

  <PropertyGroup>
    <OutputType>Exe</OutputType>
    <TargetFramework>net5.0</TargetFramework>
  </PropertyGroup>

  <ItemGroup>
    <PackageReference Include="Google.Protobuf"
      Version="3.17.3" />
    <PackageReference Include="Grpc.Net.Client"
      Version="2.38.0" />
    <PackageReference Include="Grpc.Tools" Version="2.38.1">
      <IncludeAssets>runtime; build; native; contentfiles;
        analyzers; buildtransitive</IncludeAssets>
      <PrivateAssets>all</PrivateAssets>
    </PackageReference>
```

```xml
    </ItemGroup>

</Project>
```

Next, we will need to add the following section to the project file, which references the proto file we will be using to communicate with the server:

```xml
<ItemGroup>
   <Protobuf Include="Protos\greeter.proto"
     GrpcServices="Client"
   />
</ItemGroup>
```

This will make our project file look like this:

```xml
<Project Sdk="Microsoft.NET.Sdk">

  <PropertyGroup>
    <OutputType>Exe</OutputType>
    <TargetFramework>net5.0</TargetFramework>
  </PropertyGroup>

  <ItemGroup>
    <PackageReference Include="Google.Protobuf"
      Version="3.17.3" />
    <PackageReference Include="Grpc.Net.Client"
      Version="2.38.0" />
    <PackageReference Include="Grpc.Tools" Version="2.38.1">
      <IncludeAssets>runtime; build; native; contentfiles;
        analyzers; buildtransitive</IncludeAssets>
      <PrivateAssets>all</PrivateAssets>
    </PackageReference>
  </ItemGroup>

  <ItemGroup>
    <Protobuf Include="Protos\greeter.proto"
      GrpcServices="Client" />
```

```
    </ItemGroup>

</Project>
```

This is similar to what we've done with the server application. But this time, we are telling our application to only generate code for the client components. This is why we have set the `GrpcServices` attribute to `Client`.

Because we will be connecting to the server we created previously, we need a proto file with `package`, `service`, `rpc`, and `message` definitions that are identical to what we had in our server-side proto file. However, our C# namespace can be different.

Therefore, what you'll need to do next is create a `Protos` folder inside your `BasicGrpsClient` project folder. Then, you must insert the `greeter.proto` file into this folder and ensure it has the following content:

```
syntax = "proto3";

option csharp_namespace = "BasicGrpcClient";

 package greeter;

// The greetings manager service definition.
service GreetingsManager {
  // Request the service to generate a greeting message.
  rpc GenerateGreeting (GreetingRequest) returns
    (GreetingResponse);
}

// The request message definition containing the name to be
  addressed in the greeting message.
message GreetingRequest {
  string name = 1;
}

// The response message definition containing the greeting
  text.
message GreetingResponse {
```

```
    string greetingMessage = 1;
}
```

Please note that this file is identical to the one we have in our server application project, except for the `csharp_namespace` element. This element is used by the gRPC tools inside your specific .NET project and it does not affect compatibility between the server and client versions of the proto file. However, the rest of the elements must be the same for the communication system to recognize that it's meant to be the same interface.

Some differences are tolerated (which we will talk about when we cover API versioning in *Chapter 5*, *How to Apply Versioning to the gRPC API*). But the fundamental structure of your standard gRPC element definitions must match.

Applying gRPC client components to the code

In your `BasicGrpcClient` project, locate the `Program.cs` class and change its content to the following:

```
using System;
using System.Threading.Tasks;
using Grpc.Net.Client;

namespace BasicGrpcClient
{
    class Program
    {
        static async Task Main()
        {
            // The port number(5001) must match the port of
              the gRPC server.
            using var channel =
            GrpcChannel.ForAddress("https://localhost:5001");
            var client = new
            GreetingsManager.GreetingsManagerClient(channel);
            var reply = await client.GenerateGreetingAsync(
            new GreetingRequest { Name = "BasicGrpcClient" });
            Console.WriteLine("Greeting: " + reply.
              GreetingMessage);
            Console.WriteLine("Press any key to exit...");
```

```
            Console.ReadKey();
        }
    }
}
```

Please note that the highlighted URL represents the HTTPS access point to the gRPC server. This will not be available if you are running your software on Mac. The workaround to this is described in the *Running a gRPC service on Mac* section of this chapter.

This code does the following:

1. First, it initializes the gRPC channel for the hardcoded address of `https://localhost:5001`. Please note that this is the same address that we defined in the `launchSettings.json` file in the `BasicGrpcService` project. But in a real commercial application, this will be configurable rather than hardcoded.

2. Then, it uses this channel to initialize a new instance of the gRPC client that was generated by the `GreetingsManager` service definition in our `greeter.proto` file.

3. Next, it calls the `GenerateGreetingAsync` method of the client object with a new instance of `GreetingRequest` that has its `Name` property set to `BasicGrpcClient`. Please note that it represents the `GenerateGreeting` `rpc` definition from the proto file, but the `Async` part has been added to the name. This is because, in .NET, each gRPC procedure is represented by synchronous and asynchronous methods on the client side. The async version returns an `awaitable` task, so the calling code can be set to do something else while we are waiting for the reply. The synchronous version, which has the same name as the original `rpc` definition but without "Async" at the end, blocks execution of the calling code until the result has been received.

4. From this call, we receive an instance of `GreetingResponse`.

5. Then, we read the value of its `GreetingMessage` field and print it in the console.

6. Finally, the console prompts the user to press any key to exit.

Now, you can launch both of your applications and see how they communicate with each other. It's better to launch the server application first to make sure that it has fully loaded before the client application tries to communicate with it.

The simplest way to launch both applications is to open two instances of the command-line window (cmd, PowerShell, or Terminal, depending on your operating system and your preferences). In one command-line window, navigate to the `BasicGrpcService` project folder and execute the following command:

```
dotnet run
```

This will build and run the server application for you. Once it's showing the output that indicates that the gRPC server is running, open the other instance of the command-line window, navigate to the `BasicGrpcClient` project folder, and execute the same command.

You should receive the following output, which indicates that the client was able to successfully call the method on the server via the network:

Figure 1.10 – Console output from the gRPC client application

Now, if you re-examine the code from your client and your server, you will see that it looks almost as if you are calling the code from inside the same application. And that's precisely what makes gRPC so easy to use.

In both the applications that we covered, you saw how relevant code is automatically generated from proto files. In certain scenarios, it would be useful to know how this mechanism works. This is what we will have a look at now.

Understanding how proto files generate C# code

Normally, you wouldn't need to worry about how C# classes are generated from proto files. The compiler does it all for you. But occasionally, there may be a problem with the process. Therefore, it would be useful to know how to find the generated code and what the expected output should be.

Where is auto-generated code stored?

At this point, you know that the .NET compiler generates code from the proto files. This can then be referenced from inside your application code. And you can also get it to share the same namespace as your application. But despite the ability of this code to inter-operate with your application code, it's not part of your application.

The auto-generated code is placed in the `obj` folder inside your project folder. The purpose of this folder is to store intermediate resources that are required to compile your application. Since auto-generated classes aren't part of your main application, but your application cannot be compiled without them, they are placed alongside other intermediate files in this folder.

More precisely, the location of those auto-generated files is as follows. This represents the path on the Windows system. For a Unix-based system, such as macOS or Linux, replace back-slashes (\) with forward-slashes (/):

```
{your project folder}\obj\{build configuration}\{framework name}\Ptotos
```

So, for our `BasicGrpcService` project, which is based on .NET 5's built-in `Debug` mode, the path would be as follows:

```
BasicGrpcService\obj\Debug\net5.0\Ptotos
```

For each proto file that you reference in your project, a pair of files containing C# code will be generated:

- `{PascalCase proto file name}.cs`
- `{PascalCase proto file name}Grpc.cs`

The `{PascalCase proto file name}.cs` file contains a C# representation of the proto messages that your services use, while `{PascalCased proto file name} Grpc.cs` contains a C# representation of the services themselves, whether it's overridable base classes for the server or ready-made classes for the client.

In our example, which uses the `greeter.proto` file, we would end up with two files with the following names:

- `Greeter.cs`
- `GreeterGrpc.cs`

The content of those auto-generated files would be similar to the following:

```
 1  // <auto-generated>
 2  //     Generated by the protocol buffer compiler.  DO NOT EDIT!
 3  //     source: Protos/greeter.proto
 4  // </auto-generated>
 5  #pragma warning disable 0414, 1591
 6  #region Designer generated code
 7
 8  using grpc = global::Grpc.Core;
 9
10  namespace BasicGrpcService {
11    /// <summary>
12    /// The greetings manager service definition.
13    /// </summary>
14    public static partial class GreetingsManager
15    {
16      static readonly string __ServiceName = "greeter.GreetingsManager";
17
18      static void __Helper_SerializeMessage(global::Google.Protobuf.IMessage message, grpc::SerializationContext context)
19      {
20        #if !GRPC_DISABLE_PROTOBUF_BUFFER_SERIALIZATION
21        if (message is global::Google.Protobuf.IBufferMessage)
22        {
23          context.SetPayloadLength(message.CalculateSize());
24          global::Google.Protobuf.MessageExtensions.WriteTo(message, context.GetBufferWriter());
25          context.Complete();
26          return;
27        }
28        #endif
29        context.Complete(global::Google.Protobuf.MessageExtensions.ToByteArray(message));
30      }
31
32      static class __Helper_MessageCache<T>
33      {
34        public static readonly bool IsBufferMessage = global::System.Reflection.IntrospectionExtensions.GetTypeInfo(typeof(global::Goog
35      }
36
37      static T __Helper_DeserializeMessage<T>(grpc::DeserializationContext context, global::Google.Protobuf.MessageParser<T> parser)
38      {
39        #if !GRPC_DISABLE_PROTOBUF_BUFFER_SERIALIZATION
40        if (__Helper_MessageCache<T>.IsBufferMessage)
41        {
42          return parser.ParseFrom(context.PayloadAsReadOnlySequence());
43        }
44        #endif
45        return parser.ParseFrom(context.PayloadAsNewBuffer());
46      }
```

Figure 1.11 – An example of auto-generated gRPC C# code

You can examine the structure of these files if you like. Now, let's learn how making changes to the namespaces in Protobuf will affect the auto-generated code.

Modifying Protobuf namespaces

So far, we have been using the `csharp_namespace` option inside our proto files to set the namespaces of auto-generated code classes to the same root namespace that our application uses. But it doesn't have to be this way. You can set the namespaces in auto-generated code to absolutely anything.

You can also omit the `csharp_namespace` option entirely. If you do so, the namespace that will be applied to your auto-generated code will be the PascalCase version of the package name that's specified in the `package` element of the proto file.

In our case, since the package is called `greeter`, the C# namespace that's generated from it will be `Greeter`.

Now, go ahead and remove the `csharp_namespace` element from both the client and server versions of the `greeter.proto` file. Both copies of the files should now look as follows:

```
syntax = "proto3";

 package greeter;

// The greetings manager service definition.
service GreetingsManager {
  // Request the service to generate a greeting message.
  rpc GenerateGreeting (GreetingRequest) returns
    (GreetingResponse);
}

// The request message definition containing the name to be
   addressed in the greeting message.
message GreetingRequest {
  string name = 1;
}

// The response message definition containing the greeting
   text.
message GreetingResponse {
  string greetingMessage = 1;
}
```

Now, if you try to compile the projects, they will show errors. What you need to do is add a `using` statement to both the client and the server code referencing this namespace.

The content of the `GreetingsManagerService.cs` file inside the `BasicGreeterService` project should now look as follows:

```
using System.Threading.Tasks;
using Greeter;
using Grpc.Core;

namespace BasicGrpcService
{
```

```csharp
    public class GreetingsManagerService :
        GreetingsManager.GreetingsManagerBase
    {
        public override Task<GreetingResponse>
            GenerateGreeting(GreetingRequest
                request, ServerCallContext context)
        {
            return Task.FromResult(new GreetingResponse
            {
                GreetingMessage = "Hello " + request.Name
            });
        }
    }
}
```

The content of the Program.cs file inside the BasicGreeterClient project should now look as follows:

```csharp
using System;
using System.Threading.Tasks;
using Greeter;
using Grpc.Net.Client;

namespace BasicGrpcClient
{
    class Program
    {
        static async Task Main()
        {
            // The port number(5001) must match the port of
            the gRPC server.
            using var channel =
                GrpcChannel.ForAddress("https://
                    localhost:5001");
            var client = new
                GreetingsManager.
                    GreetingsManagerClient(channel);
```

```
                var reply = await client.GenerateGreetingAsync(
                new GreetingRequest { Name = "BasicGrpcClient" });
                Console.WriteLine("Greeting: " +
                  reply.GreetingMessage);
                Console.WriteLine("Press any key to exit...");
                Console.ReadKey();

            }
        }
    }
```

Now, you know how easy it is to regenerate relevant code after making changes to the Protobuf definition. At this point, you have two copies of the `greeter.proto` file that are identical.

At this stage, you may be wondering whether having separate copies of this file would violate the **don't repeat yourself** (**DRY**) principle, which is a commonly accepted best practice when writing software. Will any problems occur if you update one of these files while forgetting to update the other? Isn't it possible to keep a single shared copy of the file that both the client and the server use?

Fortunately, you can share the same file between multiple applications in .NET. Let's have a look at how.

Sharing a proto file between the client and the server

In .NET, if you want to share common functionality between different applications, you would put this functionality into a class library and then add this library to all the projects that need to use it. The good news is that you can do the same with proto files. To share this between applications, you can just add it to a class library and then add the class library as a reference.

Let's do this with our client and server projects.

Creating a shared class library

Inside the folder that holds both the `BasicGrpcService` and `BasicGrpcClient` project folders, create a new class library project and call it `GrpcDependencies`.

If you are using an IDE, you can add a project by choosing the `Class Library` template. Please ensure that .NET 5 is selected as the framework. Otherwise, keep all other options as-is.

If you prefer to use a CLI, you can execute the following command inside the folder hosting your existing projects to create a class library:

```
dotnet new classlib -o GrpcDependencies
```

Please note that, with a class library that is shared between projects, it would be more convenient to manage them if you have all these projects, including the class library itself, added to a solution.

If you have been using an IDE up to this point with all the default options selected, unless specified otherwise, you probably have the solution set up and all of your projects will already be a part of it.

If this is what your setup already looks like, you can skip to the next section. Otherwise, you can execute the following command inside the folder that hosts all your project folders to create a solution file:

```
dotnet new sln
```

This will create a file with the `.sln` extension that has the same name as the folder that hosts it.

Now, you can add all your projects to the folder by executing the following commands:

```
dotnet sln add GrpcDependencies/GrpcDependencies.csproj
dotnet sln add BasicGrpcService/BasicGrpcService.csproj
dotnet sln add BasicGrpcClient/BasicGrpcClient.csproj
```

You should now have a solution set up and all projects added to it. If you choose the `build solution` option, all the projects will be built together. You no longer have to build them individually.

Adding shared gRPC components to the class library

Since you now have a shared library for storing proto files, you no longer need to store a copy of the `greeter.proto` file in every project that uses it. You just need to store one copy in the class library itself.

So, copy the entire proto folder from either the `BasicGrpcService` or `BasicGrpcClient` folder into the `GrpcDependencies` folder.

Next, we will need to add the right NuGet dependencies to our `GrpcDependencies` class library. The dependencies that we used to reference our client and server projects will only need to be referenced in the class library, so our dependency tree will be kept clean.

To add the required dependencies, execute the following CLI commands inside the `GrpcDependencies` folder:

```
dotnet add GrpcDependencies.csproj package Grpc.Net.Client
dotnet add GrpcDependencies.csproj package Google.Protobuf
dotnet add GrpcDependencies.csproj package Grpc.Tools
dotnet add GrpcDependencies.csproj package Grpc.AspNetCore
```

Please note that these are the standard NuGet packages that are used by both the gRPC client and server. Because our shared class library will be used by both types of applications, we need both sets of dependencies.

Now, add a proto reference to your `GrpcDependencies.csproj` file. We will amend the `GrpcServices` element to this as we need to be able to build both the client and server gRPC components from the class library. Therefore, the markup block that we need to add to the project file will look like this:

```xml
<ItemGroup>
    <Protobuf Include="Protos\greeter.proto" />
</ItemGroup>
```

Finally, remove any other `greet.proto` file references from your project file, which could have been auto-generated when you copied the file into the project folder.

Now, the content of your `GrpcDependencies.csproj` file should look similar to this:

```xml
<Project Sdk="Microsoft.NET.Sdk">

  <PropertyGroup>
    <TargetFramework>net5.0</TargetFramework>
  </PropertyGroup>

  <ItemGroup>
    <PackageReference Include="Google.Protobuf"
      Version="3.17.3" />
    <PackageReference Include="Grpc.Net.Client"
      Version="2.38.0" />
```

```xml
    <PackageReference Include="Grpc.Tools" Version="2.38.1">
      <IncludeAssets>runtime; build; native; contentfiles;
        analyzers; buildtransitive</IncludeAssets>
      <PrivateAssets>all</PrivateAssets>
    </PackageReference>
    <PackageReference Include="Grpc.AspNetCore"
      Version="2.34.0" />
  </ItemGroup>

  <ItemGroup>
    <Protobuf Include="Protos\greeter.proto" />
  </ItemGroup>
</Project>
```

Now, we are ready to use this class library in our applications.

Sharing gRPC dependencies between different projects

First, you will need to reference the newly created class library from both the `BasicGrpcService.csproj` and `BasicGrpcClient.csproj` files. To do so, add the following section to both of the files:

```xml
  <ItemGroup>
    <ProjectReference
      Include="..\GrpcDependencies\GrpcDependencies.csproj" />
  </ItemGroup>
```

Now, you can remove all the gRPC-related NuGet dependencies from both of those files. All of them are present in the shared class library, so when you reference the class library, all of those dependencies will be implicitly referenced too.

After cleaning up your project files, the `BasicGrpcService.csproj` file should look similar to this:

```xml
<Project Sdk="Microsoft.NET.Sdk.Web">

  <PropertyGroup>
    <TargetFramework>net5.0</TargetFramework>
```

```xml
    </PropertyGroup>

    <ItemGroup>
      <ProjectReference
        Include="..\GrpcDependencies\GrpcDependencies.csproj" />
    </ItemGroup>
</Project>
```

The content of the `BasicGrpcClient.csproj` file should be very similar and look like this:

```xml
<Project Sdk="Microsoft.NET.Sdk">

    <PropertyGroup>
      <OutputType>Exe</OutputType>
      <TargetFramework>net5.0</TargetFramework>
    </PropertyGroup>

    <ItemGroup>
      <ProjectReference
        Include="..\GrpcDependencies\GrpcDependencies.csproj" />
    </ItemGroup>
</Project>
```

Please note that the only differences between the two project files are the SDK type and the output type, which represent different types of applications.

Now, to verify that all the dependencies have been set up successfully, build your solution and ensure there aren't any build errors. If it builds successfully, launch your `BasicGrpcService` project, followed by the `BasicGrpcClient` project, to ensure that everything still works correctly.

The applications are expected to produce the same output that they did previously. However, this time, a single copy of the proto file will be shared between them, so you no longer run the risk of making two copies of the file incompatible while updating them.

Another important thing to note is that, just like any other class library, a library containing proto files can be published as a NuGet package.

Running a gRPC service on Mac

At the time of writing, you cannot apply TLS while running gRPC Server on Mac. This is because of missing **Application Layer Protocol Negotiation** (**ALPN**) support on the operating system. So, to make it work, you need to enable HTTP access to the server instead of HTTPS.

Configuring server-side components

First, you need to enable an unencrypted endpoint HTTP/2 endpoint inside your application. To do so, open the `Program.cs` file inside your gRPC server project. Then, add the following `using` statement on top of it:

```
using Microsoft.AspNetCore.Server.Kestrel.Core;
```

Then, inside the `Main` method (which is the entry point into the application), add the following block of code inside the call to the `ConfigureWebHostingDefaults` method:

```
webBuilder.ConfigureKestrel(options =>
{
    options.ListenLocalhost(<port number>, o => o.Protocols =
    HttpProtocols.Http2);
});
```

Replace `<port number>` with the actual port number of the HTTP endpoint, which can be found under the `applicationUrl` key in the `launchSettings.json` file, which is located in the `Properties` folder of the project.

Once you've done this, your application will be ready to accept insecure HTTP/2 requests on the specified port number.

Modifying the client-side configuration

Because TLS doesn't work on the server, you won't be able to send requests to it via the HTTPS endpoint. So, while creating the `GrpcChannel` object in the client application, you will need to pass the HTTP URL into it. The specific URL can be found under the `applicationUrl` key in the `launchSettings.json` file, which is located in the `Properties` folder of the gRPC server project.

Summary

In this chapter, we learned how to set up both the gRPC client and the server. We did so by manually adding gRPC capabilities to our .NET projects instead of creating new projects from the gRPC template. For our server, we started with a standard ASP.NET Core project template, while our client used the most basic Console Application template.

We had a look at how the gRPC compiler generates code from Protobuf files and how that auto-generated code is affected by changes that are made to the content of those files.

Finally, we covered the process of sharing the same proto file between different applications via a shared class library so that you, as a developer, would not accidentally apply incompatible Protobuf definitions to your client and the server.

In the next chapter, we will have a more detailed look at the use cases of gRPC. Although it's a great communication protocol, it has its limitations, and it's not the best solution for every situation. So, you will learn when it's best to use gRPC and when alternative solutions might be better.

Questions

Answer the following questions to test your knowledge of this chapter:

1. Please select the false statement:

    A. In Protobuf, a service is defined by the `service` keyword, while its methods are defined by the `rpc` keyword.

    B. You cannot have a Protobuf message definition without any fields.

    C. A Protobuf message can have collections of objects and can use other message definitions as field types.

    D. You have to specify a request object in a response object inside a gRPC method definition and you can only use a single object type in each of those.

2. Which platforms can you run a .NET implementation of gRPC on?

    A. Windows, Linux, and macOS

    B. Windows and macOS only

    C. Unix-based (macOS and Linux) only

    D. Windows only

3. How do you enable server-side gRPC components in .NET applications?

   A. So long as you reference the `Grpc.AspNetCore` NuGet package, it will be automatically enabled for you.

   B. You just need to add a proto file to your project; the compiler will do everything else for you.

   C. You need to define a proto element inside the project file. It can be blank or you can set its `GrpcServices` attribute to either `Server` or `Both`.

   D. You need to define a proto element inside the project file and you must set its `GrpcServices` attribute to `Server`.

4. After adding the relevant proto files to your server-side application project, what modifications do you need to make to your code?

   A. You just need to override the methods from the auto-generated C# code files with your functionality.

   B. You need to modify the auto-generated C# classes and add your functionality to them.

   C. You need to create a new class that inherits from the auto-generated base class, add gRPC to your application services via the `ConfigureServices` method of the `Startup` class, and then register the newly created class as one of the endpoints in your middleware.

   D. The system will generate all the required code for you. You just need to fill the methods with your logic.

5. Can the .NET implementation of the .NET client call RPCs both synchronously and asynchronously?

   A. It can only call methods synchronously.

   B. It can only call methods asynchronously.

   C. There is both a synchronous and asynchronous version of each method that's generated for the client to use.

   D. All auto-generated methods are asynchronous, but you can change the implementation to make them synchronous.

Further reading

To learn more about the topics that were covered in this chapter, take a look at the following resources:

- The official ASP.NET Core gRPC documentation: https://docs.microsoft.com/en-us/aspnet/core/grpc/
- C# code generation documentation: https://developers.google.com/protocol-buffers/docs/reference/csharp-generated
- Troubleshooting gRPC on .NET Core: https://docs.microsoft.com/en-us/aspnet/core/grpc/troubleshoot

2
When gRPC Is the Best Tool and When It Isn't

In this chapter, we will cover use cases for **Google Remote Procedure Call (gRPC)**. We will use sample applications to demonstrate why gRPC is a great tool to be used in some scenarios but isn't the best one for other scenarios.

The main objective of this chapter is to demonstrate how convenient it is to use gRPC for microservices architecture and asynchronous communication, but you will also be shown how inconvenient it is to use gRPC in a browser or on any platform that doesn't support the **HyperText Transfer Protocol 2 (HTTP/2)** protocol. You will also be shown alternative technologies you can use when gRPC is not the best answer.

We will cover the following topics in this chapter:

- Why gRPC is a great tool for microservices
- How gRPC can be a good tool for asynchronous communication
- Why gRPC is not the best tool for browsers
- Where SignalR would beat gRPC

By the end of this chapter, you will have learned how to decide whether or not to use gRPC in a particular situation. You will have also learned what to do if gRPC doesn't appear to be the best solution for your particular case.

Technical requirements

To follow the instructions in this chapter, you will need the following:

- A computer with either a Windows, Mac, or Linux operating system
- A supported **integrated development environment** (IDE) or code editor (Visual Studio, **Visual Studio Code** (**VS Code**), or JetBrains Rider)
- The .NET 5 **software development kit** (**SDK**)
- A self-signed development **HTTP Secure** (**HTTPS**) certificate that is enabled on your machine

Instructions on how to set all of these up were provided in the previous chapter. You can find the code files for this chapter on GitHub at `https://github.com/PacktPublishing/Microservices-Communication-in-.NET-Using-gRPC/tree/main/Chapter-02`.

Please visit the following link to check the CiA videos: `https://bit.ly/3EXh2Y2`

Why gRPC is a great tool for microservices

gRPC has been primarily developed to facilitate direct **real-time communication** (**RTC**) between microservices in a distributed application. Therefore, microservices architecture is where gRPC is often the most convenient tool to use.

To verify this assumption, we will build a solution that resembles a real-life distributed application consisting of microservices, each of which plays a distinct role. Our distributed application will consist of two microservices, as follows:

- A backend service that manages status information on connected clients
- A public-facing **REpresentational State Transfer** (**REST**) **application programming interface** (**API**) gateway that communicates with this service

Both of these will share a **Protocol Buffers** (**Protobuf**) definition via a class library.

The status manager service will maintain a collection of key-value pairs representing the client name and its status. Any connected client will be able to perform the following operations via gRPC:

- Update status information on a particular client.
- Retrieve status information about a particular client.
- Retrieve a full list of all client statuses.

In a real-world scenario, this service might be hosted on a private network and hidden from the public. Therefore, we will have another service acting as a REST API gateway that will talk to the status manager that, in a real-life scenario, would be hosted on the same private network but also exposed to the public internet, which could be done via port mapping or other techniques.

This API gateway service will act as a gRPC client. It will accept HTTP requests and translate them into gRPC calls. It will then convert Protobuf messages into standard **JavaScript Object Notation (JSON)** and return them back to the client.

Setting up a solution and shared dependencies

Let's create a solution and call it `GrpcMicroserviceSample`. If you are using an IDE such as Visual Studio or Rider, you will be able to do so while creating your first project from the relevant template. If you are using the dotnet **command-line interface (CLI)**, you can instead create a folder named `GrpcMicroserviceSample` and execute the following command inside of it to initialize the solution:

```
dotnet new sln
```

Then, inside this solution folder, you will need to create a class library that will contain shared gRPC client and server dependencies. This class library project will be called `GrpcDependencies`. If you are using the command line, execute the following command inside your solution folder to create it:

```
dotnet new classlib -o GrpcDependencies
```

Inside the `GrpcDependencies` project folder, create a folder called `Protos`, then create a `status.proto` file inside this folder. Inside this file, we will first add a standard syntax reference, the package name, and the definition of our service, as follows:

```
syntax = "proto3";
```

```
package status;
```

```
service StatusManager {
  rpc GetAllStatuses (ClientStatusesRequest) returns (stream
    ClientStatusResponse);
  rpc GetClientStatus (ClientStatusRequest) returns
    (ClientStatusResponse);
  rpc UpdateClientStatus (ClientStatusUpdateRequest) returns
    (ClientStatusUpdateResponse);
}
```

Following that, we will add definitions of the messages, as follows:

```
message ClientStatusesRequest {
}

message ClientStatusRequest {
   string clientName = 1;
}

message ClientStatusResponse {
   string clientName = 1;
   ClientStatus status = 2;
}

message ClientStatusUpdateRequest {
   string clientName = 1;
   ClientStatus status = 2;
}

message ClientStatusUpdateResponse {
   bool success = 1;
}
```

Finally, we are introducing a new data type that we need for our models—`enum`, as illustrated in the following code snippet:

```
enum ClientStatus {
    OFFLINE = 0;
    ONLINE = 1;
    BUSY = 2;
}
```

Inside this proto file, you will see some new components that we have not covered before. First of all, you see a new definition type—`enum`. This is used as a field type in some of the message definitions.

This is just a standard enumeration, equivalent to a C# enum. It can be defined as an independent object (as we have done in our example), or its definition can be nested inside a message definition. You would do the former if you wanted to use the same enum definition in different messages, while you would use the latter if it's only a specific message definition that is meant to use a specific enum type.

The values inside an enum object are expected to have sequential numeric values starting from zero.

We will cover enums in more detail in the next chapter, which is dedicated to data types supported by Protobuf.

The other new keyword that we haven't seen before is `stream`, which is located before the return message of `GetAllStatuses rpc` of the `StatusManager` service. A stream is one of the ways of transferring a collection, rather than a single object, in gRPC between the client and the server. A stream is also something that can facilitate asynchronous communication, which we will cover later in this chapter.

We will examine streaming and non-streaming gRPC calls in more detail in *Chapter 7, Using Different Call Types that gRPC Supports*.

Also, in this proto file, we have an example of a message definition with no fields: `ClientStatusesRequest`. It has been placed there to demonstrate that, while it's mandatory to have a message definition in a **remote procedure call** (**RPC**), both as an input parameter and a return value, the definition itself can be empty.

Once we've added our Protobuf definition, we just need to add all relevant dependencies to the class library project definition. The simplest way to do it would be to replace the original content of the `GrpcDependencies.csproj` file with the following code:

```xml
<Project Sdk="Microsoft.NET.Sdk">

  <PropertyGroup>
    <TargetFramework>net5.0</TargetFramework>
  </PropertyGroup>

  <ItemGroup>
    <PackageReference Include="Google.Protobuf"
      Version="3.17.3" />
    <PackageReference Include="Grpc.Net.Client"
      Version="2.38.0" />
    <PackageReference Include="Grpc.Tools" Version="2.38.1">
      <IncludeAssets>runtime; build; native; contentfiles;
        analyzers; buildtransitive</IncludeAssets>
      <PrivateAssets>all</PrivateAssets>
    </PackageReference>
    <PackageReference Include="Grpc.AspNetCore"
      Version="2.34.0" />
  </ItemGroup>

  <ItemGroup>
    <Protobuf Include="Protos\status.proto" />
  </ItemGroup>

</Project>
```

You can update the version numbers of the NuGet packages if new releases have been made available.

Now, build the project to verify that there are no compilation errors. Then, if you have been using the dotnet CLI instead of a fully-fledged IDE, add the project to the solution by executing the following command inside the `GrpcMicroserviceSample` solution folder:

```
dotnet sln add GrpcDependencies/GrpcDependencies.csproj
```

Now, we will set up our status manager microservice project that will act as a gRPC server.

Setting up the status manager microservice

Inside the solution folder, create a project named `StatusMicroservice` by using a standard `gRPC Service` project template. If you are using the dotnet CLI, run the following command from the `GrpcMicroserviceSample` solution folder to do so:

```
dotnet new grpc -o StatusMicroservice
```

It will be created with a `Protos` folder and a sample gRPC server class inside the `Services` folder. You will not need any of these as you will be using the class library we created earlier for all of your gRPC dependencies.

To add those dependencies, replace the content of the `StatusMicroservice.csproj` file with the following code:

```xml
<Project Sdk="Microsoft.NET.Sdk.Web">

  <PropertyGroup>
    <TargetFramework>net5.0</TargetFramework>
  </PropertyGroup>

  <ItemGroup>
    <ProjectReference
      Include="..\GrpcDependencies\GrpcDependencies.csproj">
      <GlobalPropertiesToRemove></GlobalPropertiesToRemove>
    </ProjectReference>
  </ItemGroup>
</Project>
```

Then, completely remove the `Protos` folder from the project. We will not need the standard `greet.proto` file for this exercise.

Next, add a `ClientStatus.cs` file to the root of our project folder. It will be an enum with the following content:

```csharp
namespace StatusMicroservice
{
    public enum ClientStatus
    {
```

```
            OFFLINE = 0,
            ONLINE = 1,
            BUSY = 2,
    }
}
```

Then, add a `StateStore.cs` file that will contain the in-memory state. This file should have a `StatusMicroservice` namespace and import a `System.Collections.Generic` package via a `using` statement. In this file, we will place an interface alongside our class. The interface should look like this:

```
public interface IStateStore
{
    IEnumerable<(string ClientName, ClientStatus ClientStatus)>
      GetAllStatuses();
    ClientStatus GetStatus(string clientName);
    bool UpdateStatus(string clientName, ClientStatus status);
}
```

Next, we will add a class that implements this interface. Its constructor and private members should look like this:

```
internal class StateStore : IStateStore
{
    private Dictionary<string, ClientStatus> statuses;

    public StateStore()
    {
        statuses = new Dictionary<string, ClientStatus>();
    }
}
```

Finally, we will insert all required methods to implement the interface. The content of the `GetAllStatuses` method will look like this:

```
    public IEnumerable<(string ClientName, ClientStatus
      ClientStatus)> GetAllStatuses()
    {
        var returnedStatuses = new List<(string ClientName,
```

```
            ClientStatus ClientStatus)>();

        foreach (var record in statuses)
        {
            returnedStatuses.Add((record.Key, record.Value));
        }

        return returnedStatuses;
    }
```

The GetStatus method will look like this:

```
    public ClientStatus GetStatus(string clientName)
    {
        if (!statuses.ContainsKey(clientName))
        {
            return ClientStatus.OFFLINE;
        }

        return statuses[clientName];
    }
```

And the UpdateStatus method will have the following implementation:

```
    public bool UpdateStatus(string clientName, ClientStatus
       status)
    {
        statuses[clientName] = status;

        return true;
    }
```

This example shows a class that implements an interface. Even though it's not strictly essential to have an interface instead of just a concrete class, we are mimicking the structure of a real-world microservices application. Therefore, we are applying the same best practices (for example, SOLID principles), as we would in a real commercial project.

In a real-world application, having an interface would allow us to replace the implementation when needed—for example, we can mock the implementation while writing unit tests and inject the mocked instance into the classes that are being tested.

After this, add a file named `StatusManagerService.cs` to the `Services` folder. The class inside of it needs to have the following package imports:

```
using System.Threading.Tasks;
using Grpc.Core;
using Status;
```

The class should import an `IStateStore` instance via its constructor, as follows:

```
public class StatusManagerService : StatusManager.
   StatusManagerBase
{
    private readonly IStateStore stateStore;

    public StatusManagerService(IStateStore stateStore)
    {
        this.stateStore = stateStore;
    }
}
```

And then, there should be a method corresponding to every **remote procedure call** (**RPC**) defined in the proto file. The implementation of the `GetAllStatuses` RPC will look like this:

```
public override async Task GetAllStatuses(ClientStatusesRequest
request, IServerStreamWriter<ClientStatusResponse>
   responseStream,
ServerCallContext context)
    {
        foreach (var record in stateStore.GetAllStatuses())
        {
            await responseStream.WriteAsync(new
               ClientStatusResponse
               {
                   ClientName = record.ClientName,
```

```
            Status = (Status.ClientStatus)record.
                ClientStatus
            });
        }
    }
```

The `GetClientStatus` implementation will look like this:

```
    public override Task<ClientStatusResponse>
    GetClientStatus(ClientStatusRequest request,
      ServerCallContext
      context)
    {
        return Task.FromResult(new ClientStatusResponse
            {
                ClientName = request.ClientName,
                Status = (Status.ClientStatus)stateStore.
                    GetStatus(request.ClientName)
            });
    }
```

Finally, the content of the `UpdateClientStatus` method will be as shown here:

```
    public override Task<ClientStatusUpdateResponse>
    UpdateClientStatus(ClientStatusUpdateRequest request,
    ServerCallContext context)
            {
                return Task.FromResult(new
                    ClientStatusUpdateResponse
                    {
                        Success = stateStore.UpdateStatus(request.
                            ClientName
                            , (ClientStatus)request.Status)
                    });
            }
```

Please note that the `GetAllStatuses` method is different in its structure from the other methods. This is because it's a server-streaming method. We will cover those in *Chapter 7, Using Different Call Types that gRPC Supports*. For now, all you need to know is that it will return a collection to your client rather than a single object.

This example shows how we insert the `IStateStore` interface into a class that needs it instead of its concrete implementation. This allows us to insert any class that implements this interface into the constructor. Choosing a concrete class to insert will be handled by our **dependency injection** (**DI**) mechanism.

Once this file has been created, please make sure that any other files are removed from the `Services` folder; otherwise, they may throw compilation errors later.

Now, we will need to register the new gRPC endpoint in our `Startup` class (or `Program.cs` file if you are using .NET 6 templates). This is also where we register services for DI. To register the newly created endpoint, please add the following line inside the call to the `UseEndpoints` method, which you will find inside the `Configure` method of the `Startup` class:

```
endpoints.MapGrpcService<StatusManagerService>();
```

Then, we will use an inbuilt DI mechanism by adding this line to the `ConfigureServices` method (or the main body of the `Program.cs` file before the `Build` event if you are using .NET 6):

```
services.AddSingleton<IStateStore, StateStore>();
```

After executing this line, any class that isn't explicitly instantiated and has a constructor parameter of the `IStateStore` type will be given an instance of the `StateStore` class, and it will always be the same instance because we are registering it as a singleton.

There is an additional step you will need to perform to the gRPC service application if you intend to host it on a Mac operating system. This can be found in the *Running a gRPC service on Mac* section of *Chapter 1, Creating a Basic gRPC Application on ASP.NET Core*.

In ASP.NET Core, controllers, gRPC services, background worker services, and some other standard class types would always accept construction parameters from DI systems as they are never instantiated explicitly in the code.

Finally, if you have been using the dotnet CLI and haven't yet added this new project to the solution, add it by executing the following command from inside the solution folder:

```
dotnet sln add StatusMicroservice/StatusMicroservice.csproj
```

Now, we will add a REST API gateway that will act as a gRPC client.

Setting up a REST API gateway service

You will now need to add a project to your `GrpcMicroserviceSample` solution by using the `ASP.Core Web API` template. We will call this project `ApiGateway`. If you are using the dotnet CLI, run the following command from the `GrpcMicroserviceSample` folder:

```
dotnet new webapi -o ApiGateway
```

In this case, you will then also need to add it to the solution by executing the following command:

```
dotnet sln add ApiGateway/ApiGateway.csproj
```

Both **HyperText Markup Language** (**HTML**) web pages and REST APIs use the HTTP protocol. However, unlike web pages, REST APIs are headless, which means they are not built with the **user interface** (**UI**), thus making them difficult to use in a browser. But we can make the process easy by adding Swagger (OpenAPI) components to our application. Once added, those components will create a web page that will allow us to manipulate any of our REST API endpoints via standard page controls (textboxes, drop-down fields, and buttons).

To enable these components, we will need to add an `NSwag.AspNetCore` NuGet package to our `ApiGateway` project. Then, since the API gateway will be acting as a gRPC client in the backend, we will also need to add a reference to the `GrpcDependencies` project we created earlier. Once done, the content of the `ApiGateway.csproj` file is expected to look similar to this:

```xml
<Project Sdk="Microsoft.NET.Sdk.Web">

  <PropertyGroup>
    <TargetFramework>net5.0</TargetFramework>
  </PropertyGroup>

  <ItemGroup>
    <PackageReference Include="NSwag.AspNetCore"
      Version="13.12.1" />
  </ItemGroup>

  <ItemGroup>
```

```xml
        <ProjectReference
            Include="..\GrpcDependencies\GrpcDependencies.csproj" />
    </ItemGroup>
</Project>
```

Next, we will add a `ClientStatus.cs` file to the `ApiGateway` project folder. It will be the same enum we used in `StatusMicroservice` but it will be intended for consumption by public clients. So, the content of the file will look like this:

```csharp
namespace ApiGateway
{
    public enum ClientStatus
    {
        OFFLINE = 0,
        ONLINE = 1,
        BUSY = 2,
    }
}
```

We will then need to add a model from which we will be generating the JSON that will be sent back to the clients of the REST API. For this, create a `ClientStatusModel.cs` file in the root of the project with the following content:

```csharp
namespace ApiGateway
{
    public class ClientStatusModel
    {
        public string Name { get; set; }
        public ClientStatus Status { get; set; }
    }
}
```

Now, we will add a `GrpcStatusClient.cs` file that will be a wrapper around our gRPC client functionality. We will first add all required dependencies to this file by putting the following statements on top of it:

```csharp
using System;
using System.Collections.Generic;
using System.Threading.Tasks;
```

```
using Grpc.Core;
using Grpc.Net.Client;
using Status;
```

Next, we will add an `ApiGateway` namespace, and inside of it, we will add an interface with the following method definitions:

```
public interface IGrpcStatusClient
{
    Task<IEnumerable<ClientStatusModel>> GetAllStatuses();
    Task<ClientStatusModel> GetClientStatus(string clientName);
    Task<bool> UpdateClientStatus(string clientName,
      ClientStatus
      status);
}
```

This will enable us to use the **dependency inversion principle** (**DIP**) in any place that will use the gRPC client wrapper. We will then add a class that implements both this interface and `IDisposable`, as follows:

```
internal class GrpcStatusClient : IGrpcStatusClient,
  IDisposable
{
    private readonly GrpcChannel channel;
    private readonly StatusManager.StatusManagerClient client;

    public GrpcStatusClient(string serverUrl)
    {
        channel = GrpcChannel.ForAddress(serverUrl);
        client = new StatusManager.
          StatusManagerClient(channel);
    }
}
```

Here, we are setting up the gRPC channel and the client based on the gRPC server **Uniform Resource Locator (URL)** provided. Next, we will need to implement an `IGrpcStatusClient` interface to make the gRPC client callable from the outside. Our `GetAllStatuses` method will have some stream-processing logic, as illustrated in the following code snippet:

```
public async Task<IEnumerable<ClientStatusModel>>
   GetAllStatuses()
{
    var statuses = new List<ClientStatusModel>();

    using var call = client.GetAllStatuses(new
      ClientStatusesRequest());

    while (await call.ResponseStream.MoveNext())
    {
        var currentStatus = call.ResponseStream.Current;
        statuses.Add(new ClientStatusModel
        {
            Name = currentStatus.ClientName,
            Status = (ClientStatus)currentStatus.Status
        });
    }

    return statuses;
}
```

The implementation of `GetClientStatus` is a simple unary method that translates a gRPC message into our own custom model, as follows:

```
public async Task<ClientStatusModel> GetClientStatus(string
   clientName)
{
    var response = await client.GetClientStatusAsync(new
      ClientStatusRequest
      {
          ClientName = clientName
```

```
    });

    return new ClientStatusModel
    {
        Name = response.ClientName,
        Status = (ClientStatus)response.Status
    };
}
```

And we apply similar principles to the implementation of the `UpdateClientStatus` method, as follows:

```
public async Task<bool> UpdateClientStatus(string clientName, ClientStatus status)
{
    var response = await client.UpdateClientStatusAsync(new
        ClientStatusUpdateRequest
    {
        ClientName = clientName,
        Status = (Status.ClientStatus)status
    });

    return response.Success;
}
```

Finally, we need to implement an `IDisposable` interface by running the following code:

```
public void Dispose()
{
    channel.Dispose();
}
```

The class will implement an interface that will be used as a constructor parameter in any class that needs to use it, and because the `GrpcChannel` instance needs to be disposed of when the class is no longer used, we need to get the class to implement an `IDisposable` interface. If we don't dispose of `GrpcChannel`, we may have a memory leak—a portion of memory not being freed even when the application is no longer running on the machine.

We will now add a controller that will use this gRPC client wrapper class. In the `ApiGateway` project folder, locate the `Controllers` folder and insert a `StatusController.cs` file into it. The namespace of the file should be `ApiGateway.Controllers` as per ASP.NET Core conventions, and we will need to add the following mandatory namespace references:

```
using System.Collections.Generic;
using System.Threading.Tasks;
using Microsoft.AspNetCore.Mvc;
```

We will add the standard REST API controller attributes to the class definition and we will pass an instance of the gRPC client wrapper via the constructor, as follows:

```
[ApiController]
[Route("[controller]")]
public class StatusController : ControllerBase
{
    private readonly IGrpcStatusClient client;

    public StatusController(IGrpcStatusClient client)
    {
        this.client = client;
    }
}
```

Finally, we will add the following endpoint methods to our controller class:

```
[HttpGet]
public async Task<IEnumerable<ClientStatusModel>>
    GetAllStatuses()
{
    return await client.GetAllStatuses();
}

[HttpGet("{clientName}")]
public async Task<ClientStatusModel> GetClientStatus(string
    clientName)
{
```

```
        return await client.GetClientStatus(clientName);
}

[HttpPost("{clientName}/{status}")]
public async Task<bool> UpdateClientStatus(string clientName,
    ClientStatus status)
{
        return await client.UpdateClientStatus(clientName, status);
}
```

This is just a standard ASP.NET Core Web API controller that has a REST-equivalent method for every RPC we have defined in our Protobuf file. Once added, we will be able to call HTTP endpoints of our application via this URL, as follows:

```
{base URL}/status
```

But the problem with it is that it's a headless API, so we wouldn't be able to easily access these endpoints via a browser. Normally, we would need software such as Fiddler or Postman to send any custom HTTP requests to REST APIs. However, because we have added `NSwag.AspNetCore`, we will have a web page that will give us access to all of these endpoints. We just need to register certain components in our application's `Startup` class (or inside `Program.cs` file if you are using .NET 6 templates, while applying appropriate modifications to the code shown next). Inside the `ConfigureServices` method, we need to enable Swagger functionality by including the following line of code:

```
services.AddOpenApiDocument();
```

Then, we actually add all required Swagger functionality to the middleware pipeline by having the following two lines inside the `Configure` methods. These lines should be placed anywhere before the call to `UseRouting`:

```
app.UseOpenApi();
app.UseSwaggerUi3();
```

In the `ConfigureServices` method, we are also adding dependency mapping so that our gRPC client wrapper can be passed to the controller that needs to use it. This is done on the following line:

```
services.AddSingleton<IGrpcStatusClient>(p => new
    GrpcStatusClient(Configuration["ServerUrl"]));
```

But this time, we are instantiating a `GrpcStatusClient` class with a concrete constructor parameter that we take from the `ServerUrl` field of the settings. We do this because it's a primitive data type and, therefore, it cannot be registered inside the DI container. So, we need to specify it explicitly.

But to get the value, we need to add a `ServerUrl` field to the `appsettings.json` file in the root of our project, which would look like this:

```
"ServerUrl": "https://localhost:35095"
```

The value of the field represents the URL or `StatusMicroservice` application. It is taken from the `applicationUrl` field of the `launchSettings.json` file of the application, which is located inside the `Properties` folder in the `StatusMicroservice` project folder. If there is more than one URL, we want the one that uses the HTTPS protocol. However, if we are running our gRPC server application on a Mac operating system, we would need to select the HTTP URL due to the limitations of the operating system. For example, the previous value was taken from a `launchSettings.json` file that had the following content:

```
{
  "profiles": {
    "StatusMicroservice": {
      "commandName": "Project",
      "applicationUrl": "http://localhost:3638;https://
        localhost:35095",
      "environmentVariables": {
        "ASPNETCORE_ENVIRONMENT": "Development"
      }
    }
  }
}
```

Now, we are set to launch our distributed application and see it in action.

Launching the distributed application

To launch our applications and get them to talk to each other, we need to open two instances of a CLI of your choice (Terminal, PowerShell, **Command Prompt** (**CMD**), and so on). One of them should be pointing at the `StatusMicroservice` folder, while the other one should be pointing at the `ApiGateway` folder.

First, launch the following command inside your `StatusMicroservice` folder:

```
dotnet run
```

Then, once the microservice is up and running, launch the same command inside the `ApiGateway` folder.

Now, you can navigate to the Swagger page of the API gateway to test its endpoints. To do so, firstly obtain the HTTPS URL of the application from the `applicationUrl` field in the `ApiGateway` section of the `launchSettings.json` file. This file is located inside the `Properties` folder in the `ApiGateway` project. Paste this URL into the browser and add `/swagger` to the address. For example, if the URL is `https://localhost:21123`, then the Swagger address will be `https://localhost:21123/swagger`.

You should now see a friendly UI that allows you to operate all REST API endpoints, as illustrated in the following screenshot:

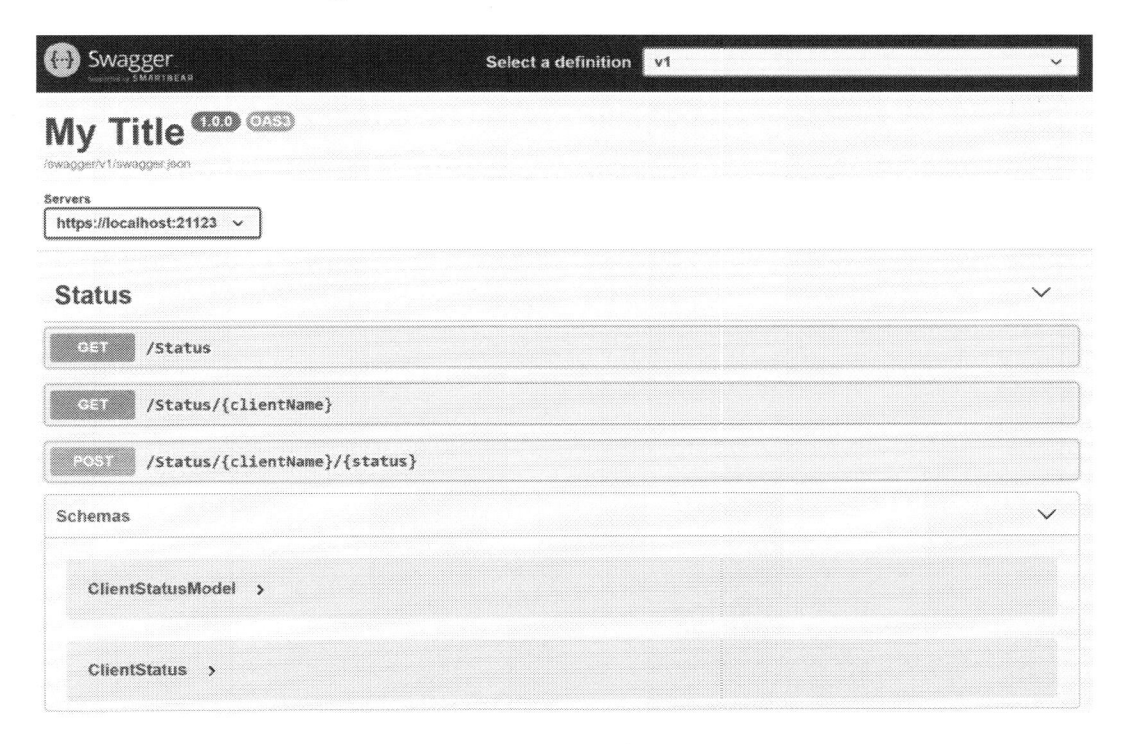

Figure 2.1 – Swagger page for ApiGateway

Now, you can see how relatively easy it is to enable direct RTC between microservices by using gRPC. We've seamlessly integrated the internal gRPC communication channel with a publicly accessible REST API, but you can also use gRPC for asynchronous long-running background tasks. In the next section, we will see how this can be achieved.

How gRPC can be a good tool for asynchronous communication

In distributed applications, it's common for one microservice to outsource a large chunk of work to another microservice in an asynchronous fashion. Perhaps the task would take a relatively long time to execute, so you wouldn't want to wait for a response. All you would be interested in is that the task has been successfully initiated.

gRPC allows you to do this. Streaming calls, which we covered earlier, aren't only suitable to pass collections—they can also be used for asynchronous task execution.

In the following example, we will add another service to our `StatusMicroservice` application. This service will use two streaming endpoints and will mimic the execution of long-running tasks of two different types. We will then add a new controller to our `ApiGateway` project to initiate asynchronous communication with the server.

Adding client-streaming and server-streaming gRPC endpoints

First, we will add another proto service definition to our `Protos` folder inside the `GrpcDependencies` project. This will be a `worker.proto` file with the following content:

```
syntax = "proto3";

package worker;

service JobManager {
  rpc SendJobs (stream SendJobsRequest) returns
    (SendJobsResponse);
  rpc TriggerJobs (TriggerJobsRequest) returns (stream
    TriggerJobsResponse);
}
```

```
message SendJobsRequest {
    int32 jobId = 1;
    string jobDescription = 2;
}

message SendJobsResponse {
   bool completed = 1;
}

message TriggerJobsRequest {
   int32 jobsCount = 1;
}

message TriggerJobsResponse {
   int32 jobSequence = 1;
   string jobMessage = 2;
}
```

Please note that we have two RPCs defined in the `JobManager` service. `SendJobs` is a client-streaming RPC as it has a `stream` keyword placed before the input parameter. `TriggerJobs`, on the other hand, is a server-streaming RPC, and the `stream` keyword placed before the return type indicates this.

We will need to register this new Protobuf definition in our `GrpcDependencies.csproj` file by adding the following line of code inside the `ItemGroup` element that contains a Protobuf reference to `status.proto`:

```
<Protobuf Include="Protos\worker.proto" />
```

Now, we will add a service definition that will implement this proto file. We will do this by placing a `JobManagerService.cs` file inside the `Services` folder of the `StatusMicroservice` project.

First, we will add the necessary package imports to the file, as follows:

```
using System;
using System.Threading.Tasks;
using Grpc.Core;
using Worker;
```

Then, we will add a class definition by inheriting from the class that has been autogenerated from our proto file, as follows:

```
namespace StatusMicroservice
{
    public class JobManagerService : JobManager.JobManagerBase
    {
    }
}
```

We will then add the following override for our server-streaming `TriggerJobs` method:

```
public override async Task TriggerJobs(TriggerJobsRequest
    request,
IServerStreamWriter<TriggerJobsResponse> responseStream,
ServerCallContext context)
{
    for (var i = 0; i < request.JobsCount; i++)
    {
        await Task.Delay(TimeSpan.FromSeconds(2));

        await responseStream.WriteAsync(new TriggerJobsResponse
        {
            JobSequence = i + 1,
            JobMessage = "Job executed successfully"
        });
    }
}
```

Then, we will add an override for our client-streaming `SendJobs` method, as follows:

```
public override async Task<SendJobsResponse>
SendJobs(IAsyncStreamReader<SendJobsRequest> requestStream,
ServerCallContext context)
{
    while (await requestStream.MoveNext())
    {
        Console.WriteLine($"Job Id: {requestStream.Current.
```

```
                JobId}.
            Job description: {requestStream.Current.
                JobDescription}");
        await Task.Delay(TimeSpan.FromSeconds(2));
    }

    return new SendJobsResponse
    {
        Completed = true
    };
}
```

This service mimics long-running tasks that the gRPC client has asked it to perform.

In the `TriggerJobs` method, we are simply told how many jobs to trigger. Perhaps there is already a list of the jobs waiting in the queue on the server, so we are telling the application how many of them we want to get executed.

In our code, we are mimicking job execution by waiting 2 seconds. Then, we place a description of the successfully executed job in the server stream.

Essentially, when a client makes a call to this RPC, a channel between the client and the server is opened and the client gets instantly notified of any new item that is placed on the server stream. So, in this case, the client will be updated on every successfully executed job at an interval of 2 seconds.

`SendJobs` is similar, but it utilizes the client stream. This method simulates a scenario where a list of specific job descriptions is sent to the server. Once again, every job takes 2 seconds to execute. However, this time, the client doesn't get notified of its execution, only getting notified when all jobs have been successfully processed. But because, just as in the first case, the process is long-running, the client is expected to keep the communication channel open and receive the response in an asynchronous manner.

We will now need to register our new service inside the `Startup` class of the `StatusMicroservice` project. To do so, just add the following line of code inside the `app.UseEndpoints()` call next to the line where you have registered `StatusManagerService` as the gRPC endpoint:

```
endpoints.MapGrpcService<JobManagerService>();
```

Next, we will configure the right client inside the `ApiGateway` project.

Configuring the gRPC client for asynchronous communication

Our REST API gateway needs a suitable JSON model that will be able to convert it (the gateway) into a `SendJobsRequest` gRPC message. This will be achieved by placing a `JobModel.cs` file in the root of the `ApiGateway` project with the following content:

```
namespace ApiGateway
{
    public class JobModel
    {
        public int JobId { get; set; }
        public string JobDescription { get; set; }
    }
}
```

Then, we will add a wrapper for our client. This will be achieved by placing a `GrpcJobsClient.cs` file in the root of the `ApiGateway` project. We will first add the necessary namespace imports, as follows:

```
using System;
using System.Collections.Generic;
using System.Threading.Tasks;
using Grpc.Core;
using Grpc.Net.Client;
using Worker;
```

Then, we will place the following interface inside the namespace definition:

```
public interface IGrpcJobsClient
{
    Task SendJobs(IEnumerable<JobModel> jobs);
    Task TriggerJobs(int jobCount);
}
```

We will add our class definition and set up our gRPC client in the constructor, as follows:

```
internal class GrpcJobsClient : IGrpcJobsClient, IDisposable
{
    private readonly GrpcChannel channel;
```

```
        private readonly JobManager.JobManagerClient client;

        public GrpcJobsClient(string serverUrl)
        {
            channel = GrpcChannel.ForAddress(serverUrl);
            client = new JobManager.JobManagerClient(channel);
        }
}
```

We will then add a client-side implementation of our client-streaming method, as follows:

```
public async Task SendJobs(IEnumerable<JobModel> jobs)
{
    using var call = client.SendJobs();

    foreach (var job in jobs)
    {
        await call.RequestStream.WriteAsync(new SendJobsRequest
        {
            JobId = job.JobId,
            JobDescription = job.JobDescription
        });
    }
    await call.RequestStream.CompleteAsync();

    await call;
}
```

Then, we will add an implementation of the server-streaming method, as follows:

```
public async Task TriggerJobs(int jobCount)
{
    using var call = client.TriggerJobs(new TriggerJobsRequest
        {
      JobsCount = jobCount });

    while (await call.ResponseStream.MoveNext())
    {
```

```
        Console.WriteLine($"Job sequence:
            {call.ResponseStream.Current.JobSequence}. Job
            description: {call.ResponseStream.Current.
            JobMessage}");
        await Task.Delay(TimeSpan.FromSeconds(2));
    }
}
```

Finally, we will implement an `IDisposable` interface to dispose of the gRPC channel object once we are done with it, as follows:

```
public void Dispose()
{
    channel.Dispose();
}
```

In the `SendJobs` method, this class will place all the job descriptions in the client stream and will then wait until the service has processed them all. In the `TriggerJobs` method, the client will send the original request to the server, then it will write into the console the content of each item that gets placed into the stream by the server. Again, this call will not be complete until the stream is closed.

Now, we will register this client, making it available for our REST API to access. To do so, add the following line of code anywhere inside the `ConfigureServices` method of the `Startup` class:

```
services.AddSingleton<IGrpcJobsClient>(p => new
GrpcJobsClient(Configuration["ServerUrl"]));
```

Finally, we will add a new controller to our application. Inside the `Controllers` folder, we will create a `JobsController.cs` file with the following content:

```
using System.Collections.Generic;
using Microsoft.AspNetCore.Mvc;

namespace ApiGateway.Controllers
{
    [ApiController]
    [Route("[controller]")]
    public class JobsController : ControllerBase
```

```csharp
{
    private readonly IGrpcJobsClient client;

    public JobsController(IGrpcJobsClient client)
    {
        this.client = client;
    }

    [HttpPost("")]
    public void SendJobs([FromBody] IEnumerable<JobModel> jobs)
    {
        _ = client.SendJobs(jobs);
    }

    [HttpPost("{jobsCount}")]
    public void TriggerJobs(int jobsCount)
    {
        _ = client.TriggerJobs(jobsCount);
    }
}
```

Here, we have an API endpoint for each of our RPC methods. In both cases, we don't care whether all the jobs have been executed successfully. After all, there may be many jobs that will take a long time to run, which will cause our HTTP client to time out. Instead, we just make sure that the jobs are triggered. It's up to the backend to actually take care of the execution.

In our case, we trigger asynchronous tasks without awaiting them by assigning return values of our client wrapper methods to `_`. This is done to explicitly let our compiler know that we don't want to wait for the outcome of the task, and we just want to move on.

Of course, we could just execute either a `SendJobs` or `TriggerJobs` method without assigning its return value to anything, but in this case, our IDE wouldn't know that it was intentional. It wouldn't know whether we actually wanted to skip the wait for the task's outcome or if we've just forgotten to put the `await` keyword, so it may warn us by highlighting the code.

We are now fully set up. Now, let's see asynchronous gRPC communication in action.

Testing asynchronous gRPC endpoints

As before, we will open the CLI in both the `ApiGateway` and `StatusMicroservice` project folders and run the following command:

```
dotnet run
```

When both applications are up and running, we will open a browser and navigate to the Swagger page of the `ApiGateway` application. You are now expected to see `Jobs` controller endpoints, as illustrated in the following screenshot:

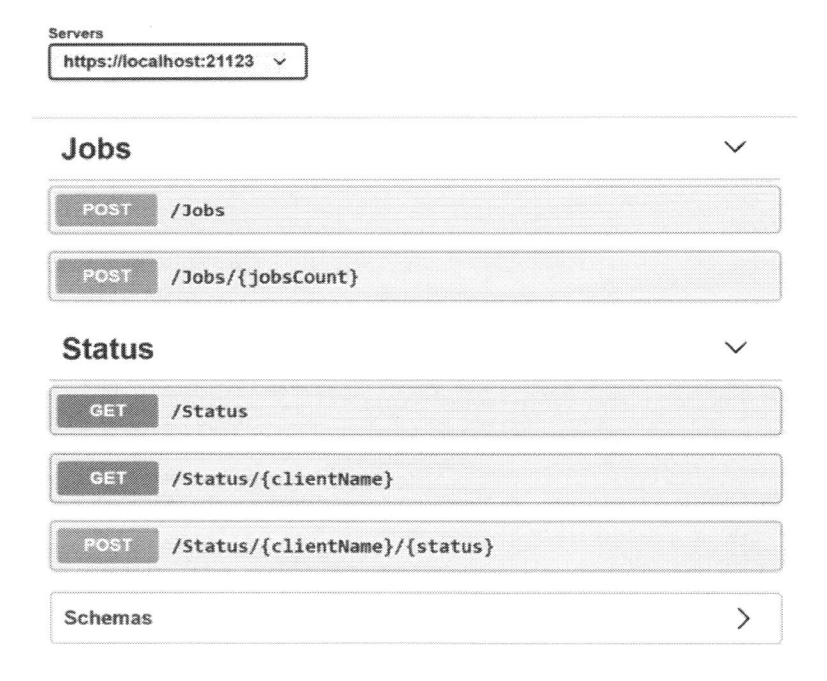

Figure 2.2 – Swagger page with new endpoints

Now, if you try the first endpoint, which corresponds to the `SendJobs` RPC and fills up the request body with sample data, you should start seeing job-status entries appearing in the command-line terminal of `StatusMicroservice` at regular intervals, as illustrated in the following screenshot:

Figure 2.3 – Job-status entries in StatusMicroservice terminal

Now, if you execute the second endpoint on the Swagger page and get it to trigger a random number of jobs, you will start seeing entries appearing in the `ApiGateway` terminal at regular intervals, as illustrated in the following screenshot:

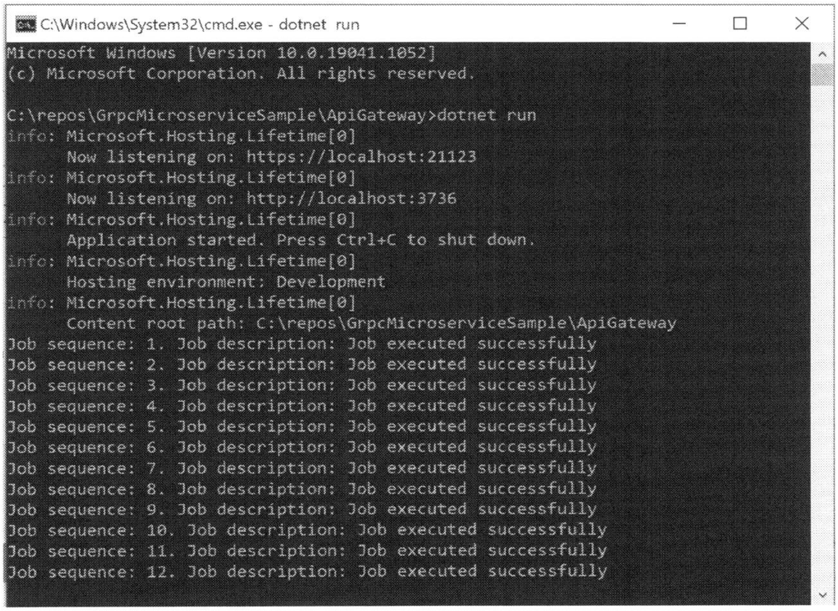

Figure 2.4 – Job-status entries in ApiGateway terminal

However, even though it took a while to execute all the jobs, in both cases the HTTP response was returned from the API immediately. So, this clearly demonstrates how gRPC communication channels can be used asynchronously.

Though gRPC is a great tool for both synchronous and asynchronous communication, it's not the best tool for all web-based communication types—for example, for use in browsers. We will now see why this is the case.

Why gRPC is not the best tool for browsers

The key reason why gRPC is not the best tool for browsers is that it relies on HTTP/2. While modern browsers support HTTP/2, they don't support all of its features, but some of those unsupported features are precisely the features that gRPC needs.

To work around these limitations, a browser-specific implementation has been developed. This is known as gRPC-Web.

However, even this implementation is not perfect. It comes with the following limitations that, arguably, nullify the utility of gRPC:

- It requires a proxy to run between the client and the server, converting browser-bound data into a format compatible with HTTP/1.1, increasing the latency and making the payload larger.
- It does not support client-streaming calls.
- It requires relaxing **cross-origin resource sharing** (**CORS**) policy on the server side, potentially creating security vulnerabilities.
- Both the client and the server require additional setup steps.

Now, to demonstrate that gRPC is not necessarily the most convenient tool to use in a browser, we will set up a **Blazor WebAssembly** project as a gRPC client. Just as with standard JavaScript, Blazor WebAssembly runs in the browser and has the same limitations as any other browser-based code.

Setting up a Blazor WebAssembly gRPC client

We will now create a .NET application that you can run in the browser after being compiled to WebAssembly. We could have used a standard JavaScript application instead, but since we have already been using .NET with our gRPC examples, we will continue to do so to minimize unnecessary cognitive load from learning new technology. In .NET, the Blazor project template allows you to compile code for execution in browsers.

In the root of `GrpcMicroserviceSample`, execute the following command to create a Blazor WebAssembly project:

```
dotnet new blazorwasm -o GrpcBlazorClient
```

Because client-side Blazor cannot use server-side ASP.NET Core framework components, you will not be able to use a `GrpcDependencies` assembly, as it contains a reference to the server-side gRPC library. Therefore, you will need to create a `Protos` folder in the `GrpcBlazorClient` project folder and copy the `status.proto` file there. After that, add the following section to the `GrpcBlazorClient.csproj` file:

```
<ItemGroup>
    <Protobuf Include="Protos\status.proto" />
</ItemGroup>
```

Next, add all necessary client-side NuGet dependencies by executing the following commands from inside the `GrpcBlazorClient` project folder:

```
dotnet add GrpcBlazorClient.csproj package Grpc.Net.Client
dotnet add GrpcBlazorClient.csproj package Google.Protobuf
dotnet add GrpcBlazorClient.csproj package Grpc.Tools
dotnet add GrpcBlazorClient.csproj package Grpc.Net.Client.Web
```

Please note that as well as adding the standard gRPC client packages, we have added the `Grpc.Net.Client.Web` package. This package is necessary for converting HTTP/2 gRPC responses from the server into HTTP/1.1 data that the client can understand.

Next, copy the `ClientStatus.cs`, `ClientStatusModel.cs`, and `GrpcStatusClient.cs` files from the root of the `ApiGateway` project to the root of the `GrpcBlazorClient` project. After you've done this, open each of the copied files and change the namespace from `ApiGateway` to `GrpcBlazorClient`.

Next, we will modify our client channel so that it can actually use gRPC-Web. To do this, add the following `using` statement to the `GrpcStatusClient.cs` file inside the `GrpcBlazorClient` project:

```
using System.Net.Http;
using Grpc.Net.Client.Web;
```

Then, inside the same file, change your constructor definition to the following:

```
public GrpcStatusClient(string serverUrl)
{
    channel = GrpcChannel.ForAddress(serverUrl, new
      GrpcChannelOptions
    {
        HttpHandler = new GrpcWebHandler(new
          HttpClientHandler())
    });

    client = new StatusManager.StatusManagerClient(channel);
}
```

This adds an HTTP handler to the channel so that gRPC communication will be converted to standard HTTP/1.1 communication that the browser client will be able to understand.

We will now need to create a page that will use our new gRPC-Web client. To do so, replace the content of the `Index.razor` file inside the `Pages` folder.

Inside this file, we will first add the path at which this page will be accessed in the browser. After that, we will inject the service that we depend on. We do this by running the following code:

```
@page "/"
@inject IGrpcStatusClient Client
```

We will then add buttons that will trigger various gRPC actions, as follows:

```
<div class="row" style="padding-top: 50px;">
    <div class="col-md-4">
        <div>
            <div>
                <label for="clientName">Client Name</label>
                <input @bind="clientName" type="text"
                  id="clientName" name="clientName" />
            </div>
            <button @onclick="() => SetStatus(1)"
```

```
                disabled="@(string.
                    IsNullOrWhiteSpace(clientName))"
                    >Set Status Online</button>
            <button @onclick="() => SetStatus(0)"
                disabled="@(string.
                    IsNullOrWhiteSpace(clientName))"
                    >Set Status Offline</button>
            <button @onclick="() => SetStatus(2)"
                disabled="@(string.
                    IsNullOrWhiteSpace(clientName))"
                    >Set Status Busy</button>
        </div>
    </div>
```

Then, we will add a panel that will display data that we will receive from the server, as follows:

```
    <div class="col-md-7">
        <p>Client Statuses</p>
        <div>
            @foreach (var status in statuses)
            {
                <div>@status</div>
            }
        </div>
        <button @onclick="GetStatuses">Get All Client
            Statuses</button>
    </div>
</div>
```

All of our C# code will go into the following section, which we will place immediately below the markup:

```
@code {

    private string clientName = string.Empty;
    private List<string> statuses = new List<string>();
```

```csharp
        private async Task SetStatus(int status)
        {
            await Client.UpdateClientStatus(clientName,
                (ClientStatus)status);
            await GetStatuses();
        }

        private async Task GetStatuses()
        {
            var newStatuses = await Client.GetAllStatuses();
            statuses = new List<string>();

            foreach (var status in newStatuses)
            {
                statuses.Add($"Client name: {status.Name}; status:
                    {status.Status}");
            }
            StateHasChanged();
        }
}
```

We have a simple web page that allows us to update client statuses and obtain the latest client status data from the gRPC server.

Finally, we need to register our gRPC client dependency. To do so, add the following line of code to the `Main` method of the `Program` class of the project:

```csharp
builder.Services.AddSingleton<IGrpcStatusClient>(p => new
 GrpcStatusClient("https://localhost:35095"));
```

Make sure that this line goes before the following line of code:

```csharp
await builder.Build().RunAsync();
```

In this example, we are hardcoding the URL because, with client-side Blazor, all settings that we have are visible to the user if they decide to view the page source. This might be acceptable for URLs but will definitely not be acceptable for sensitive private data such as secrets. Therefore, it's generally a better practice to recompile and redistribute the Blazor WebAssembly application when settings change, while populating the actual setting values in the code by an automated process.

The URL that we are using is the public HTTPS URL configured in the `launchSettings.json` file of the `StatusMicroservice` project.

Our client application is fully configured. Now, we can add the necessary modifications to our server application.

Modifying the gRPC server to enable gRPC-Web

What makes gRPC-Web difficult to use is that it's not enough to merely set up the relevant client components for it. We also need to modify our server to make it compatible with gRPC-Web.

gRPC-Web requires a proxy that will be able to translate between standard HTTP requests and gRPC, which, in a way, defeats the purpose of gRPC. Firstly, you cannot use a highly efficient Protobuf communication protocol. Secondly, you have to perform additional setup steps for enable even the most basic gRPC functionality.

We will now make the necessary changes to our `StatusMicroservice` application to demonstrate this in action. We will start by adding a `Grpc.AspNetCore.Web` NuGet reference to our `StatusMicroservice` project. We can do so by executing the following command from inside our project folder:

```
dotnet add StatusMicroservice.csproj package Grpc.AspNetCore.Web
```

Now, we will need to enable gRPC-Web components in the code. Because our calls will be done from a remote client over HTTP, we will need to tell our application to accept CORS requests with specific headers. To do so, we will add the following code into the `ConfigureServices` method of the `Startup` class:

```
services.AddCors(o => o.AddPolicy("AllowAnyGrpcWeb", builder =>
    {
            builder.AllowAnyOrigin()
                .AllowAnyMethod()
                .AllowAnyHeader()
                .WithExposedHeaders("Grpc-Status",
                    "Grpc-Message", "Grpc-Encoding",
                    "Grpc-Accept-Encoding");
    }));
```

Then, we will add both the CORS configuration and the gRPC-Web proxy to our request pipeline. To do so, locate the `app.UseRouting();` line in the `Configure` method of the `Startup` class (or the main body of the `Program.cs` file on .NET 6 template) and add the following two lines of code immediately after this:

```
app.UseGrpcWeb();
app.UseCors();
```

Finally, we will need to tell our application that a specific gRPC endpoint can be reached by gRPC-Web requests. To do so, we will replace this line of code:

```
endpoints.MapGrpcService<StatusManagerService>();
```

The preceding line of code will be replaced with the following code:

```
endpoints.MapGrpcService<StatusManagerService>().
    EnableGrpcWeb().Req
ireCors("AllowAnyGrpcWeb");
```

Now, we are ready to launch the application.

Launching the gRPC-Web application

Open a command-line terminal inside both the `StatusMicroservice` and `GrpcBlazorClient` project folders and execute a `dotnet run` command.

Once both applications are up, you can open the browser at the address configured inside the `GrpcBlazorClient` project settings (`https://localhost:5001` by default) and see gRPC-Web in action, as illustrated in the following screenshot:

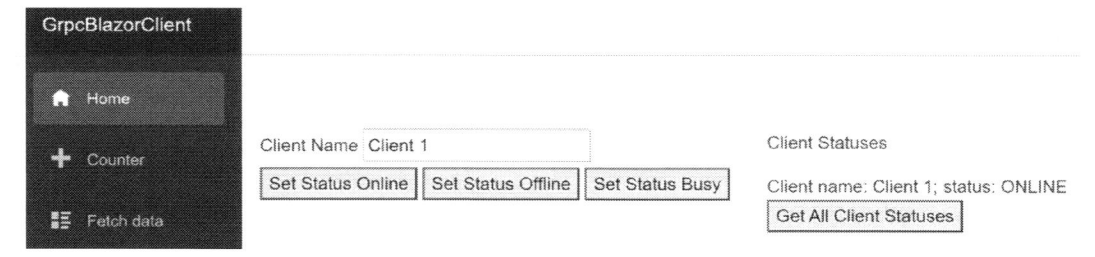

Figure 2.5 – Blazor WebAssembly using gRPC-Web

You can now appreciate why gRPC is not the best tool to be used in browsers. Setting it up involves a lot of hassle and you don't get all the gRPC benefits in return.

Luckily, .NET has other tools that will allow you to achieve the functionality in a browser equivalent to gRPC with minimal effort. SignalR is perhaps the best of such tools.

Where SignalR would beat gRPC

SignalR is an ASP.NET Core library that enables real-time two-way communication between the client and the server. It can do everything that gRPC can do (making requests, receiving responses, streaming data to and from the client, and streaming data from the server). But in addition to this, it can also send data from the server to the client without receiving a request first.

Because SignalR runs over HTTP/1.1, it requires a persistent connection and it uses a fairly verbose JSON payload, so perhaps it's not the best tool to be used in the backend of a distributed microservice application. But it's ideal for browsers and it's relatively effortless to set up too, as we will see now.

Setting up a SignalR application

Create an ASP.NET Razor Pages project by executing the following command. This command can be executed from any folder of your choice, as this will be a standalone application:

```
dotnet new webapp -o SignalrApplication
```

SignalR is already embedded in ASP.NET Core, so you won't have to add any extra dependencies.

Now, we will add the server-side SignalR functionality in a so-called SignalR hub. To do so, create a `Hubs` folder inside your project and add a `JobsHub.cs` file to it with the following content:

```
using System;
using System.Collections.Generic;
using System.Runtime.CompilerServices;
using System.Threading;
using System.Threading.Tasks;
using Microsoft.AspNetCore.SignalR;

namespace SignalrApplication.Hubs
{
    public class JobsHub : Hub
    {
    }
}
```

We will then start adding methods to the hub. `SendSingleJob` receives a single response and returns it back to the caller, as illustrated in the following code snippet:

```
public async Task SendSingleJob(string jobDescription)
{
    await Clients.Caller.SendAsync("ReceiveMessage", $"Job
      executed successfully. Description: {jobDescription}");
}
```

`StreamJobs` receives a stream of data from the client, as illustrated in the following code snippet:

```
public async Task StreamJobs(IAsyncEnumerable<int> stream)
{
    var jobsCount = 0;
    await foreach (var item in stream)
    {
        Console.WriteLine($"Job {item} executed succesfully");
        jobsCount++;
    }

    await Clients.Caller.SendAsync("ReceiveMessage",
      $"{jobsCount}
      jobs executed successfully.");
}
```

`TriggerJobs` gets initiated by the client and then sends a stream of data back to it, as illustrated in the following code snippet:

```
public async IAsyncEnumerable<string> TriggerJobs(
int jobsCount,
[EnumeratorCancellation]
CancellationToken cancellationToken)
{
    for (var i = 0; i < jobsCount; i++)
    {
        cancellationToken.ThrowIfCancellationRequested();
        yield return $"Job {i} executed succesfully";
```

```
            await Task.Delay(2000, cancellationToken);
    }
}
```

We have the following three methods here:

- `SendSingleJob` receives a single response and returns it back to the caller.
- `StreamJobs` receives a stream of data from the client.
- `TriggerJobs` gets initiated by the client and then sends a stream of data back to it.

We will now need to enable our SignalR components inside our `Startup` class, or `Program.cs` file if you are using .NET 6 template, with appropriate modifications of the following code samples. But first, we will need to add a reference to our hub namespace by adding the following `using` statement on top of the `Startup.cs` file:

```
using SignalrApplication.Hubs;
```

Then, we will need to enable SignalR by adding the following line of code to the `ConfigureServices` method:

```
services.AddSignalR();
```

Finally, we need to register the hub endpoint by adding the following line of code inside the call to the `UseEndpoints` method:

```
endpoints.MapHub<JobsHub>("/jobsHub");
```

Now, we are ready to start adding client components.

Adding a SignalR client and launching the application

Locate the `Index.cshtml` file inside the `Pages` folder and replace its content with the following:

```
@page
@model IndexModel
@{ ViewData["Title"] = "Home page"; }

<div class="row" style="padding-top: 50px;">
    <div class="col-md-6">
```

```html
            <div class="control-group">
                <div>
                    <label for="job-description">Job
                        description:</label>
                    <input type="text" id="job-description"
                        name="job-description" />
                </div>
                <button id="btn-send-single">Send Single Job
                    </button>
            </div>
            <div class="control-group">
                <div>
                    <label for="jobs-to-send">Number of jobs to
                        send:</label>
                    <input type="text" id="jobs-to-send"
                        name="jobs-to-send" />
                </div>
                <button id="btn-send-multiple">Send Multiple
                    Jobs</button>
            </div>
            <div class="control-group">
                <div>
                    <label for="jobs-to-trigger">Number of jobs to
                        trigger:</label>
                    <input type="text" id="jobs-to-trigger"
                        name="jobs-to-trigger" />
                </div>
                <button id="btn-trigger-multiple">Trigger Multiple
                    Jobs</button>
            </div>
        </div>

        <div class="col-md-7">
            <p>Responses from the server:</p>
            <pre id="signalr-message-panel"></pre>
```

```
            </div>
        </div>
        <script src="https://cdnjs.cloudflare.com/ajax/libs/microsoft-
            signalr/3.1.7/signalr.min.js"></script>
```

Please note that there is a `script` element at the bottom of the preceding code block. This is where we are adding the `SignalR` JavaScript library.

After this, locate the `site.js` file in the `wwwroot/js` folder and delete any content that's already present in it.

In this file, we will start by initializing a SignalR connection by adding the following code:

```
const connection = new signalR.HubConnectionBuilder()
    .withUrl("/jobsHub")
    .configureLogging(signalR.LogLevel.Information)
    .build();
```

Then, we will register an event. Whenever a SignalR hub on the server sends a message to the `ReceiveMessage` endpoint on the client, an `addMessage` JavaScript function will be executed. The code is illustrated in the following snippet:

```
connection.on("ReceiveMessage", (message) =>
    addMessage(message));
function addMessage(message) {
    $('#signalr-message-panel').prepend($('<div />').
        text(message));
}
```

We will then make one of our HTML buttons send a message to the `SendSingleJob` endpoint on our server-side hub by running the following code:

```
$('#btn-send-single').click(function () {
    var jobDescription = $('#job-description').val();

    connection.invoke("SendSingleJob", jobDescription).
        catch(err =>
        console.error(err.toString()));
});
```

Then, we will make another button send a stream to the `StreamJobs` endpoint, as follows:

```javascript
$('#btn-send-multiple').click(function () {
    var numberOfJobs = parseInt($('#jobs-to-send').val(), 10);
    var subject = new signalR.Subject();

    var iteration = 0;
    var intervalHandle = setInterval(() => {
        iteration++;
        subject.next(iteration);
        if (iteration === numberOfJobs) {
            clearInterval(intervalHandle);
            subject.complete();
        }
    }, 2000);

    connection.send("StreamJobs", subject);
});
```

Then, we will make another button trigger a server-side stream from the `TriggerJobs` endpoint and subscribe to it, as follows:

```javascript
$('#btn-trigger-multiple').click(function () {
    var numberOfJobs = parseInt($('#jobs-to-trigger').val(),
        10);

    connection.stream("TriggerJobs", numberOfJobs)
        .subscribe({
            next: (message) => addMessage(message)
        });
});
```

Finally, we will add some error handling to our SignalR connection object and will start the connection, as follows:

```javascript
async function start() {
    try {
        await connection.start();
```

```
        console.log('connected');
    } catch (err) {
        console.log(err);
        setTimeout(() => start(), 5000);
    }
};

connection.onclose(async () => {
    await start();
});

start();
```

Here, we are registering an event handler for the `ReceiveMessage` call from the server. We are also associating various SignalR calls with the buttons on our page, and then we instantiate a SignalR connection to the server.

We can now launch our application by executing a `dotnet run` command inside our project folder and opening it in the browser (`https://localhost:5001` by default), which will take us to the following screen:

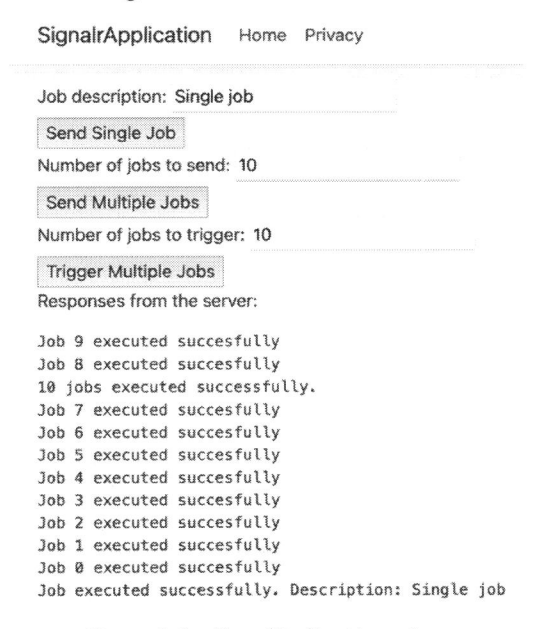

```
SignalrApplication    Home   Privacy

Job description: Single job
[Send Single Job]
Number of jobs to send: 10
[Send Multiple Jobs]
Number of jobs to trigger: 10
[Trigger Multiple Jobs]
Responses from the server:

Job 9 executed succesfully
Job 8 executed succesfully
10 jobs executed successfully.
Job 7 executed succesfully
Job 6 executed succesfully
Job 5 executed succesfully
Job 4 executed succesfully
Job 3 executed succesfully
Job 2 executed succesfully
Job 1 executed succesfully
Job 0 executed succesfully
Job executed successfully. Description: Single job
```

Figure 2.6 – SignalR client in action

This application demonstrates how SignalR allows us to do everything that we could do with gRPC but do so in a browser. Also, it shows us that, for browser-based applications, SignalR is much more effortless to set up than gRPC-Web. And, unlike gRPC-Web, SignalR is capable of performing client-streaming calls.

SignalR is also the technology that is used by server-side Blazor to allow the in-browser components to communicate with the server, and server-side Blazor is another tool that will allow you to enable gRPC-like functionality in the browser.

The main advantage of using server-side Blazor over pure SignalR is that you won't have to learn JavaScript. You can write all of your code in C# and it will be automatically converted into in-browser code and markup.

The main disadvantage of server-side Blazor is that it can only be used to communicate with the backend of the same application that has served you the web page. Unlike pure SignalR, it cannot be configured to communicate with any arbitrary service on the network.

We will not cover server-side Blazor in detail here, but you will be able to find documentation on it in the *Further reading* section.

Summary

In this chapter, we saw how the gRPC communication mechanism is most suitable to be used for direct communication between microservices, as it uses a highly efficient Protobuf messaging protocol over HTTP/2. As well as making synchronous request-response calls, gRPC is capable of asynchronously streaming data both ways between the client and the server.

gRPC cannot work in browsers as it requires HTTP/2, which browsers don't fully support. However, a gRPC-Web implementation has been created specifically to enable gRPC in the browser. However, gRPC-Web still has severe limitations, as it requires many setup steps, is much less efficient than standard gRPC, and doesn't support client-streaming calls.

A good alternative to gRPC-Web for browsers is SignalR, which is already embedded in ASP.NET Core. It supports bi-directional messaging (both singular and streaming) and takes minimal effort to set up.

After reading this chapter, you should know how to apply gRPC as a communication mechanism between ASP.NET Core microservices. You also now know how to implement gRPC-like functionality in the browser when gRPC itself is not the best solution.

In the next chapter, we will have a more detailed look at the data types that are supported by gRPC Protobuf out of the box. We will cover all of the embedded data types and explain how each of them gets converted to C#.

Questions

1. Can gRPC support asynchronous calls?

   A. No, it only supports synchronous calls.

   B. Yes, by utilizing streaming.

   C. Yes, but only by using `async/await` on the client.

   D. Yes, but only on gRPC-Web.

2. Can you use gRPC inside a browser?

   A. Not at all.

   B. Yes, it just works out of the box.

   C. Yes, but only via gRPC-Web.

   D. Yes, but it only works with a Blazor client.

3. Which one of the following is NOT a limitation of gRPC-Web?

   A. Server-streaming calls

   B. Client-streaming calls

   C. Having to convert messages to HTTP/1.1

   D. Having to use a proxy

4. Do you need to make additional modifications to enable gRPC-Web if you already have gRPC enabled?

   A. No, the framework will automatically convert gRPC to gRPC-Web.

   B. Yes, both on the server and the client.

   C. Yes, but only on the client.

   D. Yes, but only on the server.

5. What can SignalR do that gRPC can't?

    A. Bi-directional streaming

    B. Client-streaming calls

    C. Asynchronous calls

    D. Calls from the server to the client without a request from the client

Further reading

- *Core concepts, architecture, and lifecycle*: `https://grpc.io/docs/what-is-grpc/core-concepts/`
- *The state of gRPC in the browser* by Johan Brandhorst: `https://grpc.io/blog/state-of-grpc-web/`
- *Introduction to ASP.NET Core SignalR*: `https://docs.microsoft.com/en-us/aspnet/core/signalr/introduction`
- *ASP.NET Core Blazor hosting models*: `https://docs.microsoft.com/en-us/aspnet/core/blazor/hosting-models`

3
Protobuf – the Communication Protocol of gRPC

We briefly covered the structure of a proto file in *Chapter 1, Creating a Basic gRPC Application on ASP.NET Core*. In *Chapter 1, Creating a Basic gRPC Application on ASP.NET Core*, we also had a look at the most basic type of **remote procedure call** (**RPC**), the **unary call**, which is equivalent to a standard HTTP request-response call. Then, we briefly covered streaming **gRPC** calls in *Chapter 2, When gRPC Is the Best Tool and When It Isn't*.

In this chapter, we will take an in-depth look at **Protobuf** – the communication protocol that is used by gRPC. We will also cover the structure and the syntax of a proto file.

Although the Protobuf protocol was designed to be as intuitive as possible, it's not always obvious how to use some of its components most optimally. Additionally, some Protobuf features are not very well known, despite their usefulness.

The objective of this chapter is to go through all of the built-in components of a proto file, explain how they are used, and demonstrate how they get translated into **C#** code.

We will cover the following topics:

- The types of RPCs available with gRPC
- The built-in Protobuf data types
- How these data types get converted to C# data types
- How to use collections in Protobuf messages
- Special keywords in the Protobuf protocol
- How to reference other proto files from a proto file

By the end of this chapter, you will have learned how to use all of the built-in features of the Protobuf protocol and how to optimize proto definitions for the most efficient data transfer.

Technical requirements

To follow the instructions in this chapter, you will need the following:

- A computer with a **Windows**, **Mac**, or **Linux** operating system
- A supported IDE or code editor (**Visual Studio**, **Visual Studio Code**, or **JetBrains Rider**)
- The **.NET 5 software development kit** (**SDK**)
- A self-signed development HTTPS certificate enabled on your machine

For instructions on how to set up these prerequisites, please refer to *Chapter 1, Creating a Basic gRPC Application on ASP.NET Core*.

All of the code samples used in this chapter can be found in this book's **GitHub** repository: `https://github.com/PacktPublishing/Microservices-Communication-in-.NET-Using-gRPC/tree/main/Chapter-03`

The RPC types supported by gRPC

We will start by creating a solution from a standard `gRPC Service` template. We will call our project `IndepthProtobuf`. To create this project, execute the following command:

```
dotnet new grpc -o IndepthProtobuf
```

Now, we are ready to make modifications to our project to examine all the relevant Protobuf features.

The RPC types that Protobuf supports

Since we already have the `greet.proto` file placed in the `Protos` directory of our `IndepthProtobuf` project, and because we already have a basic implementation of the service represented by this file, we won't be replacing any existing functionality. Instead, we will add to it.

To make a start, we will replace the content of the `greet.proto` file with the following:

```
syntax = "proto3";

option csharp_namespace = "IndepthProtobuf";

package greet;

service Greeter {
  rpc SayHello (HelloRequest) returns (HelloReply);
    // Unary RPC
  rpc RequestManyHellos (stream HelloRequest) returns
    (HelloReply);
  // Client-streaming RPC
  rpc SayManyHellos (HelloRequest) returns (stream HelloReply);
  // Server-streaming RPC
  rpc RequestAndSayManyHellos (stream HelloRequest) returns
    (stream HelloReply); // Bi-directional streaming RPC
}

message HelloRequest {
   string name = 1; // Name of the client to say hello to
}

message HelloReply {
   string message = 1;
}
```

In this proto file, we have left the original `SayHello rpc` definition inside the `Greeter` service intact. But we have also added three additional `rpc` definitions to it, all of which reuse the same request and response objects.

The original `SayHello rpc` is a standard unary call. It receives a single request object and returns a single response object. A unary RPC call consists of an `rpc` keyword, the custom name of the RPC, and the request object type name in brackets, followed by the `returns` keyword, which is then followed by the name of the response object type in brackets. These are all of the components of a unary call. There aren't any additional keywords in use.

A newly added `RequestManyHellos rpc` is a **client-streaming call**. This is determined by the `stream` keyword being placed in front of the request message type name in brackets, but keyword needs to be present before the response message type name.

A client-streaming call allows you to send many instances of a specific message type to the server while only accepting a single response message once the entire stream of request messages has been processed. Using a client-streaming call allows you to keep the communication channel open for some time. Any new message placed in the stream by the client will be readable by the server immediately. However, the client would only expect the response to come when there are no further messages to be placed in the stream.

The messages can be added to the stream by the client in quick succession, or there can be some latency between the messages. Streaming gRPC calls are designed to be kept open for as long as necessary.

The `SayManyHellos rpc` is the opposite of `RequestManyHellos`, as it has the `stream` keyword next to the response object rather than the request object. This means that the client needs to trigger this endpoint by sending an initial singular request to it. After this request, many instances of the response message are sent back to the client. The client is notified that the stream has been closed as soon as the server-side method is complete.

Until then, the stream can be kept open for a configurable amount of time, which we will cover in *Chapter 7, Using Different Call Types that gRPC Supports*.

The final `rpc` definition that we have added, `RequstAndSayManyHellos`, has the `stream` keyword next to both the request and response objects. This is known as a bi-directional streaming call, and it works like a combination of the client-streaming and server-streaming calls.

Making comments in Protobuf

Just like in your code, you can add any arbitrary, non-executable text to your proto files as *comments*. The comments are there purely to explain the code better. They don't have any effect whatsoever on the execution of the code.

Protobuf supports two types of comments, which will be familiar to anyone who has used the C# programming language.

If you put a double forward-slash (//) on any line, the rest of the line will be treated as a single-line comment. This is where you can put any arbitrary text. The following is an example of a single-line comment:

```
// This is a single line comment
```

It can occupy the whole line or can be placed after any executable code. We have examples of the latter next to our RPC and message field definitions in the code example in the previous section. For instance, the `HelloRequest` message has the following after its definition:

```
string name = 1; // Name of the client to say hello to
```

Multi-line comments are also supported by Protobuf. They are prefixed by /*. Any content that follows this combination of characters will be treated as a comment until the closing combination (*/) is found. An example of a multi-line comment would be the following:

```
/* This is
a multiline comment */
```

We have now covered the basic structure of a proto file and had a look at every RPC type that the Protobuf protocol supports. Now, let's have a look at the built-in data types that are available with Protobuf.

Reviewing the native Protobuf data types

We will need to modify our `greet.proto` file further. Let's add the following section at the bottom of it:

```
message BasicTypes {
    int32 int_field = 1;
    int64 long_field = 2;
    uint32 unsigned_int_field = 3;
```

```
    uint64 unsigned_long_field = 4;
    sint32 signed_int_field = 5;
    sint64 signed_long_field = 6;
    fixed32 fixed_int_field = 7;
    fixed64 fixed_long_field = 8;
    sfixed32 signed_fixed_int_field = 9;
    sfixed64 signed_fixed_long_field = 10;
    float float_field = 11;
    double double_field = 12;
    bool boolean_field = 13;
    string string_field = 14;
    bytes bytes_field = 15;
}
```

This `message` definition, alongside the `enum` section that we have added, provides all of the basic built-in data types available in Protobuf. We have named each field after the data type it represents to make it easy to demonstrate each data type in action.

Please note that each field name uses the snake_case naming style (that is, the name consists of only lowercase letters and the words are separated by underscores). This is a universal convention that is independent of the Protobuf standard. When snake_case is used, any language-specific Protobuf compiler will apply standard naming conventions to the field names while converting the content of a proto file into code. For example, `int_field` would be converted into PascalCase (`IntField`) if used with C#, but camelCase (`intField`) if used with **Java**.

However, individual implementations of the Protobuf compiler can apply the correct naming conventions to field names even if snake_case conventions aren't applied. For example, if we apply camelCase field names, where we start the name with the lowercase letter and then start any new word with an uppercase letter, it will still be correctly converted into a PascalCase name in C#. We used some examples of this in *Chapter 2, When gRPC Is the Best Tool and When It Isn't*.

Please also note the sequence numbers after each field. This number is an integer and each one of them must be unique. These numbers are handy for API versioning, which we will cover in *Chapter 5, How to Apply Versioning to the gRPC API*.

Let's now go over the data types and see how each one gets converted to C# code.

Integer data types

Among the various data types, there are a few that are considered *integer* data types. We'll go through these in this section.

The int32 and int64 data types

The `int32` and `int64` data types are represented by the following fields:

```
int32 int_field = 1;
int64 long_field = 2;
```

The equivalent data types in C# would be `int` (`Int32`) and `long` (`Int64`). The `int32` type is an integer data type that consists of 32 bits, while the `int64` field is an integer data type consisting of 64 bits. Both accept positive and negative numbers. The only difference between them is the size of the number they can store.

The following C# code is generated from these fields, which can be viewed in the `Greet.cs` file in the `obj/{Build configuration}/{Framework version}/Protos` folder within the project folder:

```csharp
/// <summary>Field number for the "int_field" field.</summary>
public const int IntFieldFieldNumber = 1;
private int intField_;
[global::System.Diagnostics.DebuggerNonUserCodeAttribute]
public int IntField {
  get { return intField_; }
  set {
    intField_ = value;
  }
}

/// <summary>Field number for the "long_field" field.</summary>
public const int LongFieldFieldNumber = 2;
private long longField_;
[global::System.Diagnostics.DebuggerNonUserCodeAttribute]
public long LongField {
  get { return longField_; }
  set {
    longField_ = value;
  }
}
```

Figure 3.1 – Code generated from the int32 and int64 fields

But there is one key difference between the Protobuf and C# implementations of these data types. In C#, `int` and `long` will always occupy 32 and 64 bits of memory, respectively. In Protobuf, however, they will occupy as many bytes as needed to store a specific numeric value, up to either 32 or 64 bits. Protobuf has been designed to be very efficient. So, if you are using small numbers, those will use less storage than large numbers.

The uint32 and uint64 data types

The `uint32` and `uint64` data types are represented by the following fields:

```
uint32 unsigned_int_field = 3;
uint64 unsigned_long_field = 4;
```

These are the equivalent of the `uint` and `ulong` data types in C#.

```csharp
/// <summary>Field number for the "unsigned_int_filed" field.</summary>
public const int UnsignedIntFiledFieldNumber = 3;
private uint unsignedIntFiled_;
[global::System.Diagnostics.DebuggerNonUserCodeAttribute]
public uint UnsignedIntFiled {
  get { return unsignedIntFiled_; }
  set {
    unsignedIntFiled_ = value;
  }
}

/// <summary>Field number for the "unsigned_long_field" field.</summary>
public const int UnsignedLongFieldFieldNumber = 4;
private ulong unsignedLongField_;
[global::System.Diagnostics.DebuggerNonUserCodeAttribute]
public ulong UnsignedLongField {
  get { return unsignedLongField_; }
  set {
    unsignedLongField_ = value;
  }
}
```

Figure 3.2 – A uint32 and uint64 C# implementation

These are *unsigned integers*, which means that they don't support negative values. But because they use the same number of bytes as their standard-integer counterparts, they can store much higher positive number values.

Just like `int32` and `int64`, `uint32` and `uint64` will only use as many bytes in a Protobuf message as are strictly needed for storing a specific value.

The sint32 and sint64 data types

In our examples, the `sint32` and `sint64` data types are represented by the following fields:

```
sint32 signed_int_field = 5;
sint64 signed_long_field = 6;
```

Just like ordinary integer data types, these can store both positive and negative values. In C#, they are converted into a standard `int` and a standard `long` data type, respectively.

```csharp
/// <summary>Field number for the "signed_int_field" field.</summary>
public const int SignedIntFieldFieldNumber = 5;
private int signedIntField_;
[global::System.Diagnostics.DebuggerNonUserCodeAttribute]
public int SignedIntField {
  get { return signedIntField_; }
  set {
    signedIntField_ = value;
  }
}

/// <summary>Field number for the "signed_long_field" field.</summary>
public const int SignedLongFieldFieldNumber = 6;
private long signedLongField_;
[global::System.Diagnostics.DebuggerNonUserCodeAttribute]
public long SignedLongField {
  get { return signedLongField_; }
  set {
    signedLongField_ = value;
  }
}
```

Figure 3.3 – sint32 and sint64 representations in C#

But why do we even need separate data types for storing signed integral numbers if we already have `int32` and `int64`? Well, this is just another way to optimize Protobuf messages. Even though `sint32` and `sint64` support both positive and negative values, they encode negative values more efficiently than `int32` and `int64`. So, use signed integers when the numbers you are dealing with are likely to be negative. Otherwise, use ordinary integers.

The fixed32 and fixed64 data types

The `fixed32` and `fixed64` data types are also unsigned integer data types, which are represented by the following fields:

```
fixed32 fixed_int_field = 7;
fixed64 fixed_long_field = 8;
```

They are different from `uint32` and `uint64` by being specifically intended for storing large numbers. The `fixed32` and `fixed64` data types always occupy 32 and 64 bits, respectively. They are fixed in size, and this is the reason they are called *fixed*. But they do encode large numbers more efficiently than regular `int` data types.

In C#, unsigned integers are always fixed in size. Therefore, these data types are represented by `uint` and `ulong`.

```csharp
/// <summary>Field number for the "fixed_int_field" field.</summary>
public const int FixedIntFieldFieldNumber = 7;
private uint fixedIntField_;
[global::System.Diagnostics.DebuggerNonUserCodeAttribute]
public uint FixedIntField {
  get { return fixedIntField_; }
  set {
    fixedIntField_ = value;
  }
}

/// <summary>Field number for the "fixed_long_field" field.</summary>
public const int FixedLongFieldFieldNumber = 8;
private ulong fixedLongField_;
[global::System.Diagnostics.DebuggerNonUserCodeAttribute]
public ulong FixedLongField {
  get { return fixedLongField_; }
  set {
    fixedLongField_ = value;
  }
}
```

Figure 3.4 – fixed32 and fixed64 representations in C#

The name *fixed* is intuitively associated with just positive numeric values, so the fact that these data types don't support negative values needs to be memorized.

The sfixed32 and sfixed64 data types

The `sfixed32` and `sfixed64` data types are represented by the following fields:

```
sfixed32 signed_fixed_int_field = 9;
sfixed64 signed_fixed_long_field = 10;
```

In C#, they are represented by ordinary `int` and `long` data types.

```csharp
/// <summary>Field number for the "signed_fixed_long_field" field.</summary>
public const int SignedFixedLongFieldFieldNumber = 10;
private long signedFixedLongField_;
[global::System.Diagnostics.DebuggerNonUserCodeAttribute]
public long SignedFixedLongField {
  get { return signedFixedLongField_; }
  set {
    signedFixedLongField_ = value;
  }
}

/// <summary>Field number for the "float_field" field.</summary>
public const int FloatFieldFieldNumber = 11;
private float floatField_;
[global::System.Diagnostics.DebuggerNonUserCodeAttribute]
public float FloatField {
  get { return floatField_; }
  set {
    floatField_ = value;
  }
}
```

Figure 3.5 – sfixed32 and sfixed64 representations in C#

These are signed, fixed-width fields. They are primarily designed for processing multi-digit negative numbers.

These were all types of integers available with Protobuf. Now, let's have a look at other data types.

Non-integer numeric types

For *non-integer* numeric data types, we have the `float` and `double` data types.

The float and double data types

The `float` and `double` data types are numbers that can store decimal points. The only difference between them is how much storage space they use. The more storage space, the greater the precision. The `float` data type occupies 4 bytes (32 bits), while the `double` data type occupies 8 bytes (64 bits).

C# has equivalent data types with the same names, as follows:

```csharp
/// <summary>Field number for the "float_field" field.</summary>
public const int FloatFieldFieldNumber = 11;
private float floatField_;
[global::System.Diagnostics.DebuggerNonUserCodeAttribute]
public float FloatField {
  get { return floatField_; }
  set {
    floatField_ = value;
  }
}

/// <summary>Field number for the "double_field" field.</summary>
public const int DoubleFieldFieldNumber = 12;
private double doubleField_;
[global::System.Diagnostics.DebuggerNonUserCodeAttribute]
public double DoubleField {
  get { return doubleField_; }
  set {
    doubleField_ = value;
  }
}
```

Figure 3.6 – Protobuf float and double data types converted to C#

We have now covered all of the built-in numeric data types available in Protobuf. Please note that none of them can be set to null. The default value for all of them is 0.

We will now move on to the other data types that Protobuf supports.

Non-numeric data types

The next data types are for *non-numeric* values. In this section, we will have a look at them.

The bool data type

The `bool` data type contains a Boolean `true` or `false` value. In Protobuf, it cannot be set to null. The default value is `false` if it's not set explicitly.

In our `BasicTypes` message definition example, `bool` is represented by the following field:

```
bool boolean_field = 13;
```

C# has a fully equivalent `bool` data type.

The string data type

The `string` data type stores text. Just like any other built-in data type in Protobuf, it cannot be null. The default value is an empty string.

This is an example of a `string` field:

```
string string_field = 14;
```

In C#, on the other hand, the equivalent `string` data type can be set to null. Therefore, the C# code that's generated from a `string` Protobuf field has a null check on it.

```csharp
/// <summary>Field number for the "string_field" field.</summary>
public const int StringFieldFieldNumber = 14;
private string stringField_ = "";
[global::System.Diagnostics.DebuggerNonUserCodeAttribute]
public string StringField {
  get { return stringField_; }
  set {
    stringField_ = pb::ProtoPreconditions.CheckNotNull(value, "value");
  }
}
```

Figure 3.7 – A C# representation of a Protobuf string field with a null check

Without this check, there would have been nothing in our code to prevent us from putting a null value into this field, resulting in an error.

The bytes data type

The `bytes` data type represents an array of bytes. In our example, it's represented by the following field:

```
bytes bytes_field = 15;
```

Although a common way to process a `byte` array in C# is to have a collection of individual `byte` object entities, this is not how it's done by a C# code generator. Instead, it's converted to the `ByteString` type from the `Google.Protobuf` .NET library. However, this type has extension methods to convert to and from a standard `byte` array. This will be demonstrated in *Chapter 4, Performance Best Practices for Using gRPC on .NET*.

```csharp
/// <summary>Field number for the "bytes_field" field.</summary>
public const int BytesFieldFieldNumber = 15;
private pb::ByteString bytesField_ = pb::ByteString.Empty;
[global::System.Diagnostics.DebuggerNonUserCodeAttribute]
public pb::ByteString BytesField {
  get { return bytesField_; }
  set {
    bytesField_ = pb::ProtoPreconditions.CheckNotNull(value, "value");
  }
}
```

Figure 3.8 – A C# representation of the bytes data type

Because C# allows any custom class or struct type to be null, but Protobuf doesn't allow it for its built-in types, there is a null check in the generated code.

We have now covered all of the primitive types supported by Protobuf. Let's now move on to a more advanced topic – *enums* and *nested messages*.

Enums

Let's now add the following `enum` fields and the `enum` definition inside the `BasicTypes` message definition:

```
InternalEnum internal_enum_field = 16;
ExternalEnum external_enum_field = 17;
enum InternalEnum {
    NONE = 0;
    SINGLE = 1;
    MANY = 2;
}
```

After this, add the following enum definition anywhere outside the `BasicTypes` message definition:

```
enum ExternalEnum {
  NONE = 0;
  SINGLE = 1;
  MANY = 2;
}
```

The enum is an enumeration that is used for defining categories. It can have any number of name-value pairs. Each *name* can be any custom text consisting of alphanumeric characters. The *value* for each name is an integer number. We can use any value, but we must have an entry with 0, as this is the default value of an enum.

Because we have enum types in C#, we get an enum definition generated in the code from our Protobuf enum.

```
[global::System.Diagnostics.DebuggerNonUserCodeAttribute]
public static partial class Types {
  public enum InternalEnum {
    [pbr::OriginalName("NONE")] None = 0,
    [pbr::OriginalName("SINGLE")] Single = 1,
    [pbr::OriginalName("MANY")] Many = 2,
  }
}
```

Figure 3.9 – C# code generated from a Protobuf enum definition

But there are two types of enum definitions – *internal* and *external*. An internal enum definition is defined inside the message definition. And even though it can be referenced from the outside (as we will see in a minute), it can only be referenced by its basic name from inside the same message definition where it's defined.

This is how we represent it in our example:

```
InternalEnum internal_enum_field = 16;
```

An external enum definition, on the other hand, can be referenced from any message in our proto file, as it's defined at the root level and not inside of any specific message definition. This is an example of its usage:

```
ExternalEnum external_enum_field = 17;
```

Now, we will have a closer look at Protobuf `message` definitions and how the internal components of one `message` definition can be referenced in another `message` definition.

Nested messages

We will now modify our `HelloReply` message definition so that it will look like this:

```
message HelloReply {
  string message = 1;
  BasicTypes basic_types_field = 2;
  BasicTypes.InternalEnum internal_enum_field = 3;
  ExternalEnum external_enum_field = 4;
  NestedMessage nested_message_field = 5;
  message NestedMessage {

  }
}
```

The first field with the `string` type and the `message` name was originally present in the `message` definition. We haven't modified it.

The field with the sequence number 2 is an example of how you can use `message` definitions as the data types of fields inside other `message` definitions. This is similar to how you can use classes or structs as data types inside other classes or structs in C#:

```
/// <summary>Field number for the "basic_types_field" field.</summary>
public const int BasicTypesFieldFieldNumber = 2;
private global::IndepthProtobuf.BasicTypes basicTypesField_;
[global::System.Diagnostics.DebuggerNonUserCodeAttribute]
public global::IndepthProtobuf.BasicTypes BasicTypesField {
  get { return basicTypesField_; }
  set {
    basicTypesField_ = value;
  }
}
```

Figure 3.10 – Code generated from a field that uses a message definition as its data type

Next, we have an example of how to use an `enum` that is defined inside another `message` definition. This is what we have previously referred to as an *internal* enum definition.

```
BasicTypes.InternalEnum internal_enum_field = 3;
```

Even if an `enum` definition is defined internally inside a particular message, you can still use it in another message. You just need to specify the fully qualified name of it, including the name of the `message` definition type. In this case, because the `message` type (where we have originally defined the `InternalEnum` type) is called `BasicTypes`, our fully qualified name of the `enum` type will be `BasicTypes.InternalEnum`.

C# also supports nested types. But an important thing to note is that when C# code is generated from Protobuf, the fully qualified name of the nested object will not be `{default Proto namespace}.{top-level type name}.{nested type}`. It will actually be `{default Proto namespace}.{top-level type name}.Types.{nested type}`.

Therefore, for our `InternalEnum` reference that is nested inside `BasicTypes`, which belongs to the `IndepthProtobuf` namespace, the fully qualified name will be `IndepthProtobuf.BasicTypes.Types.InternalEnum`, as shown in the following figure:

```csharp
/// <summary>Field number for the "internal_enum_field" field.</summary>
public const int InternalEnumFieldFieldNumber = 3;
private global::IndepthProtobuf.BasicTypes.Types.InternalEnum internalEnumField_ =
    global::IndepthProtobuf.BasicTypes.Types.InternalEnum.None;
[global::System.Diagnostics.DebuggerNonUserCodeAttribute]
public global::IndepthProtobuf.BasicTypes.Types.InternalEnum InternalEnumField {
  get { return internalEnumField_; }
  set {
    internalEnumField_ = value;
  }
}
```

Figure 3.11 – Using the fully qualified names of nested enums in C#

Next, we have a field that references an `enum` defined at the root level of the proto package:

```
ExternalEnum extternal_enum_field = 4;
```

We've placed this field there purely to demonstrate how an externally defined `enum` can be shared between a `message` definition in the same proto file. We just specify the name of the type without having to fully qualify it.

Finally, we have another `message` defined inside our `HelloReply` message:

```
message NestedMessage {

}
```

As you can see, we haven't added any fields to it – we have done this to demonstrate that empty `message` definitions are still supported by Protobuf.

Just like with *nested* and *non-nested* enums, to reference a nested `message` as a field data type inside the `message` that it's been defined in, we just specify its basic name, as we have done in this field:

```
NestedMessage nested_message_field = 5;
```

However, to reference it from the outside, we will need to specify the fully qualified name, including the name of the `message` definition that this type is nested in. In our case, it will be `HelloReply.NestedMessage`.

In C#, the fully qualified namespace will also contain the `Types` word before the nested type name. So, in this instance, the name will become `HelloReply.Types.NestedMessage`:

```
#region Nested types
/// <summary>Container for nested types declared in the HelloReply message type.</summary>
[global::System.Diagnostics.DebuggerNonUserCodeAttribute]
public static partial class Types {
  public sealed partial class NestedMessage : pb::IMessage<NestedMessage>
  #if !GOOGLE_PROTOBUF_REFSTRUCT_COMPATIBILITY_MODE
      , pb::IBufferMessage
  #endif
```

Figure 3.12 – A C# representation of a nested message definition

Essentially, nested `message` definitions are analogous to nested `enum` definitions:

- You don't need to fully qualify the name of the type when it's inside the type it has been defined in.
- You need to fully qualify the name of the type when it's used outside the type it's been defined in.
- In C#, nested types aren't placed directly inside the class that represents their parent in Protobuf. Instead, `public static partial class Types` is created where the nested object is placed.

This covers all of the basic data types available in Protobuf. We have also covered how to use nesting. Now, we will have a look at how to use different types of *collections* available in Protobuf.

Using collections in Protobuf

Protobuf supports two types of collections: *repeated fields* and *maps*. Repeated fields are analogous to *arrays* or *lists* in C#. They represent a collection of singular objects. Maps are analogous to *dictionaries* in C#. They represent a collection of key-value pairs.

Repeated field collections can contain any data type, but you cannot use additional keywords inside of them. For example, you cannot have an equivalent of a multi-dimensional array by having a `repeated` keyword inside a repeated field.

Map fields can use any data type as a value, but its key needs to be either any of the integer types or a string. It cannot be a `bytes`, `enum`, `float`, or `double` data type, or any custom `message` type. Neither its key, its value, nor the whole field itself can be `repeated`. Let's discuss each type further in the next subsections.

Repeated fields

Inside the `greet.proto` file, add the following fields to the `NestedMessage` definition:

```
repeated string string_collection = 1;
repeated int32 int_collection = 2;
repeated BasicTypes object_collection = 3;
repeated ExternalEnum enum_collection = 4;
```

These fields demonstrate that any data type, regardless of whether it's built-in or custom, can be used as the data type for a `repeated` field.

In C#, a `repeated` field is represented by the `RepeatedField<T>` class of the `Google.Protobuf.Collections` namespace, where `T` is the data type of the items inside the collection. This class is similar to commonly used collection types from the `System` library of C#, such as `List<T>` from the `System.Collections.Generic` namespace. Both implement `IList<T>`, `IEnumerable<T>`, and `ICollection<T>` interfaces, so they have the same public methods for manipulating the collection.

When C# code gets generated from a Protobuf definition, `repeated` fields become read-only, as can be seen in the following figure. Each field gets initialized once as an encapsulated `private` field. The `public` property then only comes with a `getter` and doesn't have a `setter`.

```
/// <summary>Field number for the "string_collection" field.</summary>
public const int StringCollectionFieldNumber = 1;
private static readonly pb::FieldCodec<string> _repeated_stringCollection_codec
    = pb::FieldCodec.ForString(10);
private readonly pbc::RepeatedField<string> stringCollection_ = new pbc::RepeatedField<string>();
[global::System.Diagnostics.DebuggerNonUserCodeAttribute]
public pbc::RepeatedField<string> StringCollection {
  get { return stringCollection_; }
}

/// <summary>Field number for the "int_collection" field.</summary>
public const int IntCollectionFieldNumber = 2;
private static readonly pb::FieldCodec<int> _repeated_intCollection_codec
    = pb::FieldCodec.ForInt32(18);
private readonly pbc::RepeatedField<int> intCollection_ = new pbc::RepeatedField<int>();
[global::System.Diagnostics.DebuggerNonUserCodeAttribute]
public pbc::RepeatedField<int> IntCollection {
  get { return intCollection_; }
}
```

Figure 3.13 – A representation of repeated fields in C#

Making `repeated` fields read-only is done to make C# code as safe as possible. The default value for a `repeated` field in Protobuf is an empty collection. In C#, an empty collection is precisely what's created from a `repeated` field definition. You cannot replace it with a different collection, which may be set to null. You can only add items to the existing collection.

Let's have a look at how to use it in the code. In the `Services` folder, locate the `GreeterService.cs` file and replace the definition of the `SayHello` method with the following:

```
public override Task<HelloReply> SayHello(HelloRequest request,
   ServerCallContext context)
{
    var message = new HelloReply
    {
        Message = "Hello " + request.Name,
        NestedMessageField = new HelloReply.Types.
          NestedMessage()
    };
```

```
        return Task.FromResult(message);
}
```

Because we cannot manually initialize `RepeatedField` types in our C# representations of Protobuf messages, we must initialize the `message` itself before we can manipulate the collection. Therefore, we have separated the initialization of the `HelloReply` message from the `return` statement. But because the `repeated` fields we are interested in are inside a `NestedMessage` type, we need to initialize this type too, as we have done in the following example.

Now, we will insert the following code before the `return` statement:

```
message.NestedMessageField.StringCollection.Add("entry 1");
message.NestedMessageField.StringCollection.Add(new
    List<string>
{
    "entry 2",
    "entry 3"
});
```

In the preceding example, we have two examples of adding items to a collection:

- Adding a single entry
- Adding a collection of entries

Other than that, the collection can be manipulated just like any other collection in C#. You can remove items from it, you can clear the entire collection, or you can clone the whole collection into a separate variable.

Map fields

Add the following fields to the `NestedMessage` definition in `greet.proto`:

```
map<string, string> string_to_string_map = 5;
map<int64, string> int_to_string_map = 6;
map<sfixed32, BasicTypes> signedfixed_to_object_map = 7;
map<uint64, ExternalEnum> unsignedint_to_enum_map = 8;
```

These fields have been added to demonstrate the various data types that can be used as keys and values in a Protobuf map. Please note that we only have `string` and `integer` types as keys, while we also have `message` and `enum` types as values.

In C#, a Protobuf map is represented by the `MapField<TKey, TValue>` class of the `Google.Protobuf.Collections` namespace. The `TKey` and `TValue` represent any data type that can be the key or the value, respectively.

Just like `RepeatedField`, `MapField` representations are made read-only in C#:

```
/// <summary>Field number for the "string_to_string_map" field.</summary>
public const int StringToStringMapFieldNumber = 5;
private static readonly pbc::MapField<string, string>.Codec _map_stringToStringMap_codec
    = new pbc::MapField<string, string>.Codec(pb::FieldCodec.ForString(10, ""), pb::FieldCodec.ForString(18, ""), 42);
private readonly pbc::MapField<string, string> stringToStringMap_ = new pbc::MapField<string, string>();
[global::System.Diagnostics.DebuggerNonUserCodeAttribute]
public pbc::MapField<string, string> StringToStringMap {
  get { return stringToStringMap_; }
}

/// <summary>Field number for the "int_to_string_map" field.</summary>
public const int IntToStringMapFieldNumber = 6;
private static readonly pbc::MapField<long, string>.Codec _map_intToStringMap_codec
    = new pbc::MapField<long, string>.Codec(pb::FieldCodec.ForInt64(8, 0L), pb::FieldCodec.ForString(18, ""), 50);
private readonly pbc::MapField<long, string> intToStringMap_ = new pbc::MapField<long, string>();
[global::System.Diagnostics.DebuggerNonUserCodeAttribute]
public pbc::MapField<long, string> IntToStringMap {
  get { return intToStringMap_; }
}
```

Figure 3.14 – MapField representations in C#

The `MapField` class represents the standard C# collection interfaces (`IEnumerbale`, `ICollection`, and so on). But it also represents `IDictionary<TKey, TValue>`, so it can be used just like the standard `Dictionary<TKey, TValue>` class from the `System.Collection.Generics` namespace. You can add whole key-value pair entries to it and also set a value by specifying a particular key.

To see some examples of how to use `MapField` in C#, add the following code before the `return` statement of the `SayHello` method inside the `GreeterService` class:

```
message.NestedMessageField.StringToStringMap.Add("entry 1",
    "value 1");
message.NestedMessageField.StringToStringMap.Add(new
    Dictionary<string, string>
{
    { "entry 2", "value 2" },
    { "entry 3", "value 3" }
});
```

```
message.NestedMessageField.StringToStringMap["entry 4"] =
"value 4";
```

In this example, we have demonstrated three different ways of adding items to a `MapField` collection:

- As a singular key-value pair
- As a collection of key-value pairs
- Specifying a key and setting its value

Please note that each key needs to be unique. If you try to add a key-value pair with a key that already exists, an error will be thrown.

However, when you specify the key and square brackets and set its value by using the equality operator (==), as we have in the last example, it will work regardless of whether the key already exists or not. If the key doesn't exist, it will be added. However, if the key already exists, the entry will be overwritten with the new value.

So far, we have covered all of the inbuilt data types in Protobuf and collections. But Protobuf also supports some special keywords. Some of them will be analogous to what's used in various programming languages. However, there are also some that are unique to Protobuf. And this is what we will have a look at next.

Using special keywords in Protobuf

Protobuf has a range of special keywords that we haven't covered so far. Some of them are only used on rare occasions. For example, you may have to use special keywords to make your proto files compatible with an older version of Protobuf. We will not cover those in this chapter.

There are also some other Protobuf features that are only useful in a very narrow range of circumstances, such as using *extensions* and defining *custom options*. These will not be covered either due to their limited usefulness.

However, there are also some keywords that are very useful and accessible. The most prominent of them are `oneof` and `option`. These are the keywords that we will focus on now.

How the oneof keyword can make communication more efficient

Inside the `greet.proto` file, we will modify the `BasicTypes` message definition. First, we will replace the fields with the sequence numbers from `1` to `10` with the following:

```
oneof whole_number_field {
    int32 int_field = 1;
    int64 long_field = 2;
    uint32 unsigned_int_field = 3;
    uint64 unsigned_long_field = 4;
    sint32 signed_int_field = 5;
    sint64 signed_long_field = 6;
    fixed32 fixed_int_field = 7;
    fixed64 fixed_long_field = 8;
    sfixed32 signed_fixed_int_field = 9;
    sfixed64 signed_fixed_long_field = 10;
}
```

Then, we will replace the fields with the sequence numbers from `11` to `17` with the following:

```
oneof mixed_field {
    float float_field = 11;
    double double_field = 12;
    bool boolean_field = 13;
    string string_field = 14;
    bytes bytes_field = 15;
    InternalEnum internal_enum_field = 16;
    ExternalEnum external_enum_field = 17;
}
```

So, as you may have noticed, we haven't really changed any fields or their data types. We have simply wrapped two bundles of fields in a code block that started with the `oneof` keyword and an arbitrary name.

This keyword means that only one of these fields will be set. If you set the value of one of the fields and then set the value for another field in the same `oneof` block, the first field that you've set will be unset.

The benefit of using `oneof` is that the message will be smaller when it is being transferred. The only field in a `oneof` block that has any size is the one that has been set last. And if such a block consists of many fields, the saving in terms of bandwidth usage will be significant.

In the previous example, we have deliberately chosen two different variations of a `oneof` field to demonstrate that there are no restrictions on which data types you can put together. In the first example, the `whole_number_field` oneof block, we have placed different types of integers together. But in our second example, the `mixed_field` oneof block, we have fields with completely different data types together. Some of them are inbuilt scalar data types, while others are custom messages and enums.

However, `oneof` doesn't support collections, so you can't place a `repeated` or `map` field inside a `oneof` block. Neither can you use any other keywords in your fields, such as `option`, a keyword we will have a look at shortly.

Even though the `oneof` keyword is placed at a field level inside a `message` definition, it's not really a field. When a proto file is translated into code, all the fields inside a `oneof` block are still accessible at the normal field level in the object that gets generated. But there is also some additional logic that gets added to make sure that only one of the fields is used.

In C#, `oneof` gets represented by an `enum` where there is a value for every field inside the original `oneof` block:

```csharp
private object wholeNumberField_;
/// <summary>Enum of possible cases for the "whole_number_field" oneof.</summary>
public enum WholeNumberFieldOneofCase {
  None = 0,
  IntField = 1,
  LongField = 2,
  UnsignedIntFiled = 3,
  UnsignedLongField = 4,
  SignedIntField = 5,
  SignedLongField = 6,
  FixedIntField = 7,
  FixedLongField = 8,
  SignedFixedIntField = 9,
  SignedFixedLongField = 10,
}
```

Figure 3.15 – A C# enum representation of a oneof block "whole_number_field"

The name of an enum generated from a `oneof` field will have the following structure:

```
{PascalCase version of the oneof block name}OneOfField
```

There is also a `private` field of this `enum` type that is stored inside the `class` definition that represents the message where the `oneof` block was originally defined. It holds the value of the last field that has been populated.

Setting the value of a property that represents a particular field from a `oneof` block will set the value of the private `enum` field to the `enum` value that corresponds to the property that has just been set. While attempting to retrieve the value of the property, the `getter` will first check whether the `enum` has been set to the value that corresponds to this property. Otherwise, it will just return a default value for this data type:

```csharp
/// <summary>Field number for the "int_field" field.</summary>
public const int IntFieldFieldNumber = 1;
[global::System.Diagnostics.DebuggerNonUserCodeAttribute]
public int IntField {
  get { return wholeNumberFieldCase_ == WholeNumberFieldOneofCase.IntField ? (int) wholeNumberField_ : 0; }
  set {
    wholeNumberField_ = value;
    wholeNumberFieldCase_ = WholeNumberFieldOneofCase.IntField;
  }
}
```

Figure 3.16 – Using a oneof enum inside a getter and setter

This private `enum` field is also used inside the class constructor. When a Protobuf message is received, the C# representation of it will set the correct field from a `oneof` block based on the information it receives from the message. This is done via a `switch` statement, as shown in the following figure:

```csharp
switch (other.MixedFieldCase) {
  case MixedFieldOneofCase.FloatField:
    FloatField = other.FloatField;
    break;
  case MixedFieldOneofCase.DoubleField:
    DoubleField = other.DoubleField;
    break;
  case MixedFieldOneofCase.BooeanFild:
    BooeanFild = other.BooeanFild;
    break;
  case MixedFieldOneofCase.StringField:
    StringField = other.StringField;
    break;
  case MixedFieldOneofCase.BytesField:
    BytesField = other.BytesField;
    break;
  case MixedFieldOneofCase.InternalEnumField:
    InternalEnumField = other.InternalEnumField;
    break;
  case MixedFieldOneofCase.ExternalEnumField:
    ExternalEnumField = other.ExternalEnumField;
    break;
}
```

Figure 3.17 – The use of a oneof enum in a class constructor

When we use any of the fields from a `oneof` block inside our own code, they are used just like any normal fields and properties in a C# class. For example, if we place the following block of code before the `return` statement inside the `SayHello` method of the `GreeterService` class, this will still be valid:

```
message.BasicTypesField = new BasicTypes
{
    IntField = 1
};
```

However, if you then set another field from the same `oneof` block, the value you've given to `IntField` will not be used.

Customizing the behavior with the option keyword

We have already seen an example of the `option` keyword when we were setting the C# namespace, as we are using the following line inside the `greet.proto` file:

```
option csharp_namespace = "IndepthProtobuf";
```

This directive will override the default package name when generating C# code and will apply a custom namespace of `IndepthProtobuf` to any packages it generates. But there are also other modifications you can do by using the `option` keyword.

In Protobuf, `option` can be applied in three different scopes:

- Global scope
- Message-level scope
- Field-level scope

Let's discuss each scope in detail in the following subsections.

Global-level options

The previous example of `ssharp_namespace` is a global option, as it's placed at the file level. Usually, this option will contain a directive that is relevant to a specific programming language. As we are using C#, we have used a directive that is specific to C#. However, if you intend to use gRPC clients and/or servers written in other languages, here are some of the other directives you can use:

- `java_package`
- `java_outer_classname`

- `go_package`
- `optimize_for`

Message-level options

The message-level options are placed inside of the `message` and `enum` definitions at the same levels as their fields (or `enum` values). These options will modify the behavior of an entire `message` or `enum`.

To see an example of such an option, we will modify the `ExternalEnum` definition to be as follows:

```
enum ExternalEnum {
    option allow_alias = true;
    NONE = 0;
    SINGLE = 1;
    FEW = 2;
    MANY = 2;
}
```

Here, we have applied the `allow_alias` option by setting it to `true`. With this option enabled, we can assign the same value to multiple `enum` names. But why would we want to do this?

To the running code, enums are just representations of numbers. So, in this example, `FEW` is no different from `MANY`, as they both have a value of 2. However, the reason we use names in enums is to make them readable to people who read our code. And from a human perspective, there might be a benefit of knowing a distinct scenario where a particular type of situation occurs.

In the previous example, it could be that the exact amount that the `enum` refers to doesn't make a difference to the downstream logic when it's above 1. However, the system that sends the data may need to have two distinct categories depending on the amount.

Another example would be a disconnection. To the downstream system, any type of disconnection is treated the same. However, to the client, there is a difference between an on-demand disconnection and a disconnection due to failure. So, in this case, it will make sense to have two distinct `enum` aliases that share the same `enum` value.

In C#, such an `enum` will use the `OriginalName` attribute from the `Google.Protobuf.Reflection` package for each of its values with the property of `PreferredAlias` set to `false` on all but one of the entries that share the same numeric value:

```
public enum ExternalEnum {
  [pbr::OriginalName("NONE")] None = 0,
  [pbr::OriginalName("SINGLE")] Single = 1,
  [pbr::OriginalName("FEW")] Few = 2,
  [pbr::OriginalName("MANY", PreferredAlias = false)] Many = 2,
}
```

Figure 3.18 – A C# representation of a Protobuf enum with the allow_alias option enabled

Field-level options

Finally, there are also field-level options in Protobuf. These are placed after the sequence number next to a relevant field, but before the semicolon (;). In this case, you don't have to use the `option` keyword. You can just apply any option directly by wrapping it in square brackets ([]).

One of the most commonly used field-level options in Protobuf is `deprecated`. Let's see how this gets applied.

In the `HelloReply` message definition in our `greet.proto` file, locate `nested_message_field` and replace it with the following:

```
NestedMessage nested_message_field = 5 [deprecated = true];
```

When the code gets generated, it will apply `ObsoleteAttribute` to the property that represents this field:

```
/// <summary>Field number for the "nested_message_field" field.</summary>
public const int NestedMessageFieldFieldNumber = 5;
private global::IndepthProtobuf.HelloReply.Types.NestedMessage nestedMessageField_;
[global::System.ObsoleteAttribute]
[global::System.Diagnostics.DebuggerNonUserCodeAttribute]
public global::IndepthProtobuf.HelloReply.Types.NestedMessage NestedMessageField {
  get { return nestedMessageField_; }
  set {
    nestedMessageField_ = value;
  }
}
```

Figure 3.19 – A C# representation of the deprecated option being set to true

If we use an IDE or a relevant code styling extension for our code editor, a warning will be generated whenever we attempt to use this field. If we have a look at the code in our `GreeterService` class, every instance of this field is highlighted to warn us that it has been deprecated:

```csharp
public override Task<HelloReply> SayHello(HelloRequest request, ServerCallContext context)
{
    var message = new HelloReply
    {
        Message = "Hello " + request.Name,
        NestedMessageField = new HelloReply.Types.NestedMessage()
    };

    message.NestedMessageField.StringCollection.Add("entry 1");
    message.NestedMessageField.StringCollection.Add(new List<string>
    {
        "entry 2",
        "entry 3"
    });

    message.NestedMessageField.StringToStringMap.Add("entry 1", "value 1");
    message.NestedMessageField.StringToStringMap.Add(new Dictionary<string, string>
    {
        { "entry 2", "value 2" },
        { "entry 3", "value 3" }
    });

    message.NestedMessageField.StringToStringMap["entry 4"] = "value 4";

    message.BasicTypesField = new BasicTypes
    {
        IntField = 1
    };

    return Task.FromResult(message);
}
```

Figure 3.20 – Visual Studio showing the deprecation warning

These are the most used Protobuf options, and they are the only ones that most developers will ever need.

Protobuf allows you to specify your own custom options, but this is reserved for very specific use cases. Therefore, we will not cover this here. But you will find a link to the relevant documentation in the *Further reading* section of this chapter.

There are also reserved keywords that we haven't covered. But, since these are mainly intended for enabling easy updates to proto file definitions, we will fully cover their use in *Chapter 5, How to Apply Versioning to the gRPC API*.

Now, we will cover how to reference other proto files from a proto file and how to create Protobuf libraries – that is, proto file definitions specifically intended to be referenced.

Referencing other proto files

In any programming language, you can create reusable bundles of code and package them up into libraries that can be referenced by any application. In .NET, for example, you can create a project of a *Class Library* type that you can reference from your main application project. Or, if such a library is meant to be accessible by other projects that aren't part of your solution, you can publish it as a **NuGet** package.

Similar principles are available in Protobuf. You can reference other proto files from inside your proto file. Another similarity between Protobuf and any major programming language is that you can add references to both internal and external proto files. We will have a look at how to apply them both.

Just like you would use namespaces in C# to import external libraries, you use the equivalent in Protobuf. The `package` directive in a proto file is what sets the name of the Protobuf package. Then, if any other proto file will need to reference this package, it will use this package name as a prefix to refer to the `message`, `enum`, and `service` types defined in this package. For example, if the package name inside our `greet.proto` file is `greet` and we have a `HelloReply` message defined inside the proto file, then any other proto file that will reference `greet.proto` will have to use a fully qualified name to refer to the `HelloReply` object (that is, `greet.HelloReply`).

Importing external proto packages

Importing either an internal or external package in proto files is done via the `import` directive. You would put this directive before the `package` directive on top of the proto file. The format would be as follows:

```
import "{path to proto file}"
```

We will now import one of the proto files from Google's collection of so-called *well-known types*, which we will examine in more detail in *Chapter 8, Using Well-Known Types to Make Protobuf More Handy*. But for now, we will import a package representing one of its data types, `Any`.

We will start by adding the following directive above our `package` directive inside the `greet.proto` file:

```
import "google/protobuf/any.proto";
```

This is a path to the `any.proto` file that contains the data type we need. It will be recognized by the Protobuf compiler, as the paths to the packages published by Google are pre-configured in the gRPC tools.

We will now use this field in one of our messages. Inside the `HelloReply` message definition, add the following field after the last field:

```
google.protobuf.Any external_reference_field = 6;
```

As you can see, we are specifying the fully qualified data type name. The data type is called `Any`, and it comes from the `google.protobuf` package.

In this case, because the package was intended to be used by gRPC clients and servers written in any language, it doesn't have any language-specific package name or namespace directive. Therefore, when the code is generated, the C# namespace is created by applying the camelCase format to the original package name, as per C# naming conventions:

```csharp
/// <summary>Field number for the "external_reference_field" field.</summary>
public const int ExternalReferenceFieldFieldNumber = 6;
private global::Google.Protobuf.WellKnownTypes.Any externalReferenceField_;
[global::System.Diagnostics.DebuggerNonUserCodeAttribute]
public global::Google.Protobuf.WellKnownTypes.Any ExternalReferenceField {
  get { return externalReferenceField_; }
  set {
    externalReferenceField_ = value;
  }
}
```

Figure 3.21 – An imported external Protobuf object translated to C#

This is how external proto files can be referenced. Now, we will create some internal proto files and then see how to reference them.

Referencing internal proto files

Create a `reference.proto` file in the `Protos` folder of your project and populate it with the following content:

```
syntax = "proto3";

option csharp_namespace = "IndepthProtobuf.Reference";

package greet.reference;

message ReferenceMessage {
  string description = 1;
}
```

We are adding a package with the `ReferenceMessage` definition. As this proto file has no `service` definitions, the file is intended to be used purely as a reference package.

When we reference this file inside other proto files, we will need to use the `greet.reference` package name to use the `ReferenceMessage` definition. However, when the C# code gets generated, the namespace of the class that represents the message will be `IndepthProtobuf.Reference`, as we have specified in the `csharp_namespace` option.

We will need to ensure that the `reference.proto` file is recognized by our project. To do so, we will locate the `ItemGroup` section inside of `IndepthProtobuf.csproj` that contains the Protobuf reference to the `greet.proto` file and replace it with the following:

```
<ItemGroup>
  <Protobuf Include="Protos\greet.proto" GrpcServices="Server"
    />
  <Protobuf Include="Protos\reference.proto"
    GrpcServices="Server" />
</ItemGroup>
```

Now, we will import this file into our `greet.proto` file. We will do so by adding the following directive before the `package` directive:

```
import "Protos/reference.proto";
```

This is a Unix-style path to the file relative to the root of the project.

Now, we will use a custom data type from the `reference.proto` file. We do so by adding the following field to the `HelloReply` message definition:

```
greet.reference.ReferenceMessage internal_reference_field = 7;
```

The fully-qualified name of the `ReferenceMessage` custom data type uses the original Protobuf package name, which is `greet.reference`. But the C# code generated from it uses the namespace defined in the `csharp_namespace` option directive in the `reference.proto` file:

```
/// <summary>Field number for the "internal_reference_field" field.</summary>
public const int InternalReferenceFieldFieldNumber = 7;
private global::IndepthProtobuf.Reference.ReferenceMessage internalReferenceField_;
[global::System.Diagnostics.DebuggerNonUserCodeAttribute]
public global::IndepthProtobuf.Reference.ReferenceMessage InternalReferenceField {
  get { return internalReferenceField_; }
  set {
    internalReferenceField_ = value;
  }
}
```

Figure 3.22 – A namespace conversion for a package with the csharp_namespace option

So, the process of importing internal and external Protobuf packages is broadly the same. But there is one additional handy feature that Protobuf has when working with internal packages. If you need to move the reference package to another location for whatever reason, you can still do so without changing any code inside the file that imports the package.

Using proto files as relays

If you move your proto file to a different location (for example, to make it accessible by other projects), you may still do so without changing any code in the proto files that reference it. However, you will still need to make some changes to enable this.

We will start by creating another file inside our `Protos` folder, which we will call `new.proto`. And then we will copy the entire content from the `reference.proto` file.

Please note that we will still need our `reference.proto` file to be exactly where it was before. We will just need to change its content to make the file act purely as a relay. We will do so by replacing its content with the following:

```
syntax = "proto3";

option csharp_namespace = "IndepthProtobuf.Reference";

import public "Protos/new.proto";

package greet.reference;
```

The directive that makes this file act as a relay for new.proto is import public. With this directive in place, the reference.proto file will act as if the content of the new.proto file is its own content. So, anything that imports reference.proto will implicitly import new.proto. And this is why, as long as you don't change anything in the proto file that you have moved, every proto file that used to import the content from the old proto file will still be valid.

The final change that we need to make is to add a new.proto reference to our IndepthProtobuf.csproj file so that it's recognized by the internal gRPC tools:

```
<ItemGroup>
  <Protobuf Include="Protos\greet.proto" GrpcServices="Server"
    />
  <Protobuf Include="Protos\reference.proto"
    GrpcServices="Server" />
  <Protobuf Include="Protos\new.proto" GrpcServices="Server" />
</ItemGroup>
```

If your code doesn't compile after making these changes, you may need to delete the .vs, obj, and bin folders from your project folder and try again. But other than this, everything is expected to work as before, and identical code is expected to be generated.

Summary

In this chapter, you learned how to use all of the core structural components of Protobuf. You now know all of the rpc types supported by Protobuf. You also learned all of the possible ways of annotating your Protobuf elements with comments.

You learned about all of the inbuilt data types in Protobuf and how they get converted to C# data types. We covered all of the types of integers available in Protobuf and how to choose the right data type depending on what kind of values it's intended to represent. We also covered other scalar types, such as bool, string, and float. In addition to this, you learned how to use nested message and enum definitions.

You also learned how to use two types of collections in Protobuf – repeated fields and maps – and learned that the former is used for creating collections of single values, while the latter is used for creating a dictionary-like collection of key-value pairs. You also learned which data types and keywords aren't compatible with Protobuf collections.

We also covered the use of the keywords that are unique to Protobuf. You learned how to create bundles of mutually exclusive fields by using the `oneof` keyword. You also learned how to modify the default behavior of Protobuf objects by adding the `option` directive at the file, message, and field levels.

Finally, you learned how to reference other proto files from a single proto file, both internally and externally. You now also know how to use a proto file as a relay for another proto file if one has been moved elsewhere, so your original code can remain unchanged.

We have now completed an overview of gRPC and its messaging protocol, Protobuf. In the next part of the book, we will cover some best practices for using gRPC in ASP.NET Core applications. In the next chapter, we will have a look at the techniques you can apply to optimize the performance of this communication mechanism.

Questions

1. What is the equivalent of the `fixed64` data type in C#?

    A. `long`

    B. `ulong`

    C. `int`

    D. `uint`

2. What is the difference between `int32` and `fixed32`?

    A. The `int32` data type will have only as many bytes allocated as necessary, while `fixed32` always occupies 4 bytes.

    B. There is no difference. Two data types exist purely for backward compatibility.

    C. The `int32` data type only accepts positive numbers, while `fixed32` accepts negative numbers.

    D. The `int32` data type accepts only whole numbers, while `fixed32` accepts decimal point numbers.

3. How do you create a multi-dimensional array in Protobuf?

    A. Apply the `repeated repeated` keyword to the field.

    B. There is no way of creating anything that resembles a multi-dimensional array in Protobuf.

    C. Create a repeated field of a message that itself has a repeated field.

    D. You can only do it if you apply a custom option.

4. What happens if you assign a value on a field within a `oneof` block if another field has already been set?

    A. A compiler error is thrown.

    B. The original field gets unset, and the new field gets set.

    C. The original field remains set, and nothing happens to the new field.

    D. A runtime error is thrown.

5. How can you keep your main proto file unchanged if you must move one of the files that it references?

    A. You will have no choice but to change the `import` directive.

    B. The only option is to move all your files to the same location and change the references in the `csproj` file.

    C. You will have no choice but to change both your proto file and your code.

    D. You can keep the original proto file that is specified in the `import` directive but get it to import the new proto file via the `import public` directive.

Further reading

- The official Protobuf language guide:

    https://developers.google.com/protocol-buffers/docs/proto3

- Specifying custom options in Protobuf:

    https://developers.google.com/protocol-buffers/docs/proto#extensions

Section 2: Best Practices of Using gRPC

This part covers best practices of using gRPC. It will show you how to use it in the most optimal way in code, how to scale it, and how to apply API versioning. The following chapters will be covered in this part:

- *Chapter 4, Performance Best Practices of Using gRPC on .NET*
- *Chapter 5, How to Apply Versioning to the gRPC API*
- *Chapter 6, Scaling a gRPC Application*

4
Performance Best Practices for Using gRPC on .NET

Since gRPC is often used for processing large volumes of data inside a distributed application, this communication mechanism must be optimized for the best performance. In this chapter, we will cover some best practices when it comes to using gRPC on ASP.NET Core to optimize its performance as much as possible.

If you don't know how to optimize gRPC for the best performance, you are running the risk of not being able to cope with the volume of data that your application is intended to process. Alternatively, you may need to scale your application out, which would require you to use additional software and hardware resources. If you are running your application under a cloud subscription, such as Microsoft Azure or Amazon AWS, unnecessarily scaling your application out will probably cost you some additional money. This is why it's important to use gRPC to its maximum potential before scaling out is required.

In this chapter, we will cover the following topics:

- Why you need to reuse a gRPC channel
- How to not get held up by a concurrent stream limit

- Ensuring that your connection remains alive
- When streaming is better than individual calls
- Using binary payloads to decrease the data's size

By the end of this chapter, you will have learned how to fine-tune your gRPC client and server applications to make them suitable for optimally handling large amounts of data.

Technical requirements

To follow the instructions in this chapter, you will need the following:

- A computer with either the Windows, Mac, or Linux operating system installed
- A supported IDE or code editor (Visual Studio, Visual Studio Code, or JetBrains Rider)
- .NET 5 SDK
- A self-signed development HTTPS certificate enabled on the machine

The instructions for how to set all of these up were provided in *Chapter 1*, *Creating a Basic gRPC Application on ASP.NET Core*.

All of the code samples used in this chapter can be found in this book's GitHub repository: https://github.com/PacktPublishing/Microservices-Communication-in-.NET-Using-gRPC/tree/main/Chapter-04

Please visit the following link to check the CiA videos: https://bit.ly/3m1Eg7I

Why you need to reuse a gRPC channel

When you connect the gRPC client to the server, you do so via a configurable channel. When the channel is opened, the following things happen:

1. A socket is opened
2. The TCP connection is established
3. **Transport Layer Security** (**TLS**) is negotiated and applied
4. An HTTP/2 connection is started

Once these steps have been completed, gRPC calls can be made to the server.

Because opening a channel requires all these steps to take place, which represent multiple roundtrips to the server, it's better to reuse the channel while you can. If you already have an existing channel open, you can start making gRPC calls on it right away. However, if you recreate the channel every time you make a call, you will need to perform all these steps every single time. If you need to make many calls, this may slow down your system substantially.

In C#, the gRPC channel is represented by the `GrpcChannel` class from the `Grpc.Net.Client` namespace. An object of this type needs to be reused rather than an implementation of the gRPC client.

The gRPC client's implementation is nothing but a thin layer of abstraction around the Protobuf definition. It's there merely to provide strongly typed representations of the Protobuf RPCs that you can call. All the heavy lifting is done by `GrpcChannel`. Therefore, it doesn't matter if we reuse the client object or instantiate a new one every time we need to make a call. What matters is that we reuse the channel if we can.

Let's set up some gRPC server and client applications to see how the channel object can be reused.

Setting up the server application

First, we need to create a solution that will hold both our client and server applications, along with their shared gRPC dependencies. To do so, we'll create a folder called `GrpcBestPractices` and run the following command inside it to create a solution with the same name:

```
dotnet new sln
```

Then, while still in the same folder, we will create a gRPC service application by executing the following command:

```
dotnet new grpc -o PerformanceService
```

Then, we will add the newly created project to the solution by executing the following command:

```
dotnet sln add PerformanceService/PerformanceService.csproj
```

Now, we will add a console application that will hold the shared gRPC dependencies between the client and the server.

Adding a library with shared Protobuf dependencies

We can create a shared library project by executing the following command:

```
dotnet new classlib -o GrpcDependencies
```

We can add this project to our solution by executing the following command:

```
dotnet sln add GrpcDependencies/GrpcDependencies.csproj
```

Now, let's add all the required NuGet dependencies to our shared class library project. We can do so by navigating to the `GrpcDependencies` project folder and executing the following commands:

```
dotnet add GrpcDependencies.csproj package Grpc.Net.Client
dotnet add GrpcDependencies.csproj package Google.Protobuf
dotnet add GrpcDependencies.csproj package Grpc.Tools
dotnet add GrpcDependencies.csproj package Grpc.AspNetCore
```

Now, we will add a Protobuf definition to our shared library. To do so, we will create a `Protos` folder inside the `GrpcDependencies` project folder and add a `performance.proto` file to it. The content of this file will be as follows:

```
syntax = "proto3";

package performance;

service Monitor {
    rpc GetPerformance (PerformanceStatusRequest) returns
      (PerformanceStatusResponse);
}

message PerformanceStatusRequest {
    string client_name = 1;
}

message PerformanceStatusResponse {
    double cpu_percentage_usage = 1;
    double memory_usage = 2;
    int32 processes_running = 3;
    int32 active_connections = 4;
}
```

It's a simple service definition with a single unary RPC called `GetPerformance`. The service that we are building is emulating a performance monitor. It receives a request with a client name, and it returns performance statistics, including CPU and memory usage, the number of active processes that are running, and the number of active connections.

But don't worry. We won't have to be monitoring a actual system. We are purely emulating these statistics for demonstration purposes.

To finish off our reference library, we need to insert the following section anywhere inside the `<Project>` element in the `GrpcDependencies.csproj` file:

```xml
<ItemGroup>
    <Protobuf Include="Protos\performance.proto" />
</ItemGroup>
```

This project now contains all the gRPC dependencies that both the server and the client applications need. Therefore, it's no longer essential to have them explicitly defined in either of those projects.

Now, we will add this library to our server project while removing all the redundant dependencies from it.

Adding a shared Protobuf library to the server project

Inside `GrpcBestPractices`, navigate to the `PerformanceService` project folder and replace the content of the `PerformanceService.csproj` file with the following:

```xml
<Project Sdk="Microsoft.NET.Sdk.Web">

  <PropertyGroup>
    <TargetFramework>net5.0</TargetFramework>
  </PropertyGroup>

  <ItemGroup>
    <ProjectReference
      Include="..\GrpcDependencies\GrpcDependencies.csproj" />
  </ItemGroup>
</Project>
```

Now that all the necessary dependencies are in place, we are ready to implement the server-side components for our solution. But first, we need to remove the auto-generated gRPC service implementation for the default `greet.proto` file. As we no longer use this file, we will need to remove the `GreeterService.cs` file from the `Services` folder inside the `PerformanceService` project folder. Otherwise, we will get a compiler error.

Implementing server-side gRPC components

Once we've deleted all the redundant files, we can put the `PerformanceMonitor.cs` file in its place. The content of this file will be as follows:

```csharp
using System;
using System.Threading.Tasks;
using Grpc.Core;
using Performance;

namespace PerformanceService
{
    public class PerformanceMonitor : Monitor.MonitorBase
    {
        public override Task<PerformanceStatusResponse>
          GetPerformance(PerformanceStatusRequest request,
            ServerCallContext context)
        {
            var randomNumberGenerator = new Random();

            return Task.FromResult(new
              PerformanceStatusResponse
              {
                  CpuPercentageUsage =
                    randomNumberGenerator.NextDouble() * 100,
                  MemoryUsage = randomNumberGenerator.
                    NextDouble() * 100,
                  ProcessesRunning = randomNumberGenerator.
                    Next(),
                  ActiveConnections = randomNumberGenerator.
                    Next()
              });
        }
    }
}
```

Essentially, the implementation of the `GetPerformance` RPC accepts a request from the client and returns a single response with emulated performance statistics. All of these statistics are completely random numbers.

Now, we need to register this gRPC service implementation. To do so, we need to open the `Startup.cs` file inside the project folder and, inside the `Configure` method, locate a call to `UseEndpoints`. If you are using .NET 6 template, this call will be located in the main body of `Program.cs` class. Inside this call, locate the line with a call to `MapGrpcService`. We will replace this line with the following code:

```
endpoints.MapGrpcService<PerformanceMonitor>();
```

> **Note**
> If you are running your server-side application on a Mac, you will need to apply some modifications to it. Instructions on how to do so can be found in the *Running a gRPC service on a Mac* section of *Chapter 1, Creating a Basic gRPC Application on ASP.NET Core*.

Now, you can compile the application to ensure that we have added all the components correctly and haven't missed anything. If so, we are ready to start adding our client application.

Setting up the client application

Our client application will be a standard ASP.NET Core web API. To create it from a relevant template, open your command-line terminal inside the `GrpcBestPractices` solution folder and execute the following command:

```
dotnet new webapi -o ApiGateway
```

Next, we will add it to our solution by executing the following command:

```
dotnet sln add ApiGateway/ApiGateway.csproj
```

After this, we will add all the required gRPC dependencies to our project. We will also add a NuGet package to give us access to Swagger. So, we will replace the content of `ApiGateway.csproj` with the following:

```
<Project Sdk="Microsoft.NET.Sdk.Web">

  <PropertyGroup>
    <TargetFramework>net5.0</TargetFramework>
```

```xml
    </PropertyGroup>

    <ItemGroup>
      <PackageReference Include="NSwag.AspNetCore"
        Version="13.12.1" />
    </ItemGroup>

    <ItemGroup>
      <ProjectReference
        Include="..\GrpcDependencies\GrpcDependencies.csproj" />
    </ItemGroup>

</Project>
```

The API endpoints of the application will return a JSON representation of the `PerformanceStatusResponse` message from our `performance.proto` file. We will also measure how long it takes to execute various types of calls. Therefore, the return object will also contain a field to store the time in milliseconds.

To represent the response object, we will create a `ResponseModel.cs` file in the root of our `ApiGateway` project and populate it with the following content:

```csharp
using System.Collections.Generic;

namespace ApiGateway
{
    public class ResponseModel
    {
        public List<PerformanceStatusModel> PerformanceStatuses
        {
            get; } = new();
        public double RequestProcessingTime { get; set; }

        public class PerformanceStatusModel
        {
            public double CpuPercentageUsage { get; set; }
            public double MemoryUsage { get; set; }
            public int ProcessesRunning { get; set; }
```

```
                public int ActiveConnections { get; set; }
            }
        }
}
```

To demonstrate the importance of reusing a gRPC channel, we will set up three different types of clients in our application.

The first one will be a wrapper class, where a new `client` object is created every time a new call is made, but the channel remains active until the wrapper object is disposed of. This wrapper class will be inside the `GrpcPerformanceClient.cs` file, which we will place in the root of the `ApiGateway` project folder. Inside this file, we will place all the required `using` statements, `namespace`, and the class definition. So, it will look as follows initially:

```
using System;
using System.Threading.Tasks;
using Grpc.Net.Client;
using Performance;

namespace ApiGateway
{
    internal class GrpcPerformanceClient
    {
    }
}
```

Inside the namespace, we will add the interface definition for our class:

```
public interface IGrpcPerformanceClient
{
    Task<ResponseModel.PerformanceStatusModel>
        GetPerformanceStatus(string clientName);
}
```

Next, we will add a constructor to our class, which will set the client channel when it's initialized:

```
private readonly GrpcChannel channel;

public GrpcPerformanceClient(string serverUrl)
{
    channel = GrpcChannel.ForAddress(serverUrl);
}
```

After this, we will ensure that our class implements both the `IGrpcPerformanceClient` and `IDisposable` interfaces. The class needs to implement the method that we have defined in the interface. Likewise, we need to ensure that we dispose of the channel once an instance of this class is destroyed. Therefore, we will change the class definition line to the following:

```
internal class GrpcPerformanceClient : IGrpcPerformanceClient,
IDisposable
```

Now, let's implement the `IGrpcPerformanceClient` interface by adding the following method to our class:

```
public async Task<ResponseModel.PerformanceStatusModel>
  GetPerformanceStatus(string clientName)
{
    var client = new Monitor.MonitorClient(channel);

    var response = await client.GetPerformanceAsync(new
      PerformanceStatusRequest
    {
        ClientName = clientName
    });

    return new ResponseModel.PerformanceStatusModel
    {
        CpuPercentageUsage = response.CpuPercentageUsage,
        MemoryUsage = response.MemoryUsage,
        ProcessesRunning = response.ProcessesRunning,
        ActiveConnections = response.ActiveConnections
```

```
        };
}
```

Then, we will implement an `IDisposable` interface by adding the following method to the class:

```
public void Dispose()
{
    channel.Dispose();
}
```

Now, we need to register this wrapper class alongside our other dependencies. So, we will apply some changes to the `Startup.cs` file, (or `Program.cs` file if you are on a .NET 6 template), which is located within the root of the `ApiGateway` project folder.

First, we will ensure that the class imports all the necessary namespaces. The full collection of `using` statements should be as follows:

```
using System;
using Microsoft.AspNetCore.Builder;
using Microsoft.AspNetCore.Hosting;
using Microsoft.Extensions.Configuration;
using Microsoft.Extensions.DependencyInjection;
using Microsoft.Extensions.Hosting;
using Performance;
```

Then, we will ensure that we inject all the necessary dependencies into our code by placing the following content inside the `ConfigureServices` method. If you are using .NET 6 template, the following code will go into the main body of `Program.cs` file before the Build event. And you will need to replace `services` with `builder.Services`:

```
services.AddControllers();
services.AddOpenApiDocument();
services.AddSingleton(Configuration);
services.AddSingleton<IGrpcPerformanceClient>(p => new
    GrpcPerformanceClient(Configuration["ServerUrl"]));
services.AddGrpcClient<Monitor.MonitorClient>(o =>
{
    o.Address = new Uri(Configuration["ServerUrl"]);
});
```

Here, we are adding API controllers. Then, we are adding `Swagger` dependencies so that we can generate web pages based on REST API endpoints. Then, we are making the application configuration available to the other classes (we will need this to instantiate gRPC clients on demand). After this, we are registering an instance of our wrapper class that we have just created.

The final registration method, `AddGrpcClient`, is an in-built way to register a gRPC client inside the ASP.NET Core application without using any custom wrapper. If we have this registration call, then we can inject the client type (in this case, `Monitor.MonitorClient`) into the constructors of our controllers and it will get resolved to a functioning instance. This makes client registration more convenient. However, as we will see later, outsourcing client registration to the underlying framework doesn't necessarily improve its performance.

Next, we will need to add `Swagger` elements to our pipeline. To do so, we will place the following lines into the `configure` method. They will need to be placed anywhere before the calls to `UseRouting` and `UseHttpsRedirection`:

```
app.UseOpenApi();
app.UseSwaggerUi3();
```

As you may have noticed, we have inserted the value of the `ServerUrl` element from our configuration. So, we will need to add it to our `appsetting.json` file. The value of the element will be the secure (HTTPS) application URL we defined in the `applicationUrl` element of the `launchSettings.json` file from the `PerformanceService` project. However, if you are running the gRPC service application on a Mac, you will need to use the HTTP URL. In my case, the URL is `https://localhost:5001`. So, let's add the following field to the `appsettings.json` file of the `ApiGateway` project:

```
"ServerUrl": "https://localhost:5001"
```

Also, since we are adding a Swagger page to our project, we can make things easier for us by enabling automatic navigation to this page whenever the application is launched. To do so, open the `launchSettings.json` file in the `ApiGateway` project and replace the values of all the `launchUrl` elements with `swagger`.

Now, we are ready to add the controller that will provide the interface between the gRPC client and the outside world. Before we do this, we will remove any existing files from the `Controllers` folder inside the `ApiGateway` project. We won't need them anymore. Then, we will create the `PerformanceController.cs` file inside this folder.

We will start by populating this file with the basic ASP.NET Core Web API controller structure:

```csharp
using System.Diagnostics;
using System.Threading.Tasks;
using Grpc.Net.Client;
using Microsoft.AspNetCore.Mvc;
using Microsoft.Extensions.Configuration;
using Performance;

namespace ApiGateway.Controllers
{
    [ApiController]
    [Route("[controller]")]
    public class PerformanceController : ControllerBase
    {
    }
}
```

Then, we will add the constructor and the `private` fields:

```csharp
private readonly Monitor.MonitorClient factoryClient;
private readonly IGrpcPerformanceClient clientWrapper;
private readonly string serverUrl;

public PerformanceController(Monitor.MonitorClient
   factoryClient,
    IGrpcPerformanceClient clientWrapper,
    IConfiguration configuration)
{
    this.factoryClient = factoryClient;
    this.clientWrapper = clientWrapper;
    serverUrl = configuration["ServerUrl"];
}
```

Here, we are inserting a dependency of `IGrpcPerformanceClien` – the gRPC client wrapper that we created earlier. We are also inserting the `Monitor.MonitorClient` instance, which we registered via `AddGrpcClient` in the `Startup` class (or `Program.cs` file, depending on your platform version). Finally, we are inserting `configuration` so that we can store the URL of the gRPC server for later.

Now, let's add three endpoints that have identical logical flows but use different gRPC client types. We will start by adding an endpoint that uses the client that was created by the internal factory method of ASP.NET Core. This method will look as follows:

```csharp
[HttpGet("factory-client/{count}")]
public async Task<ResponseModel>
    GetPerformanceFromFactoryClient(int count)
{
    var stopWatch = Stopwatch.StartNew();
    var response = new ResponseModel();
    for (var i = 0; i < count; i++)
    {
        var grpcResponse = await
            factoryClient.GetPerformanceAsync(new
                PerformanceStatusRequest { ClientName =
                    $"client {i + 1}" });
        response.PerformanceStatuses.Add(new
            ResponseModel.PerformanceStatusModel
            {
                CpuPercentageUsage = grpcResponse.
                    CpuPercentageUsage,
                MemoryUsage = grpcResponse.MemoryUsage,
                ProcessesRunning = grpcResponse.ProcessesRunning,
                ActiveConnections = grpcResponse.ActiveConnections
            });
    }
    response.RequestProcessingTime = stopWatch.
        ElapsedMilliseconds;
    return response;
}
```

Why you need to reuse a gRPC channel   145

What we have done here is accept a parameter containing a count of the gRPC calls we are about to make. Then, we generate that many gRPC requests on the client that we have inserted into our controller directly. The client is expected to reuse the channel, but we don't know how else it has been configured internally.

Now, let's add an endpoint that uses the gRPC client wrapper, which will have the following content:

```csharp
[HttpGet("client-wrapper/{count}")]
public async Task<ResponseModel>
  GetPerformanceFromClientWrapper(int
  count)
{
    var stopWatch = Stopwatch.StartNew();
    var response = new ResponseModel();

    for (var i = 0; i < count; i++)
    {
        var grpcResponse = await
            clientWrapper.GetPerformanceStatus($"client
            {i + 1}");
        response.PerformanceStatuses.Add(grpcResponse);
    }

    response.RequestProcessingTime = stopWatch.
        ElapsedMilliseconds;
    return response;
}
```

The principle here is the same, but we are making all the gRPC calls via the wrapper that we created previously. Here, we have full control over the gRPC client. We are reusing the same channel between the calls but are creating a new client for every call.

Finally, we will add a method where we will be recreating a new instance of the gRPC channel and the client every time we make a gRPC call:

```csharp
[HttpGet("initialized-client/{count}")]
public async Task<ResponseModel>
  GetPerformanceFromNewClient(int
```

```
    count)
{
    var stopWatch = Stopwatch.StartNew();
    var response = new ResponseModel();

    for (var i = 0; i < count; i++)
    {
        using var channel = GrpcChannel.ForAddress(serverUrl);
        var client = new Monitor.MonitorClient(channel);
        var grpcResponse = await client.GetPerformanceAsync(new
            PerformanceStatusRequest { ClientName =
                $"client {i + 1}" });
        response.PerformanceStatuses.Add(new
            ResponseModel.PerformanceStatusModel
            {
                CpuPercentageUsage = grpcResponse.
                    CpuPercentageUsage,
                MemoryUsage = grpcResponse.MemoryUsage,
                ProcessesRunning = grpcResponse.ProcessesRunning,
                ActiveConnections = grpcResponse.ActiveConnections
            });
    }
    response.RequestProcessingTime = stopWatch.
        ElapsedMilliseconds;
    return response;
}
```

Here, we are, once again, making a specified number of gRPC calls. However, we are also creating a new channel and a new client for every call.

Now, we are in a position to launch our application and see which of the endpoints performs best.

Comparing the performance of different client types

First, we need to launch the application that represents the gRPC server. To do so, execute the `dotnet run` command from the `PerformanceService` project folder. Then, execute the same command from the `ApiGateway` project folder.

Once both applications are running, navigate to the API gateway's Swagger page in your browser. The address will be the secure URL from the `launchUrl` element of the `launchSettings.json` file of the `ApiGateway` project, followed by the `/swagger` path. For example, the URL that I have in my `launchSettings` file is `https://localhost:36670`. Therefore, the web page I need to access will be located at `https://localhost:36670/swagger`.

You will be presented with visual representations of all three endpoints that we have added to the controller:

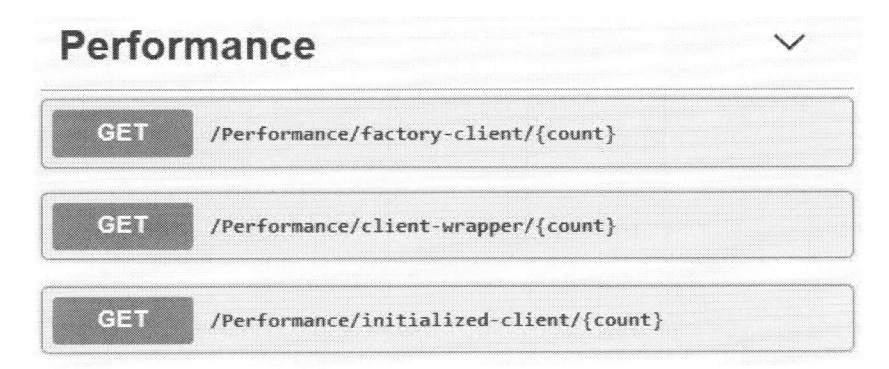

Figure 4.1 – Swagger representation of PerformanceController

Now, let's try each endpoint with the same `count` parameter to see how they perform. Let's pick up a relatively high number – for example, 1,000 – and see how long it takes to process the request on each of the endpoints.

The best-performing endpoint will be the one that uses a client wrapper. This is where we have full control over the client and we reuse the same channel:

Figure 4.2 – A request on the client-wrapper endpoint taking just over 15 seconds

Unsurprisingly, the endpoint that creates a new gRPC channel for every call has performed worse. Unlike the client wrapper endpoint, which took approximately 15 seconds to execute, the endpoint that uses a new channel for every call took approximately 25 seconds:

```
{
    "cpuPercentageUsage": 73.52017721790828,
    "memoryUsage": 22.799029072187388,
    "processesRunning": 931767674,
    "activeConnections": 171368762
  },
  {
    "cpuPercentageUsage": 70.10974896611168,
    "memoryUsage": 2.944346053034228,
    "processesRunning": 784356151,
    "activeConnections": 1837297110
  }
  ],
  "requestProcessingTime": 24186
}
```

Figure 4.3 – A request on the initialized-client endpoint taking around 25 seconds

However, the surprising outcome was that the client that was created by the framework had the worst performance. Even though it used the same channel for all its calls, it probably wasn't configured optimally by the framework:

```
{
    "cpuPercentageUsage": 55.91410363834076,
    "memoryUsage": 88.68799232351034,
    "processesRunning": 499050749,
    "activeConnections": 835356275
  },
  {
    "cpuPercentageUsage": 59.17895560114596,
    "memoryUsage": 77.78339217313723,
    "processesRunning": 901384749,
    "activeConnections": 1973813494
  }
  ],
  "requestProcessingTime": 51024
}
```

Figure 4.4 – A request on the factory-client endpoint taking around 50 seconds

The conclusion is that reusing the gRPC channel on your client does improve performance. However, if you want to get the best performance, you need to control how you create your client as much as possible. You can outsource this task to the framework, which will mean that there will be less code to write. However, what you gain in convenience might be lost in terms of performance.

Reusing the gRPC channel on your client is just one of the ways of improving performance. There is also a limit on the number of streams that can be used at the same time inside the same server connection. And if this limit is exceeded, any additional calls need to be queued. But there is a way to work around this, which we will have a look at in the next section.

How to not get held up by a concurrent stream limit

The HTTP/2 connection that gRPC relies on has a limit on concurrent streams on a connection that can be applied at the same time. If this limit is exceeded, the subsequent calls cannot be made right away. They have to be queued.

The default concurrent connection limit is normally set to 100 streams. This can be configured on the server; however, this approach is not recommended. This can introduce separate performance issues, such as connection packet loss, resulting in all the TCP calls to the server being blocked. There can also be a conflict between different threads trying to write to the same connection.

The recommended way to work around this concurrent stream limit is to configure your client channel to open additional connections when the concurrency limit is exceeded. And this is easy enough to achieve using the .NET implementation of the gRPC client.

Configuring connection concurrency on the gRPC client

In this section, we will create a new controller with two endpoints that are identical to each other except for one detail: the gRPC client that's used by one endpoint will have a default single-connection configuration applied, while the other client will be configured to open additional connections when needed.

In our `ApiGateway` project folder, place the `ConcurrencyController.cs` file inside the `Controllers` folder. First, let's add the following content to this file:

```
using System.Collections.Generic;
using System.Diagnostics;
using System.Net.Http;
using System.Threading.Tasks;
using Grpc.Net.Client;
using Microsoft.AspNetCore.Mvc;
```

```
using Microsoft.Extensions.Configuration;
using Performance;

namespace ApiGateway.Controllers
{
    [ApiController]
    [Route("[controller]")]
    public class ConcurrencyController : ControllerBase
    {
    }
}
```

Now, let's add the private member and the constructor to the class:

```
private readonly string serverUrl;

public ConcurrencyController(IConfiguration configuration)
{
    serverUrl = configuration["ServerUrl"];
}
```

Following this, we will add an endpoint that uses a standard gRPC client to make the specified number of concurrent gRPC calls to the server:

```
[HttpGet("single-connection/{count}")]
public ResponseModel GetDataFromSingleConnection(int count)
{
    using var channel = GrpcChannel.ForAddress(serverUrl);
    var stopWatch = Stopwatch.StartNew();
    var response = new ResponseModel();
    var concurrentJobs = new List<Task>();
    for (var i = 0; i < count; i++)
    {
        var client = new Monitor.MonitorClient(channel);
        concurrentJobs.Add(Task.Run(() =>
        {
            client.GetPerformance(new PerformanceStatusRequest
            {
```

```
                ClientName = $"client {i + 1}" });
        }));
    }

    Task.WaitAll(concurrentJobs.ToArray());
    response.RequestProcessingTime = stopWatch.
        ElapsedMilliseconds;
    return response;
}
```

We create this concurrency by generating as many tasks that are specified in the count parameter as quickly as possible.

Finally, we will add another endpoint, which has very similar logic but one notable difference, as highlighted in the following code block:

```
[HttpGet("multiple-connections/{count}")]
public ResponseModel GetDataFromMultipleConnections(int count)
{
    using var channel = GrpcChannel.ForAddress(serverUrl, new
        GrpcChannelOptions
    {
        HttpHandler = new SocketsHttpHandler
        {
            EnableMultipleHttp2Connections = true,
        }
    });
    var stopWatch = Stopwatch.StartNew();
    var response = new ResponseModel();
    var concurrentJobs = new List<Task>();
    for (var i = 0; i < count; i++)
    {
        concurrentJobs.Add(Task.Run(() =>
        {
            var client = new Monitor.MonitorClient(channel);
            client.GetPerformance(new PerformanceStatusRequest
            {
                ClientName = $"client {i + 1}" });
```

```
        }));
    }
    Task.WaitAll(concurrentJobs.ToArray());
    response.RequestProcessingTime = stopWatch.
      ElapsedMilliseconds;
    return response;
}
```

In this case, when we are creating the channel, we are passing the `GrpcChannelOptions` object into it. Inside this object, we are setting a custom `HttpHandler`. To allow our client to open additional connections when needed, we are setting this field to a new instance of `SocketsHttpHandler`. Then, we are setting its `EnableMultipleHttp2Connections` field to `true`.

This is all we need to do to make our client open additional HTTP/2 connections when needed. Now, let's launch our application and test it.

Comparing the performance between a single connection and multiple connections

We will launch both of our applications by running the `dotnet run` command inside both the `PerformanceService` and `ApiGateway` project folders. Then, we will navigate to the Swagger page of the `ApiGateway` application, where we should be able to see our new concurrency controller endpoints:

Concurrency

- GET `/Concurrency/single-connection/{count}`
- GET `/Concurrency/multiple-connections/{count}`

Performance

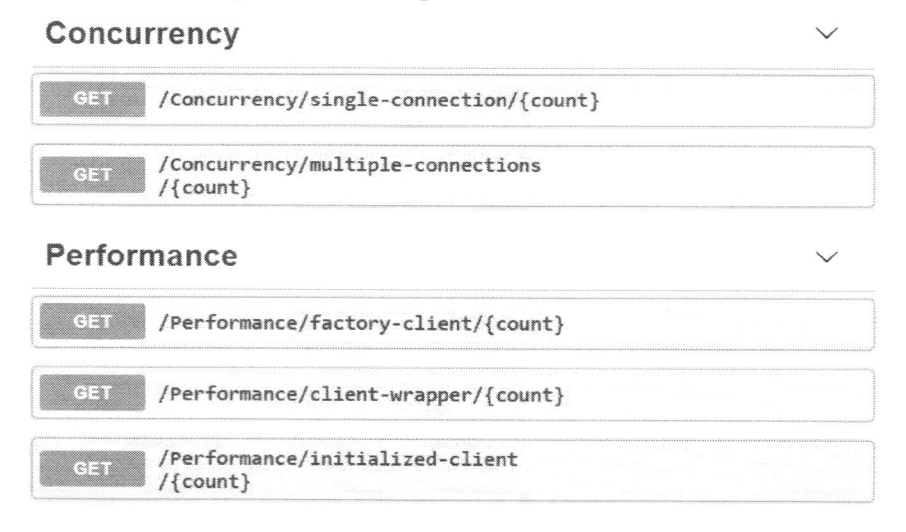

- GET `/Performance/factory-client/{count}`
- GET `/Performance/client-wrapper/{count}`
- GET `/Performance/initialized-client/{count}`

Figure 4.5 – The ConcurrencyController endpoints on the Swagger page

This time, it may not be enough to run each endpoint once because when you use a high number, creating so many tasks may have a performance overhead. This is why, if you run each endpoint once, you may get overlapping numbers. However, this is still perhaps the simplest demonstration of concurrent calls. And, as such, it will still take advantage of multiple connection settings.

The best way to test the performance difference between these two endpoints is to run each of them multiple times and check the average. In my case, after running each endpoint 50 times, the average request processing time for a `single-connection` endpoint was around 35 seconds, while it was 30 seconds for a `multiple-connections` one. That's not a huge difference, but it's still significant. Therefore, it makes sense to apply the `EnableMultipleHttp2Connections` setting to `HttpHandler` of the gRPC client if you expect many concurrent calls to be made by it.

Ensuring that your connection remains alive

Your application, which acts as a gRPC client, might experience prolonged periods of idleness where no gRPC calls are made to the server. In this period, your connection to the server may get interrupted. Therefore, while reusing a gRPC channel is good for performance, you need to ensure that the channel can still be used every time you need to rely on it.

Fortunately, ensuring that the connection remains alive is relatively easy to implement. To some extent, this functionality will already be configured by default. But you can also fine-tune it to suit your needs.

Setting up keep-alive pings on the gRPC client

Inside the `ConcurrencyController` class of the `ApiGateway` application, locate the `GetDataFromMultipleConnections` method. Inside this method, replace the initialization of the `channel` variable with the following code:

```
using var channel = GrpcChannel.ForAddress(serverUrl, new
    GrpcChannelOptions
    {
        HttpHandler = new SocketsHttpHandler
        {
            PooledConnectionIdleTimeout =
                System.Threading.Timeout.InfiniteTimeSpan,
            KeepAlivePingDelay = TimeSpan.FromSeconds(60),
            KeepAlivePingTimeout = TimeSpan.FromSeconds(30),
```

```
            EnableMultipleHttp2Connections = true,
        }
});
```

We have retained the client's ability to create new HTTP/2 connections whenever the concurrent stream limit is exceeded. However, we have also added several options to fine-tune keep-alive pings to make sure that the connection remains active.

The `PooledConnectionIdleTimeout` setting controls how long a connection can be idle before it can be considered reusable. In our case, we have set it to an infinite time to keep the connection reserved.

`KeepAlivePingDelay` is a setting that controls the interval at which keep-alive pings are sent to the server. These pings are lightweight requests. Their purpose is to keep the connection active. In this case, they are sent every 60 seconds.

`KeepAlivePingTimeout` is a setting that controls the time window that the response from the keep-alive ping is expected to be received within. If nothing is received within this time window after sending the ping, the client will close the connection. The default value is 20 seconds, but in this example, we are setting it to 30 seconds.

The main performance benefit of correctly applied keep-alive ping settings is that these pings will keep your connection fresh. Your client will still work if you use it once the connection has been closed, but it will require establishing a new connection, which is almost equivalent to creating a new channel. And this is where the performance penalty comes from when you submit the first request after a period of inactivity.

But if the connection was kept alive all this time, it has already been fully prepared for you. When you make the first request after a period of inactivity, the client will not have to establish a new connection. You will be able to use a fully functioning connection in the same way as if the period of inactivity didn't happen at all.

So, reusing your channels, opening additional connections for concurrent calls, and configuring keep-alive pings will improve your performance to an extent. But there is a way to improve your performance by an order of magnitude if you need to create communication-heavy applications. This is what we will have a look at now.

When streaming is better than individual calls

So far, we have only had one RPC in our solution. This was a unary RPC, `GetPerformance`, which is where we've been sending a single response message and retrieving a single request message. Having a unary RPC is acceptable in scenarios where it's only meant to be called occasionally.

However, we haven't been using it this way. We have been bombarding this endpoint with many repeated calls. And this is precisely the type of situation where a unary RPC is not the best tool for the job. A bi-directional streaming RPC would be a better option as it will improve our performance significantly.

Setting up a bi-directional streaming RPC

Let's open the `performance.proto` file, which resides inside the `Protos` folder of the `GrpcDependencies` project. Now, add the following RPC to the `Monitor service` definition:

```
rpc GetManyPerformanceStats (stream PerformanceStatusRequest)
    returns (stream PerformanceStatusResponse);
```

This RPC uses the same request and response messages as `GetPerformance`, but it uses both of those inside streams.

Now, we need to implement this RPC definition on the server side. To do so, open the `PerformanceMonitor` class of the `PerformanceService` project and add the following method to it:

```
public override async Task
    GetManyPerformanceStats(IAsyncStreamReader<PerformanceStatus
        Request> requestStream, IServerStreamWriter<Performance
        StatusResponse> responseStream, ServerCallContext
            context)
{
    while (await requestStream.MoveNext())
    {
        var randomNumberGenerator = new Random();
        await responseStream.WriteAsync(new
            PerformanceStatusResponse
            {
                CpuPercentageUsage = randomNumberGenerator.
                    NextDouble()
                    * 100,
                MemoryUsage = randomNumberGenerator.NextDouble() *
                    100,
                ProcessesRunning = randomNumberGenerator.Next(),
                ActiveConnections = randomNumberGenerator.Next()
```

```
        });
    }
}
```

In this method, we are doing a similar thing to what we have been doing in the `GetPerformance` method. But instead of just accepting a single request and sending back a single response, we read all the messages from the request stream. Then, for each of those, we write a response message into the response stream.

The principle remains the same – we process the request messages in the same order as they come in and we produce a response for every request. But we no longer have to make separate gRPC calls to process multiple messages.

Now, let's make the necessary changes to our client. First, in the `GrpcPerformanceClient.cs` file of the `ApiGateway` project, add the following `using` statements to the top of the file:

```
using System.Collections.Generic;
using Grpc.Core;
```

Following this, add the following method signature to the `IGrpcPerformanceClient` interface:

```
Task<IEnumerable<ResponseModel.PerformanceStatusModel>>
    GetPerformanceStatuses(IEnumerable<string> clientNames);
```

Now, we need to implement this method inside the `GrpcPerformanceClient` class. We will start by adding the method definition:

```
public async Task<IEnumerable<ResponseModel.
    PerformanceStatusModel>>
    GetPerformanceStatuses(IEnumerable<string> clientNames)
{
}
```

Now, let's create a gRPC client from the existing channel and open a streaming call:

```
var client = new Monitor.MonitorClient(channel);
using var call = client.GetManyPerformanceStats();
var responses = new List<ResponseModel.
    PerformanceStatusModel>();
```

Following this, we will create an asynchronous task that will listen for any response messages being placed on the server stream. We will convert each of these messages into `ResponseModel.PerformanceStatusModel` and add it to the list of responses as soon as we receive it:

```
var readTask = Task.Run(async () =>
{
    await foreach (var response in
      call.ResponseStream.ReadAllAsync())
    {
        responses.Add(new ResponseModel.PerformanceStatusModel
        {
            CpuPercentageUsage = response.CpuPercentageUsage,
            MemoryUsage = response.MemoryUsage,
            ProcessesRunning = response.ProcessesRunning,
            ActiveConnections = response.ActiveConnections
        });
    }
});
```

Then, we must populate the client stream with a list of request messages that correspond to the collection of client names that we have received as the method parameter:

```
foreach (var clientName in clientNames)
{
    await call.RequestStream.WriteAsync(new
      PerformanceStatusRequest
    {
        ClientName = clientName
    });
}
```

Finally, we will close the client stream, wait for all the messages to be extracted from the response stream, and return the collection of responses to the caller.

Now, let's create an endpoint inside our `PerformanceController` class that will use this method.

First, ensure that your `PerformanceController.cs` file contains the following `using` statement:

```
using System.Collections.Generic;
```

Then, add the following method to the class:

```
[HttpGet("streaming-call/{count}")]
public async Task<ResponseModel>
  GetPerformanceFromStreamingCall(int
  count)
{
    var stopWatch = Stopwatch.StartNew();
    var response = new ResponseModel();
    var clientNames = new List<string>();

    for (var i = 0; i < count; i++)
    {
        clientNames.Add($"client {i + 1}");
    }

    response.PerformanceStatuses.AddRange(await
      clientWrapper.GetPerformanceStatuses(clientNames));
    response.RequestProcessingTime = stopWatch.
      ElapsedMilliseconds;
    return response;
}
```

This endpoint takes the same parameter as the other endpoints in this controller and returns the same object type. But this time, we are just making a single RPC call and populating the request stream with multiple messages. Let's see how it performs compared to making a unary call multiple times.

Monitoring the performance of the bi-directional streaming call

Launch both the `PerformanceService` and `ApiGateway` applications and navigate to the Swagger page of `ApiGateway`. You should be able to see the new `streaming-call` endpoint on the `Performance` controller:

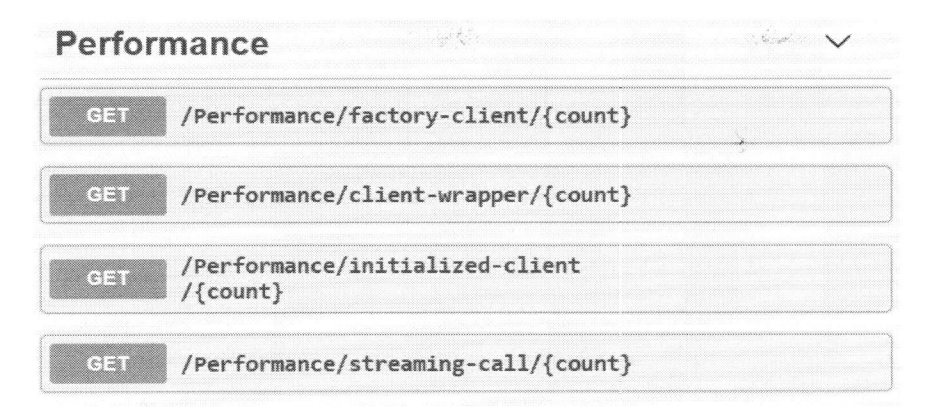

When streaming is better than individual calls 159

Figure 4.6 – The Swagger representation of PerformanceController with the streaming-call endpoint

Now, we will run this endpoint with the `count` parameter set to 1,000, as we did with the other endpoints before this:

Figure 4.7 – A request on the streaming-call endpoint taking around 3 seconds

Our call was fully processed in just over 3 seconds. This is five times faster than our previous fastest call, although we have submitted the same number of requests and have received the same number of response objects.

So, if you expect your gRPC application to process a large number of messages regularly – create streaming RPCs for them. They are faster than individual unary calls by a large margin.

There is also a modification you can apply to your Protobuf messages to transfer them faster due to the reduced bandwidth that they would require. This is what we will have a look at next.

Using binary payloads to decrease the data's size

If you want to minimize a Profobuf message's size while fitting as much data as possible into it, you can convert your data into a binary form. In Protobuf, there is a `bytes` data type that exists specifically for this.

Even though this data type is represented by the `ByteString` type from the `Google.Protobuf` library in C#, there are multiple ways of inserting a standard `byte` array into the fields of this type, which makes it compatible with any byte-processing functionality available in C#.

Let's have a look at various ways of writing data into this field and reading data from it.

Adding binary fields to Protobuf

In the `GrpcDependencies` project, open the `performance.proto` file inside the `Protos` folder and add the following fields to the `PerformanceStatusResponse` message definition:

```
bytes data_load_1 = 5;
bytes data_load_2 = 6;
```

Now, let's apply some modifications to the `PerformanceMonitor` class from the `PerformanceService` project. First, we will add the following `using` statement to the top of the file containing the class:

```
using Google.Protobuf;
```

Because both of the public endpoint methods will use similar functionality, we will refactor the class. First, we will add the following `private` method to it:

```
private PerformanceStatusResponse GetPerformaceResponse()
{
    var randomNumberGenerator = new Random();
    var dataLoad1 = new byte[100];
    var dataLoad2 = new byte[100];
    randomNumberGenerator.NextBytes(dataLoad1);
    randomNumberGenerator.NextBytes(dataLoad2);
    return new PerformanceStatusResponse
    {
```

Using binary payloads to decrease the data's size 161

```
            CpuPercentageUsage = randomNumberGenerator.NextDouble()
                * 100,
            MemoryUsage = randomNumberGenerator.NextDouble() * 100,
            ProcessesRunning = randomNumberGenerator.Next(),
            ActiveConnections = randomNumberGenerator.Next(),
            DataLoad1 = UnsafeByteOperations.UnsafeWrap(dataLoad1),
            DataLoad2 = ByteString.CopyFrom(dataLoad2)
        };
}
```

Now, we will change both public endpoint methods to the following:

```
public override Task<PerformanceStatusResponse>
    GetPerformance(PerformanceStatusRequest request,
        ServerCallContext
        context)
{
    return Task.FromResult(GetPerformaceResponse());
}

public override async Task
    GetManyPerformanceStats(IasyncStreamReader
        <PerformanceStatusRequest> requestStream,
        IServerStreamWriter
        <PerformanceStatusResponse>
responseStream, ServerCallContext context)
{
    while (await requestStream.MoveNext())
    {
        await responseStream.
            WriteAsync(GetPerformaceResponse());
    }
}
```

So, to populate the two `bytes` fields that we've added, we are generating two `byte` arrays, each with a length of 100, and populating those with randomly generated bytes.

Then, we are using two different methods to write the data from these two `byte` arrays into the `bytes` fields:

- `UnsafeByteOperations.UnsafeWrap`, which is similar to adding the `byte` array to a `ByteString` field by reference. It's not merely the data that gets copied. If you do anything to the original `byte` array after you've added it this way, modifying this array may corrupt the data. The advantage of using this method is that it's faster than copying.
- `ByteString.CopyFrom` copies the original array into the `ByteString` field. This method is safer but slower.

Now, let's modify our client so that it can read the data.

First, we will add the following field to the `PerformanceStatusModel` class, which is nested inside the `ResponseModel` class of the `ApiGateway` project:

```
public byte[] DataLoad1 { get; set; }
public byte[] DataLoad2 { get; set; }
```

Now, let's make some changes to the `GrpcPerformanceClient` class so that it can read the `bytes` data from the newly added fields. But first, we will need to add the following `using` statement to the top of the file containing the class:

```
using System.Runtime.InteropServices;
```

Now, let's add the following `private` method to the class:

```
private ResponseModel.PerformanceStatusModel
ReadResponse(PerformanceStatusResponse response)
{
    return new ResponseModel.PerformanceStatusModel
    {
        CpuPercentageUsage = response.CpuPercentageUsage,
        MemoryUsage = response.MemoryUsage,
        ProcessesRunning = response.ProcessesRunning,
        ActiveConnections = response.ActiveConnections,
        DataLoad1 = response.DataLoad1.ToByteArray(),
        DataLoad2 =
            MemoryMarshal.TryGetArray(response.DataLoad2.Memory,
                out var segment) ? segment.Array :
```

```
            response.DataLoad2.Memory.ToArray()
    };
}
```

Here, once again, we have two different ways of converting `ByteString` into a `byte` array:

- `ToByteArray` will convert `ByteString` into a `byte` array.
- `MemoryMarshal.TryGetArray` will try to obtain a specific array segment. If this fails, we can try to convert the read-only memory segment of the `ByteString` object into the byte array by calling the `ToArray` method.

Now, we can apply this `private` method to both of our `public` methods. In the `GetPerformanceStatus` method, change the `return` statement to the following:

```
return ReadResponse(response);
```

In the `GetPerformanceStatuses` method, replace the statement that starts with `responses.Add` with the following code:

```
responses.Add(ReadResponse(response));
```

Now, we can get this data on our Swagger page:

```
{
  "performanceStatuses": [
    {
      "cpuPercentageUsage": 81.90360515467059,
      "memoryUsage": 67.90969272512463,
      "processesRunning": 1432912527,
      "activeConnections": 1384382367,
      "dataLoad1": "smRYixhm3401EP5A5CIrViyz9qhUfnoC0vy8OdpjlIz8AE0
+r5WcVnyK34JPpaCZwhLhxFOb4zTqVbkbqqWy0ntyROPV7KaWF58ryZ/3sy1bInfIgc
85YR0ZVFncgKzX1wwG3Q==",
      "dataLoad2": "Yb3E1mtKrbRvGZXyooy/hy7qUKw448W8mE261vJU8ZLw1su
eXqBcNyKE8QODYbZQwCWo7LxapH33CD0dkBbBGygDAczAISiNjRmKs/HCODaWatXMqw
TWljJNplZiP6YLw9XbgA=="
    },
```

Figure 4.8 – The HTTP response data with byte array fields

Even though we used raw bytes in this example, any kind of data can be packaged into this binary format. C# has a lot of in-built tools for working with bytes and converting them into other data types.

Summary

In this chapter, you learned that reusing existing gRPC channels is good for performance, while performance isn't affected by reusing a client object. You also saw that even though it's convenient to outsource the process of creating a gRPC client to the framework, this isn't necessarily good for performance. Therefore, for optimal performance, it's better to control how the client is created as much as possible.

We covered the fact that there is a streaming limit on active HTTP/2 connections. But you also learned that there is a setting that allows you to create a new connection from your gRPC client when this limit is about to be exceeded.

Then, we covered how to keep the gRPC connection between the client and the server alive while you aren't actively using it. This allows you to start using it as soon as you need it without having to reestablish it.

After that, we learned how using bi-directional streaming instead of unary calls improves the processing speed by an order of magnitude when repeated calls need to be made.

Finally, we covered how to transfer binary data in Protobuf messages, which significantly reduces the message's size and minimizes the bandwidth usage.

In the next chapter, we will cover the best practices surrounding gRPC API versioning. You will learn how to update your server-side API in such a way that it doesn't break the existing clients.

Questions

1. For the best performance in terms of gRPC communication, which of the following client-side objects would you need to reuse?

    A. Client

    B. Channel

    C. Both the client and the channel

    D. Neither

2. What is the default concurrent stream limit on the HTTP/2 connection?

    A. 1,000

    B. 10

    C. 100

    D. 1

3. What happens if no data is received within the timeout window after sending a keep-alive ping?

   A. The connection is terminated

   B. The next ping is sent

   C. The connection is marked as idle

   D. This configuration parameter is made redundant

4. How do you define a bi-directional streaming call in Protobuf?

   A. Apply the `stream` keyword before the `rpc` keyword

   B. Apply the `stream` keyword after the `rpc` keyword

   C. Apply the `stream` keyword before the input parameter

   D. Apply the `stream` keyword before both the input and output parameters

5. When shouldn't you use `UnsafeByteOperations.UnsafeWrap` to populate `ByteString`?

   A. When you intend to modify the original byte array after this call

   B. You should be able to use it in any situation

   C. When you haven't made a copy of the original array

   D. When you want higher performance

Further reading

- Performance best practices for gRPC: https://docs.microsoft.com/en-us/aspnet/core/grpc/performance.

5
Applying Versioning to the gRPC API

So far, we have had a look at the uses of **gRPC** in **ASP.NET Core** where both the client and server applications are present in the same solution and rely on the same reference library. When this is the case and the applications at both ends of gRPC communication are in the same repository, then those components are probably meant to be deployed together. This is where API versioning is not critical, as you can simply apply Protobuf changes to both the client and server at the same time. Even if these are *breaking changes*, only the applications from the same repository will be affected.

But not all gRPC implementations are like this. Quite often, your client and your server will be in different repositories and will be deployed as separate components. It might even be the case that the client and the server are developed by separate teams or even separate organizations. Just like with a **REST API**, your server might have a public gRPC endpoint that any authorized client should be able to access.

This is where **API versioning** becomes critically important. If you make updates to your server, these changes should not cause the existing clients to break or behave in an unexpected manner. Luckily, Protobuf has been designed for easy API versioning. And this is what we will have a look at in this chapter.

We will cover the following topics:

- Why an API versioning strategy is important
- What the sequence numbers in the proto file represent
- Why you must not modify existing fields in future Protobuf versions
- How to deprecate old, unused fields in gRPC
- How to factor in API versioning at the design stage

By the end of this chapter, you will have learned how to apply API versioning so that you can make changes to the gRPC server without breaking any of its existing clients.

Technical requirements

To follow the instructions in this chapter, you will need the following:

- A computer with a **Windows**, **Mac**, or **Linux** operating system
- A supported IDE or code editor (**Visual Studio**, **Visual Studio Code**, or **JetBrains Rider**)
- The .NET 5 **software development kit** (**SDK**) (or newer)
- A self-signed development HTTPS certificate enabled on your machine

For instructions on how to set up all of these prerequisites, please refer to *Chapter 1, Creating a Basic gRPC Application on ASP.NET Core*.

All of the code samples used in this chapter can be found in this book's **GitHub** repository:

```
https://github.com/PacktPublishing/Microservices-Communication-in-.NET-Using-gRPC/tree/main/Chapter-05
```

Please visit the following link to check the CiA videos: `https://bit.ly/3pT2hPA`

Why an API versioning strategy is important

We will begin by setting up two applications. We will pretend that these two applications are developed by different teams and they don't have access to shared gRPC dependencies. This setup will be done to demonstrate why API versioning is so important.

For convenience, while using an IDE, you may add these applications to the same solution. But this is not necessary, as these applications will not share any dependencies.

Creating a server application

We will start by executing the following command to create an ASP.NET Core application based on the `gRPC Service` template:

```
dotnet new grpc -o GrpcServer
```

In the `GrpcServer` project folder that has been created, we will remove the default `greet.proto` file from the `Protos` folder. Then, we will place the `stats.proto` file in there with the following service definition:

```
syntax = "proto3";

package stats;

service Status {
    rpc GetStatus (StatusRequest) returns (StatusResponse);
}
```

The definition of the `StatusRequest` message will be as follows:

```
message StatusRequest {
    string client_name = 1;
    string client_description = 2;
    bool ready = 3;
    bool authorized = 4;
}
```

And the definition of the `StatusResponse` message should be as follows:

```
message StatusResponse {
    string server_name = 1;
    string server_description = 2;
    int32 number_of_connections = 3;
    double cpu_usage = 4;
    double memory_usage = 5;
    uint64 errors_logged = 6;
    uint32 catastrophic_failures_logged = 7;
    bool active = 8;
}
```

Essentially, our server application will receive some basic information from a client and will send back its performance statistics, such as memory usage, the number of errors logged, and so on. Of course, all of these measurements will be mocked, as the scope of this exercise is purely gRPC communication and not the collection of any internal metrics.

This newly added file will need to be registered in the server role in the project. To do so, we need to ensure that the following section is added to the `GrpcServer.csproj` file:

```xml
<ItemGroup>
    <Protobuf Include="Protos\stats.proto" GrpcServices="Server"
    />
</ItemGroup>
```

We are now ready to implement the server-side components of this Protobuf definition.

Implementing the server-side gRPC components

Since we have removed the default `greet.proto` file, we need to remove the `GreeterService.cs` file from the `Services` folder of the `GrpcServer` project. We will also need to remove the line that references the `GreeterService` class from our `Startup.cs` file (or `Program.cs` file if you are using .NET 6 template). Otherwise, our code won't compile.

Once we have done this, we will create a `StatusService.cs` file in the `Services` folder. The file will contain a class definition with the following namespace imports:

```csharp
using System;
using System.Threading.Tasks;
using Grpc.Core;
using Stats;

namespace GrpcServer
{
    public class StatusService : Stats.Status.StatusBase
    {
    }
}
```

The class will have the following override method, which will output the details of the request into the console:

```
public override Task<StatusResponse> GetStatus(StatusRequest
   request, ServerCallContext context)
{
    Console.WriteLine($"Client name is {request.ClientName}");
    Console.WriteLine($"Client description is
      {request.ClientDescription}");
    Console.WriteLine($"Is client ready? {request.Ready}");
    Console.WriteLine($"Is client authorized?
      {request.Authorized}");
}
```

At the end of the method, we will insert the following block, which will return a response object populated by some randomized values:

```
var randomNumberGenerator = new Random();

return Task.FromResult(new StatusResponse
{
    ServerName = "TestServer",
    ServerDescription = "This is a test server that is used for
      generating status metrics",
    NumberOfConnections = randomNumberGenerator.Next(),
    CpuUsage = randomNumberGenerator.NextDouble() * 100,
    MemoryUsage = randomNumberGenerator.NextDouble() * 100,
    ErrorsLogged = (ulong)randomNumberGenerator.Next(),
    CatastrophicFailuresLogged = (uint)randomNumberGenerator.
      Next(),
    Active = true
});
```

Now, we will need to register this gRPC service implementation as an endpoint. To do so, add the following line to the expression inside the `app.UseEndpoints` call, which is inside the `Configure` method in the `Startup` class (or the main body of `Program.cs` class for .NET 6):

```
endpoints.MapGrpcService<StatusService>();
```

> **Note**
> If you are running your server-side application on a Mac, you will need to apply some modifications to it. The instruction on how to do so can be found in the *Running a gRPC service on Mac* section of *Chapter 1, Creating a Basic gRPC Application on ASP.NET Core*.

Now, we are ready to configure the client that will communicate with our gRPC server application.

Creating the gRPC client application

Our client application will be nothing more than a basic console app, as we will be focusing purely on gRPC communication. We will create the application project by executing the following command in any folder outside of any of our .NET project folders:

```
dotnet new console -o GrpcClient
```

We will then add all **NuGet** packages to the project that are required for the gRPC client implementation. This will be done by executing the following commands from inside the `GrpcClient` project folder:

```
dotnet add GrpcClient.csproj package Grpc.Net.Client
dotnet add GrpcClient.csproj package Google.Protobuf
dotnet add GrpcClient.csproj package Grpc.Tools
```

After we've added all the dependencies, we will create a `Protos` folder in the `GrpcClient` project folder. We will then copy the `stats.proto` file from the `Protos` folder of the `GrpcServer` project to this newly created `Protos` folder in the `GrpcClient` project. Once done, we need to register this Protobuf definition in the `GrpcClient.csproj` file by adding the following section to it:

```
<ItemGroup>
   <Protobuf Include="Protos\stats.proto" GrpcServices="Client"
    />
</ItemGroup>
```

There is an important reason why we copied the proto file instead of getting two applications to share it. This is what we will probably have to do in real life too – when the client is developed separately from the server.

Of course, even in this case, you may have a separate class library that holds the proto files that both your client and your server will reference, even if they are completely separate from each other. For example, you may have the class library published as a NuGet package on a NuGet feed that both the client and the server can access.

This will only work if both the client and the server are .NET applications. However, if your gRPC server is meant to be accessible to external clients, it's unreasonable to assume that all of those clients will be built on the same technology stack. The developers of the client application will know the API specification (in this case, a Protobuf definition), and it will be up to them to choose the technology to build the client on. Therefore, when you make your gRPC API available to the outside, the best way to share the API specifications is to publish the proto files, which the developers can copy into their own client applications. And this is what we are emulating here.

Now, we will need to implement the client logic.

Implementing the gRPC client logic

To make it simple, all of our client-side gRPC logic will be placed into the entry point method of the `Program.cs` file of the `GrpcClient` application. First, we will add all of the required namespace references to the class by placing the following `using` statements at the top of the file:

```
using System;
using System.Threading.Tasks;
using Grpc.Net.Client;
```

Then, replace the content of the `Main` method of the `Program` class with the following lines:

```
Console.WriteLine("Please enter gRPC server address:");
var serverUrl = Console.ReadLine();

var client = new
    Stats.Status.StatusClient(GrpcChannel.ForAddress(serverUrl));

Console.WriteLine("Please enter client name:");
var clientName = Console.ReadLine();

Console.WriteLine("Please enter client description:");
var clientDescription = Console.ReadLine();
```

We have added an interactive script, where we specified the address of the gRPC server to connect to. Next, we type in the name and the description of our client, which will be placed into the `request` object during the gRPC call.

We then create the `request` object and make a call to the server:

```
var response = await client.GetStatusAsync(new Stats.
  StatusRequest
{
    ClientName = clientName,
    ClientDescription = clientDescription,
    Ready = true,
    Authorized = true
});
```

Finally, we print out the data we received from the server in the console:

```
Console.WriteLine($"Server name: {response.ServerName}");
Console.WriteLine($"Server description:
  {response.ServerDescription}");
Console.WriteLine($"Number of connections:
  {response.NumberOfConnections}");
Console.WriteLine($"CPU usage: {response.CpuUsage}");
Console.WriteLine($"Memory usage: {response.MemoryUsage}");
Console.WriteLine($"Errors logged: {response.ErrorsLogged}");
Console.WriteLine($"Catastrophic failures logged:
  {response.CatastrophicFailuresLogged}");
Console.WriteLine($"Active: {response.Active}");

Console.ReadKey();
```

Now, we will launch both of our applications to verify that they are working correctly.

Verifying that the client can talk to the server

We will first need to launch our server application. To do so, execute the `dotnet run` command from the `GrpcServer` project folder. Then, once our server is running and is ready to start accepting calls, we execute the same command from the `GrpcClient` folder.

Once the console application is launched, you will be asked to provide the address of your gRPC server application, which can be found in the `applicationUrl` field of the `launchSettings.json` file that is located in the `Properties` folder of the `GrpcServer` project. It should be `https://localhost:5001` by default. However, if you are running the gRPC service application on Mac, you would need to use the HTTP version, which is `http://localhost:5000` by default.

Following this, you will be asked to provide the name of the client and its description, both of which can be any arbitrary text.

Once you have provided those, you should see the following response from the server in your console window if your setup has worked correctly.

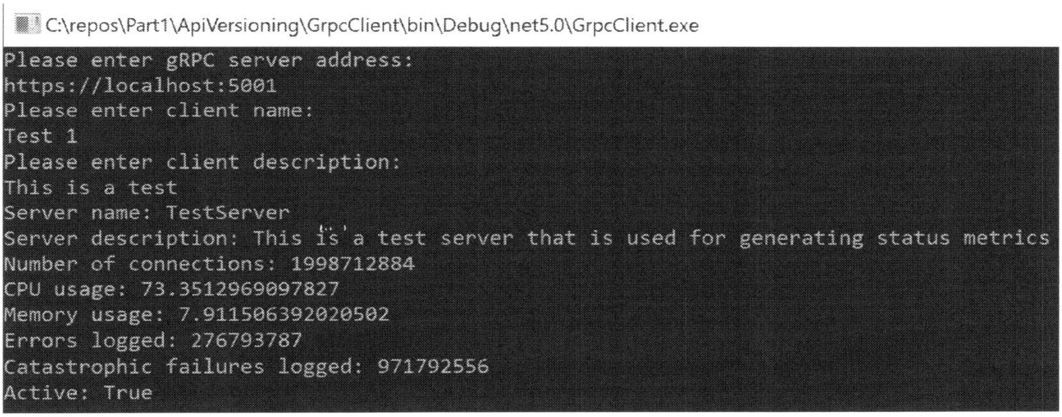

Figure 5.1 – The server response logged in the client console window

Once the connection has been verified from the client side, you can now also verify that the server application has printed the client data into its own console:

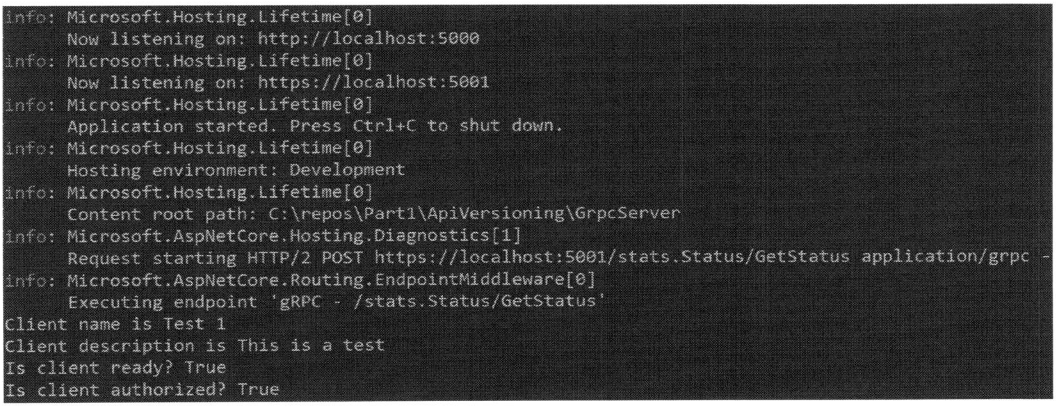

Figure 5.2 – Client request data being printed to the server console

So, we have established that both of our client and server applications are working correctly, despite having independent copies of the Protobuf definition. But to make sure the applications can communicate with each other, we rely on these copies to match each other.

In our example, because the client and the server use independent copies of the proto file, there is nothing that stops either copy from being modified to such an extent that it becomes incompatible with the other. And this is what may happen in a real-life scenario.

Developers of the server applications don't have control over what the developers of the client application are doing. And the developers of the client application don't have access to the code of the server applications. So, if the team maintaining the server application needs to update the Protobuf definition, the copy of the proto files that the client uses will become outdated.

Depending on the complexity of the server application and how many client applications are using it, bringing all clients up to date may take a relatively long time. And until this happens, the existing clients are expected to still function correctly. And this is precisely why you need to apply the API versioning strategy.

The good news is that the Protobuf protocol was designed from the outset to make API versioning as painless as possible. The sequence numbers next to the fields in the Protobuf `message` definitions are there to help with this task.

What the sequence numbers in the proto file represent

What makes Protobuf different from any other communication protocols or data storage formats is that each field, in its objects, has an equality sign (==) at the end, followed by a unique integer number. The equality sign followed by a numeric value is how you would normally assign a numeric value to a variable, but in Protobuf, it represents a unique sequence number of the field.

The reason these sequence numbers exist is that they are the only field identifiers that are used when the message is being transferred between the client and the server. The Protobuf messaging format has been designed to be as efficient as possible. Using arbitrary byte arrays to represent human-readable field names isn't very efficient. Instead, using numeric identifiers is the simplest way of both keeping track of each unique field and keeping the data payload size as small as possible.

Another feature that makes Protobuf so efficient is that you don't have to set every single field in each message. If you don't explicitly set the value of any given field, the field will simply be omitted from the message.

Each data type has its default value. And when the gRPC middleware in your application receives a message with a field missing, it will simply assign the default value to this field. The application that consumes this message will not see that any of the fields in it haven't been populated.

Also, when there are sequence numbers in a particular `message` payload that aren't defined in the proto file of the consuming application, no error is thrown. Instead, these are simply ignored.

These behavioral characteristics make the sequence numbers in the `message` definitions so useful for API versioning. If you add any new fields to the Protobuf definition on the server side, they will not be relevant to the old client and will simply be ignored.

Likewise, if any field is removed from `message` on the server-side Protobuf definition, old clients will still be able to consume data from the server. The client will still see this field, but the field will always contain the default value for its data type.

We still have to be careful in this situation though. If the consuming application did expect something other than the default value, it may be a breaking behavior change. Nevertheless, at the very least, adding or removing fields in a Protobuf definition of one application would not cause its interface to be incompatible with the other application that was designed to communicate with it.

Now, we will make some changes to the Protobuf definition on both the client and server applications and see whether they still work afterward.

Modifying the Protobuf definition in the server application

Let's open the `stats.proto` file in the `Protos` folder of the `GrpcServer` application and make some changes to it.

Let's pretend that we no longer care how many errors were logged by the server application. And we also realize that having an active flag is redundant because the server just wouldn't respond if it was not active. But we also want to know whether or not the server is busy, which we didn't previously have a metric for.

So, we remove the `errors_logged` and `active` fields from the `StatusResponse` message definition and we add the `busy` field to it with a new sequence number. Our `StatusResponse` message definition in the server application will now look like this:

```
message StatusResponse {
    string server_name = 1;
    string server_description = 2;
    int32 number_of_connections = 3;
    double cpu_usage = 4;
    double memory_usage = 5;
    uint32 catastrophic_failures_logged = 7;
    bool busy = 9;
}
```

Now, we will need to modify the logic inside the `StatusService` class. We will change the `return` statement in the `GetStatus` method to the following:

```
return Task.FromResult(new StatusResponse
{
    ServerName = "TestServer",
    ServerDescription = "This is a test server that is used for
       generating status metrics",
    NumberOfConnections = randomNumberGenerator.Next(),
    CpuUsage = randomNumberGenerator.NextDouble() * 100,
    MemoryUsage = randomNumberGenerator.NextDouble() * 100,
    CatastrophicFailuresLogged = (uint)randomNumberGenerator.
       Next(),
    Busy = true
});
```

Now, we will make some changes to our client too. But not the ones we have applied on the server.

Modifying the Protobuf definition in the client application

Let's pretend that the developers of the client application are unaware of the changes that have been applied on the server. But, at the same time, they have realized that one of the fields in the `StatusRequest message` definition is redundant.

Why does the client need to explicitly tell the server that it's ready when the fact that the client could connect to the server already implies that it's ready? So, we will remove the `ready` field from the `StatusRequest message` definition of the `stats.proto` file that's located in the `Protos` folder of the `GrpcClient` project. The `message` definition should now look like this:

```
message StatusRequest {
    string client_name = 1;
    string client_description = 2;
    bool authorized = 4;
}
```

To make sure that the code of the client application still compiles, we need to remove all the references to the field that no longer exists in the `message` definition. We only had one, and it was being applied during the request to the server. So, in the `Main` method of the `Program` class, modify the statement that makes the request so that it looks like this:

```
var response = await client.GetStatusAsync(new Stats.
    StatusRequest
    {
        ClientName = clientName,
        ClientDescription = clientDescription,
        Authorized = true
    });
```

Now, we will launch our applications to see how their behavior has changed.

Launching modified applications

Execute the `dotnet run` command from the `GrpcServer` project folder. Then, once the server application is up and running, execute the same command from the `GrpcClient` folder.

In the console window of the client application, enter the server application address followed by any arbitrary client name and client description. Now, you will be able to see how both of the applications behave.

180   Applying Versioning to the gRPC API

You will see in your client console window that the number of errors reported by the server is 0, while the server also appears to be inactive. This is because the `errors_logged` and `active` fields have been removed from the `StatusReponse message` definition on the server side, so they are populated with default values (which happen to be `false` for `bool` and `0` for `uint64`). Your console window will look similar to this:

```
Please enter gRPC server address:
https://localhost:5001
Please enter client name:
Test Client
Please enter client description:
This is a test client
Server name: TestServer
Server description: This is a test server that is used for generating status metrics
Number of connections: 186299282
CPU usage: 25.271901453506157
Memory usage: 65.48899019392626
Errors logged: 0
Catastrophic failures logged: 75945647
Active: False
```

Figure 5.3 – The Errors logged and Active fields on the client side being populated with default values

Our server application is unaware that the `active` field is no longer used in the `StatusRequest message` definition on the client. But it hasn't been removed from the corresponding `message` definition on the server. So it just gets populated with the default value of `false`, as can be seen in the following console output:

```
info: Microsoft.Hosting.Lifetime[0]
      Now listening on: http://localhost:5000
info: Microsoft.Hosting.Lifetime[0]
      Now listening on: https://localhost:5001
info: Microsoft.Hosting.Lifetime[0]
      Application started. Press Ctrl+C to shut down.
info: Microsoft.Hosting.Lifetime[0]
      Hosting environment: Development
info: Microsoft.Hosting.Lifetime[0]
      Content root path: C:\repos\Part2\ApiVersioning\GrpcServer
info: Microsoft.AspNetCore.Hosting.Diagnostics[1]
      Request starting HTTP/2 POST https://localhost:5001/stats.Status/GetStatus application/grpc -
info: Microsoft.AspNetCore.Routing.EndpointMiddleware[0]
      Executing endpoint 'gRPC - /stats.Status/GetStatus'
Client name is Test Client
Client description is This is a test client
Is client ready? False
Is client authorized? True
```

Figure 5.4 – The Active field of the StatusRequest message definition
being populated with the default value of false

This demonstrates that the removal and addition of fields in your Protobuf `message` definitions is the safest way to update your gRPC API. Neither of these changes will make the interface incompatible with the old applications that use it. Removed fields will be populated with default values, while additional fields will be ignored.

Of course, this doesn't make API updates 100% safe. Therefore, it's up to developers to verify whether any specific changes will result in unintended behavior. From the application's perspective, the concept of *no data* may be treated differently from `0`, an empty string, or a Boolean value of `false`. So, we need to be mindful of the fact that removing a field from the Protobuf definition of one application may completely change the meaning of the message to the application that communicates with it.

Well-known types from the **Google** library will allow you to easily distinguish between *no data* and any specific value. We will cover these types in *Chapter 8, Using Well-Known Types to Make Protobuf More Handy*. But even with these types applied, you need to make sure that any given field doesn't have a special meaning in the application that consumes the message.

As well as adding or removing fields, you can make modifications to the existing fields when updating Protobuf definitions. However, this is rarely a good idea – let's see why.

Why you must not modify existing fields in future Protobuf versions

Protobuf doesn't prevent you from changing data types on your fields. But not all data types are compatible with each other. If you change the data type of just one of your fields to a data type that isn't compatible with it, you will make your whole interface incompatible with the existing clients.

In the following list, each bullet contains the data types that can be interchanged with each other:

- `int32`, `uint32`, `int64`, `uint64`, and `bool`
- `int32`, `uint32`, `int64`, `uint64`, and `enum` values
- `sint32` and `sint64`
- `string` and `bytes`, but only if the `bytes` value uses UTF-8 encoding
- `fixed32` and `sfixed32`
- `fixed64` and `sfixed64`

However, just because you can change the data type of a field, it doesn't mean that you should. For example, what would happen if you sent a negative value as `int32`, but consumed it as a positive-only `uint32` data type on the other side? The original value cannot be held into the destination's data type. So how will it be modified?

What would happen if you sent a large `int64` value and consumed it as `int32`? The target data type won't be able to store such a large value, so it will have to truncate it, potentially breaking your logic.

The same arguments can be applied to all data type conversions. Every one of these conversions may cause a situation where data is either lost or it is altered to such an extent that it's no longer useful. This is why, despite the fact that you can convert certain data types without breaking the interface, you shouldn't do so unless absolutely necessary and you know that the risk of such action is low.

The same applies to field names. We have already established that the actual human-readable field names from `message` definitions are not used during communication. And this is what allows us to change the field names. As long as the sequence number of the field stays the same and it has the same (or a compatible) data type, the interface will still work.

The same can be applied to the names of `message` or `enum` definitions. Even though you don't apply specific numeric identifiers to the definitions of these objects, from the perspective of Protobuf, they are simply object placeholders. And as long as their structure remains the same, they will still be correctly interpreted by the consuming application.

But, once again, because the option to change field names and message names exists, it doesn't mean that you should use it. By changing the name, you may change the verbal meaning of it. And you may make it harder for yourself to update your application once the new version of the Protobuf definition has been published.

What you cannot make changes to in Protobuf are `rpc` names. Each RPC is represented as a path in an HTTP URL, so its name must match. Otherwise, if your client and server implementations of Protobuf have different names specified for the same RPC, you will get an `UNIMPLEMENTED` error code.

We will now make some changes to our application to see how it behaves if we modify some Protobuf fields at one end, but leave them unmodified at the other end.

Modifying Protobuf definitions on the client side

Open the `stats.proto` file in the `Protos` folder of the `GrpcClient` project. In this file, change the sequence number of the `authorized` field in the `StatusRequest` `message` definition from 4 to 3. Let's pretend that a new developer has joined a team and they don't fully understand what the sequence numbers are for. The developer sees that the numbers aren't sequential, so they make them sequential again.

Your `message` definition should now look like this:

```
message StatusRequest {
   string client_name = 1;
   string client_description = 2;
   bool authorized = 3;
}
```

Now, we will modify some fields in the `StatusResponse` message definition. We will change the data type of the `number_of_connections` field from `int32` to `uint32`. Then, we will set the data types of the `errors_logged` and `catastrophic_failures_logged` fields to `int32`. Your `StatusResponse` message definition should now look like this:

```
message StatusResponse {
   string server_name = 1;
   string server_description = 2;
   uint32 number_of_connections = 3;
   double cpu_usage = 4;
   double memory_usage = 5;
   int32 errors_logged = 6;
   int32 catastrophic_failures_logged = 7;
   bool active = 8;
}
```

Let's launch our applications and see what effect these changes have.

Launching the applications

After executing the `dotnet run` command in both the `GrpcServer` and `GrpcClient` project folders and typing the required information in the console window of the client app, you should expect to see that the applications are able to communicate with one another.

The client was able to read the data from the server, even where the data types of the fields were different. This can be seen in the following console output:

```
Please enter gRPC server address:
https://localhost:5001
Please enter client name:
Test Client
Please enter client description:
This client is used for testing
Server name: TestServer
Server description: This is a test server that is used for generating status metrics
Number of connections: 1188454209
CPU usage: 25.405058555959286
Memory usage: 82.5813088950614
Errors logged: 0
Catastrophic failures logged: 801045433
Active: False
```

Figure 5.5 – The successful conversion between signed and unsigned int data types

However, an interesting thing happens when we look at the console window of the server application. It seems to think that the client application had its `ready` field populated, even though this field no longer exists on the client. Moreover, the server read the value of the `authorized` field as `false`, even when the client had set it to `true`.

```
info: Microsoft.Hosting.Lifetime[0]
      Now listening on: http://localhost:5000
info: Microsoft.Hosting.Lifetime[0]
      Now listening on: https://localhost:5001
info: Microsoft.Hosting.Lifetime[0]
      Application started. Press Ctrl+C to shut down.
info: Microsoft.Hosting.Lifetime[0]
      Hosting environment: Development
info: Microsoft.Hosting.Lifetime[0]
      Content root path: C:\repos\Part3\ApiVersioning\GrpcServer
info: Microsoft.AspNetCore.Hosting.Diagnostics[1]
      Request starting HTTP/2 POST https://localhost:5001/stats.Status/GetStatus application/grpc -
info: Microsoft.AspNetCore.Routing.EndpointMiddleware[0]
      Executing endpoint 'gRPC - /stats.Status/GetStatus'
Client name is Test Client
Client description is This client is used for testing
Is client ready? True
Is client authorized? False
```

Figure 5.6 – The server reading the value of the authorized field of the
client as the value of the ready field

So, how is this even possible? Well, the answer is simple. Because field names are irrelevant to gRPC communication, we haven't really assigned a value to the `authorized` field on the client. We have merely reinstated the field with the sequence number of 3 and changed the label on it from `ready` to `authorized`. But our code on the client side didn't change at all, as all of the field names that we used were already present in the code that was generated from the proto file.

However, the server sees it differently. We have retained the original `StatusRequest` structure on the server with both the `ready` and `authorized` fields present. And `ready` happens to be the label of the field with the sequence number of 3, which was populated by the client.

This demonstrates why you should avoid modifying definitions of individual fields in Protobuf. A subtle change may cause the client and the server to get lost in translation. When we thought that we were sending the `authorized` attribute to the server, this is not what the server saw.

Now, we will make a further change to our client to eliminate any misunderstanding between it and the server.

Making further changes to the client application

In the `stats.proto` file of the `GrpcClient` project, rename the `authorized` field of the `StatusRequest` message definition to `allowed` and change its sequence number back to 4. Your `message` definition should now look like this:

```
message StatusRequest {
    string client_name = 1;
    string client_description = 2;
    bool allowed = 4;
}
```

After this, we will need to make a change to our code to make sure it still compiles. In the `Main` method of the `Program` class, replace the gRPC request statement with the following:

```
var response = await client.GetStatusAsync(new Stats.
    StatusRequest
{
    ClientName = clientName,
    ClientDescription = clientDescription,
    Allowed = true
});
```

Now, let's see whether our applications can still intercommunicate after all these changes.

Re-launching the applications

After launching both applications, the server application was still able to read the value of the `authorized` field, even though it was renamed to `allowed` on the client side:

```
info: Microsoft.Hosting.Lifetime[0]
      Now listening on: http://localhost:5000
info: Microsoft.Hosting.Lifetime[0]
      Now listening on: https://localhost:5001
info: Microsoft.Hosting.Lifetime[0]
      Application started. Press Ctrl+C to shut down.
info: Microsoft.Hosting.Lifetime[0]
      Hosting environment: Development
info: Microsoft.Hosting.Lifetime[0]
      Content root path: C:\repos\Part3\ApiVersioning\GrpcServer
info: Microsoft.AspNetCore.Hosting.Diagnostics[1]
      Request starting HTTP/2 POST https://localhost:5001/stats.Status/GetStatus application/grpc -
info: Microsoft.AspNetCore.Routing.EndpointMiddleware[0]
      Executing endpoint 'gRPC - /stats.Status/GetStatus'
Client name is Test Client
Client description is This client is used for testing
Is client ready? False
Is client authorized? True
```

Figure 5.7 – The server reading the value from the authorized field,
despite its name being different on the client

In our experiment, we have confirmed that changing the human-readable name of a Protobuf `message` field doesn't affect its functionality, even if the name doesn't match any field names of the proto file on the other side. Nevertheless, the fact that the applications can still communicate with each other actually represents a risk that we need to be mindful of, as we saw when we changed the sequence number of the original `authorized` field.

This is why it's important to know what sequence numbers in Protobuf represent. And this is why it's important not to modify fields when updating your interface unless it's absolutely necessary.

There is also another problem in Protobuf we need to be aware of. We may modify our interface definition by removing some fields, which, as we have already established, won't be a breaking change. But what if somebody who was not aware of the original fields joins our team and adds completely new fields with the old sequence numbers? If there are still some clients that used the old interface with the original fields, they will no longer be able to communicate with the server.

The chances are that the old fields will be incompatible with the new fields, which will make the whole interface incompatible and prevent any communication from happening. But even if those fields happened to have compatible data types, their meaning would be different, so it still may be a breaking behavioral change for the existing clients.

In the next section, you will learn how to mitigate this problem. In a similar way, the same technique can minimize the chances of somebody accidentally changing sequence numbers on the existing fields.

How to deprecate old, unused fields in gRPC

To prevent anyone from inserting fields into proto files with the same sequence numbers as the ones of the fields that have been removed, you can use the `reserved` keyword. To use it, you just need to place it into your `message` definition at the same level that you put your fields in.

To specify the field sequence numbers that you don't want anyone to use, you just place them after the `reserved` keyword. If you need to specify multiple sequence numbers, you just separate them by a comma. Otherwise, you can specify a sequential range by using the `to` keyword. For example, if you use `6 to 12`, all sequence numbers starting from `6` and ending with `12` will be unavailable. If you try to use them, you will receive an error when trying to generate code from the proto file.

There is also another way that you can use the `reserved` keyword. Instead of specifying field *sequence numbers*, you can specify field *names*. If you do so, you will not be able to use these field names in any of the fields.

However, as field names are purely there to provide human-readable field definitions, this approach is less useful than reserving field sequence numbers. Even though it will stop you from using specific field names, it will not stop you from accidentally inserting fields with the same sequence numbers as the ones that have already been removed.

Nevertheless, we will have a look at both approaches.

Applying the reserved keyword to the server-side Protobuf interface

In our `stats.proto` file in the `Protos` folder of the `GrpcServer` project, we will remove the `busy` field with the sequence number `9` from the `StatusResponse` `message` definition. Perhaps we have decided that this field is redundant, as we can establish how busy the server is by looking at its CPU and memory usage data.

We also found out the `server_description` field isn't really useful on the client side. So, we will remove this field too.

Now, we will add two `reserved` blocks to our `message` definition. The first one will contain the field sequence numbers 6, 8, and 9. It will look like this:

```
reserved 6,8 to 9;
```

The second `reserved` block will specify the `server_description` field by name:

```
reserved "server_description";
```

Your `message` definition should now look like this:

```
message StatusResponse {
    string server_name = 1;
    int32 number_of_connections = 3;
    double cpu_usage = 4;
    double memory_usage = 5;
    uint32 catastrophic_failures_logged = 7;
    reserved 6,8 to 9;
    reserved "server_description";
}
```

Now, if you try to add the following field to your `message` definition, the errors shown in *Figure 5.8* will be displayed if you try to compile the project:

```
string server_description = 6;
```

The errors will be displayed as follows:

⊗	☐	0	Field "server_description" uses reserved number 6.
⊗	☐	18	Field name "server_description" is reserved.

Figure 5.8 – Error messages during an attempt to use reserved fields

Let's now remove this field.

But another thing that we need to do to get our project to compile is to remove all the unwanted fields from the code. To do so, go to the `StatusService` class and replace the `return` statement of the `GetStatus` method with the following:

```
return Task.FromResult(new StatusResponse
{
    ServerName = "TestServer",
    NumberOfConnections = randomNumberGenerator.Next(),
```

```
        CpuUsage = randomNumberGenerator.NextDouble() * 100,
        MemoryUsage = randomNumberGenerator.NextDouble() * 100,
        CatastrophicFailuresLogged = (uint)randomNumberGenerator.
            Next()
});
```

We are now ready to test it with our client to see what changes in behavior it caused.

Testing the application

As usual, we will execute the `dotnet run` command in both the `GrpcServer` and `GrpcClient` projects. If we then fill in the required details in the console window of the client application, we will see that we are no longer receiving a `server_description` field from the server. The value of this field is blank.

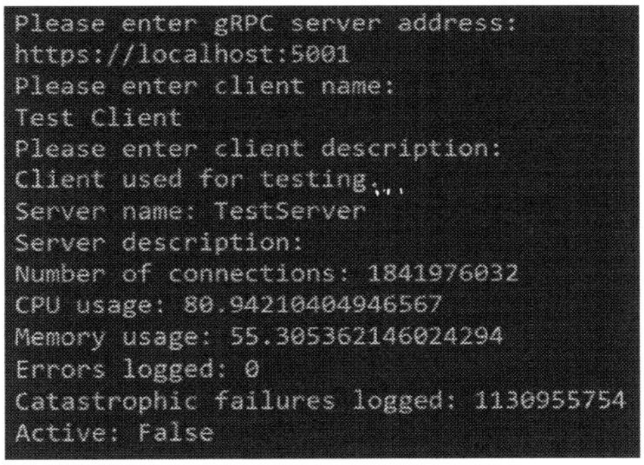

Figure 5.9 – No server_description field is returned to the client

This shows how the `reserved` keyword acts as a safety mechanism against accidental field insertions while not altering any other gRPC behavior.

So far, we have gone through the techniques you can use in gRPC to ensure that you don't introduce any breaking changes when updating your interface. But, as we have already covered, those only apply to the interface itself. You can still cause breaking behavioral changes.

Also, if you keep updating your application on a regular basis, you will probably eventually encounter a situation where you will need to introduce some breaking changes.

Even though the techniques that we have covered will minimize problems during API updates, the best way to deal with API versioning is to factor it in at the design stage. You can design your application in such a way that making updates to it will be easy. This way, you will never accidentally introduce breaking behavioral changes. And introducing breaking interface changes will become easy.

This is what we will cover in the next section.

How to factor in API versioning at the design stage

There are some standard ways of applying versioning to REST APIs. Usually, you will have some subpath in your URL that contains the version number. This way, you can host several different versions of the API simultaneously. And your clients will never communicate with the wrong version, as the version number will be written into the address that they submit requests to.

For example, you may have a URL like this:

```
https://example.com/status/v1
```

In this example, `v1` would represent the API version number. Then, if you need to update your API, you will not modify the original endpoints. Instead, you will host another version of it at the address that ends with `v2`. This way, the functionality of the existing clients will not change at all, as nothing in the backend that they are talking to would have changed. And this is why you don't have to worry about your new API being compatible with the old clients.

The same principles can be applied to gRPC. After all, gRPC is simply a middleware wrapper around the HTTP protocol. It still uses standard HTTP addresses. If you examine the console window of a server-side gRPC application, you will see that every gRPC call is just a `POST` request to a specific address. And this address will have the following pattern:

```
{base URL}/{Protobuf package name}.{Protobuf service name}/{rpc name}
```

This is precisely why, in order to make the gRPC client compatible with the server, at the very least, the following details in the Protobuf definitions should match exactly:

- gRPC package name
- Service name
- RPC name

Therefore, if we are to apply API versioning at the design stage, it would be a good practice to specify the version identifier in the `package` statement of a proto file. Likewise, by convention, your proto file name should be the same as your package name. So, if you have changed your package name from `stats` to `stats.v1`, a good practice would be to also change the name of the file from `stats.proto` to `stats.v1.proto`.

If you don't specify additional namespace modifiers in your proto files, such as `csharp_namespace`, different Protobuf versions will be placed into different namespaces of the generated code. Therefore, you can maintain multiple versions of a Protobuf definition and run them in parallel inside the same application.

Let's now see what this might look like in practice.

Adding multiple Protobuf versions to the server application

As we have modified our `stats.proto` file since the beginning of this chapter, we will pretend that we are now on version two of it. Therefore, inside the `Protos` folder of the `GrpcServer` project, we will rename the file `stats.v2.proto`. And we will also change the `package` definition inside this file to the following:

```
package stats.v2;
```

Now, we will make a copy of this file and rename it `stats.v1.proto`. Its `package` name will also be changed to `stats.v1`.

In the `stats.v1.proto` file, we will restore the `StatusResponse` message definition to its original state. But we will mark all fields that don't exist in the second version as `deprecated`. So, our `message` definition will now look like this:

```
message StatusResponse {
    string server_name = 1;
    string server_description = 2 [deprecated = true];
    int32 number_of_connections = 3;
    double cpu_usage = 4;
    double memory_usage = 5;
    uint64 errors_logged = 6 [deprecated = true];
    uint32 catastrophic_failures_logged = 7;
    bool active = 8 [deprecated = true];
}
```

We will now need to ensure that both of our proto files are registered in the project. To do so, we need to open the `GrpcServer.csproj` file and add the following section to it:

```
<ItemGroup>
  <Protobuf Include="Protos\stats.v1.proto"
    GrpcServices="Server" />
  <Protobuf Include="Protos\stats.v2.proto"
    GrpcServices="Server" />
</ItemGroup>
```

There should be no other `Protobuf` elements in this file and no references to any other proto files.

Now, we will need to make some changes to our code to allow it to use both API versions.

Allowing the server application to use multiple Protobuf versions

After applying these changes, our `StatusService` class – the representation of the Protobuf service – will no longer compile, as the classes it inherits from are no longer present in its original namespace. So, we will need to update the namespace references.

But first, we will rename the `StatusService.cs` file to `StatusServiceV2.cs`. And we will rename the class inside it from `StatusService` to `StatusServiceV2`.

Then, we will need to update all the namespace references. To do so, we will replace the existing `using` statements inside the file with the following:

```
using System;
using System.Threading.Tasks;
using Grpc.Core;
using Stats.V2;
```

Then, we will change the line with the class definition to the following:

```
public class StatusServiceV2 : Stats.V2.Status.StatusBase
```

Now, we have a service implementation of version two of our Protobuf. Let's implement version one too. To do so, we will copy the `StatusServiceV2.cs` class and rename the newly created file to `StatusServiceV1.cs`.

Inside this file, we will replace the class name with `StatusServiceV1`. Then, we will also replace all `V2` namespace references with `V1`.

Finally, because `stats.v1.proto` has more fields in the `StatusResponse` message definition than `stats.v2.proto`, we will apply these additional fields to the `return` object. The `return` statement inside the `GetStatus` method of the `StatusServiceV1` class will be as follows:

```
return Task.FromResult(new StatusResponse
{
    ServerName = "TestServer",
    ServerDescription = "This is a test server that is used for
      generating status metrics",
    NumberOfConnections = randomNumberGenerator.Next(),
    CpuUsage = randomNumberGenerator.NextDouble() * 100,
    MemoryUsage = randomNumberGenerator.NextDouble() * 100,
    ErrorsLogged = (ulong)randomNumberGenerator.Next(),
    CatastrophicFailuresLogged = (uint)randomNumberGenerator.
      Next(),
    Active = true
});
```

Now, we need to register both services as gRPC endpoints. To do so, we will need to open the `Startup` class (or `Program.cs` file if you are using .NET 6 template) and locate the line that contains this statement:

```
endpoints.MapGrpcService<StatusService>();
```

We will need to replace it with the following:

```
endpoints.MapGrpcService<StatusServiceV1>();
endpoints.MapGrpcService<StatusServiceV2>();
```

Now, we have two implementations of the `Status` gRPC service. But because we have changed our namespace, neither of them will be compatible with the existing client.

Assuming we are running our application on localhost, our old service implementation was accessible via the `https://localhost:5001/stats.Status/` URL.

But now, we have two separate URLs for the separate service implementations:

- `https://localhost:5001/stats.v1.Status/`
- `https://localhost:5001/stats.v2.Status/`

So, we need to apply some changes to our client to make it compatible with the server once again.

Making the gRPC client implementation version-specific

We will pretend that we have an old version of the client that talks to version one of the server API. To do so, we will need to rename the `stats.proto` file in the `Protos` folder of the `GrpcCleint` project to `stats.v1.proto`. And then we will change the `package` name inside this file to `stats.v1`.

We then need to verify that the following section is present inside the `GrpcClient.csproj` file:

```
<ItemGroup>
  <Protobuf Include="Protos\stats.v1.proto"
  GrpcServices="Client" />
</ItemGroup>
```

There should be no other `Protobuf` elements present in the file and no references to any other proto files. Then, we need to update the namespaces inside the code. There are only two places in the `Main` method of the `Program` class where we need to do this.

The line where we are instantiating a `client` variable needs to be replaced with the following:

```
var client = new
  Stats.V1.Status.StatusClient(GrpcChannel.
    ForAddress(serverUrl));
```

Then, the statement where we are making a gRPC request needs to be replaced with the following:

```
var response = await client.GetStatusAsync(new
  Stats.V1.StatusRequest
{
    ClientName = clientName,
    ClientDescription = clientDescription,
    Allowed = true
});
```

Now, we are ready to test our application to see whether it can still reach the server.

Making a gRPC call to a versioned endpoint

As we have done multiple times, we will execute the `dotnet run` command inside the `GrpcServer` project folder and, once the application is up and running, we'll execute the same command in the `GrpcClient` project folder.

After filling in all the details in the console window of the client application, we can see that all the fields in the server response have been populated, which confirms that we have been able to reach version one of the endpoint. The console will display an output similar to the following:

```
Please enter gRPC server address:
https://localhost:5001
Please enter client name:
Tester Client
Please enter client description:
Client for testing
Server name: TestServer
Server description: This is a test server that is used for generating status metrics
Number of connections: 833049075
CPU usage: 27.64067464863913
Memory usage: 37.44751710325829
Errors logged: 1460164990
Catastrophic failures logged: 1683121737
Active: True
```

Figure 5.10 – The fields from the stats.v1 Protobuf definitions are present in the server response

Additionally, if we look at the server-side console, we can confirm that it was the URL associated with the `v1` endpoint that the request was submitted to:

```
info: Microsoft.AspNetCore.Hosting.Diagnostics[1]
      Request starting HTTP/2 POST https://localhost:5001/stats.v1.Status/GetStatus application/grpc -
info: Microsoft.AspNetCore.Routing.EndpointMiddleware[0]
      Executing endpoint 'gRPC - /stats.v1.Status/GetStatus'
Client name is Tester Client
Client description is Client for testing
Is client ready? False
Is client authorized? True
info: Microsoft.AspNetCore.Routing.EndpointMiddleware[1]
      Executed endpoint 'gRPC - /stats.v1.Status/GetStatus'
info: Microsoft.AspNetCore.Hosting.Diagnostics[2]
      Request finished HTTP/2 POST https://localhost:5001/stats.v1.Status/GetStatus application/grpc -
- 200 - application/grpc 237.1542ms
```

Figure 5.11 – The server logs indicating that the v1 gRPC endpoint has been triggered

So, we have confirmed that behavioral changes associated with version two of the Protobuf definition, such as the removal of certain fields, will not affect any clients that have been pre-configured to communicate with version one. In fact, it would be impossible for the client to communicate with other versions of the endpoint, even by accident. From the perspective of gRPC middleware, those versions are represented by different gRPC packages, which this client wasn't configured to use.

This example demonstrates that, by far, the easiest way to apply API versioning to your gRPC applications is to implement an API versioning strategy at the design stage. This way, you will have much more freedom when updating your API. If you do it correctly, then you will not be running the risk of breaking any compatibility with the existing clients. Old clients and new clients will be able to work with your server application in parallel.

Summary

In this chapter, you have learned why API versioning in gRPC is important when using public endpoints or clients that have been developed by external teams. You now know that the sequence numbers of Protobuf fields are used as field identifiers during the transit of the message, while human-readable field names are simply labels. However, despite the fact that changing the field name to any arbitrary value will not break interface compatibility, modifying the existing fields in any way is still not a good practice.

You have learned that the safest way to change a Protobuf definition without causing compatibility issues is to either remove some fields or add new fields with new sequence numbers. Any fields that haven't been populated will be populated with default values by gRPC middleware. Any fields that don't exist in a Protobuf definition will be ignored if they are present in the message.

You are now aware that to prevent anyone from accidentally adding new fields with the same sequence numbers as the fields that have been removed, a good practice is to use the `reserved` keyword to specify all the sequence numbers that aren't to be used.

But, as you have learned, the easiest way to apply API versioning in gRPC is to factor in an API versioning strategy at the design stage. This way, you can create multiple distinct versions of gRPC services and each client will only be talking to a specific version.

In the next chapter, you will learn the best practices for scaling your gRPC application. *Scaling* is important when your distributed application is expected to handle a large amount of data or deal with large numbers of simultaneous requests. The gRPC framework has a number of ways of achieving this, and we will cover them all.

Questions

1. What would happen if you changed the name of one of your fields in the Protobuf `message` definition on your client but not on the server?

   A. It will make the interface incompatible with the server.

   B. It will throw an error unless you also change the sequence number.

   C. It will not affect the functionality.

   D. The server will associate the value with the wrong field.

2. Which of these data types cannot be interchanged?

   A. `Bytes` and `string`

   B. `sfixed32` and `int32`

   C. `uint64` and `int32`

   D. `uint64` and `bool`

3. What would happen if you removed a field from a Protobuf response `message` definition on the server, but not on the client?

   A. It will be populated with the default value on the client.

   B. It will make the client incompatible with the server.

   C. The client will have mismatching field values.

   D. No error will be thrown, but the client will not be able to interpret the data.

4. What's the best way to prevent new fields from being accidentally reinstated with the sequence numbers of the old fields that have been removed?

   A. Only add sequence numbers that are bigger than the last one.

   B. Maintain up-to-date documentation.

   C. Use the `reserved` keyword, followed by a list of the removed field names.

   D. Use the `reserved` keyword, followed by the sequence numbers of the removed fields.

5. What's the best way of minimizing the risk of breaking changes during the gRPC API update?

   A. Never modifying the data types of the fields
   B. Never modifying the names of the fields
   C. Using separate Protobuf definitions for separate API versions
   D. Using the `reserved` keyword

Further reading

- *Versioning gRPC services*:

  https://docs.microsoft.com/en-us/aspnet/core/grpc/versioning

- *Protobuf Language Guide, Updating a Message Type*:

  https://developers.google.com/protocol-buffers/docs/proto3#updating

- *Protobuf Language Guide, Reserved Fields*:

  https://developers.google.com/protocol-buffers/docs/proto3#reserved

6
Scaling a gRPC Application

If you expect your web application to support a high number of connections, running a single instance of it will not be enough. You will have to scale it.

There are two types of scaling you can do – scaling up and scaling out. Scaling up is when you add more hardware to the machine running the server-side components of your application. This is a pure hardware solution and it has its limits. Therefore, we will not cover it in this chapter.

Scaling out, on the other hand, is when you run multiple instances of the same application, so any particular instance of it will not be overwhelmed by an excessive number of connections. The connections will be distributed evenly between the running instances.

The ability to easily scale out granular components of a distributed application is one of the main purposes of microservices architecture. This is what we will cover in this chapter.

To evenly distribute incoming connections between multiple instances of an application, you would need a load balancer. In this chapter, we will focus on how to apply different types of load balancing in the context of gRPC.

We will cover the following topics:

- Introduction to load balancing
- Client-side load balancing with gRPC
- Proxy load balancing with gRPC

By the end of this chapter, you will have learned how to evenly distribute incoming connections between multiple instances of a gRPC service so that you can prevent excessive latency and bottlenecks.

Technical requirements

To follow the instructions in this chapter, you will need the following:

- A computer with either a Windows, Macintosh, or Linux operating system
- A supported IDE or code editor (Visual Studio, Visual Studio Code, or JetBrains Rider)
- A .NET 5 SDK
- A self-signed development HTTPS certificate enabled on the machine

The instructions on how to set all of these up were provided in *Chapter 1, Creating a Basic gRPC Application on ASP.NET Core*. All the code samples used in this chapter can be found at `https://github.com/PacktPublishing/Microservices-Communication-in-.NET-Using-gRPC/tree/main/Chapter-06`.

Please visit the following link to check the CiA videos: `https://bit.ly/3IKF76x`

Introduction to load balancing

When you have multiple instances of the same service running in the backend of your server, you will need to implement some kind of a gateway that will decide which particular instance any particular client would connect to. This gateway software would need to have a logic that will decide which specific instance any specific client connection will need to go to. This is what load balancing is.

A load balancer is a piece of software that is positioned between the client and the server-side application instances. It can be a component of the client application itself, or it can be a proxy that the client communicates directly with.

But regardless of what type of load balancer you use, its operation principles will be the same. When it receives the instruction from the client to send a request to the server, it will decide which specific server-side endpoints the request should go to.

We will now build a basic distributed application to demonstrate the fundamental principles of load balancing.

Adding shared gRPC dependencies

We will first create a solution that will contain all our projects:

1. To do so, create a folder called `GrpcLoadBalancing`. Then, run the following command inside this folder:

   ```
   dotnet new sln
   ```

2. Now, we create a class library that will contain all our gRPC dependencies. To do so, execute the following command inside the solution folder:

   ```
   dotnet new classlib -o GrpcDependencies
   ```

3. We now add this project to our solution by executing the following command:

   ```
   dotnet sln add GrpcDependencies/GrpcDependencies.csproj
   ```

4. Next, we navigate to the `GrpcDependencies` project folder. From there, we execute the following commands to add necessary NuGet packages to the project:

   ```
   dotnet add GrpcDependencies.csproj package Grpc.Net.Client
   dotnet add GrpcDependencies.csproj package Google.Protobuf
   dotnet add GrpcDependencies.csproj package Grpc.Tools
   dotnet add GrpcDependencies.csproj package Grpc.AspNetCore
   ```

5. Next, we create the `Protos` folder inside the `GrpcDependencies` project folder and add the `data_processor.proto` file to it. The content of the file is as follows:

   ```
   syntax = "proto3";

   package data_processor;

   service Ingestor {
       rpc ProcessData (DataRequest) returns
         (DataResponse);
   ```

```
    }

    message DataRequest {
        int32 id = 1;
        string name = 2;
        string description = 3;
    }

    message DataResponse {
        bool success = 1;
    }
```

6. Finally, we register this file inside the `GrpcDependencies.csproj` file by adding the following markup to it:

```
<ItemGroup>
    <Protobuf Include="Protos\data_processor.proto" />
</ItemGroup>
```

Now, we create another class library that will contain all the server-side logic that will be shared between gRPC service instances.

Creating a shared library for server-side application instances

We now navigate back to the `GrpcLoadBalancing` solution folder. From there, we execute the following command to create a new class library project:

```
dotnet new classlib -o GrpcServerCommon
```

Next, we add this new project to the solution by executing the following command:

```
dotnet sln add GrpcServerCommon/GrpcServerCommon.csproj
```

Next, we will navigate to `GrpcServerCommon` project folder. From there, we will open the `GrpcServerCommon.csproj` file and add the following markup snippet to it:

```
<ItemGroup>
    <ProjectReference Include="..
```

```
        \GrpcDependencies\GrpcDependencies.csproj" />
</ItemGroup>
```

This project now references the class library that contains all shared gRPC dependencies. So, we are ready to start adding custom logic to our library. To do so, create an `IngestorService.cs` file in the project folder. The content of the file will be as follows:

```
using System;
using System.Threading.Tasks;
using DataProcessor;
using Grpc.Core;
namespace GrpcServerCommon
{
    public class IngestorService : Ingestor.IngestorBase
    {
        public override Task<DataResponse>
          ProcessData(DataRequest request,
            ServerCallContext context)
        {
            Console.WriteLine($"Object id: {request.Id}");
            Console.WriteLine($"Object name:
              {request.Name}");
            Console.WriteLine($"Object description:
              {request.Description}");
            return Task.FromResult(new DataResponse
            {
                Success = true
            });
        }
    }
}
```

Essentially, we receive a request object from the client, print out the data from the request object, and return a response object back with the value of the `Success` field set to `true`.

Now, we are ready to create multiple instances of the server-side gRPC application.

Creating multiple instances of the server-side application

In a real-life scenario, you would create a single application and then launch multiple instances of it to scale it. But in our case, we will be creating two identical applications to mimic this process. This way, it will be much simpler to demonstrate the principle of load balancing in action. You will just be able to launch both of these applications from your solution at the same time, and you won't have to do any additional configuration or complex orchestration that you would have to do in a real-life scenario.

This is precisely why we moved the core logic into a class library. We want our web application projects to be as lightweight as possible. We will start by creating the first application:

1. To do so, navigate to the `GrpcLoadBalancing` solution folder and execute the following command:

    ```
    dotnet new web -o GrpcServer1
    ```

2. Next, add this project to the solution by executing the following command:

    ```
    dotnet sln add  GrpcServer1/GrpcServer1.csproj
    ```

3. After this, navigate to the `GrpcServer1` project folder and modify the `GrpcServer1.csproj` file by registering a reference to the `GrpcServerCommon` project in it. This can be achieved by adding the following markup snippet:

    ```
    <ItemGroup>
        <ProjectReference Include="..\GrpcServerCommon
    \GrpcServerCommon.csproj" />
    </ItemGroup>
    ```

4. Now, your server application will be able to use all the server-side gRPC logic. We just need to register the endpoint in its `Startup` class (or `Program.cs` file if you have .NET 6 project template). To do so, add the following `using` statement on top of the `Startup.cs` or `Program.cs` file as per your .NET version:

    ```
    using GrpcServerCommon;
    ```

5. Then, add the following line to the `ConfigureServices` method:

    ```
    Services.AddGrpc();
    ```

6. After this, add the following line inside the call of the `app.UseEndpoints`:

   ```
   endpoints.MapGrpcService<IngestorService>();
   ```

   > **Important Note**
   > If you are running your server-side application on a Macintosh, you will need to apply some modifications to it. The instruction on how to do so can be found in the *Running gRPC Service on Mac* section in *Chapter 1, Creating a Basic gRPC Application on ASP.NET Core*.

Your first instance of the server-side application is now ready to start accepting requests from the connected clients. We now need to create a second instance.

To do so, create another project inside the `GrpcLoadBalancing` solution folder via the following command:

```
dotnet new web -o GrpcServer2
```

After this, finalize it by following the same process you did to prepare the `GrpcServer1` project. Repeat the steps from *2* to *5*, but this time, use `GrpcServer2` as the project name. Don't forget to make an additional modification to the project if you intend to run it on Macintosh.

Now, you have two identical web application projects in your solution that can run as two instances of the same gRPC service application. They will be absolutely identical in their functionality. The only difference would be their access URLs, which would have been auto-generated by the `dotnet new` command. Because the project-creation process allocates randomized port numbers to ASP.NET Core projects, it is unlikely that there will be any port clash between these projects and any of your existing applications running on the machine. But if the clash does occur, you can change those endpoints by modifying the URLs listed under the `applicationUrl` key of the `launchSettings.json` file that can be found in the `Properties` folder inside the project folder.

Now, we are ready to create the client application.

Creating a client application

Our client application will be a web API web application. It will receive REST API HTTP requests and those will trigger gRPC requests to one of our gRPC service application instances.

First, we create a new project by running the following command from the `GrpcLoadBalancing` solution folder:

```
dotnet new webapi -o ApiGateway
```

We then add the project to the solution by executing the following command:

```
dotnet sln add ApiGateway/ApiGateway.csproj
```

Next, we navigate to the `ApiGateway` project folder and register the shared class library as a dependency by adding the following snippet inside the `ApiGateway.csproj` file:

```xml
<ItemGroup>
  <ProjectReference Include="..\GrpcDependencies
    \GrpcDependencies.csproj" />
</ItemGroup>
```

Next, we install the Swagger library to the project by running the following command:

```
dotnet add ApiGateway.csproj package NSwag.AspNetCore
```

Now, we are ready to start adding logic to our application.

Adding backend components

The first class we add will be the representation of the REST API response that the application will return to the HTTP clients. We will create the `ApiResponse.cs` file inside the `ApiGateway` project folder. The content of this file will be as follows:

```csharp
namespace ApiGateway
{
    public class ApiResponse
    {
        public int DataItemsProcessed { get; set; }
        public double RequestProcessingTime { get; set; }
    }
}
```

Then, we add a wrapper for our gRPC client objects. To do so, we add the GrpcClientWrapper.cs file to the ApiGateway project folder. The file will have the following using statements:

```csharp
using System;
using System.Collections.Generic;
using System.Threading.Tasks;
using DataProcessor;
using Grpc.Net.Client;
```

Then, we add the namespace and the interface definition to this file:

```csharp
namespace ApiGateway
{
    public interface IGrpcClientWrapper
    {
        Task<int> SendDataViaStandardClient(int
            requestCount);
        Task<int> SendDataViaLoadBalancer(int
            requestCount);
    }
}
```

Below the interface definition, we add a class definition that will be implementing this interface, along with its constructor and private methods:

```csharp
internal class GrpcClientWrapper : IGrpcClientWrapper,
IDisposable
{
    private int currentChannelIndex = 0;
    private readonly GrpcChannel standardChannel;
    private readonly List<GrpcChannel> roundRobinChannels;

    public GrpcClientWrapper(List<string> addresses)
    {
        roundRobinChannels = new List<GrpcChannel>();
        standardChannel =
            GrpcChannel.ForAddress(addresses[0]);
```

```
            foreach (var address in addresses)
            {
                roundRobinChannels.Add(GrpcChannel.ForAddress(
                    address));
            }
        }
    }
```

Essentially, we are creating three gRPC channels. One will be reserved for a client that doesn't use load balancing, while the two other channels that are added to the list are there to demonstrate the basic principles of load balancing.

We then add a method that will use a single client without any load balancing applied:

```
public async Task<int> SendDataViaStandardClient(int requestCount)
{
    var count = 0;

    for (var i = 0; i < requestCount; i++)
    {
        var client = new
            Ingestor.IngestorClient(standardChannel);
        await client.ProcessDataAsync
            (GenerateDataRequest(i));
        count++;
    }

    return count;
}
```

This method will accept an arbitrary number as a parameter and then make as many gRPC calls as the number specifies. Then, we add another method that demonstrates the principles of load balancing:

```
public async Task<int> SendDataViaLoadBalancer(int requestCount)
{
    var count = 0;
```

```
    for (var i = 0; i < requestCount; i++)
    {
        var client = new Ingestor.IngestorClient
            (roundRobinChannels[GetCurrentChannelIndex()]);
        await
            client.ProcessDataAsync(GenerateDataRequest(i));
        count++;
    }

    return count;
}
```

This method is similar, but this time, the calls get alternated between two different endpoints. This is done in a round-robin fashion, which means that endpoints are always called in the same sequence.

This is how the most basic load balancing logic works. Instead of sending all the requests to the same server application instance, the calls are evenly spread between multiple instances. So each instance will receive only half as many calls. This will help to prevent the instance from reaching its maximum capacity.

We then add the private method to perform the actual sequence selection:

```
private int GetCurrentChannelIndex()
{
    if (currentChannelIndex == roundRobinChannels.Count - 
      1)
        currentChannelIndex = 0;
    else
        currentChannelIndex++;

    return currentChannelIndex;
}
```

But we also need to add the method that will generate the response object:

```
private DataRequest GenerateDataRequest(int index)
{
    return new DataRequest
```

```
        {
            Id = index,
            Name = $"Object {index}",
            Description = $"This is an object with the index of
                {index}."
        };
}
```

Finally, we need to add a method to dispose of the gRPC channels to prevent the locking up of available resources:

```
public void Dispose()
{
    standardChannel.Dispose();

    foreach (var channel in roundRobinChannels)
    {
        channel.Dispose();
    }
}
```

You may have noticed that this class violates the single responsibility principle. There is no relationship between load-balanced and non-load-balanced clients. That means that there is low cohesion between the methods that use them, which would make them good candidates to be moved into separate classes.

However, this is intentional. Both methods have been placed into the same class because this way of setting up the solution requires far less code. But in a real-life scenario, you would need to follow the accepted standards and place these two methods into separate classes.

Adding the controller

We now create a controller that will generate our REST API endpoints. To do so, add the `DataController.cs` file to the `Controllers` folder of the `ApiGateway` project folder. The class definition, along with all its namespace imports, will look as follows:

```
using System.Diagnostics;
using System.Threading.Tasks;
using Microsoft.AspNetCore.Mvc;
```

```csharp
namespace ApiGateway.Controllers
{
    [ApiController]
    [Route("[controller]")]
    public class DataController : ControllerBase
    {
        private readonly IGrpcClientWrapper clientWrapper;

        public DataController(IGrpcClientWrapper
            clientWrapper)
        {
            this.clientWrapper = clientWrapper;
        }
    }
}
```

We then add an endpoint method for triggering a gRPC client that doesn't use any load balancing:

```csharp
[HttpPost("standard-client/{count}")]
public async Task<ApiResponse>
PostDataViaStandardClient(int count)
{
    var stopWatch = Stopwatch.StartNew();
    var processedCount = await
        clientWrapper.SendDataViaStandardClient(count);

    return new ApiResponse
    {
        DataItemsProcessed = processedCount,
        RequestProcessingTime =
            stopWatch.ElapsedMilliseconds
    };
}
```

Then, we add an endpoint method that triggers a load-balanced client:

```
[HttpPost("load-balancer/{count}")]
public async Task<ApiResponse> PostDataViaLoadBalancer(int count)
{
    var stopWatch = Stopwatch.StartNew();
    var processedCount = await
      clientWrapper.SendDataViaLoadBalancer(count);

    return new ApiResponse
    {
        DataItemsProcessed = processedCount,
        RequestProcessingTime =
          stopWatch.ElapsedMilliseconds
    };
}
```

After this, we need to register all relevant dependencies in the `Startup` class (or `Program.cs` file) of the `ApiGateway` project.

Registering required dependencies

All of our custom gRPC components have now been added. We have also added all the relevant REST API endpoints. Now, we need to register our custom components inside the dependency injection system to make them accessible to any classes that need to use them. Also, we need to apply Swagger dependencies to make our REST API accessible via a browser:

1. First, we need to make sure that the `Startup` class of the `ApiGateway` (or `Program.cs` file if you are on .NET 6) project has all of the following `using` statements:

    ```
    using System.Collections.Generic;
    using Microsoft.AspNetCore.Builder;
    using Microsoft.AspNetCore.Hosting;
    using Microsoft.Extensions.Configuration;
    using Microsoft.Extensions.DependencyInjection;
    using Microsoft.Extensions.Hosting;
    ```

2. Then, we register the gRPC client dependency by adding the following code to the `ConfigureServices` method:

   ```
   var addresses = Configuration.
     GetSection("ServerAddresses").Get<List
     <string>>();
   services.AddSingleton<IGrpcClientWrapper>(new
     GrpcClientWrapper(addresses));
   ```

3. Then, we add Swagger dependencies. To do so, we place this line anywhere inside the `ConfigureServices` method. If you are using .NET 6 project template, this code will need to be inserted into the main body of `Program.cs` file before the `Build` event, while `services` would need to be replaced with `builder.Services`:

   ```
   services.AddOpenApiDocument();
   ```

4. Then, we add these lines anywhere in the `Configure` method before the call to `app.UseRouting()`:

   ```
   app.UseOpenApi();
   app.UseSwaggerUi3();
   ```

5. If there is an existing call to `app.UseSwagger()` inside the `Configure` method that has been added by the template, remove it. This came from another Swagger library, which will be in conflict with yours.

6. Finally, we will need to add the URLs of our server application instances to the `appsetting.json` file of the `ApiGateway` project. This is done by adding the following section to it:

   ```
   "ServerAddresses": [
       "https://localhost:6992",
       "https://localhost:46785"
   ]
   ```

The URLs presented here can be found under the `applicationUrl` key in the `launchSettings.json` files from the `GrpcServer1` and `GrpcServer2` projects. Normally, you would use an HTTPS URL. However, if you are running your gRPC server applications on a Macintosh, you would not be able to use TLS with it. So, in this case, use an HTTP URL.

Now, we are ready to run our applications to see how load balancing works.

Running a load-balanced application

To launch all instances of the application, you will first need to navigate to the `GrpcServer1` project folder and execute the `dotnet run` command. Then, do the same from the `GrpcServer2` project folder. Finally, once both applications are up and their console output indicates that they are ready to receive calls, execute the same command from the `ApiGateway` folder.

If you navigate to the HTTPS address specified under the `applicationUrl` key of `launchSettings.json` file of the `ApiGateway` project and then add the `/swagger` path to this URL, you will be presented with the following page, which displays both of the endpoints:

Figure 6.1 – Swagger page of the ApiGateway application

If you then execute the `standard-client` endpoint with an arbitrary value of the `count` parameter, you will see that all of the requests will go to only one of the available gRPC server application instances. You will expect only one console window to be filled with sequential data from the client, while the console window of the other instance would remain empty, as shown here:

Introduction to load balancing 215

Figure 6.2 – Only one gRPC service instance receives requests

However, if you submit a request to a load-balancer endpoint, you will see that both instances receive the requests. But, as shown here, the requests aren't duplicated. Instead, different requests go to different instances of the server-side application:

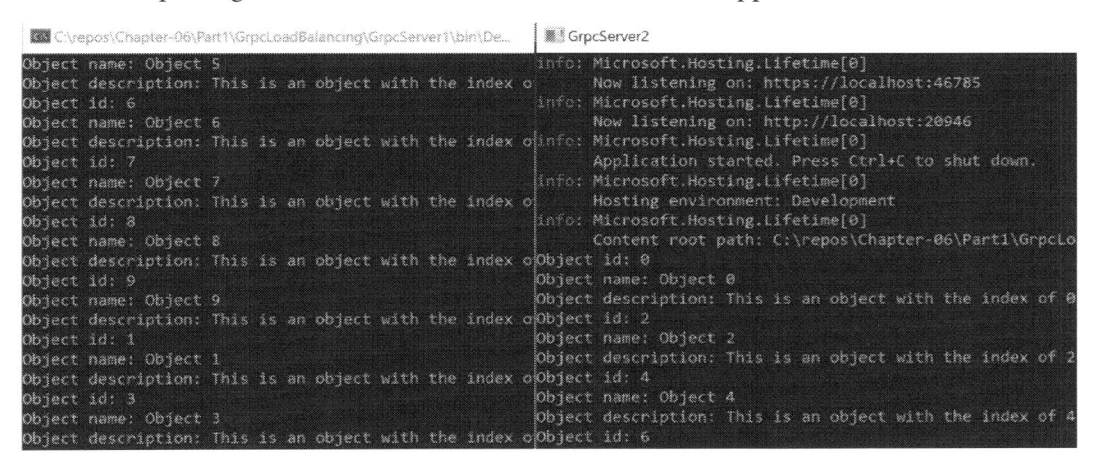

Figure 6.3 – The requests are evenly distributed between both instances of the gRPC service application

If both of these gRPC service application instances were connected to the same backend system, as they would be in real life, then it wouldn't matter whether it's not the same application instance that receives all the data. All the data will still reach its intended destination.

But because requests get evenly distributed between multiple instances, there isn't any single application instance that can become a bottleneck. Adding only one instance increases the number of simultaneous requests the system can handle without slowing down by an order of magnitude. Adding any subsequent instances increases this capacity even further. This is why load balancing is so important when the application is intended to interact with many simultaneous connections.

But this was only a very basic representation of load-balancing logic. Next, we will have a look at some in-built mechanisms for performing client load balancing that are available in the gRPC libraries for .NET.

Client-side load balancing with gRPC

Client-side load balancing is similar in principle to the example that we previously looked at. This is where the client decides which server endpoints to connect to. Then, client-side gRPC middleware connects to those endpoints directly.

gRPC .NET libraries have inbuilt components that enable client-side load balancing. But, at the time of writing, those are only available in preview. Therefore, we need to update one of our NuGet packages to a prerelease version.

The caveat is that the specific code implementations may change once the feature is fully released. But even if this happens, the principles of applying it will remain the same.

Updating the NuGet package

All the client-side load balancing components are available in the `Grpc.Net.Client` NuGet package, but they are only available in the package versions that have a pre-release tag. However, since by default the `dotnet` CLI command will apply the latest full-release version, we need to rerun this command while explicitly defining the version we want.

The earliest package version where client-side load balancing was made available is `2.39.0-pre1`. However, any later version with a `pre` tag will have this feature too.

At the time of writing, `2.40.0-pre1` was the latest version. However, this is just an example. You need to make sure that the pre-release version that you choose is higher than the version of your existing `Grpc.Net.Client` package. Otherwise, you will get a package downgrade error and your code won't compile. To apply this, you need to navigate to the `GrpcDependencies` project folder and execute the following command:

```
dotnet add package Grpc.Net.Client -v 2.40.0-pre1
```

If the command has executed successfully, you should see the following entry inside the `GrpcDependencies.csproj` file:

```xml
<PackageReference Include="Grpc.Net.Client"
 Version="2.40.0-pre1" />
```

Now, we are ready to start registering the relevant components in the gRPC client application.

Enabling client-side load balancing components

Some of the load-balancing components we are about to implement require an instance of `IServiceProvider` – the same object that is used for the inbuilt dependency injection mechanism in ASP.NET Core. This implementation (and all the dependencies it contains) is automatically passed to any object that the dependency injection system knows. For this to work, the class that the object is constructed from needs to have an instance of `IServiceProvider` as one of its interface parameters. Also, that class needs to be registered without an explicit call to its constructor.

To make our `GrpcClientWrapper` class inside the `ApiGateway` project compatible with this mechanism, we need to change its constructor. So, we replace the existing one with the following:

```csharp
public GrpcClientWrapper(IConfiguration configuration,
    IServiceProvider serviceProvider)
{
    this.serviceProvider = serviceProvider;
    roundRobinChannels = new List<GrpcChannel>();

    var addresses =
        configuration.GetSection("ServerAddresses")
            .Get<List<string>>();
    standardChannel = GrpcChannel.ForAddress(addresses[0]);

    foreach (var address in addresses)
    {
        roundRobinChannels.Add
            (GrpcChannel.ForAddress(address));
    }
}
```

We need to add the following `private` field to the class:

```
private readonly IServiceProvider serviceProvider;
```

We also need to add the following `using` statements to the top of the file, as we will need this later:

```
using Grpc.Core;
using Grpc.Net.Client.Configuration;
using Microsoft.Extensions.Configuration;
```

The rest of the structure remains the same. But because we no longer have a generic collection of primitive `string` data types as a constructor parameter, we no longer have to explicitly call the constructor when registering the class instance. All required parameters will be resolved automatically.

Now, we need to change the structure of the `ConfigureServices` method in the `Startup` class of the `ApiGateway` project. The easiest way would be to replace its content with the following:

```
services.AddControllers();
services.AddOpenApiDocument();
services.AddSingleton(Configuration);
services.AddSingleton<IGrpcClientWrapper,
GrpcClientWrapper>();
```

If you are using .NET 6 project template, you will need to insert these lines in `Program.cs` file in the place of all the lines that start with `builder.Services` and modify the code accordingly. We no longer need to resolve values from the application settings, as we are now doing it inside the constructor of the `GrpcClientWrapper` class. But we will need to add the instance of an `IConfiguration` object to our dependency injection system, which we are doing by passing the `Configuration` variable to it via the `AddSingleton` method.

Now, we are ready to add different types of load balancers to our application.

Enabling a DNS resolver for the load balancer

Selection of a specific resolver for the client-side load balancer is done when the `GrpcChannel` object is instantiated. The resolver type is selected by applying a URL schema. But instead of the protocol (HTTP, HTTPS, TCP, WS, and so on), you provide the name of the resolver type. And if this is a type the system knows about, you will have a specific type of object that will resolve all relevant endpoints for load balancing.

The first resolver type we will have a look at is the DNS resolver, which can be selected by specifying the following URI while creating a gRPC channel:

```
dns://{DNS host name}
```

The DNS hostname will represent a key in the DNS table accessible by your machine. All endpoints that match this key will be returned, and this will be your list of addresses of the available gRPC service instances.

Configuring DNS on your machine is very OS-specific and is beyond the scope of this book. Also, if you do it incorrectly, you may end up not being able to access anything on the web. But links to some instructions will be provided in the *Further reading* section of this chapter if you want to try it.

However, as it's one of the inbuilt resolvers available with the standard gRPC client NuGet package, we will still cover it here. And to demonstrate its implementation, we will add the following code to the `GrpcClientWrapper` class:

```
public async Task<int> SendDataViaDnsLoadBalancer(int
requestCount)
{
    using var channel =
      GrpcChannel.ForAddress("dns://myhost", new
        GrpcChannelOptions
    {
        Credentials = ChannelCredentials.SecureSsl,
        ServiceProvider = serviceProvider,
        ServiceConfig = new ServiceConfig {
          LoadBalancingConfigs = { new PickFirstConfig() }
        }
    });

    var client = new Ingestor.IngestorClient(channel);
```

```
        var count = 0;
        for (var i = 0; i < requestCount; i++)
        {
            await
                client.ProcessDataAsync(GenerateDataRequest(i));
            count++;
        }

        return count;
}
```

In the preceding example, `myhost` is just an arbitrary hostname that we expect to be present in the DNS table. When we are defining `GrpcChannelOptions`, we are specifying `Credentials` as `ChannelCredentials.SecureSsl`. However, this is only applicable if the endpoints that we will be accessing are protected by TLS and use HTTPS protocol. Otherwise, you would use `ChannelCredentials.Insecure` credentials. This will be applicable if the server-side gRPC applications are running on a Macintosh.

Next, we are specifying the load-balancing config. We can manually populate various values, but we can also just use the inbuilt `PickFirstConfig` class. With this setting applied, the client doesn't evenly distribute the load between different server instances. Instead, it just stays connected to the first instance it was able to successfully connect to. But if it can't connect to any specific instance within a particular period of time, it will try to connect to a different one.

This type of load balancing is more reactive than proactive. Instead of evenly distributing the load from the start, it attempts to add the load to a service that's already under a high load.

The rest of the logic is identical to what we had in the other methods of the client wrapper class. Now, we need to add the signature of this method to the `IGrpcClientWrapper` interface by adding the following line to it:

```
Task<int> SendDataViaDnsLoadBalancer(int requestCount);
```

Finally, we can add the following endpoint method to the `DataController` class:

```
[HttpPost("dns-load-balancer/{count}")]
public async Task<ApiResponse>
PostDataViaDnsLoadBalancer(int count)
```

```
{
    var stopWatch = Stopwatch.StartNew();
    var processedCount = await
        clientWrapper.SendDataViaDnsLoadBalancer(count);

    return new ApiResponse
    {
        DataItemsProcessed = processedCount,
        RequestProcessingTime =
            stopWatch.ElapsedMilliseconds
    };
}
```

Now, we will have a look at another inbuilt load balancer available with the gRPC client NuGet package.

Using a static resolver for the load balancer

Another type of load balancer resolver that's available in the gRPC client NuGet package is a static resolver. But unlike the DNS resolver, you need to configure it and register it in the dependency injection system before you can use it.

The static resolver doesn't attempt to retrieve any endpoints based on a hostname listed in DNS records. Instead, it will have a preconfigured list of endpoints. But the rest of its functionality is identical.

We will register an instance of the static resolver and populate it with entries from the application settings. To do so, we add the following snippet to the `ConfigureServices` method of the `Startup` class of the `ApiGateway` project (or the main body of the `Program.cs` file if you are using .NET 6 template):

```
var addresses = Configuration.GetSection("ServerAddresses").
    Get<List<string>>();
services.AddSingleton<ResolverFactory>
    (new StaticResolverFactory(addr => addresses
        .Select(a => new DnsEndPoint(a.Replace("//",
            string.Empty).Split(':')[1],
                int.Parse(a.Split(':')[2])))
                    .ToArray()));
```

We also need the following `using` statements to make it work:

```
using Grpc.Net.Client.Balancer;
using System.Net;
```

This will register an instance of the `StaticResolverFactory` class and create an endpoint for every URL entry we have in the `ServerAddresses` section of the `appsetting.json` file. In our case, because we have them as fully qualified URIs, we will need to remove the protocol and split the hostname from the port number. This is because a pure hostname and port number are the constructor parameters of the `DnsEndPoint` class, which the static resolver uses to represent the endpoints. Whether the protocol is HTTP or HTTPS will be controlled at the time when the gRPC channel is created by using either `Insecure` or `SecureSsl` as the channel credential configuration.

Now, we can start using the static load balancer resolver inside a gRPC client. To do so, we will add the following method to the `GrpcClientWrapper` class:

```csharp
public async Task<int> SendDataViaStaticLoadBalancer(int requestCount)
{
    using var channel =
      GrpcChannel.ForAddress("static://localhost", new
        GrpcChannelOptions
        {
            Credentials = ChannelCredentials.SecureSsl,
            ServiceProvider = serviceProvider,
            ServiceConfig = new ServiceConfig {
               LoadBalancingConfigs = { new RoundRobinConfig() }
            }
        });

    var client = new Ingestor.IngestorClient(channel);
    var count = 0;
    for (var i = 0; i < requestCount; i++)
    {
        await
           client.ProcessDataAsync(GenerateDataRequest(i));
        count++;
```

```
        }

        return count;
}
```

The implementation is almost identical to the DNS resolver, but we are using the `static` keyword in the gRPC channel URI instead of `dns`. In this case, the hostname can be absolutely anything, as it's purely a label for our convenience. It doesn't actually represent a real hostname.

The only major difference is that we have used a different load-balancing configuration here. We have applied `RoundRobinConfig`. This class will make our load balancer work similar to the primitive load-balancing mechanism we have previously built ourselves. It will make endpoint requests in a round-robin fashion.

To be able to use this newly added method, we need to add the signature of this method to the `IGrpcClientWrapper` interface and then add the following endpoint method to our `DataController` class:

```
[HttpPost("static-load-balancer/{count}")]
public async Task<ApiResponse>
PostDataViaStaticLoadBalancer(int count)
{
    var stopWatch = Stopwatch.StartNew();
    var processedCount = await
        clientWrapper.SendDataViaStaticLoadBalancer(count);

    return new ApiResponse
    {
        DataItemsProcessed = processedCount,
        RequestProcessingTime =
            stopWatch.ElapsedMilliseconds
    };
}
```

But those are not the only types of endpoint resolvers and load balancers you can use with your gRPC clients. You can also create custom resolvers and custom load balancers.

Creating custom load balancers and resolvers

What if we wanted to read endpoint URIs from a file on the disk? Or what if we could query a specific website to retrieve the list of the endpoints? Well, with available components, you can achieve either of these.

All existing resolvers inherit from the `Resolver` base class, and you can write your own resolvers to do the same.

As an example, we will create a resolver that will read from a file on the disk. To do so, we will add the `addresses.txt` file to the `ApiGateway` application project.

The content of the file will be the addresses of the gRPC server applications without the protocol and with the hostname and the port number separated by whitespace. For example, if your addresses are `https://localhost:6992` and `https://localhost:46785`, the content of this file will be as follows:

```
localhost 6992
localhost 46785
```

To make sure that this file is moved into the application folder during the build, we will add the following snippet to the `ApiGateway.csproj` file:

```xml
<ItemGroup>
    <None Update="addresses.txt">
        <CopyToOutputDirectory>Always</CopyToOutputDirectory>
    </None>
</ItemGroup>
```

Now, we are ready to create the resolver. To do so, we create the `DiskResolver.cs` file inside our `ApiGateway` application folder. The namespace imports and the general structure of the file will be as follows:

```csharp
using Grpc.Net.Client.Balancer;
using System;
using System.Collections.Generic;
using System.IO;
using System.Net;
using System.Threading;
using System.Threading.Tasks;

namespace ApiGateway
```

```
{
    public class DiskResolver : Resolver
    {
        private readonly Uri _address;
        private Action<ResolverResult> _listener;

        public DiskResolver(Uri address)
        {
            _address = address;
        }
}
```

Now, we can add logic to it that will read the file from the disk and extract endpoint addresses from it:

```
public override Task RefreshAsync(CancellationToken
  cancellationToken)
{
    var addresses = new List<DnsEndPoint>();

    foreach (var line in File.ReadLines(_address.Host))
    {
        var addresComponents = line.Split(' ');
        addresses.Add(new DnsEndPoint(addresComponents[0],
          int.Parse(addresComponents[1])));
    }

    _listener(ResolverResult.ForResult(addresses,
      serviceConfig: null));

    return Task.CompletedTask;
}
```

Then, we need to add a method that will start the resolver:

```
public override void Start(Action<ResolverResult> listener)
{
    _listener = listener;
}
```

But this is not all. Inside the same file, we need to put a resolver factory class. This is the class that will map our newly created resolver to a `disk` keyword in the URI schema. It will look like this:

```
public class DiskResolverFactory : ResolverFactory
{
    public override string Name => "disk";

    public override Resolver Create(ResolverOptions
       options)
    {
        return new DiskResolver(options.Address);
    }
}
```

But what if, as well as being unsatisfied with existing resolvers, we also aren't satisfied with the existing load-balancer rules? What if we want the load balancer to access endpoints at random? Well, we can do this too.

We add the `RandomizedBalancer.cs` file to the `ApiGateway` project folder. The basic structure of the class inside the file will be as follows:

```
using Grpc.Net.Client.Balancer;
using Microsoft.Extensions.Logging;
using System;
using System.Collections.Generic;

namespace ApiGateway
{
    public class RandomizedBalancer :
        SubchannelsLoadBalancer
    {
```

```
            public RandomizedBalancer(IChannelControlHelper
        controller, ILoggerFactory loggerFactory)
            : base(controller, loggerFactory)
        {
        }
    }
}
```

Then, we add the following class inside the `RandomizedBalancer` class. This is a nested class with the `private` access modifier:

```
private class RandomizedPicker : SubchannelPicker
{
    private readonly IReadOnlyList<Subchannel>
        _subchannels;
    private readonly Random _randomNumberGenerator;

    public RandomizedPicker(IReadOnlyList<Subchannel>
        subchannels)
    {
        _subchannels = subchannels;
        _randomNumberGenerator = new Random();
    }

    public override PickResult Pick(PickContext context)
    {
        return
            PickResult.ForSubchannel(_subchannels
                [_randomNumberGenerator.Next
                    (0, _subchannels.Count)]);
    }
}
```

After this, we add the necessary override method that uses this class:

```
protected override SubchannelPicker
    CreatePicker(IReadOnlyList<Subchannel> readySubchannels)
{
```

```
        return new RandomizedPicker(readySubchannels);
}
```

Finally, we add the following factory class to the same file at the same level that `RandomizedBalancer` is positioned at:

```
public class RandomizedBalancerFactory :
LoadBalancerFactory
{
    public override string Name => "randomized";

    public override LoadBalancer Create(LoadBalancerOptions
        options)
    {
        return new RandomizedBalancer(options.Controller,
            options.LoggerFactory);
    }
}
```

Now, we need to register both the resolver and the load balancer in the `ConfigureServices` method of the `Startup` class (or the main body of the `Program.cs` file if you are using .NET 6 template):

```
services.AddSingleton<ResolverFactory, DiskResolverFactory>();
services.AddSingleton<LoadBalancerFactory,
    RandomizedBalancerFactory>();
```

Now we can use them both by adding the following method to the `GrpcClientWrapper` class:

```
public async Task<int> SendDataViaCustomLoadBalancer(int
requestCount)
{
    using var channel =
        GrpcChannel.ForAddress("disk://addresses.txt", new
            GrpcChannelOptions
        {
            Credentials = ChannelCredentials.SecureSsl,
            ServiceProvider = serviceProvider,
```

```
                ServiceConfig = new ServiceConfig {
                    LoadBalancingConfigs = { new
                        LoadBalancingConfig("random") } }
                });
    var client = new Ingestor.IngestorClient(channel);
    var count = 0;
    for (var i = 0; i < requestCount; i++)
    {
        await
            client.ProcessDataAsync(GenerateDataRequest(i));
        count++;
    }
    return count;
}
```

To access the custom resolver we've created, we use disk as the resolver name. Then, we specify the file path, which, in our case, is addresses.txt, as the file is located in the same folder where the compiled application is.

Now, to use it from the outside, we need to add the signature of this method to the IGrpcClientWrapper interface and add the following method to DataController:

```
[HttpPost("custom-load-balancer/{count}")]
public async Task<ApiResponse>
    PostDataViaCustomLoadBalancer(int count)
{
    var stopWatch = Stopwatch.StartNew();
    var processedCount = await
        clientWrapper.SendDataViaCustomLoadBalancer(count);

    return new ApiResponse
    {
        DataItemsProcessed = processedCount,
        RequestProcessingTime =
            stopWatch.ElapsedMilliseconds
    };
}
```

Even though client-side load balancing is effective, it's not always a viable solution. Quite often, the client wouldn't know the addresses of the individual endpoints. But fortunately, there is a solution for this. Load balancing can be done by a proxy running on a server.

Proxy load balancing with gRPC

Proxy load balancing is the most popular type of load balancing used by standard web applications. With it in place, the client doesn't know the exact addresses of individual endpoints. It only knows the address of a single endpoint that the proxy is hosted on. And it's the job of the proxy to then redirect the request to the actual endpoints.

Large-scale user-facing applications would use this type of load balancing. Because web applications like Facebook or YouTube would not be able to support the number of requests they receive if they just ran as a single instance, they have to be scaled out and run as many duplicate instances. The number of these instances may change as the number of requests changes. Also, the instances may get moved to different hardware if the original machine fails, which regularly happens in data centers.

As the user, you would never be expected to know the ever-changing list of the endpoint addresses. All you have to do is type a standard address in the browser. And this is precisely how the proxy works. When you type the address, it resolves to the IP address of the proxy, and it's then the proxy that redirects the request to the actual application.

And you can do exactly the same type of load balancing with gRPC. The only caveat is that you would need a proxy that supports HTTP/2. But luckily, there are several that do. A few examples would be Envoy, Linkerd, and YARP.

But there are several more. All you need to do is to check whether any particular product supports HTTP/2.

But to demonstrate how proxy load balancing works, we will build our own. Luckily, we will have to do minimal work, as the bulk of load-balancing logic has already been added to the YARP NuGet package.

Building a web application to act as a proxy

We navigate to the `GrpcLoadBalancing` solution folder and execute the following command to create an empty ASP.NET Core application project:

```
dotnet new web -o Http2Proxy
```

Then, we add the new project to the solution by executing the following command:

```
dotnet sln add Http2Proxy/Http2Proxy.csproj
```

Next, we navigate to the `Http2Proxy` project folder and add the `Yarp.ReverseProxy` NuGet package. At the time of writing, this NuGet package was available in preview only. Therefore, you would need to specify the version while running the command:

```
dotnet add package Yarp.ReverseProxy -v 1.0.0-
   preview.12.21451.3
```

If you are using an IDE, you can find the latest version via the NuGet package manager.

Next, we add the necessary dependency to the `Startup` class of the `Http2Proxy` application, or `Program.cs` file if it's based on .NET 6 template. First, we need to ensure that the following `using` statements are present:

```
using Microsoft.AspNetCore.Builder;
using Microsoft.AspNetCore.Hosting;
using Microsoft.Extensions.Configuration;
using Microsoft.Extensions.DependencyInjection;
using Microsoft.Extensions.Hosting;
```

Next, we need to make sure that the application configuration is passed to the class, as it may not be for an empty ASP.NET Core application by default. To do so, we need to make sure that the following property and the following constructor are present:

```
public IConfiguration Configuration { get; }

public Startup(IConfiguration configuration)
{
    Configuration = configuration;
}
```

Next, we register the reverse proxy by adding this to the `ConfigureServices` method:

```
var proxyBuilder = services.AddReverseProxy();
proxyBuilder.LoadFromConfig(Configuration.GetSection("Rever
   seProxy"));
```

Then, inside the `Configure` method, we replace the call to `app.UseEndpoints` with the following:

```
app.UseEndpoints(endpoints =>
{
    endpoints.MapReverseProxy();
});
```

Now, we need to configure our proxy to talk to specific endpoints. To do so, add the following section to the `appsettings.json` file:

```
"ReverseProxy": {
  "Routes": {
    "route1": {
      "ClusterId": "cluster1",
      "Match": {
        "Path": "{**catch-all}"
      },
    }
  },
  "Clusters": {
    "cluster1": {
      "Destinations": {
        "cluster1/destination1": {
          "Address": "https://localhost:6992"
        },
        "cluster1/destination2": {
          "Address": "https://localhost:46785"
        }
      }
    }
  }
}
```

Here, we are adding a cluster of endpoints. The cluster has two destinations, which contain the addresses of the `GrpcServer1` and `GrpcServer2` applications. Normally, you would use HTTPS addresses, but if you are running those applications on a Macintosh, then you would use HTTP addresses.

Finally, we modify the `launchSettings.json` file that is located inside the `Properties` folder of the `Http2Proxy` project. Because it's no longer a normal web application, we need to prevent it from automatically running in the browser. And we won't use IIS Express. To enable these changes, replace the content of this file with the following:

```
{
  "profiles": {
    "Http2Proxy": {
      "commandName": "Project",
      "dotnetRunMessages": "true",
      "launchBrowser": false,
      "applicationUrl":
          "https://localhost:5001;http://localhost:5000",
      "environmentVariables": {
        "ASPNETCORE_ENVIRONMENT": "Development"
      }
    }
  }
}
```

Now, our proxy application is ready to act as a load balancer. We will just need to configure the client application to connect to it. To do so, just replace the first entry in the `ServerAddresses` section of the `appsettings.json` file from the `ApiGateway` project folder with the address of the `Http2Proxy` application. If you are running the `Http2Proxy` application on a Macintosh, use the HTTP address; otherwise, use the HTTPS one.

Launching the HTTP/2 proxy

To launch the application, execute the `dotnet run` command from inside the `GrpcServer1`, `GrpcServer2`, `Http2Proxy`, and `ApiGateway` application folders. Then, open the Swagger page of `ApiGateway` application in the browser and execute the `standard-client` endpoint with an arbitrarily defined value of the `count` parameter.

Now, if you look at the console output of the `GrpcServer1` and `GrpcServer2` applications, you will see that requests have been distributed between both of them. This can be seen on the following screenshot:

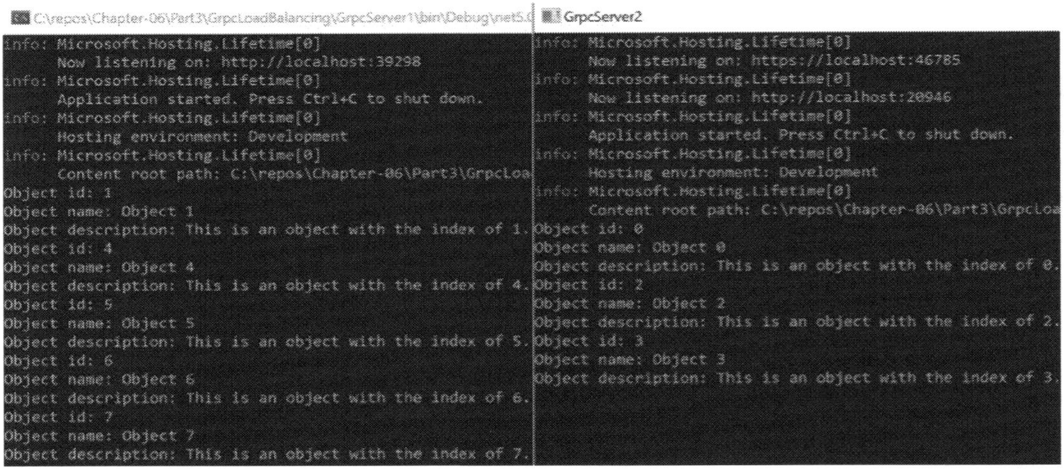

Figure 6.4 – Proxy load balancing has distributed requests between two instances

As we have demonstrated, both client-side and proxy load balancers work well. The choice of the load balancer type would depend on the situation.

If you need to run a load balancer on an internal network, then perhaps client-side load balancing would be the best. With it, you would not have to add additional components, such as services that are acting as proxies.

But if you expect clients to connect to your network from the outside, then proxy load balancing would be better suited. The clients won't have to know the addresses of all of your endpoints. All they need to know is a single address that will take them to the proxy.

Summary

In this chapter, you have learned that load balancing is needed when the number of connections you expect to receive would exceed what a single instance of an application would be able to handle. Load balancing is performed by having several instances of the application and distributing requests between them.

You saw multiple ways that load balancing can be done. A common way is to call the endpoints in a round-robin fashion. But it's also possible to get the load balancer to connect to the first available endpoint and maintain the connection for as long as it can.

You now know that client-side load balancing is performed by getting the client to directly connect to the individual endpoints. In order to obtain these addresses, the gRPC client would need to use a resolver.

You have also learned that proxy load balancing is performed by a proxy service on the server that the client connects to. For gRPC, you can use any proxy that supports HTTP/2.

And now we have completed the section about gRPC best practices. Next, we will start going into various gRPC concepts in depth. In the next chapter, we will cover different types of gRPC calls in more detail. You will also learn how to apply various configuration options to them.

Questions

1. Why would you need load balancing?

    A. To improve the application performance

    B. To split queries into smaller sub-queries

    C. To split a large number of requests between multiple instances of the application

    D. To protect your server-side components from hacking

2. How is client-side load balancing done?

    A. By sending requests to a server endpoint, which then redirects the call

    B. By getting the server hostname resolved into a list of IP addresses

    C. By getting the list of individual endpoint addresses and calling them directly

    D. By trying to call all addresses specified in the local DNS configuration

3. Which one of these is a valid type of load balancing?

    A. Connecting to endpoints in a round-robin fashion

    B. Connecting to the first available endpoint

    C. Connecting to endpoints at random

    D. All of the above

4. How does a proxy load balancer work?

    A. The client connects to the proxy endpoint and the proxy redirects it to individual application instances.

    B. The client requests the full list of addresses from the proxy and connects directly to them.

    C. The client obtains the address of the server that will contain the list of endpoints it will connect to.

    D. The client requests a single address to the endpoint that it will connect to next.

5. What's required to enable proxy load balancing with gRPC?

    A. Protobuf on the proxy

    B. GRPC middleware on the proxy

    C. Support for HTTP/2

    D. An SSL certificate on the proxy

Further reading

- gRPC client-side load balancing: https://docs.microsoft.com/en-us/aspnet/core/grpc/loadbalancing
- Envoy proxy: https://www.envoyproxy.io/
- Linkerd proxy: https://linkerd.io/
- YARP reverse proxy: https://microsoft.github.io/reverse-proxy/
- DNS fundamentals: https://www.thegeekstuff.com/2013/12/dns-basics/

- Local DNS configuration on the Macintosh: `https://markinns.com/archive/how-to-setup-a-local-dns-host-file-on-mac-os-x.html`
- Local DNS configuration on Windows: `https://helpdeskgeek.com/networking/edit-hosts-file/`
- Local DNS configuration on Linux: `https://www.thegeekstuff.com/2014/01/install-dns-server/`

Section 3: In-Depth Look at gRPC on .NET

This part delves deeper into gRPC functionality on .NET. It covers all supported types of gRPC calls, gRPC security, and different ways of debugging gRPC applications. This section comprises the following chapters:

- *Chapter 7, Using Different Call Types That gRPC Supports*
- *Chapter 8, Using Well-Known Types to Make Protobuf More Handy*
- *Chapter 9, Securing gRPC Endpoints in Your ASP.NET Core Application with SSL/TLS*
- *Chapter 10, Applying Authentication and Authorization to gRPC Endpoints*
- *Chapter 11, Using Logging, Metrics, and Debugging in gRPC on .NET*

7
Using Different Call Types Supported by gRPC

In the previous chapters, we covered several ways you can make a gRPC call to and from a .NET application. In this chapter, we will have an in-depth look at how to make these calls and what happens in the background when these calls are made.

In this chapter, you will not only learn how to make the different types of calls that are available with gRPC, but you will also learn what happens in the background while these calls are being made. We will cover how Protobuf RPC definitions are resolved by gRPC middleware into paths that are understood by the HTTP protocol, as well as how gRPC middleware deals with errors.

You will also learn how to apply various configuration options, both to the gRPC channel and to individual calls. Finally, you will learn how to extract metadata from gRPC calls, both on the client and the server.

In this chapter, we will cover the following topics:

- Making unary calls on gRPC
- Streaming data from the client
- Reading streams from the server
- Enabling bi-directional streaming

By the end of this chapter, you will have learned how to use all the available gRPC call types optimally and how to prevent unintentional errors while using them.

Technical requirements

To follow the instructions in this chapter, you will need the following:

- A computer with either Windows, Mac, or Linux installed
- A supported IDE or code editor (Visual Studio, Visual Studio Code, or JetBrains Rider)
- .NET 5 SDK
- A self-signed development HTTPS certificate that's enabled on your machine

The instructions on how to set all of these up were provided in *Chapter 1, Creating a Basic gRPC Application on ASP.NET Core*. All the code samples for this chapter can be found at `https://github.com/PacktPublishing/Microservices-Communication-in-.NET-Using-gRPC/tree/main/Chapter-07`.

Please visit the following link to check the CiA videos: `https://bit.ly/3m5o8SR`

Making unary calls on gRPC

In this section, we will learn how to make the most basic gRPC call—a unary call. Even though we have used this call type in previous chapters, we will look into it in more detail here. You will learn the difference between blocking and non-blocking unary call implementations on .NET, as well as how to work with its metadata.

We will also provide examples of unary calls that cover other fundamental aspects of gRPC and its .NET implementation. For example, you will learn how the URI path to RPCs gets constructed based on whether or not you use the `package` keyword inside a Protobuf definition. You will also learn how to extract metadata from the requests and responses, both on the client and the server.

But first, we will set up our solution.

Setting up shared gRPC dependencies

We will place all of our projects into the same solution with shared dependencies. Let's get started:

1. To create the solution, create the `GrpcCallTypes` folder. Then, execute the following command inside it:

   ```
   dotnet new sln
   ```

2. Then, execute the following command inside the solution folder to create a class library that will hold all shared dependencies:

   ```
   dotnet new classlib -o GrpcDependencies
   ```

3. Next, add this project to the solution by executing the following command:

   ```
   dotnet sln add GrpcDependencies/GrpcDependencies.csproj
   ```

4. After this, navigate to the `GrpcDependencies` project folder and add all the necessary `NuGetDependencies` by executing the following commands:

   ```
   dotnet add GrpcDependencies.csproj package Grpc.Net.Client
   dotnet add GrpcDependencies.csproj package Google.Protobuf
   dotnet add GrpcDependencies.csproj package Grpc.Tools
   dotnet add GrpcDependencies.csproj package Grpc.AspNetCore
   ```

We are now ready to start adding Protobuf definitions. But this time, we will do something unusual – we will add three files with almost identical content. The only difference between them will be in the way they use the `package` keyword. We will do this later to demonstrate how the .NET implementations of the Protobuf definitions are generated under different scenarios. You will also learn how the `package` attribute (or its absence) affects the URI path to the RPC endpoint.

The first definition will have the package keyword, but no csharp_namespace. The second definition will have no package keyword; it will have the csharp_namespace attribute instead. The third package will have neither. The following steps show you how these files can be set up:

1. We will start by creating the Protos folder inside the GrpcDependencies project folder. Next, we will place the device_management.proto file in this folder. In this file, we must define the service:

    ```
    syntax = "proto3";
    package device_management;

    service DeviceManager {
        rpc UpsertDeviceStatus (DeviceDetails) returns
            (UpsertDeviceResponse);
        rpc GetDevice (GetDeviceRequest) returns
            (DeviceDetails);
    }
    ```

2. Then, we must add the message and enum definitions:

    ```
    message DeviceDetails {
        int32 device_id = 1;
        string name = 2;
        string description = 3;
        DeviceStatus status = 4;
    }

    message GetDeviceRequest {
        int32 device_id = 1;
    }

    message UpsertDeviceResponse {
        bool success = 1;
    }
    enum DeviceStatus {
        OFFLINE = 0;
        ONLINE = 1;
        BUSY = 2;
    ```

```
        ERRORED = 3;
}
```

3. Now, we must copy this file and rename the copy `device_management_cs_namespace.proto`. In this file, we will replace the `package` definition with the following code:

   ```
   option csharp_namespace = "GrpcDependencies.Protos";
   ```

4. After this, make another copy of the `device_management.proto` file and call it `device_management_no_package.proto`. Inside this file, we will remove the `package` directive altogether.

5. Next, we will register all of these Protobuf definitions by inserting this section into the `GrpcDependencies.csproj` file:

   ```
   <ItemGroup>
     <Protobuf Include="Protos\device_management.proto" />
     <Protobuf
       Include="Protos\device_management_cs_namespace.proto"
       />
     <Protobuf
       Include="Protos\device_management_no_package.proto"
       />
   </ItemGroup>
   ```

Now, we are ready to start creating server-side implementations of all three Protobuf definitions we have added.

Creating server-side implementations of the Protobuf definitions

Inside the `GrpcCallTypes` solution folder, we will create a project based on the gRPC template. Then, we will link this project to the class library we have created and create implementations of the Protobuf definitions we have added to it. Let's get started:

1. Execute the following command to create a project from the gRPC service template:

   ```
   dotnet new grpc -o DeviceManagerService
   ```

2. Then, add it to the solution by executing the following command:

```
dotnet sln add DeviceManagerService/DeviceManagerService.csproj
```

3. Now, navigate to the `DeviceManagerService` project folder and link the shared class library to it by adding the following snippet to the `DeviceManagerService.csproj` file:

```xml
<ItemGroup>
    <ProjectReference
      Include="..\GrpcDependencies\GrpcDependencies.csproj"
      />
</ItemGroup>
```

Now, we can remove the direct gRPC NuGet references from this file since we have already defined them in the class library. Once we've done this, we can add the implementation for our Protobuf definitions. We will start by placing the `ManagerService.cs` file in the `Services` folder. The class definition inside the file will look as follows:

```csharp
using System;
using System.Threading.Tasks;
using Grpc.Core;

namespace DeviceManagerService.Services
{
    public class ManagerService :
        DeviceManagement.DeviceManager.DeviceManagerBase
    {
    }
}
```

This is the implementation for the `device_management.proto` file. Now, we can add the implementation of the `UpsertDeviceStatus` rpc to this class, as follows:

```csharp
public override Task<DeviceManagement.
    UpsertDeviceResponse>
UpsertDeviceStatus(DeviceManagement.DeviceDetails
    request,
```

```
        ServerCallContext context)
    {
        Console.WriteLine($"DeviceManagerService triggered.
          Peer:
            {context.Peer}. Host: {context.Host}.");
        Console.WriteLine($"Device id: {request.DeviceId},
          Name:
            {request.Name}, Description: {request.Description},
              Status {request.Status}.");

        return Task.FromResult(new
            DeviceManagement.UpsertDeviceResponse
            {
                Success = true
            });
    }
}
```

We will not include the implementation of `GetDevice rpc`. We've done this on purpose so that we can demonstrate what will happen if the client attempts to make a call to this endpoint later. But for now, let's examine the server-side implementation of a unary gRPC call on .NET.

A unary call will always be an `override` of a method that has been added to auto-generated code by gRPC tools on .NET. The format of the method signature will always be as follows:

```
public override Task<{return message type}> {RPC name}({request
   message type} request, ServerCallContext context)
```

Of course, just like with any C# `Task`, you can add the `async` keyword to it if you intend to use the `await` keyword inside the method. Both the return object and the input message types will vary, depending on the `rpc` definition in Protobuf. But there will always be an input parameter of the `ServerCallContext` type. This is the parameter that contains the metadata of the request.

This object will contain information such as the request headers, if any were applied. Some standard metadata fields are represented by class properties. For example, you can extract information about logged-in users.

In the preceding example, we are extracting peer and host information from the `context` parameter. The former represents the address of the client, while the latter represents the address of the host running the application. We output this information to the console. Then, we output the data from the input message itself. Let's continue:

1. First, we will copy this file and name the copy `ManagerServiceCsNamespace.cs`. We will change the class signature inside the file to the following since we are now implementing the `device_management_cs_namespace.proto` file:

   ```
   public class ManagerServiceCsNamespace :
   GrpcDependencies.Protos.DeviceManager.DeviceManagerBase
   ```

2. Then, we will replace the implementation of the `UpsertDeviceStatus` rpc with the following:

   ```
   public override Task<GrpcDependencies.Protos.
     UpsertDeviceResponse>
     UpsertDeviceStatus(GrpcDependencies.Protos.
     DeviceDetails
       request, ServerCallContext context)
   {
       Console.WriteLine($"ManagerServiceCsNamespace
         triggered.
         Peer: {context.Peer}. Host: {context.Host}.");
       Console.WriteLine($"Device id: {request.DeviceId},
         Name:
         {request.Name}, Description: {request.Description},
           Status {request.Status}.");

       return Task.FromResult(new
         GrpcDependencies.Protos.UpsertDeviceResponse
         {
             Success = true
         });
   }
   ```

3. Next, we will make another copy of the `ManagerService.cs` file and rename it `ManagerServiceNoPackage.cs`. Inside this file (which is the implementation of `device_management_no_package.proto`), we will change the class signature to the following:

```
public class ManagerServiceNoPackage : DeviceManager.
    DeviceManagerBase
```

4. Then, we will replace the implementation of the `UpsertDeviceStatus` rpc with the following:

```
public override Task<UpsertDeviceResponse>
UpsertDeviceStatus(DeviceDetails request,
    ServerCallContext
    context)
{
    Console.WriteLine($"ServiceNoPackage triggered. Peer:
        {context.Peer}. Host: {context.Host}.");
    Console.WriteLine($"Device id: {request.DeviceId},
        Name:
        {request.Name}, Description: {request.Description},
        Status {request.Status}.");

    return Task.FromResult(new UpsertDeviceResponse
    {
        Success = true
    });
}
```

Please note that we haven't used any additional namespace imports in this file. This is because the `service` and `message` implementations won't have any namespaces in auto-generated code if they represent a Protobuf definition that has neither `package` nor `csharp_namespace` defined.

5. Now, we have all implementations of all three Protobuf definitions we created previously. Let's make them accessible to the clients. To do so, we need to make sure that the `Startup` class inside the `DeviceManagerService` project (or `Program.cs` file if you are using .NET 6 template) has the following using statements specified:

```
using DeviceManagerService.Services;
using Microsoft.AspNetCore.Builder;
using Microsoft.AspNetCore.Hosting;
using Microsoft.AspNetCore.Http;
using Microsoft.Extensions.DependencyInjection;
using Microsoft.Extensions.Hosting;
```

6. Then, we will need to add the following statements inside the call to `app.UseEndpoints`:

```
endpoints.MapGrpcService<ManagerService>();
endpoints.MapGrpcService<ManagerServiceCsNamespace>();
endpoints.MapGrpcService<ManagerServiceNoPackage>();
```

We now have an application with three almost identical gRPC service implementations. However, they are based on Protobuf definitions with different `package` configurations, so there are differences in how they can be accessed by gRPC clients. Each service implementation will input its class name into the console. So, we will now be able to build a client and see if we can reliably reach the service we want to reach.

> **Note**
> If you are running your server-side application on a Mac, you will need to make some modifications to it. The instructions on how to do so can be found in the *Running the gRPC service on Mac* section of *Chapter 1, Creating a Basic gRPC Application on ASP.NET Core*.

Building the gRPC client

Our gRPC client will be a standard ASP.NET Core web API application. As we did previously, we will add Swagger dependencies to it to make all the API endpoints accessible via a standard browser. Let's get started:

1. First, we must navigate to the `GrpcCallTypes` solution folder and execute the following command to create a project from the Web API template:

   ```
   dotnet new webapi -o ApiGateway
   ```

2. Then, we must add this project to the solution by executing the following command:

   ```
   dotnet sln add ApiGateway/ApiGateway.csproj
   ```

3. Next, we must navigate to the `ApiGateway` project folder and insert the following snippet into the `ApiGateway.csproj` file to link it to the class library that contains all the shared dependencies:

   ```xml
   <ItemGroup>
     <ProjectReference
       Include="..\GrpcDependencies\GrpcDependencies.csproj"
     />
   </ItemGroup>
   ```

4. Next, we must add the Swagger dependency to the project by executing the following command:

   ```
   dotnet add ApiGateway.csproj package NSwag.AspNetCore
   ```

5. Next, we must create a class that will represent the API response and request object. We will create the `DeviceDetails.cs` file inside the `ApiGateway` project folder. The content of this file is as follows:

   ```csharp
   namespace ApiGateway
   {
       public class DeviceDetails
       {
           public int Id { get; set; }
           public string Name { get; set; }
           public string Description { get; set; }
           public DeviceStatus Status { get; set; }
   ```

```
    }

    public enum DeviceStatus
    {
        OFFLINE = 0,
        ONLINE = 1,
        BUSY = 2,
        ERRORED = 3
    }
}
```

Please note that the `class` and `enum` names have been intentionally chosen to be the same as the corresponding `message` and `enum` names from the Protobuf definitions. This was done to demonstrate how any potential naming conflicts are resolved by C# when we are dealing with auto-generated gRPC abstractions that don't use namespaces, such as the ones that are based on the `device_management_no_package.proto` file.

6. Now, we must add the `ClientType.cs` file to the root of the `ApiGateway` project. It will be an `enum` that allows us to select a specific client implementation:

```
namespace ApiGateway
{
    public enum ClientType
    {
        PackageName,
        NoPackage,
        CsNamespace
    }
}
```

7. Next, we must add a class that will act as a wrapper for gRPC clients that are based on different Protobuf definitions. The file will be called `GrpcClientWrapper.cs` and it will be placed in the root of the `ApiGateway` project folder. This file will have the following `using` statements and the following namespace definition:

```
using System;
using System.Threading.Tasks;
using Grpc.Core;
using Grpc.Net.Client;
```

```
using Microsoft.Extensions.Configuration;

namespace ApiGateway
{
}
```

8. Now, we must place the following interface definition inside the namespace:

```
public interface IGrpcClientWrapper
{
    DeviceDetails GetDevice(ClientType clientType, int
        deviceId);
    bool UpsertDeviceStatus(ClientType clientType,
        DeviceDetails details);
    Task<bool> UpsertDeviceStatusAsync(ClientType
        clientType, DeviceDetails details);
}
```

9. Next, we must add a class that will implement this interface. This class will reuse the same gRPC channel for all its calls since all Protobuf implementations are hosted by the same server-side application:

```
internal class GrpcClientWrapper : IGrpcClientWrapper,
IDisposable
{
    private readonly GrpcChannel channel;

    public GrpcClientWrapper(IConfiguration
        configuration)
    {
        channel = GrpcChannel.ForAddress(configuration
            ["ServerUrl"], new GrpcChannelOptions
            {
                Credentials = ChannelCredentials.SecureSsl,
            });
    }
}
```

Please note that we are using `GrpcChannelOptions` as one of the constructor parameters for the channel. We've done this to demonstrate how the gRPC channel can be configured.

We are applying the `Credential` options and setting them to `ChannelCredentials.SecureSsl`, which will ensure that the channel will only be able to connect to HTTPS endpoints. This option is relevant so long as the machine hosting your gRPC service application can support TLS or SSL (which will not be the case with a Mac, so you will need to remove this option if you are running your setup on a Mac). However, you also have the following options that you can apply to your channel:

- `CompressionProviders`: This option allows you to customize how message compression is performed.
- `HttpClient`: You can reuse an `HttpClient` instance as the client for gRPC communication. This option allows you to set such a client. There might be some valid reasons to reuse an existing HTTP client. For example, it might have already been pre-populated with request headers you want to reuse, such as authentication tokens.
- `DisposeHttpClient`: If you are using a custom instance of `HttpClient`, this option, when set to true, will dispose of this instance when the instance of `GrpcChannel` is disposed of.
- `HttpHandler`: This option allows you to apply some custom middleware logic that will be triggered when gRPC calls are made. For example, you may want to record some metrics for every gRPC response you receive. Using an HTTP handler will allow you to apply the code for it in one central place.
- `LoggerFactory`: This allows you to apply custom loggers to gRPC calls. We will cover this in more detail in *Chapter 11*, *Using Logging, Metrics, and Debugging in gRPC on .NET*.
- `MaxReceiveMessageSize`: This option controls the maximum size of a single message that can be received from the server. By default, it's set to 4 megabytes. Setting it to `null` will remove this limit.
- `MaxSendMessageSize`: This option limits the size of the request message. The default value is `null`, which means that there is no limit.

There are also some other options available, but at the time of writing, they are marked as experimental APIs that are subject to being changed or removed. Therefore, we will not cover them here.

Applying different types of client-side call implementations

Now, let's get back to building the rest of our class since we need implementations for both the `IGrpcClientWrapper` and `IDisposable` interfaces:

1. To implement the `IDisposable` interface, we must add the following method, where we will dispose of the channel:

    ```
    public void Dispose()
    {
        channel.Dispose();
    }
    ```

2. Then, we must add a `private` method that will be used by a number of our `public` methods:

    ```
    private DeviceDetails GetDeviceDetails(int id, string
        name,
    string description, DeviceStatus status)
    {
        return new DeviceDetails
        {
            Id = id,
            Name = name,
            Description = description,
            Status = status
        };
    }
    ```

3. After this, we must add an implementation of the `GetDevice` method from the `IGrpcClientWrapper` interface:

    ```
    public DeviceDetails GetDevice(ClientType clientType, int
        deviceId)
    {
        switch(clientType)
        {
        }
    }
    ```

4. The `switch` statement will be populated by the following cases:

```
case ClientType.PackageName:
    var packageClient = new DeviceManagement.
      DeviceManager.
      DeviceManagerClient(channel);
    var packageResponse = packageClient.GetDevice(new
      DeviceManagement.GetDeviceRequest { DeviceId =
        deviceId
      });
    return GetDeviceDetails(packageResponse.DeviceId,
      packageResponse.Name, packageResponse.Description,
        (DeviceStatus)packageResponse.Status);
case ClientType.CsNamespace:
    var csNamespaceClient = new
      GrpcDependencies.Protos.DeviceManager.
        DeviceManagerClient(channel);
    var csNamespaceResponse = csNamespaceClient.
      GetDevice(new
      GrpcDependencies.Protos.GetDeviceRequest
        { DeviceId = deviceId });
    return GetDeviceDetails(csNamespaceResponse.DeviceId,
      csNamespaceResponse.Name, csNamespaceResponse
        .Description, (DeviceStatus)
          csNamespaceResponse.Status);
default:
    var client = new
      DeviceManager.DeviceManagerClient(channel);
    var response = client.GetDevice(new GetDeviceRequest
      {
        DeviceId = deviceId });
    return GetDeviceDetails(response.DeviceId, response.
      Name,
        response.Description, (DeviceStatus) response.
          Status);
```

5. Now, we must add the implementation of the `UpsertDeviceStatus` method. First, we will add the method definition:

```
public bool UpsertDeviceStatus(ClientType clientType,
DeviceDetails details)
{
       switch (clientType)
       {
       }
}
```

6. Then, we will add the following `case` block to our `switch` statement:

```
case ClientType.PackageName:
    var packageClient = new
      DeviceManagement.DeviceManager.
        DeviceManagerClient(channel);
    var packageResponse = packageClient.
      UpsertDeviceStatus(new
      DeviceManagement.DeviceDetails
      {
        DeviceId = details.Id,
        Name = details.Name,
        Description = details.Description,
        Status = (DeviceManagement.DeviceStatus)details.
          Status
      });
    return packageResponse.Success;
```

7. Then, we will add a `case` block for `ClientType.CsNamespace`:

```
case ClientType.CsNamespace:
    var csNamespaceClient = new
      GrpcDependencies.Protos.DeviceManager
        .DeviceManagerClient(channel);
    var csNamespaceResponse =
      csNamespaceClient.UpsertDeviceStatus(new
        GrpcDependencies.Protos.DeviceDetails
        {
```

```
            DeviceId = details.Id,
            Name = details.Name,
            Description = details.Description,
            Status = (GrpcDependencies.Protos.DeviceStatus)
                details.Status
        });
        return csNamespaceResponse.Success;
```

8. After this, we will add the `default` case:

```
    default:
        var client = new
            DeviceManager.DeviceManagerClient(channel);
        var response = client.UpsertDeviceStatus(new
          global::DeviceDetails
          {
            DeviceId = details.Id,
            Name = details.Name,
            Description = details.Description,
            Status = (global::DeviceStatus)details.Status
        });
        return response.Success;
```

This is a good example of how the .NET compiler resolves naming conflicts. We have the `DeviceDetails` class and the `DeviceStatus` enum defined in the local namespace. However, they are also defined without any namespaces in auto-generated code for gRPC implementations.

Having the same names in gRPC and REST API objects is not uncommon as those objects often have the same meaning. But the .NET compiler is capable of dealing with situations where an object with the same name exists in the local namespace and outside of any namespace. When you're specifying the object name without fully qualifying it, the compiler will assume that you mean the object that exists in the local namespace. The object that doesn't have a namespace then needs to be qualified by applying the `global::` prefix to it.

Now, let's add the implementation of the `UpsertDeviceStatusAsync` method. It will be similar to the previous method, but it will be using an asynchronous version of the gRPC calls:

1. The method can be defined as follows:

    ```
    public async Task<bool> UpsertDeviceStatusAsync(ClientType
    clientType, DeviceDetails details)
    {
        switch (clientType)
        {
        }
    }
    ```

2. The first `case` block inside the `switch` statement will look as follows:

    ```
    case ClientType.PackageName:
        var packageClient = new DeviceManagement.
           DeviceManager.DeviceManagerClient(channel);
        var packageResponseCall =
           packageClient.UpsertDeviceStatusAsync(new
              DeviceManagement.DeviceDetails
        {
            DeviceId = details.Id,
            Name = details.Name,
            Description = details.Description,
            Status = (DeviceManagement.DeviceStatus)details.
               Status
        });
        var packageResponse = await
           packageResponseCall.ResponseAsync;
        return packageResponse.Success;
    ```

    Now, you can add blocks for the `ClientType.CsNamespace` and `default` cases to use asynchronous calls on the `CsNamespace` and `NoPackage` clients, respectively, as per the examples from the `UpsertDeviceStatus` method.

We now have two methods that make a unary call to the same gRPC endpoint; that is, `UpsertDeviceStatus`. However, one implementation uses synchronous blocking calls, while the other implementation uses asynchronous calls and waits for the results to be available. The .NET gRPC client implementation of unary calls gives us this choice by generating code for both of these call types. The blocking synchronous call will be the same as the original `rpc` name, while a non-blocking asynchronous call will have the `Async` suffix added to its name.

Other than one call being blocking while the other being non-blocking, there is also another significant difference between them. Blocking calls will always return just the response message. However, the asynchronous version can also give us metadata that's been sent by the server.

There are two ways to use the asynchronous call – await it as it's being made or store it in a variable. If we await the call as its being made, it will work similarly to awaiting a standard asynchronous `Task`. However, implementations of unary gRPC calls don't use `Task`. They use `AsyncUnaryCall`, which gives us more options.

If we store the call in a variable, as we did in the preceding example, we can retrieve the output message from it at any time by awaiting the `ResponseAsync` property of the object. However, if we also need the metadata, we can extract it by awaiting on the `ResponseHeadersAsync` property.

With that, we have completed the wrapper for all of our client implementations. Now, let's register this class and add a controller that will use it.

Using gRPC dependencies in the client application

First, we will apply all the necessary configurational changes to the `Startup` class of the `ApiGateway` application, or `Program.cs` file if you have created the project from .NET 6 template:

1. Replace the content of the `ConfigureServices` method with the following. If you are using .NET 6 template, you would need to place this code before the Build event and replace `services` with `builder.Services`:

    ```
    services.AddOpenApiDocument();
    services.AddSingleton(Configuration);
    services.AddSingleton<IGrpcClientWrapper,
      GrpcClientWrapper>();
    services.AddControllers();
    ```

2. Then, place the following lines anywhere at the beginning of the `Configure` method:

   ```
   app.UseOpenApi();
   app.UseSwaggerUi3();
   ```

3. If the template already contains a line stating `app.UseSwagger();`, remove it. This will cause conflicts with the components from the `NSwag` library.

4. To complete the configuration, we will need to add the following section to the `appsettings.json` file:

   ```
   "ServerUrl": "https://localhost:5001"
   ```

The value will be `https://localhost:5001` by default. However, if you are using a Mac, you will need to use `http://localhost:5000`. These URLs can be found inside the `launchSettings.json` file of the `DeviceManagerService` project.

Now, let's add the controller that we will be able to call:

1. Add the `DeviceController.cs` class to the `Controllers` folder. Add the following content to the file:

   ```
   using System.Threading.Tasks;
   using Microsoft.AspNetCore.Mvc;

   namespace ApiGateway.Controllers
   {
       [ApiController]
       [Route("[controller]")]
       public class DevicesController : ControllerBase
       {
           private readonly IGrpcClientWrapper
               clientWrapper;

           public DevicesController(IGrpcClientWrapper
               clientWrapper)
           {
               this.clientWrapper = clientWrapper;
           }
       }
   }
   ```

2. Then, add the following endpoint methods to the class:

```csharp
[HttpGet("{clientType}/{deviceId}")]
public DeviceDetails GetDevice(ClientType clientType, int
   deviceId)
{
    return clientWrapper.GetDevice(clientType, deviceId);
}


[HttpPost("{clientType}")]
public async Task PostDeviceStatus(ClientType clientType,
    [FromBody] DeviceDetails deviceDetails, [FromQuery]
    bool
    async = false)
{
    if (async)
        await clientWrapper.UpsertDeviceStatusAsync
            (clientType, deviceDetails);
    else
        clientWrapper.UpsertDeviceStatus(clientType,
            deviceDetails);

}
```

Now that both our client and server applications have been completed, we are ready to start testing them.

Testing different types of unary call endpoints

We will launch both the `DeviceManagerService` and `ApiGateway` applications by executing the `dotnet run` command in each of those folders. Then, you will be able to open the Swagger page for the `ApiGateway` application in your browser, which can be accessed by writing the base application URL into the address bar, followed by the `/swagger` path.

First, we will call the `GetDevice` API endpoint, which corresponds to a gRPC method that we haven't implemented on the server. Calling this method will give us an `Unimplemented` error. This error will have also been thrown if we hadn't registered the server-side endpoint. `Unimplemented` is the error that is thrown if the client was able to successfully connect to the server, but the path couldn't be resolved as any specific RPC. The Swagger page is expected to produce an output similar to the following:

```
Grpc.Core.RpcException: Status(StatusCode="Unimplemented", Detail="")
    at Grpc.Net.Client.Internal.HttpClientCallInvoker.BlockingUnaryCall[
    at Grpc.Core.Interceptors.InterceptingCallInvoker.<BlockingUnaryCall
    at Grpc.Core.ClientBase.ClientBaseConfiguration.ClientBaseConfigurat
kingUnaryCallContinuation`2 continuation)
    at Grpc.Core.Interceptors.InterceptingCallInvoker.BlockingUnaryCall[
    at DeviceManagement.DeviceManager.DeviceManagerClient.GetDevice(GetD
g\net5.0\Protos\DeviceManagementGrpc.cs:line 150
    at DeviceManagement.DeviceManager.DeviceManagerClient.GetDevice(GetD
hapter-07\Part1\GrpcCallTypes\GrpcDependencies\obj\Debug\net5.0\Protos\
    at ApiGateway.GrpcClientWrapper.GetDevice(ClientType clientType, Int
    at ApiGateway.Controllers.DevicesController.GetDevice(ClientType cli
```

Figure 7.1 – Unimplemented gRPC error returned while attempting to reach a non-existent server endpoint

Then, we can call the `PostDeviceStatus` endpoint. If we specify the client with an index of 0, which is based on the `device_management.proto` file, we are expected to receive an HTTP status code indicating success. In the console of the gRPC service application, we can see the full path that was called, as shown in the following screenshot:

```
info: Microsoft.AspNetCore.Hosting.Diagnostics[1]
      Request starting HTTP/2 POST https://localhost:5001/device_management.DeviceManager/UpsertDeviceStatus application
/grpc -
info: Microsoft.AspNetCore.Routing.EndpointMiddleware[0]
      Executing endpoint 'gRPC - /device_management.DeviceManager/UpsertDeviceStatus'
DeviceManagerService triggered. Peer: ipv6:[::1]:55833. Host: localhost:5001.
Device id: 1, Name: Test, Description: Test, Status Offline.
info: Microsoft.AspNetCore.Routing.EndpointMiddleware[1]
      Executed endpoint 'gRPC - /device_management.DeviceManager/UpsertDeviceStatus'
info: Microsoft.AspNetCore.Hosting.Diagnostics[2]
      Request finished HTTP/2 POST https://localhost:5001/device_management.DeviceManager/UpsertDeviceStatus application
/grpc - - 200 - application/grpc 145.4204ms
```

Figure 7.2 – Console output from the gRPC service application showing the full URL of the request

Under the default configuration, a URL pointing at a gRPC endpoint will have the following structure:

```
{base URL}/{gRPC package name}.{gRPC service name}/{gRPC rpc
   name}
```

However, if no package name was specified in a Protobuf file, then the URL will be as follows:

```
{base URL}/{gRPC service name}/{gRPC rpc name}
```

This creates a conflict for us as we have two Protobuf files with identical object names. There was no conflict while generating the code as one of them had the `csharp_namespace` directive, while the other one didn't. This ensured that the code was generated with completely different fully qualified names. But how would these services behave if we were to attempt to make a gRPC call to them?

The short answer is that the gRPC middleware will throw an error. If the path that's specified by the gRPC client can match more than one object, you will receive an `Unknown` error code. The output on the Swagger page will look similar to the following:

```
Grpc.Core.RpcException: Status(StatusCode="Unknown", Detail="Bad gRPC response. HTTP status code: 500")
   at ApiGateway.GrpcClientWrapper.UpsertDeviceStatusAsync(ClientType clientType, DeviceDetails details)
ne 125
   at ApiGateway.Controllers.DevicesController.Use(ClientType clientType, DeviceDetails deviceDetails,
s\DevicesController.cs:line 29
   at lambda_method480(Closure , Object )
   at Microsoft.AspNetCore.Mvc.Infrastructure.ActionMethodExecutor.AwaitableResultExecutor.Execute(IActi
bject[] arguments)
   at Microsoft.AspNetCore.Mvc.Infrastructure.ControllerActionInvoker.<InvokeActionMethodAsync>g__Awaite
   at Microsoft.AspNetCore.Mvc.Infrastructure.ControllerActionInvoker.<InvokeNextActionFilterAsync>g__Aw
cope, Object state, Boolean isCompleted)
   at Microsoft.AspNetCore.Mvc.Infrastructure.ControllerActionInvoker.Rethrow(ActionExecutedContextSeale
   at Microsoft.AspNetCore.Mvc.Infrastructure.ControllerActionInvoker.Next(State& next, Scope& scope, Ob
   at Microsoft.AspNetCore.Mvc.Infrastructure.ControllerActionInvoker.<InvokeInnerFilterAsync>g__Awaited
Object state, Boolean isCompleted)
   at Microsoft.AspNetCore.Mvc.Infrastructure.ResourceInvoker.<InvokeFilterPipelineAsync>g__Awaited|19_0
e, Boolean isCompleted)
```

Figure 7.3 – An unknown gRPC error is returned when the specified path matches multiple gRPC endpoints

However, an interesting thing will happen if you open the `Startup` class of the `DeviceManagementService` project, or `Program.cs` file if you are using .NET 6 template, and remove the `MapGrpcService` statement, which registers either `ManagerServiceCsNamespace` or `ManagerServiceNoPackage`. Then, if you execute the `PostDeviceStatus` endpoint from the Swagger page, selecting either 1 or 2 as the client type index (`NoPackage` or `CsNamespace`, respectively) will route the call to the same service – the remaining service that is still mapped.

In the following example, we have an unregistered `ManagerServiceNoPackage` service. Both implementations of the client that were based on Protobuf files without the `package` definition have successfully reached the `ManagerServiceCsNamespace` service. This is because even though the client implementations were based on different Protobuf definitions, they produced identical URLs and the objects that they worked with had identical structures. Here is the console output from the gRPC service application that demonstrates this:

```
ManagerServiceCsNamespace triggered. Peer: ipv6:[::1]:56087. Host: localhost:5001.
Device id: 1, Name: Test, Description: Test, Status Offline.
info: Microsoft.AspNetCore.Routing.EndpointMiddleware[1]
      Executed endpoint 'gRPC - /DeviceManager/UpsertDeviceStatus'
info: Microsoft.AspNetCore.Hosting.Diagnostics[2]
      Request finished HTTP/2 POST https://localhost:5001/DeviceManager/UpsertDeviceStatus application/grpc - - 200
- application/grpc 735.2744ms
info: Microsoft.AspNetCore.Hosting.Diagnostics[1]
      Request starting HTTP/2 POST https://localhost:5001/DeviceManager/UpsertDeviceStatus application/grpc -
info: Microsoft.AspNetCore.Routing.EndpointMiddleware[0]
      Executing endpoint 'gRPC - /DeviceManager/UpsertDeviceStatus'
ManagerServiceCsNamespace triggered. Peer: ipv6:[::1]:56087. Host: localhost:5001.
Device id: 1, Name: Test, Description: Test, Status Offline.
info: Microsoft.AspNetCore.Routing.EndpointMiddleware[1]
      Executed endpoint 'gRPC - /DeviceManager/UpsertDeviceStatus'
info: Microsoft.AspNetCore.Hosting.Diagnostics[2]
      Request finished HTTP/2 POST https://localhost:5001/DeviceManager/UpsertDeviceStatus application/grpc - - 200
- application/grpc 12.5724ms
```

Figure 7.4 – Two separate gRPC client implementations that generate identical URLs that will reach the same endpoint

So, when you make a gRPC call, remember that the middleware will construct a URL to reach the server. You also need to make sure that the endpoint that's specified in the URL is only implemented once.

But gRPC is not only limited to unary calls. You can also use it to stream data. This is what we will talk about next, starting with the client-streaming call type.

Streaming data from the client

Another type of call that gRPC supports is the client-streaming call. With this call, a client can send a stream of messages while the server still returns only a single message as the response.

For the remainder of this chapter, we will only be using client and server implementations of the `device_management.proto` file. The other Protobuf files are now redundant as they have already served their purpose to demonstrate how gRPC middleware resolves the URL path and how it deals with conflicts.

Adding a client-streaming call to the server application

We will start by adding a new client-streaming `rpc` to the service definition inside a Protobuf definition. Then, we will implement this `rpc` as a C# method in the gRPC service application:

1. Add the following `rpc` to the `DeviceManager` service definition inside the `device_management.proto` file, which is located in the `GrpcDependencies` project:

    ```
    rpc UpsertDeviceStatuses (stream DeviceDetails) returns (UpsertDeviceResponse);
    ```

2. Now, add the following method to the `ManagerService` class inside the `DeviceManagerService` project:

    ```csharp
    public override async Task<DeviceManagement.
      UpsertDeviceResponse> Upsert
      DeviceStatuses(IAsyncStreamReader<DeviceManagement.
        Device
        Details> requestStream, ServerCallContext context)
    {
        await foreach (var status in requestStream.
          ReadAllAsync())
        {
            Console.WriteLine($"Device id: {status.DeviceId}, 
              Name: {status.Name}, Description:
                {status.Description}, Status {status.
                  Status}.");
        }

        return new DeviceManagement.UpsertDeviceResponse
        {
            Success = true
        };
    }
    ```

Here is the breakdown of what we've done. In the `proto` file, we have defined a client-streaming call by placing the `stream` keyword before the request message, while the response message was still defined as singular.

The server-side implementation of a client-streaming method has the following signature. As we did previously, we can also use the `async` keyword in the signature if we wish to use the `await` keyword inside the method, as we did in the preceding example:

```
public override Task<{response message name}> {RPC
    name}(IAsyncStreamReader<request message name> requestStream,
        ServerCallContext context)
```

Inside this method, there are two ways we can extract individual messages from the `requestStream` parameter. First, we can call the `ReadAllAsync` method in a `foreach` loop, where we will need to `await` on `foreach`, as we did in the previous example. Alternatively, we can call the `MoveNext` method inside a `while` loop and access each message by using the `Current` property. The `MoveNext` method will return `true` if there are still items in the stream and return `false` if there aren't any. It will also move the iterator to the next item so that the `Current` property will be referring to it.

In the preceding example, we are simply iterating through all the request objects, printing their data to the console, and returning a response object once we have processed all of the objects. Next, we will add some client logic that will call this method.

Adding client logic for a client-streaming gRPC call

Let's add a new method to the gRPC client wrapper class. Then, we will add a REST API endpoint to call this method:

1. Add the following `using` statement to the top of the file:

    ```
    using System.Collections.Generic;
    ```

2. Add the following method signature to the `IGrpcClientWrapper` interface in the `ApiGateway` project:

    ```
    Task<bool>
    UpsertDeviceStatusesAsync(IEnumerable<DeviceDetails>
        devices);
    ```

3. Then, add the following method implementation to the `GrpcClientWrapper` class:

    ```
    public async Task<bool>
    UpsertDeviceStatusesAsync(IEnumerable<DeviceDetails>
        devices)
    {
    ```

```csharp
            var client = new DeviceManagement.DeviceManager
                .DeviceManagerClient(channel);
            using var call = client.UpsertDeviceStatuses();
            foreach (var device in devices)
            {
                await call.RequestStream.WriteAsync(new
                    DeviceManagement.DeviceDetails
                    {
                        DeviceId = device.Id,
                        Name = device.Name,
                        Description = device.Description,
                        Status = (DeviceManagement.DeviceStatus)
                            device.Status
                    });
            }
            await call.RequestStream.CompleteAsync();
            var response = await call;
            return response.Success;
        }
```

4. After, add the following endpoint method to the `DevicesController` class:

```csharp
[HttpPost("")]
public async Task PostDeviceStatuses([FromBody]
IEnumerable<DeviceDetails> deviceDetails)
{
    await clientWrapper.UpsertDeviceStatusesAsync
        (deviceDetails);
}
```

Here, a collection of device status objects are being posted to the API endpoint. Then, we created an instance of `AsyncClientStreamingCall` by calling the implementation of the `UpsertDeviceStatuses` method on the client. For each item in the device's status collection, we are creating an implementation of the `DeviceDetails` Protobuf message and immediately placing it on the stream by calling the `WriteAsync` method on the `RequestStream` property of the `AsyncClientStreamingCall` object instance. As soon as we do that, this message becomes available to the server application, which consumes the stream.

Then, we closed the stream by calling the `CompleteAsync` method on the `RequestStream` property. Then, we `await` for the `AsyncClientStreamingCall` instance to extract the response object from it.

Reading streams from the server

A server-streaming gRPC call is the opposite of the client-streaming one. The client sends a singular object in its request. This is what will trigger the server stream to open. While the stream is open, multiple response objects can be sent to the client.

Server streaming is frequently used to retrieve a collection of items from a server. This is what we will use it for in the following example.

Adding a server-streaming RPC to Protobuf

First, we will add a server-streaming *rpc* to the Protobuf definition. In the following example, we will use an empty request object, which is one of the so-called well-known types that we will cover in *Chapter 8, Using Well-Known Types to Make Protobuf More Handy*:

1. Add the following `import` statement above the package directive in the `device_management.proto` file in the `GrpcDependencies` project:

   ```
   import "google/protobuf/empty.proto";
   ```

2. Then, add the following `rpc` definition to the `DeviceManager` service:

   ```
   rpc GetAllStatuses (google.protobuf.Empty) returns
       (stream DeviceDetails);
   ```

In this example, we have imported a Protobuf definition of the `Empty` message type from the Google library of well-known types. This will allow us to send a request that doesn't contain any data in it. The server-streaming `rpc` definition can be identified by the presence of the `stream` keyword in front of the response object, while it's absent in front of the `request` object.

Setting up a server-streaming call on the server side

Now, let's implement the server-streaming call on the server. But before we do that, we will add an object that will store the in-memory cache of device status objects. This will allow us to test the insertion functionality alongside the retrieval functionality:

1. Add the `DeviceStatusCache.cs` file to the root of the `DeviceManagerService` project. The file will contain the following interface definition:

    ```
    using System.Collections.Generic;

    namespace DeviceManagerService
    {
        public interface IDeviceStatusCache
        {
            void UpsertDeviceDetail(DeviceManagement.
              DeviceDetails
              status);
            List<DeviceManagement.DeviceDetails>
              GetAllDeviceDetails();
        }
    }
    ```

2. Then, add the following class to implement it:

    ```
    internal class DeviceStatusCache : IDeviceStatusCache
    {
        private readonly List<DeviceManagement.DeviceDetails>
          deviceStatuses;

        public DeviceStatusCache()
        {
            deviceStatuses = new
              List<DeviceManagement.DeviceDetails>();
        }

        public List<DeviceManagement.DeviceDetails>
          GetAllDeviceDetails()
    ```

```
        {
            return deviceStatuses;
        }

        public void
            UpsertDeviceDetail(DeviceManagement.DeviceDetails
                status)
        {
            deviceStatuses.Add(status);
        }
    }
```

3. Now, let's register this class in the dependency injection system by adding the following statement to the `ConfigureServices` method of the `Startup` class. If you are using .NET 6 template, this statement will need to go into the main body of `Program.cs` file and modified accordingly:

   ```
   services.AddSingleton<IDeviceStatusCache,
       DeviceStatusCache>();
   ```

4. Then, add the following constructor and the `private` field to the `ManagerService` class:

   ```
   private readonly IDeviceStatusCache deviceStatusCache;
   public ManagerService(IDeviceStatusCache
       deviceStatusCache)
   {
       this.deviceStatusCache = deviceStatusCache;
   }
   ```

5. Next, we will add the following `using` statement above the class:

   ```
   using Google.Protobuf.WellKnownTypes;
   ```

6. Then, we will add the following line anywhere inside the `UpsertDeviceStatus` method, before the `return` statement:

   ```
   deviceStatusCache.UpsertDeviceDetail(request);
   ```

7. Now, we will add the following line inside the `foreach` loop of the `UpsertDeviceStatuses` method:

```
deviceStatusCache.UpsertDeviceDetail(status);
```

8. Now, let's add the implementation of the `GetAllStatuses` rpc, as follows:

```
public override async Task GetAllStatuses(Empty request,
IServerStreamWriter<DeviceManagement.DeviceDetails>
responseStream, ServerCallContext context)
{
    foreach (var device in
      deviceStatusCache.GetAllDeviceDetails())
    {
        if (DateTime.UtcNow.AddSeconds(1) > context.
 Deadline)
            break;
        await responseStream.WriteAsync(device);
        await Task.Delay(500);
    }
}
```

The method signature of the server-side server-streaming RPC implementation is as follows:

```
public override Task {RPC name}({request message type}
request, IServerStreamWriter<{response message type}>
responseStream, ServerCallContext context)
```

It doesn't have a return type (other than a plain `Task`) since the client will receive every message as soon as it gets written into the response stream.

In the preceding example, we also demonstrated how to use an important per-call configuration option – deadline. Deadline is a time value that the call is expected to complete. If the call hasn't been completed by the deadline, the call will be terminated and an error will be returned. The deadline configuration parameter can be accessed with any gRPC call type, but it's especially relevant for the calls that deal with streams, as these types of calls are more likely to deal with large volumes of data that take a long time to process.

Because the deadline can be accessed on the server, it can be used to make sure that at least some data is returned instead of the whole call being terminated. In the preceding code, we added a condition that will stop processing the stream when it is within 1 second of the deadline. We also added a delay to make it easier to test the deadline logic.

Making a server-streaming call from a gRPC client

In our `ApiGateway` project, we will add a client implementation of the server-streaming RPC. Then, we will add an API endpoint to call it:

1. First, we need to add the following `using` statement to the `GrpcClientWrapper.cs` file:

    ```
    using Google.Protobuf.WellKnownTypes;
    ```

2. Then, we must add the following method signature to the `IGrpcClientWrapper` interface:

    ```
    Task<IEnumerable<DeviceDetails>> GetAllDevices(int deadlineSeconds = 0);
    ```

3. Now, let's add the implementation of this method to the `GrpcClientWrapper` class. First, we will create an instance of `AsynServerStreamingCall`. We will do so by passing the request object into it. But this time, we will also apply the optional `deadline` parameter:

    ```
    public async Task<IEnumerable<DeviceDetails>>
    GetAllDevices(int deadlineSeconds = 0)
    {
        var client = new DeviceManagement.DeviceManager.
          DeviceManagerClient(channel);
        DateTime? deadline = deadlineSeconds > 0 ?
          DateTime.UtcNow.AddSeconds(deadlineSeconds) : null;
        var call = client.GetAllStatuses(new Empty(),
          deadline:
          deadline);
    }
    ```

4. We will complete this method by reading it from the response stream:

```
var devices = new List<DeviceDetails>();
while (await call.ResponseStream.MoveNext())
{
    var device = call.ResponseStream.Current;
    devices.Add(GetDeviceDetails(device.DeviceId, device.
      Name,
        device.Description, (DeviceStatus)device.Status));
}
return devices;
```

5. Then, we will add the following method to the `DevicesController` class:

```
[HttpGet("")]
public async Task<IEnumerable<DeviceDetails>>
    GetAllDevices([FromQuery] int deadlineSeconds = 0)
{
    return await clientWrapper.
        GetAllDevices(deadlineSeconds);
}
```

Now, we can insert the data into an in-memory cache and retrieve it. We can also verify how our server-streaming call behaves if we adjust the `deadlineSeconds` value. So long as there aren't any processes that interfere with your deployment and create additional latency, you should expect the `GetAllDevices` endpoint to always return data. However, the quantity of data you receive is expected to vary, depending on the deadline's duration.

With that, we have covered how gRPC can be used to stream data either from the client to the server or from the server to the client. But it's also possible to stream data in both directions at the same time. This is what we will cover next.

Enabling bi-directional streaming

We have now reached the final type of gRPC call—a bi-directional streaming RPC. As the name suggests, this RPC can have both client-initiated and server-initiated streams – and those streams don't necessarily have to depend on one another.

Enabling server-side components for bi-directional streaming

As we did previously, first, we will add a bi-directional `rpc` to the relevant `proto` file. Then, we will add the method's implementation to our C# code:

1. First, we will add the following `rpc` definition to the `DeviceManager` service definition in the `device_management.proto` file, which is located in the `GrpcDependencies` project:

   ```
   rpc UpdateAndConfirmBatch (stream DeviceDetails) returns
   (stream DeviceDetails);
   ```

2. Add the following method signature to the `IDeviceStatusCache` interface of the `DeviceManagerService` project:

   ```
   DeviceManagement.DeviceDetails GetDevice(int deviceId);
   ```

3. Add the following method implementation to the `DeviceStatusCache` class:

   ```csharp
   public DeviceManagement.DeviceDetails GetDevice(int
      deviceId)
   {
       return deviceStatuses.FirstOrDefault(d => d.DeviceId
          == deviceId);
   }
   ```

4. Now, add the following implementation of this method to the `ManagerService` class inside the `DeviceManagerService` project:

   ```csharp
   public override async Task
   UpdateAndConfirmBatch(IAsyncStreamReader
   <DeviceManagement.Devi
      ceDetails> requestStream, IServerStreamWriter
         <DeviceManagement.DeviceDetails> responseStream,
            ServerCallContext context)
   {
       await foreach (var device in requestStream.
          ReadAllAsync())
       {
           deviceStatusCache.UpsertDeviceDetail(device);
   ```

```
            var newDevice =
                deviceStatusCache.GetDevice(device.DeviceId);

            if (newDevice is not null)
                await responseStream.WriteAsync(newDevice);
            await Task.Delay(500);
        }
    }
```

In a `proto` file, a bi-directional streaming `rpc` can be identified by the `stream` keyword, which is next to both the request and response message definitions. The method signature of the C# implementation of a bi-directional streaming method is as follows:

```
public override Task {RPC name}(IAsyncStreamReader<{request
    message name}> requestStream, IServerStreamWriter<{response
        message name}>
responseStream, ServerCallContext context)
```

In this example, we are inserting multiple `DeviceDetails` objects into the memory cache and, for each of them, we query the cache to verify that it has been inserted successfully. This is an example of using a bi-directional stream in a request-response fashion. For each read of the client stream, there is a write into the server stream. But it doesn't have to be like this. The streams can be made completely independent of each other.

We have also added a delay to the method. It was placed there so you can see what happens if a gRPC call exceeds a deadline.

Adding a client-side implementation of a bi-directional streaming call

Now, let's update the gRPC client wrapper inside the `ApiGateway` project and add a REST API endpoint to call the bi-directional streaming method:

1. In the `IGrpcClientWrapper` interface, add the following method signature:

    ```
    Task<IEnumerable<DeviceDetails>>
    UpdateAndConfirmBatch(IEnumerable<DeviceDetails> devices,
        int
    deadlineSeconds = 0);
    ```

2. Then, add the implementation of this method to the `GrpcClientWrapper` class. First, create an instance of the client and initiate a bi-directional streaming call:

   ```
   public async Task<IEnumerable<DeviceDetails>>
   UpdateAndConfirmBatch(IEnumerable<DeviceDetails> devices,
     int
     deadlineSeconds = 0)
   {
       var client = new DeviceManagement.DeviceManager.
         DeviceManagerClient(channel);
       DateTime? deadline = deadlineSeconds > 0 ?
         DateTime.UtcNow.AddSeconds(deadlineSeconds) : null;
       var call = client.UpdateAndConfirmBatch(deadline:
         deadline);


   }
   ```

3. Next, add a task that will listen to the server stream and populate a local collection variable from it:

   ```
   var outputDevices = new List<DeviceDetails>();
   var readTask = Task.Run(async () =>
   {
       await foreach (var device in
         call.ResponseStream.ReadAllAsync())
       {
           outputDevices.Add(GetDeviceDetails(device.
             DeviceId, device.Name, device.Description,
               (DeviceStatus) device.Status));
       }
   });
   ```

4. Then, populate the request stream:

   ```
   foreach (var device in devices)
   {
       await call.RequestStream.WriteAsync(new
         DeviceManagement.DeviceDetails
         {
   ```

```
            DeviceId = device.Id,
            Name = device.Name,
            Description = device.Description,
            Status = (DeviceManagement.DeviceStatus)device.
            Status
        });
    }
```

5. We will complete the method by closing the request stream and waiting for the response stream listener to finish:

    ```
    await call.RequestStream.CompleteAsync();
    await readTask;
    return outputDevices;
    ```

6. Finally, add the following endpoint method to the `DevicesController` class:

    ```
    [HttpPost("batch")]
    public async Task<IEnumerable<DeviceDetails>>
      PostDeviceStatusBatch(
            [FromBody] IEnumerable<DeviceDetails>
                deviceDetails,
            [FromQuery] int deadlineSeconds = 0)
    {
        return await clientWrapper.UpdateAndConfirmBatch
          (deviceDetails, deadlineSeconds);
    }
    ```

Now, we can launch our application and see how the streaming methods operate. We will also be able to see how they deal with deadline configuration.

Testing how to stream gRPC calls

Let's launch our applications by executing the `dotnet run` command in both the `DeviceManagerService` and `ApiGateway` project folders. By doing this, we can see how the `deadline` parameter affects the execution of the call.

We don't have any deadline-handling logic in the backend of the `UpdateAndConfirmBatch` gRPC call. So, if we call the `POST Devices/batch` endpoint via the Swagger page with a collection of input values while setting the `deadlineSeconds` parameter to 1, we expect to receive a `DeadlineExceeded` error, as shown in the following screenshot:

```
Grpc.Core.RpcException: Status(StatusCode="DeadlineExceeded", Detail="")
   at Grpc.Net.Client.Internal.HttpContentClientStreamReader`2.MoveNextCore(CancellationToken cancellationToken)
   at Grpc.Core.AsyncStreamReaderExtensions.ReadAllAsyncCore[T](IAsyncStreamReader`1 streamReader, CancellationToken ca
   at Grpc.Core.AsyncStreamReaderExtensions.ReadAllAsyncCore[T](IAsyncStreamReader`1 streamReader, CancellationToken ca
e<System.Boolean>.GetResult()
   at ApiGateway.GrpcClientWrapper.<>c__DisplayClass8_0.<<UpdateAndConfirmBatch>b__0>d.MoveNext() in C:\repos\Chapter-0
--- End of stack trace from previous location ---
   at ApiGateway.GrpcClientWrapper.<>c__DisplayClass8_0.<<UpdateAndConfirmBatch>b__0>d.MoveNext() in C:\repos\Chapter-0
--- End of stack trace from previous location ---
   at ApiGateway.GrpcClientWrapper.UpdateAndConfirmBatch(IEnumerable`1 devices, Int32 deadlineSeconds) in C:\repos\Chap
202
   at ApiGateway.Controllers.DevicesController.PostDeviceStatusBatch(IEnumerable`1 deviceDetails, Int32 deadlineSeconds
lers\DevicesController.cs:line 50
   at lambda_method479(Closure , Object )
   at Microsoft.AspNetCore.Mvc.Infrastructure.ActionMethodExecutor.AwaitableObjectResultExecutor.Execute(IActionResultT
ler, Object[] arguments)
   at Microsoft.AspNetCore.Mvc.Infrastructure.ControllerActionInvoker.<InvokeActionMethodAsync>g__Awaited|12_0(Controll
```

Figure 7.5 – The DeadlineExceeded error is displayed if the gRPC call could not be completed before the deadline

However, if we insert a collection of device statuses via the `POST Devices/` endpoint, we will still be able to retrieve them via the `GET Devices/` endpoint. It just won't be the full collection if we set a short deadline. For example, setting the deadline to 2 seconds causes the endpoint to return two out of the four items that are stored in the cache, as shown in the following screenshot:

```
[
    {
        "id": 1,
        "name": "Test1",
        "description": "Test 1",
        "status": 0
    },
    {
        "id": 2,
        "name": "Test2",
        "description": "Test 2",
        "status": 0
    }
]
```

Figure 7.6 – A deadline of 2 seconds prevented the full collection from being returned

This is because the gRPC method that was called, `GetAllStatuses`, had deadline-handling logic in the backend. And instead of just terminating the call and returning no data, it returned as much data as it could.

With that, we have covered the different types of gRPC calls in detail. Now, let's summarize what we have learned.

Summary

In this chapter, you learned that gRPC supports four types of calls – unary, client streaming, server streaming, and bi-directional streaming. You learned that in a Protobuf definition, the type of the call is controlled by the `stream` keyword or a lack thereof.

We looked at the server-side method signatures that are used for implementing gRPC calls of different kinds. Each of these signatures includes the `context` parameter, as well as the actual request and response data. This parameter is used for extracting metadata from the call, which may include user information and request headers.

You also learned that a gRPC channel can be configured by using the `GrpcChannelOptions` object. This object allows you to restrict the message's size, reuse `HttpClient`, apply any custom middleware logic, and more.

We also looked at what happens when multiple gRPC implementations correspond to the same HTTP path. If those paths have identical `service` and `rpc` names, an error will be returned. If you don't implement any specific gRPC method in the server-side application, the gRPC middleware will also return an error.

You then learned that individual gRPC calls can have a deadline configured. The call will fail if the deadline is exceeded. However, because the deadline can be accessed by the server-side implementations of RPCs, you can use it on the server to make sure that a valid result is always returned before the deadline is exceeded.

In the next chapter, we will look at how to use the so-called well-known types from the Google Protobuf library so that you can easily handle nullable objects, empty messages, and other data types that aren't available in Protobuf natively, such as date and time representations.

Questions

Answer the following questions to test your knowledge of this chapter:

1. Can you use Protobuf with no package defined?

    A. No

    B. Yes

    C. Only if there is a `csharp_namespace` directive

    D. Only if you import another Protobuf definition

2. How can you extract response metadata from a unary gRPC call?

    A. It's not possible.

    B. Only when you make blocking synchronous calls.

    C. Only when you make asynchronous calls.

    D. When you make either a synchronous or an asynchronous call.

3. What exception will be thrown if there is a clash between server-side Protobuf implementations?

    A. `Unknown`

    B. `NotFound`

    C. `Unimplemented`

    D. `Unresolved`

4. What is the `deadline` parameter used for in a gRPC call?

    A. To set the delay on the call

    B. To let the server know the client's preferences regarding the response duration

    C. To set a strict timeout on the call's completion time

    D. To synchronize the clocks between the server and the client

5. How do you define a bi-directional streaming call in Protobuf?

    A. By using the `stream` keyword before the request message definition

    B. By using the `stream` keyword before the response message definition

    C. By using the `stream` keyword before the RPC name

    D. By using the `stream` keyword between both the request and response message definitions

Further reading

To learn more about the topics that were covered in this chapter, take a look at the following resources:

- *ASP.NET Core gRPC call types*: https://docs.microsoft.com/en-us/aspnet/core/grpc/client
- *gRPC for .NET Configuration*: https://docs.microsoft.com/en-us/aspnet/core/grpc/configuration
- *gRPC and Deadlines*: https://grpc.io/blog/deadlines/

8
Using Well-Known Types to Make Protobuf More Handy

We learned in *Chapter 3, Protobuf – the Communication Protocol of gRPC*, that data types that are native to Protobuf cannot be null and must have the default value. The default value will be applied if you don't explicitly set the value in the code. For example, the default value for the `string` data type is an empty `string` value. The default value for any of the integer data types is 0. The default value for `bool` is `false`.

This presents a problem. Sometimes, you will be in a situation where you will need to distinguish between a value that has been deliberately set and a value that was automatically set to the default. For example, the count of 0 has a different meaning than "no data." Likewise, Boolean `false` has a very different meaning from "no answer has been given."

Luckily, there is a neat solution to this problem. Protobuf has access to a library of so-called "well-known types." This library provides you with a collection of wrapper data types that make the standard Protobuf data types nullable. The default value of a nullable data type is `null`. And this is what makes them ideal for the scenarios where it's important to know the difference between the absence of data and any value that has been deliberately assigned.

But the library of well-known types doesn't stop there. It also provides you with commonly used data types that aren't natively available in Protobuf. These include representations of dates and time durations.

These libraries also give you a mechanism of putting an empty message in either the request or the response. Finally, it has a mechanism of applying any arbitrary message type to a field without having to write a complex `oneof` block.

We will cover the following topics:

- Using nullable types in Protobuf
- Using dates and times in Protobuf
- Exchanging empty messages
- Using loosely-types fields in a Protobuf message

By the end of this chapter, you will have learned how to make your Protobuf definitions much more flexible without having to make them excessively complex and less readable.

Technical requirements

To follow the instructions in this chapter, you will need the following:

- A computer with either a Windows, Macintosh, or Linux operating system
- A supported IDE or code editor (Visual Studio, Visual Studio Code, or JetBrains Rider)
- .NET 5 SDK (or later)
- A self-signed development HTTPS certificate enabled on the machine

The instructions on how to set all of these up were provided in *Chapter 1, Creating a Basic gRPC Application on ASP.NET Core*.

All code samples used in this chapter can be found at `https://github.com/PacktPublishing/Microservices-Communication-in-.NET-Using-gRPC/tree/main/Chapter-08`.

Please visit the following link to check the CiA videos: `https://bit.ly/3ywE4Ta`

Using nullable types in Protobuf

Natively, there are no nullable data types in Protobuf. Any primitive non-message data type, such as `string` or `int32`, has a default value. The default value will be used if the field hasn't been deliberately set to anything. Therefore, if a field of a particular data type in Protobuf returns its default value, it's not easy to determine whether this value was set deliberately or whether the field hasn't been set to anything at all.

The `proto2` version of Protobuf dealt with this option by having the `optional` keyword. However, this keyword was removed from the `proto3` syntax.

Another way of determining whether or not a particular field has been deliberately set is by using a `oneof` block. For example, such a block may have two fields, one carrying the value we are interested in and one telling us whether this value has been set. If the second field is set, then we know that the original field hasn't been set.

But this solution creates some issues. If you have multiple fields of this sort, then your Protobuf definition may be excessively complex and difficult to follow. Therefore, Google has introduced a much more elegant solution – having wrappers for native data types in its importable library.

Wrappers are `message` definitions that encapsulate a primitive data type. So, because a `message` field, unlike a primitive data type, can be set to null, any field that has such `message` definition as its data type is nullable. And because there is a primitive value inside the message, this value can still be transmitted when needed.

But these `message` wrapper definitions aren't treated like any standard `message` definition by the language-specific Protobuf compilers. When you use these fields in the code, you won't have to create a new object and then set a field on it. Instead, the field will be resolved to a nullable data type specific to that language.

For example, if you use an `Int32Value` data type on one of your `message` fields, the C# representation of that type won't be a class called `Int32Value`. It would actually be an `int?` data type, which is a nullable version of `int`.

Wrapper data type names are written in the following format:

```
{PascalCase name of the original primitive data type}Value
```

The full list includes the following:

- `DoubleValue`
- `FloatValue`
- `Int64Value`
- `UInt64Value`
- `Int32Value`
- `UInt32Value`
- `BoolValue`
- `StringValue`
- `BytesValue`

All of these are available in the `google/protobuf/wrappers.proto` Protobuf package, which needs to be imported into your own Protobuf definition before you can start using them. We will now create a sample application that uses these nullable types.

Setting up a gRPC server application

As previously, we will create a solution, which we will then populate with gRPC server application, gRPC client application, and a library that contains shared dependencies:

1. We will create a `GrpcWellKnownTypes` folder and instantiate a solution with the same name inside of it by executing the following command:

   ```
   dotnet new sln
   ```

2. We will then instantiate a gRPC service project inside this folder by executing the following command:

   ```
   dotnet new grpc -o GrpcServiceApp
   ```

3. Next, we will add this project to the solution by executing the following command:

   ```
   dotnet sln add GrpcServiceApp/GrpcServiceApp.csproj
   ```

4. We are now ready to add well-known nullable types to our Protobuf definition. By default, our `GrpcServiceApp` project was created with the `greet.proto` file inside the `Protos` folder. We will open this file and add the following statement after the `syntax = "proto3";` line:

   ```
   import "google/protobuf/wrappers.proto";
   ```

5. Now, we can use nullable types inside our `message` definitions. We will use all of the available types by replacing the content of the `HelloReply` message with the following:

```
message HelloReply {
  google.protobuf.StringValue message = 1;
  google.protobuf.UInt32Value message_processed_count =
     2;
  google.protobuf.UInt64Value message_length_in_bytes =
     3;
  google.protobuf.Int32Value message_length_in_letters =
     4;
  google.protobuf.Int64Value milliseconds_to_deadline =
     5;
  google.protobuf.FloatValue seconds_to_deadline = 6;
  google.protobuf.DoubleValue minutes_to_deadline = 7;
  google.protobuf.BoolValue last_name_present = 8;
  google.protobuf.BytesValue message_bytes = 9;
}
```

We have now added representations of all wrapper fields to the Protobuf definition. Now, we can build the application and have a look at how these fields are represented in C#.

Examining auto-generated code for wrapper fields

If we open the `Greet.cs` file that should have been placed inside the `Protos` folder in the `obj` folder of the `GrpcWellKnownTypes` project, we can have a look at the code that has been generated for our `HelloReply` message definition that is populated by wrapper data types of every kind. Let's first examine the representation of the following field:

```
google.protobuf.StringValue message = 1;
```

This field is represented by `string` data type in C#, which makes it no different from a regular `string` Protobuf field. This is because the `string` type in C# is nullable already. This can be seen in the following screenshot:

```csharp
/// <summary>Field number for the "message" field.</summary>
0 references
public const int MessageFieldNumber = 1;
21 references
private static readonly pb::FieldCodec<string> _single_message_codec = pb::FieldCodec.ForClassWrapper<string>(10);
56 references
private string message_;
[global::System.Diagnostics.DebuggerNonUserCodeAttribute]
[global::System.CodeDom.Compiler.GeneratedCode("protoc", null)]
81 references
public string Message {
  get { return message_; }
  set {
    message_ = value;
  }
}
```

Figure 8.1 – C# representation of a StringValue field

Next, let's have a look at C# code for the following field:

```
google.protobuf.UInt32Value message_processed_count = 2;
```

As the following screenshot shows, the `UInt32Value` data type is represented by the `uint?` data type in C#, which is a nullable version of `uint`:

```csharp
/// <summary>Field number for the "message_processed_count" field.</summary>
0 references
public const int MessageProcessedCountFieldNumber = 2;
21 references
private static readonly pb::FieldCodec<uint?> _single_messageProcessedCount_codec = pb::FieldCodec.ForStructWrapper<uint>(18);
56 references
private uint? messageProcessedCount_;
[global::System.Diagnostics.DebuggerNonUserCodeAttribute]
[global::System.CodeDom.Compiler.GeneratedCode("protoc", null)]
81 references
public uint? MessageProcessedCount {
  get { return messageProcessedCount_; }
  set {
    messageProcessedCount_ = value;
  }
}
```

Figure 8.2 – C# representation of UInt32Value data type

We will then move on to the following field:

```
google.protobuf.UInt64Value message_length_in_bytes = 3;
```

As the following screenshot demonstrates, the `UInt64Value` data type is represented by `ulong?`, which is a nullable version of `ulong`:

```
/// <summary>Field number for the "message_length_in_bytes" field.</summary>
0 references
public const int MessageLengthInBytesFieldNumber = 3;
21 references
private static readonly pb::FieldCodec<ulong?> _single_messageLengthInBytes_codec = pb::FieldCodec.ForStructWrapper<ulong>(26);
66 references
private ulong? messageLengthInBytes_;
[global::System.Diagnostics.DebuggerNonUserCodeAttribute]
[global::System.CodeDom.Compiler.GeneratedCode("protoc", null)]
81 references
public ulong? MessageLengthInBytes {
  get { return messageLengthInBytes_; }
  set {
    messageLengthInBytes_ = value;
  }
}
```

Figure 8.3 – C# representation of the UInt64Value data type

Next, we will examine the following field:

```
google.protobuf.Int32Value message_length_in_letters = 4;
```

In C#, the `Int32Value` data type is represented by the `int?` data type – a nullable version of `int`. This can be seen on the following screenshot:

```
/// <summary>Field number for the "message_length_in_letters" field.</summary>
0 references
public const int MessageLengthInLettersFieldNumber = 4;
21 references
private static readonly pb::FieldCodec<int?> _single_messageLengthInLetters_codec = pb::FieldCodec.ForStructWrapper<int>(34);
58 references
private int? messageLengthInLetters_;
[global::System.Diagnostics.DebuggerNonUserCodeAttribute]
[global::System.CodeDom.Compiler.GeneratedCode("protoc", null)]
81 references
public int? MessageLengthInLetters {
  get { return messageLengthInLetters_; }
  set {
    messageLengthInLetters_ = value;
  }
}
```

Figure 8.4 – C# representation of the Int32Value data type

Next, let's examine the following field:

```
google.protobuf.Int64Value milliseconds_to_deadline = 5;
```

C# representation of this data type would be `long?` – a nullable version of `long`. It can be confirmed by looking at this code:

Figure 8.5 – C# representation of the Int64Value data type

Then, we move on to the data types containing floating-point numbers. We will first examine the following field:

```
google.protobuf.FloatValue seconds_to_deadline = 6;
```

As demonstrated by the following screenshot, in C# this field is represented by a nullable `float` data type:

Figure 8.6 – C# representation of the FloatValue data type

It's the same principle for the following field:

```
google.protobuf.DoubleValue minutes_to_deadline = 7;
```

Using nullable types in Protobuf 291

As the following screenshot demonstrates, the `DoubleValue` data type is represented by a nullable `double` in C#:

Figure 8.7 – C# representation of the DoubleValue data type

Next, we will have a look at the nullable Boolean, which is represented by this field:

```
google.protobuf.BoolValue last_name_present = 8;
```

C# uses a nullable `bool` data type to represent `BoolValue`. This can be seen in the following screenshots:

Figure 8.8 – C# representation of the BoolValue data type

Finally, we have reached the following `BytesValue` field:

```
google.protobuf.BytesValue message_bytes = 9;
```

As the following screenshot demonstrates, C# representation of it is not different from the representation of the standard bytes data type. This is because `ByteString` is a class, which is always nullable in C#:

Figure 8.9 – C# representation of the ByteString data type

We have now had a look at representations of all nullable wrapper data types in C#. Next, we will add some logic to our application to see how these fields are used inside our code.

Adding logic to gRPC server application

We will now add a service to our `GrpcWellKnownTypes` project that keeps count of how many requests have been processed. Then, we will modify the server-side implementation of our Protobuf definition to use this service so that we can populate all the fields that we have added to the `message` response:

1. Add the `MessageCounter.cs` file to the `GrpcWellKnownTypes` project folder and populate it with the following content:

```
namespace GrpcServiceApp
{
    public class MessageCounter
    {
        private uint messageCount = 0;

        public uint IncrementCount()
        {
            messageCount++;
            return messageCount;
        }
    }
}
```

2. Register this class in the dependency injection container by adding the following line to the `ConfigureServices` method of the `Startup` class:

   ```
   services.AddSingleton<MessageCounter>();
   ```

3. Ensure that the `GreeterService.cs` file inside the `Services` folder has the following `using` statements:

   ```
   using System;
   using System.Text;
   using System.Threading.Tasks;
   using Grpc.Core;
   ```

4. Add a constructor and the following private field to the `GreeterService` class:

   ```
   private readonly MessageCounter counter;

   public GreeterService(MessageCounter counter)
   {
       this.counter = counter;
   }
   ```

5. Replace the content of the `SayHello` method with the following:

   ```
   if (!string.IsNullOrWhiteSpace(request.Name))
   {
       var message = "Hello " + request.Name;
       var timeToDeadline = context.Deadline - DateTime.
         UtcNow;
       var messageBytes = Encoding.ASCII.GetBytes(message);

       return Task.FromResult(new HelloReply
       {
           Message = message,
           MessageProcessedCount = counter.IncrementCount(),
           MessageLengthInBytes = (ulong)messageBytes.
             Length,
           MessageLengthInLetters = message.Length,
           MillisecondsToDeadline = timeToDeadline.
             Milliseconds,
   ```

```
            SecondsToDeadline =
                (float)timeToDeadline.TotalSeconds,
            MinutesToDeadline = timeToDeadline.TotalMinutes,
            LastNamePresent = request.Name.Split(' ').Length
                > 1,
            MessageBytes = Google.Protobuf.ByteString.
                CopyFrom(messageBytes)
        });
    }
    return Task.FromResult(new HelloReply());
```

The application is now looking at the content of the request message and populates the response accordingly. If we receive a blank string as the name field of the request, we just return an empty response. Otherwise, we populate each field of the response.

Now, let's move the dependencies to a shared library so that we won't need to duplicate the Protobuf definition in our gRPC client project.

Setting up shared dependencies

We will create a class library inside our solution, which will contain all gRPC references alongside the shared Protobuf definition.

1. Execute the following command inside the GrpcWellKnownTypes solution folder to create the class library:

   ```
   dotnet new classlib -o GrpcDependencies
   ```

2. Add this project to the solution by executing the following command:

   ```
   dotnet sln add GrpcDependencies/GrpcDependencies.csproj
   ```

3. Next, add all relevant NuGet packages to the class library by executing the following command inside the GrpcDependencies project folder:

   ```
   dotnet add GrpcDependencies.csproj package Grpc.Net.Client
   dotnet add GrpcDependencies.csproj package Google.Protobuf
   dotnet add GrpcDependencies.csproj package Grpc.Tools
   ```

```
dotnet add GrpcDependencies.csproj package Grpc.
   AspNetCore
```

4. We will next create the `Protos` folder inside the `GrpcDependencies` project folder and will move the `greet.proto` file there from the `GrpcServiceApp` project. We will then register this Protobuf definition inside the `GrpcDependencies.csproj` file by adding the following snippet to it:

```
<ItemGroup>
    <Protobuf Include="Protos\greet.proto" />
</ItemGroup>
```

5. Next, we will reference this newly created class library from the `GrpcServiceApp.csproj` file. We will also remove any redundant gRPC NuGet dependencies from this file. After doing this, the content of your `GrpcServiceApp.csproj` file should look similar to this:

```
<Project Sdk="Microsoft.NET.Sdk.Web">

    <PropertyGroup>
        <TargetFramework>net5.0</TargetFramework>
    </PropertyGroup>

    <ItemGroup>
        <ProjectReference Include=
            "..\GrpcDependencies\GrpcDependencies.csproj" />
    </ItemGroup>
</Project>
```

We can verify our setup by rebuilding the `GrpcServiceApp` project. Because we haven't changed the `csharp_namespace` directive inside the `greet.proto` file, our code is expected to compile without any further changes.

> **Important Note**
>
> If you are running your server-side application on a Macintosh, you will need to apply some modifications to it. The instruction on how to do so can be found in the *Running a gRPC Service on Mac* section of *Chapter 1, Creating a Basic gRPC Application on ASP.NET Core*.

Next, we will set up the gRPC client. We will then use it to see how nullable data types are handled by the logic that we've placed in our code.

Setting up the gRPC client

This time, for the sake of simplicity, our gRPC client will be a basic console application:

1. Execute the following command inside the `GrpcWellKnownTypes` solution folder to create the console application project:

   ```
   dotnet new console -o GrpcClient
   ```

2. Add the project to the solution by executing the following command:

   ```
   dotnet sln add GrpcClient/GrpcClient.csproj
   ```

3. Reference the shared class library from the console application by adding the following snippet to the `GrpcClient.csproj` file:

   ```
   <ItemGroup>
     <ProjectReference Include=
       "..\GrpcDependencies\GrpcDependencies.csproj" />
   </ItemGroup>
   ```

4. Now, open the `Program.cs` class and ensure that the following `using` statements are applied:

   ```
   using System;
   using GrpcServiceApp;
   using Grpc.Net.Client;
   using System.Threading.Tasks;
   ```

5. Change the signature of `Main` method inside `Program` class to the following:

   ```
   static async Task Main()
   ```

6. Insert the following content into the method:

   ```
   Console.WriteLine("Please enter the gRPC service URL.");
   var url = Console.ReadLine();
   using var channel = GrpcChannel.ForAddress(url);
   var client = new Greeter.GreeterClient(channel);
   ```

```
var proceed = true;

while (proceed)
{
}

Console.WriteLine("Press any key to exit...");
Console.ReadKey();
```

7. Insert the following code into the `while` statement:

```
Console.WriteLine("Please enter the name.");
var name = Console.ReadLine();
var reply = await client.SayHelloAsync( new HelloRequest
  {
   Name = name }, deadline: DateTime.UtcNow.
     AddMinutes(1));
Console.WriteLine("Message: " + reply.Message);
Console.WriteLine("Messages processed: " +
   reply.MessageProcessedCount);
Console.WriteLine("Message length in bytes: " +
   reply.MessageLengthInBytes);
Console.WriteLine("Message length in letters: " +
   reply.MessageLengthInLetters);
Console.WriteLine("Milliseconds to deadline: " +
   reply.MillisecondsToDeadline);
Console.WriteLine("Seconds to deadline: " +
   reply.SecondsToDeadline);
Console.WriteLine("Minutes to deadline: " +
   reply.MinutesToDeadline);
Console.WriteLine("Last name present: " +
   reply.LastNamePresent);
Console.WriteLine("Message bytes: " + reply.
   MessageBytes);
```

We are now ready to run our application and see how it performs with different inputs.

Running the application

To launch the applications, execute `dotnet run` command in `GrpcServiceApp` folder. Then do the same in `GrpcClient` folder. Once the console application is up and running, you will be prompted to type the URL of the gRPC service, which can be found in the `launchSettings.json` file of the `GrpcServiceApp` project. It should be `https://localhost:5001` by default. However, if you are using Mac, it will be `http://localhost:5000`.

Once the application is up and running, you will be able to apply any custom value to the `name` field of the request object. We do so when by typing the value in the console when prompted. And we will get a response object with all of its fields populated, as can be seen on the following screenshot:

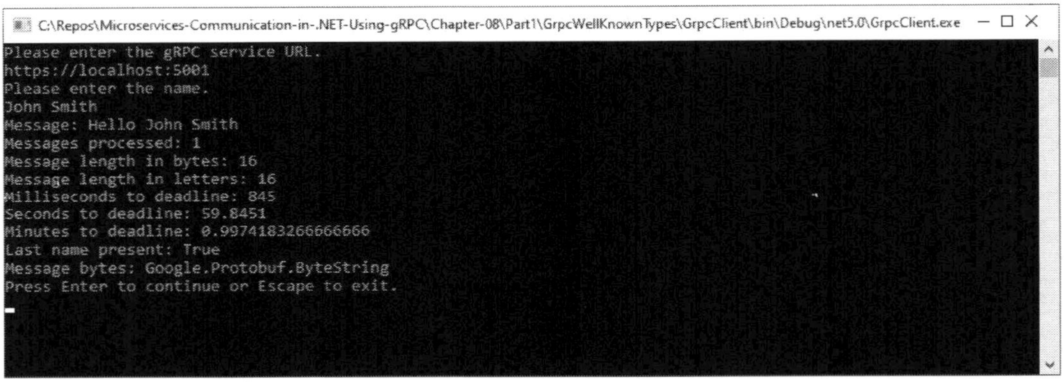

Figure 8.10 – Console output when the name is provided

However, when we don't provide the name, all the fields in our response object will be set to `null` and show as blank in the console. This can be seen in the following screenshot:

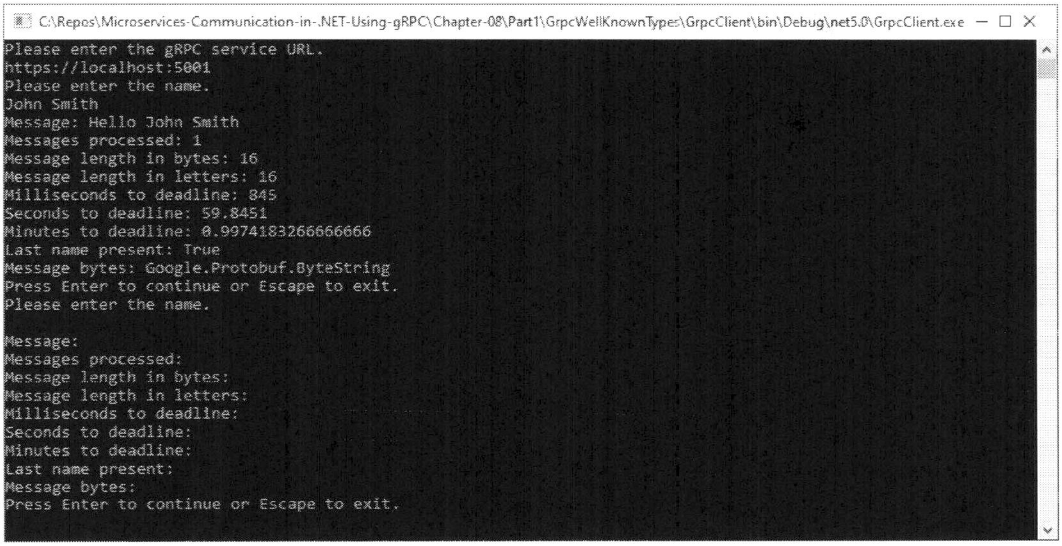

Figure 8.11 – Console output when no name is provided

And this concludes our overview of nullable wrapper data types in Protobuf. Next, we will have a look at data types related to dates and times, which are also missing from the native Protobuf syntax.

Using dates and times in Protobuf

Date and time values are frequently used by software developers. So are data types representing durations. But they are completely missing from Protobuf.

There are some workarounds that can be applied. For example, we can transfer an integer value that represents a number of milliseconds from a specific date. Alternatively, we can construct our own `message` definitions that store days, months, years, hours, minutes, and seconds. But these workarounds are not necessarily easy to implement. For example, if we choose to represent a date as milliseconds only, there is no guarantee that both the client and the server use the same date as the standard origin. Likewise, if we opt to use a custom `message` definition, we will need to write additional code to convert it into proper date and time data in both the client and the server applications.

Luckily, Google's library of well-known types has a much better solution for it. It has two data types to represent time – `Timestamp` and `Duration`. `Timestamp` represents a point in time. It consists of all recognizable date and time components – hours, days, years, and so on. It is equivalent to either `DateTime` or `DateTimeOffset` in C#. `Duration` also contains a recognizable date and time components. But it represents a difference between two points in time rather than a single date/time value. In C#, the closest equivalent is `TimeSpan`. And, just like subtracting one `DateTime` value from another will give you a `TimeSpan` in C#, subtracting one `Timestamp` value from another will give you a `Duration`.

We will now add both of these data types to our application. You will then be able to examine them more closely.

Adding timestamp and duration to the server

We will first add the necessary `import` statements and fields to our Protobuf definition. Then, we will populate these fields in our server-side gRPC application.

1. Open `greet.proto` file in `GrpcDependencies` project and add the following `import` statements to it:

    ```
    import "google/protobuf/duration.proto";
    import "google/protobuf/timestamp.proto";
    ```

2. Then, add the following field to the `HelloRequest` message definition:

    ```
    google.protobuf.Timestamp request_time_utc = 2;
    ```

3. Now, add the following fields to `HelloReply` message definition:

    ```
    google.protobuf.Timestamp response_time_utc = 10;
    google.protobuf.Duration call_processing_duration = 11;
    ```

4. We will now slightly change the implementation of `SayHello` method in `GreeterService` class of `GrpcServiceApp` project. Replace the list of local variables before the first `return` statement with the following:

    ```
    var message = "Hello " + request.Name;
    var currentTime = DateTime.UtcNow;
    var timeToDeadline = context.Deadline - currentTime;
    var messageBytes = Encoding.ASCII.GetBytes(message);
    ```

5. Then, add the following field assignment to the response class initialization inside the `return` statement (don't forget to add a comma at the end of the previous field assignment):

   ```
   ResponseTimeUtc = Timestamp.FromDateTime(currentTime),
   CallProcessingDuration = Timestamp.
     FromDateTime(currentTime) - request.RequestTimeUtc
   ```

6. To make it compile, we will need to add the following `using` statement to the class:

   ```
   using Google.Protobuf.WellKnownTypes;
   ```

Here, we have provided an example of how we can populate `Timestamp` and `Duration` fields from C# code. These are represented in C# by classes of the same names. But they can be easily populated from the standard `TimeSpan`, `DateTime`, and `DateTimeOffset` data types from the `System` library.

`Timestamp` can be populated from `DateTime` or `DateTimeOffset` by using either the `FromDateTime` or `FromDateTimeOffset` static method respectively. `Duration` can be populated from `TimeSpan` by using the `FromTimeSpan` static method, but it can also be calculated by subtracting one `Timestamp` value from another.

Next, we will set up our client and test our application.

Applying changes to the gRPC client and launching the app

We will make slight modifications to our client. Then, we will see how `Timestamp` and `Duration` values are represented inside the console:

1. In the `Main` method of the `Program` class of `GrpcClient` project, add the following `using` statement:

   ```
   using Google.Protobuf.WellKnownTypes;
   ```

2. Then, replace the call to the `SayHelloAsync` method on the client object with the following:

   ```
   var reply = await client.SayHelloAsync(
     new HelloRequest { Name = name, RequestTimeUtc =
       Timestamp.FromDateTime(DateTime.UtcNow) }, deadline:
         DateTime.UtcNow.AddMinutes(1));
   ```

3. Then, add the following lines to the block of console outputs:

```
Console.WriteLine("Call processing duration: " +
    reply.CallProcessingDuration);
Console.WriteLine("Response time UTC: " +
    reply.ResponseTimeUtc);
```

We have finished adding `Timestamp` and `Duration` to both our client and our server. Next, we will launch both of these applications to see how this data is processed.

After launching both of the applications, specifying the address of the gRPC server, and entering an arbitrary name, we can see console output similar to the one displayed in the following screenshot:

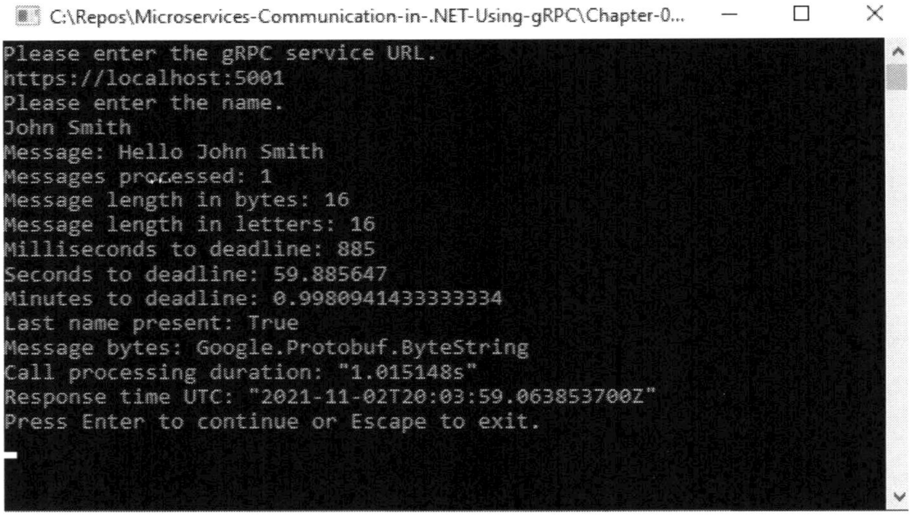

Figure 8.12 – Console output now includes Timestamp and Duration

As we can see, both `Timestamp` and `Duration` are written in a nice human-readable format. This is because both of them have an implementation of the `ToString` method in C#, which gets called automatically when they are used in a `string` context. And it's this method that is set to output the values in a nice human-readable format.

Next, we will have a look at how to use empty requests and responses in Protobuf, which can be really convenient in certain use cases.

Exchanging empty messages

Each remote procedure call in gRPC must have a request and a response message defined. You cannot have an RPC that doesn't accept an input parameter or doesn't return an output object. However, there are many use cases where either a request parameter or a response object would be redundant. For example, if you would want to retrieve a full unfiltered collection of data, you wouldn't need to specify the request attributes. Likewise, if you want to submit a new entry to the server, you probably won't expect to receive any data back. All you'll need is a basic confirmation that your action was successful.

When you use standard HTTP, both of these actions are easily achievable. A simple `GET` request that contains only a URL path and no parameters can be made to obtain an unfiltered collection of data. Likewise, when you submit a `PUT`, `POST`, `PATCH`, or `DELETE` request, you won't usually receive any data back (although in some situations you could). All you will usually care about is that your action was successful. And this would be indicated by an HTTP response code in the correct range (200 to 204).

But luckily, on gRPC, even though you must define both a `message` request and response, you don't necessarily need to have any fields in either of them. A completely empty `message` definition is still a valid `message` definition according to Protobuf. Therefore, if you really don't need to use any specific parameters in any given situation, you can just create a `message` definition with no fields.

But there is an even better way than creating your own empty `message` definition. There is already the `Empty` data type that is available via the Google library of well-known types. The disadvantage of using a custom empty `message` definition is that there is no guarantee that someone would not misunderstand the intention behind it and wouldn't add some fields to it in the future. But if you use the `Empty` type from the library of well-known types, the intention behind it will be clear to everyone using the code.

Next, we will make some changes to our application to demonstrate the usage of the `Empty` data type.

Adding the Empty data type to the server-side application

We will start by adding some `rpc` definitions to our Protobuf file. Then, we will implement these RPCs on the server side:

1. In the `greet.proto` file inside the `GrpcDependencies` project, we will add the following `import` statement:

   ```
   import "google/protobuf/empty.proto";
   ```

2. Then, add the following two `rpc` definitions to the `Greeter` service:

```
rpc GetMessageProcessedCount (google.protobuf.Empty) 
  returns 
    (MessageCount);
rpc SynchronizeMessageCount (MessageCount) returns
    (google.protobuf.Empty);
```

3. Then, add the following `message` definition to the file:

```
message MessageCount {
    uint32 count = 1;
}
```

4. We will now modify the `MessageCounter` class inside the `GrpcServiceApp` project. We will add the following two methods to it:

```
public uint GetCurrentCount()
{
    return messageCount;
}

public void UpdateCount(uint count)
{
    messageCount = count;
}
```

5. Next, we will make some changes to the `GreeterService` class. We will first add the implementation of `GetMessageProcessedCount` that has an empty request:

```
public override Task<MessageCount>
  GetMessageProcessedCount(Empty request,
    ServerCallContext
    context)
{
    return Task.FromResult(new MessageCount
    {
        Count = counter.GetCurrentCount()
```

```
    });
}
```

6. Then, we will add the implementation of `SynchronizeMessageCount` that has an empty response:

```
public override Task<Empty>
    SynchronizeMessageCount(MessageCount request,
        ServerCallContext context)
{
    counter.UpdateCount(request.Count);
    return Task.FromResult(new Empty());
}
```

So, here is what we've done. Previously, the count of processed messages was incremented every time the `SayHello` RPC was called, but it only happened if the name attribute was provided. Also, there was no way to retrieve the count without incrementing it.

Now, we have added an RPC specifically to retrieve the count. Because there is only one kind of count, we don't really need to specify anything in the request parameters. Therefore, we are using an empty request.

We have also added an RPC to update the count. For example, our client might count every message and not just the ones that had the name parameter defined. In this case, it may tell our server what the count should be updated to. And because we only care that this action is successful, we don't need any data in the server response. Therefore the response is empty.

Now, we will modify our client so that it can interact with our new RPCs.

Applying an Empty object on the client

We will now modify our gRCP client console application so that it won't be limited to only a single action. We will be able to choose which RPC to call:

1. At the beginning of the `while` loop inside the `Main` method of the `Program` class of the `GrpcClient` project, add the following prompt:

```
Console.WriteLine("Which acion you would like to take?");
Console.WriteLine("1 - get a greeting.");
Console.WriteLine("2 - Receive message count");
```

```
    Console.WriteLine("3 - Update message count");

    var action = Console.ReadLine();
```

2. Then, immediately after this, add the following `switch` statement:

```
switch (action)
{
    case "1":
        break;
    case "2":
        var couterResponse = await client.
            GetMessageProcessed
            CountAsync(new Empty());
        Console.WriteLine("Message processed count: " +
            couterResponse.Count);
        break;
    case "3":
        Console.WriteLine("Please type new message
            count:");
        var messageCount = Console.ReadLine();
        await client.SynchronizeMessageCountAsync(new
            MessageCount { Count = uint.Parse(messageCount)
                });
        Console.WriteLine("Message count successfully
            updated to " + messageCount);
        break;
    default:
        Console.WriteLine("Invalid selection option.");
        break;
}
```

3. Then, cut and paste all the lines starting with `Console.WriteLine("Please enter the name.");` and ending with `Console.WriteLine("Response time UTC: " + reply.ResponseTimeUtc);` inside the `case "1"` condition.

And this concludes our client setup. We can now launch our applications and verify that both of our new gRPC endpoints work correctly. As the following screenshot demonstrates, we should be able to update the message count to any arbitrary number. Then, this will be the number the server will return to us:

```
Please enter the gRPC service URL.
https://localhost:5001
Which action you would like to take?
1 - get a greeting.
2 - Receive message count
3 - Update message count
3
Please type new message count:
125
Message count successfully updated to 125
Press Enter to continue or Escape to exit.
Which action you would like to take?
1 - get a greeting.
2 - Receive message count
3 - Update message count
2
Message processed count: 125
Press Enter to continue or Escape to exit.
```

Figure 8.13 – gRPC console output indicating that both of our newly added endpoints are working

To recap, you would use an empty request in a situation where there you cannot (or don't want to) apply a specific configuration to your query. For example, this will apply when you would want to retrieve a complete and unfiltered collection of items. Likewise, it would apply if there is only one kind of value that the endpoint can return (only one count value, as per the preceding example, or any other type of unconfigurable data).

An empty response is appropriate when you are performing an operation that creates, updates, or deletes some record or multiple records. All you would want in this case is that the operation was successful. And for this, an absence of errors in the response would be sufficient.

Next, you will learn what to do if the data type of any particular Protobuf field cannot be known in advance. The library of well-known types has an answer for this situation too.

Using loosely typed fields in a Protobuf message

So far, we have only used examples of strongly typed Protobuf definitions, which means that, if we have set the data type of any particular field, it cannot just dynamically change to a different data type. Yes, some data types are compatible with each other. For example, you can send an `int32` value to an `int64` field. But what you can't do is send a `string` value where `int64` is expected.

But there might be cases where you will need the ability to change the data type of a variable depending on the situation. For example, this could be relevant when your system is expected to interoperate with loosely typed programming languages, such as JavaScript or PHP, or schema-less messaging formats, such as JSON.

Even C# has this capability, despite being a strongly typed language. In C#, there is a data type called `dynamic`. It can change to any data type depending on requirements.

Luckily, this is possible with gRPC too. There are two data types that allow you to do just that, `Any` and `Value`. If a Protobuf field uses the `Any` data type, its value can be set to any `message` definition. The `Value` data type, on the other hand, is used for basic data types, such as `string`, `bool`, and numeric types.

Without using either of these data types, you would probably be limited to either using byte arrays or writing excessively complex `oneof` statements. It will also be up to you to write complete logic to convert the data into its intended types. But these two well-known types have a range of convenient properties that will make your job much easier. We will now apply them both in our application.

Adding Any and Value data types to the gRPC server

We will first add some additional fields to our Protobuf definition. Then, we will modify our server-side logic to demonstrate how these data types are used in C#:

1. Add the following `import` statements to the `greet.proto` file in the `GrpcDependencies` project:

    ```
    import "google/protobuf/any.proto";
    import "google/protobuf/struct.proto";
    ```

2. Now, add the following two fields to the `HelloRequest` message definition:

    ```
    google.protobuf.Any payload = 3;
    google.protobuf.Value additional_payload = 4;
    ```

3. Add the following `message` definitions at the bottom of the file:

   ```
   message IntegerPayload {
     uint32 value = 1;
   }

   message DoublePayload {
     double value = 1;
   }

   message BooleanPayload {
     bool value = 1;
   }

   message CollectionPayload {
       repeated string list = 1;
       map<string, string> dictionary = 2;
   }
   ```

4. We will now add the following lines at the beginning of the `SayHello` method of the `GreeterService` class of the `GrpcServiceApp` project:

   ```
   Console.WriteLine($"Payload type is: {request.Payload?.
      TypeUrl ?? "No payload provided"}");

   var payloadExtracted = request.Payload is null;
   ```

5. Below it, we will add the following condition, which will check whether we have been provided with an `integer` payload:

   ```
   if (!payloadExtracted && request.Payload.
      Is(IntegerPayload.Descriptor))
   {
         Console.WriteLine($"Extracted the following integer
            value from the payload: {request.Payload.Unpack
               <IntegerPayload>().Value}" );
         Console.WriteLine($"Extracted the following integer
            value from the additional payload: {Convert.ToInt32
   ```

```
        (request.AdditionalPayload.NumberValue)}");
    payloadExtracted = true;
}
```

6. Then, we will add the following condition, which will check whether we have received a double payload:

```
if (!payloadExtracted && request.Payload.TryUnpack
    <DoublePayload>(out var doublePayload))
{
    Console.WriteLine($"Extracted the following double
        value from the payload: {doublePayload.Value}");
    Console.WriteLine($"Extracted the following double
        value from the additional payload:
            {request.AdditionalPayload.NumberValue}");
    payloadExtracted = true;
}
```

7. After this, we will add the following condition, which will check whether we received a Boolean payload:

```
if (!payloadExtracted && request.Payload.TryUnpack
    <BooleanPayload>(out var booleanPayload))
{
    Console.WriteLine($"Extracted the following Boolean
        value from the payload: {booleanPayload.Value}");
    Console.WriteLine($"Extracted the following Boolean
        value from the additional payload:
            {request.AdditionalPayload.BoolValue}");
    payloadExtracted = true;
}
```

8. Finally, there is another condition, to check for a collection payload:

```
if (!payloadExtracted && request.Payload.Is
  (CollectionPayload.Descriptor))
{
    var primaryPayload =
      request.Payload.Unpack<CollectionPayload>();
    var secondaryPayload =
      request.AdditionalPayload.StructValue;

    foreach (var item in primaryPayload.List)
    {
        Console.WriteLine($"Item extracted from the list
          in the primary payload: {item}");
    }

    foreach (var item in primaryPayload.Dictionary)
    {
        Console.WriteLine($"Item extracted from the
          dictionary in the primary payload: key - {item.
            Key}, value - {item.Value}");
    }

    foreach (var field in secondaryPayload.Fields)
    {
        Console.WriteLine($"Item extracted from the
          fields in the secondary payload: key - {field.
            Key}, value - {field.Value.StringValue}");
    }
}
```

In this example, we are processing `Any` and `Value` types simultaneously for the sake of simplicity. We had additional two fields added to the `HelloRequest` message – `payload` and `additional_payload`. The former is of the `Any` type, while the latter is of the `Value` type. Please note that, while the `Any` data type comes from the `any.proto` file of the `google/protobuf` namespace, the `Value` data type comes from the `struct.proto` definition.

We have added some `message` definitions purely for the sake of demonstrating how the `Any` data type works, and we have applied multiple conditional statements to it to demonstrate the different ways this data type can be read.

In its original state, the `Any` data type has two fields – `TypeUrl` and `Value`. `TypeUrl` is a string that contains the fully qualified name of the `message` definition that it holds. The `Value` field holds the actual data as a collection of bytes.

In C#, we are extracting the data from the `Any` data type by calling the `Unpack<T>` method on it, where `T` is the type that we are trying to extract. We can call `Unpack` directly if we know the data type we expect, or we can call `TryUnpack<T>` if we aren't sure about the data type. We can also check whether or not the field contains a message of a particular type by calling the `Is` method on the `Any` data type, which takes the static `Descriptor` property of the message type as its parameter.

The `Value` field works differently. To extract a specific data type from it, we need to call a corresponding static method on the class that represents the `Value` type in C#. The following options are available:

- `NullValue`: Represents `null`
- `NumberValue`: Equivalent to `double`
- `StringValue`: Represents `string`
- `BoolValue`: Represents `bool`
- `ListValue`: Represents a collection of `Value` items
- `StructValue`: `Struct` data type, which is equivalent to a dictionary

In this context, the `Struct` data type is very different from the `struct` keyword available in C#. The `Struct` data type from the `Google.Protobuf` library is a collection of dynamically typed fields, where the field name (which can also be seen as a dictionary key) is a `string`, while the field value is the `Value` data type. In the preceding example, we are unpacking a `Struct` object and outputting all of its keys and values into the console.

Our server-side part of the application is now complete. Next, we will modify our client to populate the `payload` and `additional_payload` fields in the `HelloRequest` message.

Populating the Any and Value fields from the gRPC client

We will add some logic to our gRPC client console application to populate the `Any` and `Value` fields. Then, we will launch both of our applications to see whether the server interprets the data correctly:

1. In the `Main` method of the `Program` class of the `GrpcClient` application, locate the following lines:

    ```
    Console.WriteLine("Please enter the name.");
    var name = Console.ReadLine();
    ```

2. Underneath them, insert the following:

    ```
    Console.WriteLine("Please enter the payload type:");
    Console.WriteLine("1 - integer");
    Console.WriteLine("2 - double");
    Console.WriteLine("3 - boolean");
    Console.WriteLine("4 - collection");

    var payloadType = Console.ReadLine();

    Any payload = null;
    Value additionalPayload = null;
    ```

3. Immediately after this, insert the following `switch` block:

    ```
    switch (payloadType)
    {
        case "1":
            payload = Any.Pack(new IntegerPayload() { Value = 1 });
            additionalPayload = Value.ForNumber(1);
            break;
        case "2":
    ```

```csharp
        payload = Any.Pack(new DoublePayload() { Value =
            1.5 });
        additionalPayload = Value.ForNumber(1.5);
        break;
    case "3":
        payload = Any.Pack(new BooleanPayload() { Value =
            true });
        additionalPayload = Value.ForBool(true);
        break;
    case "4":
        break;
    default:
        Console.WriteLine("No payload value provided.");
        break;
}
```

4. Then, insert the following logic under the `case "4"` statement:

```csharp
var collection = new List<string> { "item1", "item2",
    "item3" };
var dictionary = new Dictionary<string, string> { { "1",
    "item1" }, { "2", "item2" }, { "3", "item3" } };

var collectionPayload = new CollectionPayload();

collectionPayload.List.Add(collection);
collectionPayload.Dictionary.Add(dictionary);

payload = Any.Pack(collectionPayload);
additionalPayload = Value.ForStruct(new Struct
{
    Fields =
        {
            ["1"] = Value.ForString("item1"),
            ["2"] = Value.ForString("item2")
        }
});
```

5. Now, replace the call to the `client.SayHelloAsync` method with the following:

```
var reply = await client.SayHelloAsync(
    new HelloRequest
    {
        Name = name,
        RequestTimeUtc =
            Timestamp.FromDateTime(DateTime.
                UtcNow),
        Payload = payload,
        AdditionalPayload = additionalPayload
    }, deadline: DateTime.UtcNow.AddMinutes(1));
```

Let's quickly overview what we have done. To populate a field that has the `Any` data type, what you need to do is call the static `Pack` method on the `Any` class. Any class that implements the `IMessage` interface (which would be any class that represents a Protobuf message definition) would be a suitable parameter.

To populate a field of `Value` type, we need to call a static method on the `Value` class that corresponds to this data type. The following methods are available:

- `ForNull`: Allows you to set the field to `null`
- `ForNumber`: Allows you to set the field to `double`
- `ForString`: Allows you to set the field to `string`
- `ForBool`: Allows you to set the field to `bool`
- `ForList`: Allows you to set the field to a collection of `Value` items
- `ForStruct`: Allows you to use the `Struct` data type in the field

We now know both how to write data into loosely typed Protobuf fields and how to then read it from them. If we will now launch our applications, we will be able to see whether the data sent by the client gets correctly interpreted by the server.

From the following screenshot of the server-side console, we can see that we have been able to extract the correct types of payload from both the `Any` and `Value` fields:

```
Payload type is: type.googleapis.com/greet.IntegerPayload
Extracted the following integer value from the payload: 1
Extracted the following integer value from the additional payload: 1
info: Microsoft.AspNetCore.Routing.EndpointMiddleware[1]
      Executed endpoint 'gRPC - /greet.Greeter/SayHello'
info: Microsoft.AspNetCore.Hosting.Diagnostics[2]
      Request finished HTTP/2 POST https://localhost:5001/greet.Greeter/Say
grpc 512.7934ms
info: Microsoft.AspNetCore.Hosting.Diagnostics[1]
      Request starting HTTP/2 POST https://localhost:5001/greet.Greeter/Say
info: Microsoft.AspNetCore.Routing.EndpointMiddleware[0]
      Executing endpoint 'gRPC - /greet.Greeter/SayHello'
Payload type is: type.googleapis.com/greet.DoublePayload
Extracted the following double value from the payload: 1.5
Extracted the following double value from the additional payload: 1.5
info: Microsoft.AspNetCore.Routing.EndpointMiddleware[1]
      Executed endpoint 'gRPC - /greet.Greeter/SayHello'
info: Microsoft.AspNetCore.Hosting.Diagnostics[2]
      Request finished HTTP/2 POST https://localhost:5001/greet.Greeter/Say
grpc 14.5028ms
info: Microsoft.AspNetCore.Hosting.Diagnostics[1]
      Request starting HTTP/2 POST https://localhost:5001/greet.Greeter/Say
info: Microsoft.AspNetCore.Routing.EndpointMiddleware[0]
      Executing endpoint 'gRPC - /greet.Greeter/SayHello'
Payload type is: type.googleapis.com/greet.BooleanPayload
Extracted the following Boolean value from the payload: True
Extracted the following Boolean value from the additional payload: True
```

Figure 8.14 – gRPC server has correctly extracted data from the Any and Value fields

The following screenshot demonstrates that, when we populate our loosely typed payload fields with collections of items, the server was also able to successfully extract the correct data from them:

```
Payload type is: type.googleapis.com/greet.CollectionPayload
Item extracted from the list in the primary payload: item1
Item extracted from the list in the primary payload: item2
Item extracted from the list in the primary payload: item3
Item extracted from the dictionary in the primary payload: key - 1, value - item1
Item extracted from the dictionary in the primary payload: key - 2, value - item2
Item extracted from the dictionary in the primary payload: key - 3, value - item3
Item extracted from the fields in the secondary payload: key - 1, value - item1
Item extracted from the fields in the secondary payload: key - 2, value - item2
```

Figure 8.15 – Collections from the Any and Value fields were also correctly processed

We have now completed the overview of loosely typed fields in Protobuf messages. Let's now summarize everything we've covered in this chapter.

Summary

In this chapter, you have learned that it's possible to use nullable data types in Protobuf messages. Even though nullable data types aren't natively available in Protobuf, they can be added to it by importing wrapper data types from Google's library of well-known types.

You have also learned that although there is no native support for time and duration data in Protobuf, there are `Timestamp` and `Duration` data types that have been designed specifically for this purpose. These data types need to be imported into your Protobuf definitions individually.

You now also know that although it is possible to create a Protobuf `message` definition with no fields, the library of well-known types already has a standardized `message` definition specifically to be used as an empty object. Unsurprisingly, it is called `Empty`.

We have also covered two ways you can use loosely typed fields in Protobuf. There is the `Any` data type, which you can use to assign any arbitrary `message` definition to a field. There is also the `Value` type, which allows you to assign any primitive type to a field.

With the help of the examples that we used, you can probably now appreciate how much well-known types simplify the process of writing the code. With the help of various helper methods, there is a convenient way you can convert any of these data types into objects that you can use in your code.

And this concludes the chapter on well-known types. In the next chapter, we will have a detailed look at how to enable and disable encrypted communication while using gRPC, which is an important topic from the perspective of cybersecurity. You will learn how to use any custom TLS certificate in gRPC, as well as create your own.

Questions

1. Which proto file do you need to import to use the `BoolValue` data type?

    A. `google/protobuf/boolvalue.proto`.

    B. `google/protobuf/value.proto`.

    C. `goggle/protobuf/wrappers.proto`.

    D. `google/protobuf/wellknowntypes.proto`.

2. Which of the following does not exist among well-known types in Protobuf?

    A. `Int32Value`.

    B. `Int64Value`.

    C. `Fixed64Value`.

    D. `UInt32Value`.

3. Which of the following statements is incorrect?

    A. `Duration` is equivalent to `DateTimeOffset`.

    B. `Timespan` is equivalent to `DateTimeOffset`.

    C. `Timespan` is equivalent to `DateTime`.

    D. `Duration` is equivalent to `TimeSpan`.

4. Which of these scenarios is suitable for using the `Empty` message in an RPC response?

    A. When updating data.

    B. When inserting data.

    C. When deleting data.

    D. All of the above.

5. How would you unpack a string value from a field of `Any` type?

    A. `Any.SringValue`.

    B. `Any.ForString`.

    C. The `Any` data type cannot store strings.

    D. `Any.Unpack<string>`.

Further reading

- Protocol Buffers well-known types: `https://developers.google.com/protocol-buffers/docs/reference/google.protobuf`
- `google/protobuf/wrappers.proto` Protobuf definition: `https://github.com/protocolbuffers/protobuf/blob/master/src/google/protobuf/wrappers.proto`
- `google/protobuf/empty.proto` Protobuf definition: `https://github.com/protocolbuffers/protobuf/blob/master/src/google/protobuf/empty.proto`
- `google/protobuf/timestamp.proto` Protobuf definition: `https://github.com/protocolbuffers/protobuf/blob/master/src/google/protobuf/timestamp.proto`
- `google/protobuf/duration.proto` Protobuf definition: `https://github.com/protocolbuffers/protobuf/blob/master/src/google/protobuf/duration.proto`
- `google/protobuf/any.proto` Protobuf definition: `https://github.com/protocolbuffers/protobuf/blob/master/src/google/protobuf/any.proto`
- `google/protobuf/struct.proto` Protobuf definition: `https://github.com/protocolbuffers/protobuf/blob/master/src/google/protobuf/struct.proto`

9
Securing gRPC Endpoints in Your ASP.NET Core Application with SSL/TLS

In this chapter, we will learn how to secure your **ASP.NET Core gRPC** service application with **SSL/TLS** certificates. We briefly touched on this topic in *Chapter 1, Creating a Basic gRPC Application on ASP.NET Core*, where we saw how to use the .NET **command-line interface** (**CLI**) to create a self-signed development certificate. We also saw how this allows you to map your hosted application to a port that is accessible via **HTTPS**.

However, a self-signed development certificate is not something you would want to use in production. In a real-life scenario, you would want to protect your application with a bespoke certificate that has been issued by a recognized certification authority. This chapter will cover how such certificates work in detail.

We will cover the following topics:

- Configuring the gRPC client and server for unencrypted communication
- Creating and trusting a self-signed certificate
- Applying certificate authentication on the gRPC client and server

By the end of this chapter, you will have learned how an ASP.NET Core gRPC service application can be hosted for both **HTTP/2** and **HTTP/1.1** with no TLS enabled. You will also have learned how to create and sign your own TLS certificate with custom data. Finally, you will have learned how to use any custom certificate to secure your gRPC service application.

Technical requirements

To follow the instructions in this chapter, you will need the following:

- A computer with either a **Windows** or **Linux operating system** (**OS**) (or a Windows or Linux **virtual machine** (**VM**) if you are using **macOS**)
- A supported **integrated development environment** (**IDE**) or code editor (**Visual Studio**, **Visual Studio Code**, or **JetBrains Rider**)
- The .NET 5 **software development kit** (**SDK**)

> **Note**
> Due to the lack of **Application-Layer Protocol Negotiation** (**ALPN**) support on macOS, it won't be possible to secure HTTP/2 ports with TLS on Macs. Therefore, if you are a Mac user, you will not be able to follow some of the instructions from this chapter. However, you will be able to implement the code samples if you set up either a Windows or Linux VM on your Mac.

The instructions on how to set all of these up were provided in *Chapter 1, Creating a Basic gRPC Application on ASP.NET Core*. All of the code samples used in this chapter can be found at https://github.com/PacktPublishing/Microservices-Communication-in-.NET-Using-gRPC/tree/main/Chapter-09.

Please visit the following link to check the CiA videos: https://bit.ly/3DVcy2F

Configuring the gRPC client and server for unencrypted communication

Before we start talking about the process of securing gRPC endpoints with a custom certificate, we will cover the base case – that is, how to set up your application to run without any such certificate. This is useful for real-life scenarios, as even though gRPC was originally intended to primarily run over TLS, there are situations where using a certificate just adds unnecessary overhead. For example, if a gRPC endpoint represents a microservice that is only ever hosted on your internal network and is never exposed to the public internet, encrypting the communication within it (and going through the entire process of obtaining a valid certificate from a certification authority) might not be necessary.

Likewise, it's not necessary to use encryption when you are writing the software on your development machine. Even though a project created from the gRPC service .NET template will have encryption enabled by default and will work with a self-signed development certificate created by the **dotnet CLI**, it will not work on Mac. An attempt to bind an HTTPS port for a gRPC endpoint will fail. Therefore, if you intend for your software to run on any development machine, it makes sense to apply additional configuration to your project so that it doesn't even attempt to use HTTPS when development mode is applied.

But before we go through the process of configuring gRPC for communication without TLS, let's briefly remind ourselves what TLS is used for.

The role of TLS certificates

TLS stands for **Transport Layer Security**. It is a successor to the **Secure Sockets Layer** (**SSL**) protocol. Even though SSL is now deprecated and isn't being used to secure modern applications, it is very common to hear the terms TLS and SSL used interchangeably. Even some parts of the inbuilt .NET libraries mention *SSL* where it should more accurately be *TLS*. This is why – even though it is technically incorrect – we have included *SSL* in some headings within this chapter.

Server certificates

TLS is a protocol that is designed to encrypt communication between the *client* and the *server*. In TLS, the data is transferred as a collection of seemingly random bytes that only the intended recipient can decrypt. If the message is intercepted, it would be meaningless to the entity that has intercepted it. This is why TLS (and the corresponding **HTTPS**, which stands for **Hypertext Transfer Protocol Secure**) is always used for the transfer of sensitive information such as personal details.

The encryption for TLS is achieved by using **cryptographic keys**. There are two types of keys that are stored by the server application – a public key and a private key. A *public key* is given to the client that wants to communicate with the server. The client can then use it to encrypt the data. But the same key cannot be used to decrypt the data. This can only be done by the *private key*, which the server application *never shares* with anyone.

The keys have been designed in such a way that it's impossible to calculate the private key even if you know the public key. And this is what makes the communication channel *secure*.

Now that we understand how encryption keys are used, we can assess the role of the *certificate*. No TLS communication is possible without one. The *digital certificate* (also known as a *public key certificate*) is a digital document that stores the public key and proves its ownership. The certificate includes information such as the hostname, which tells the connected client that the certificate definitely belongs to the correct server and hasn't been forged.

And here is where the **certification authority (CA)** has its role to play. A CA is a third-party organization that is universally recognized as a valid provider of certificates. The reason why a digital signature from such an organization is necessary is that it is not difficult to create your own digital signature. So, if the client connects to an endpoint that is protected by a *self-signed certificate*, there is no guarantee that such a certificate wasn't forged by a malicious agent. But if the certificate has been signed by a CA, it is guaranteed that you are dealing with a real certificate that has been issued specifically to protect the domain that you are connecting to.

Client certificates

So far, we have covered server-side certificates. But client-side certificates can also be used in TLS. Their purpose, however, is slightly different. And, unlike server-side certificates, they don't necessarily need to be signed by a third-party CA.

Client-side certificates contain information about the client that is trying to connect to the server. They are used for authentication to prove that the client is what it says it is. They are rarely used for browser-based clients because such clients store authentication information in the browser cache and cookies. However, client certificates are useful with **remote procedure calls (RPCs)**.

In this chapter, we will cover both server-side and client-side certificates. But by now, you can probably appreciate that despite the benefits of enabling encryption, TLS certificates create quite a lot of overhead in terms of setup. This means they would affect the performance of your application, as additional computation would be required to encrypt and decrypt messages. This is why it is useful to know how to run your applications without using TLS, which we will demonstrate in the next section.

Setting up a gRPC service application

In this section, we will set up a gRPC service application that will be accessible via both HTTP/1.1 and HTTP/2 without encryption. Our application will be expected to work on any OS, including macOS.

The reason why we need both HTTP/1.1 and HTTP/2 access is that we will be exposing our **proto** files to the clients over standard **REST API** endpoints, and these endpoints will require HTTP/1.1 to function. Please complete the following steps:

1. Run the following command to create a project based on the gRPC service template:

   ```
   dotnet new grpc -o UserInfoManager
   ```

2. Inside the project folder that was created, open the Protos folder and create a users.proto file with the following content:

   ```
   syntax = "proto3";
   package users;
   import "google/protobuf/empty.proto";
   import "google/protobuf/timestamp.proto";
   service UserManager {
       rpc GetAllUsers (google.protobuf.Empty) returns
           (stream UserInfo);
   }

   message UserInfo {
       string first_name = 1;
       string surname = 2;
       string gender = 3;
       google.protobuf.Timestamp date_of_birth = 4;
       string nationality = 5;
       AddressInfo address = 6;
   ```

```
}

message AddressInfo {
    string first_line = 1;
    string town = 2;
    string postcode_or_zip_code = 3;
    string country = 4;
}
```

3. The gRPC service application will deliver personal user information to the client as a stream. This data will originate from the `UserDataCache` class inside the `UserInfoManager` project. So, we will place a `UserDataCache.cs` file into the root of the project folder. The initial file structure will be as follows:

```
using System;
using System.Collections.Generic;
using Google.Protobuf.WellKnownTypes;
using Users;

namespace UserInfoManager
{
    public class UserDataCache
    {
        private readonly List<UserInfo> users;

        public UserDataCache()
        {
            users = new List<UserInfo>();
        }

        public IEnumerable<UserInfo> GetUsers()
        {
            return users;
        }
    }
}
```

4. We can now add as many entries to the list of users as we want. To do so, we can start adding entries at the end of our constructor block in the following way:

```
users.Add(new UserInfo
{
    FirstName = "John",
    Surname = "Smith",
    Gender = "M",
    DateOfBirth =
        Timestamp.FromDateTime(DateTime.UtcNow
            .AddYears(-20)),
    Nationality = "English",
    Address = new AddressInfo
    {
        FirstLine = "51 Park Lane",
        PostcodeOrZipCode = "SW2 5BL",
        Town = "London",
        Country = "UK"
    }
});
```

5. We can now add the `UserInfoService.cs` file to the `Services` folder inside our project. The content of the file will be as follows:

```
using System.Threading.Tasks;
using Google.Protobuf.WellKnownTypes;
using Grpc.Core;
using Users;

namespace UserInfoManager.Services
{
    public class UserInfoService :
        UserManager.UserManagerBase
    {
        private readonly UserDataCache userDataCache;
        public UserInfoService(UserDataCache
            userDataCache)
        {
```

```csharp
            this.userDataCache = userDataCache;
        }
        public override async Task GetAllUsers(Empty
            request, IServerStreamWriter<UserInfo>
            responseStream, ServerCallContext context)
        {
            foreach (var item in
                userDataCache.GetUsers())
            {
                await responseStream.WriteAsync(item);
            }
        }
    }
}
```

6. Now, we need to register all of the components that we have added. First, we will need to add the following markup to the `UserInfoManager.csproj` file:

```xml
<ItemGroup>
    <Protobuf Include="Protos\users.proto"
        GrpcServices="Server" />
</ItemGroup>
```

7. Then, we will add the following statement to the `ConfigureServices` method of the `Startup` class. Alternatively, if we are using .NET 6 project template, we will add this statement to `Program.cs` file before the `Build` event and replace services with `builder.Services`:

```csharp
services.AddSingleton<UserDataCache>();
```

8. Finally, we will add the following statement inside the call to `app.UseEndpoints` in the `Startup` class (or in the main body of `Program.cs` file if we are using .NET 6, replacing endpoints with app):

```csharp
endpoints.MapGrpcService<UserInfoService>();
```

We have now registered our custom endpoints and our application is already pre-configured to use gRPC without TLS. To verify this, we can open the `appsetting.json` file. Inside the `Kestrel` section, it will have a section called `EndpointDefaults`. This section will have an entry called `Protocols`, which should be set to `Http2`. This will mean that both HTTP and HTTPS ports will work with gRPC. However, there are some caveats.

This configuration wouldn't work on macOS, as it will still attempt to bind an HTTPS port for gRPC and fail. As a workaround, you can remove the HTTPS URL from the `launchSettings.json` file. But there is an additional caveat.

This time, we have decided to share **Protobuf** definitions with the clients via REST API endpoints. And in order for these to work, we need to have HTTP/1.1 available. To do so, we could just change the `Protocols` value to `Http1AndHttp2`. But there is an additional caveat to this. gRPC on ASP.NET Core is set up in such a way that if you use the `Http1AndHttp2` option, both protocol versions will work with the HTTPS endpoint. However, any HTTP calls will use HTTP/1.1, which will make the gRPC endpoints unreachable. Therefore, we will need to apply some additional configurations to accommodate these caveats.

Removing TLS on both HTTP/1.1 and HTTP/2

The best way to enable both HTTP/1.1 and HTTP/2 communication in your ASP.NET Core application is to explicitly assign a specific protocol to each specific port. If you assign only HTTP/1.1 to a port, you won't be able to use this port for gRPC. However, it will still be fully accessible by any HTTP client, including your browser. If you assign only HTTP/2 to a specific port, this port will not be accessible by normal HTTP clients. But you will be able to enable unencrypted gRPC communication via this port.

Configuring different ports for different protocol versions can be done via configuration. But we can also do it directly in the code, which will override the configuration. In our case, we will use port `5000` for unencrypted gRPC communication. And we will dedicate port `5002` to unencrypted HTTP communication. To do so, we will open the `Program` class inside the `UserInfoManager` project and replace the `CreateHostBuilder` method with the following. If you are using .NET 6, the `ConfigureKestrel` method will need to be placed after `builder.WebHost.UseKestrel` call in `Program.cs` file.:

```
public static IHostBuilder CreateHostBuilder(string[] args) =>
    Host.CreateDefaultBuilder(args)
        .ConfigureWebHostDefaults(webBuilder =>
        {
```

```
                webBuilder.ConfigureKestrel(options =>
                {
                    options.ListenLocalhost(5002, o =>
                        o.Protocols =
                        HttpProtocols.Http1);
                    options.ListenLocalhost(5000, o =>
                        o.Protocols =
                        HttpProtocols.Http2);
                });
                webBuilder.UseStartup<Startup>();
            });
```

To make it work, we need to include the following `using` statement in the class:

```
using Microsoft.AspNetCore.Server.Kestrel.Core
```

We have added two listeners, both of which are listening on the default IP address of the host machine, which is 127.0.0.1 and is also associated with the `localhost` domain. This is done by calling the `ListenLocalhost` method. And then, we are associating ports 5002 and 5000 with HTTP/1.1 and HTTP/2, respectively.

Please note that our setup would still work if we associated `Http1AndHttp2` with port 5002. In this case, the unencrypted request would be routed to HTTP/1.1 by default. However, it is mandatory to restrict the gRPC port to HTTP/2 to prevent the same from happening.

Next, we will create a REST API endpoint to demonstrate why both HTTP/1.1 and HTTP/2 ports had to be enabled in our gRPC service application in the previous sections.

Exposing Protobuf definitions to clients

Our application will be exposing its Protobuf definitions so that the clients can always get up-to-date information on the schema that the server expects. If you are using Visual Studio on Windows as your IDE, you will be able to automate the process of synchronizing your client with the service application, as will be demonstrated later. But first, we will need to perform the following steps:

1. Add the following line to the `ConfigureServices` method of the `Startup` class of your application (or relevant section of `Program.cs` file if you are using .NET 6 template):

   ```
   services.AddControllers();
   ```

2. Insert the following statement into the `app.UseEndpoints` call:

   ```
   endpoints.MapControllers();
   ```

3. Create a `Controllers` folder inside the project and place a `ProtosController.cs` file into the folder. The content of the file should be as follows:

   ```
   using System.IO;
   using System.Linq;
   using System.Threading.Tasks;
   using Microsoft.AspNetCore.Hosting;
   using Microsoft.AspNetCore.Mvc;

   namespace UserInfoManager.Controllers
   {
       [Route("[controller]")]
       [ApiController]
       public class ProtosController : ControllerBase
       {

           private readonly string baseDirectory;

           public ProtosController(IWebHostEnvironment
               webHost)
           {
               baseDirectory = webHost.ContentRootPath;
           }
       }
   }
   ```

4. Add the following method to the `Controller` class:

```
[HttpGet("")]
public ActionResult GetAll()
{
    return
        Ok(Directory.GetFiles($"{baseDirectory}/Protos")
            .Select(Path.GetFileName));
}
```

5. Then, add the following method:

```
[HttpGet("{protoName}")]
public async Task<ActionResult> GetFileContent(string
    protoName)
{
    var filePath =
        $"{baseDirectory}/Protos/{protoName}";

    if (System.IO.File.Exists(filePath))
        return Content(await
            System.IO.File.ReadAllTextAsync(filePath));

    return NotFound();
}
```

We have now added two endpoints. One of them lists all of the available proto files in our application. The other one returns the content of a selected proto file as plain text. Both of them use the GET HTTP verb. Therefore, they both can be accessed via a normal browser.

We can now launch our application by executing the `dotnet run` command inside the project folder. If we have configured everything correctly, the following content is expected to be displayed if you enter `http://localhost:5002/protos/users.proto` in your browser address bar:

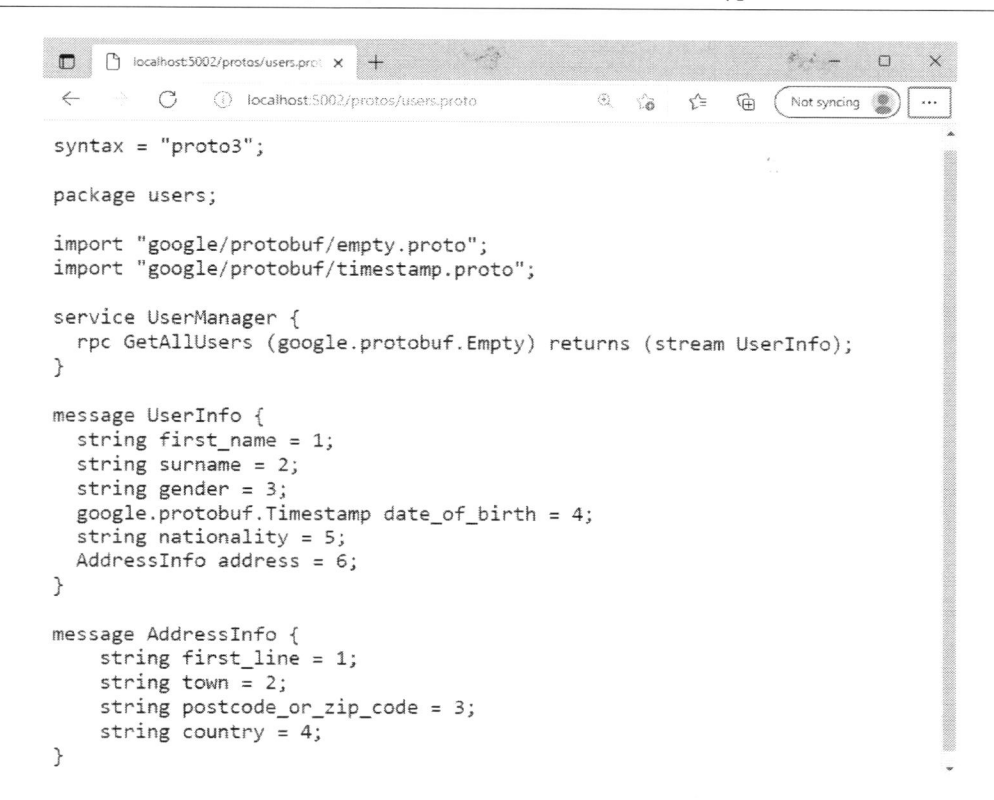

```
syntax = "proto3";

package users;

import "google/protobuf/empty.proto";
import "google/protobuf/timestamp.proto";

service UserManager {
  rpc GetAllUsers (google.protobuf.Empty) returns (stream UserInfo);
}
message UserInfo {
  string first_name = 1;
  string surname = 2;
  string gender = 3;
  google.protobuf.Timestamp date_of_birth = 4;
  string nationality = 5;
  AddressInfo address = 6;
}
message AddressInfo {
    string first_line = 1;
    string town = 2;
    string postcode_or_zip_code = 3;
    string country = 4;
}
```

Figure 9.1 – The content of the users.proto file displayed in a browser window

By performing this action, we have verified that we can use this endpoint to extract the Protobuf definition and build a client with it. And this is precisely what we will do next. Keep this application running, as you will need it to build the client.

Building the client for gRPC communication

Execute the following command to build a new project from the `Console Application` template:

```
dotnet new console -o UserManagementClient
```

Your next action will depend on which IDE you use. At the time of writing, only Visual Studio for Windows has the option of pulling a gRPC reference from the server and building the client based on it. However, if you use a different IDE, a similar option may be available for it.

Configuring the gRPC client via a service reference

The following series of steps apply if the option of adding a gRPC service reference is available for the IDE that you are using. Depending on the IDE, the exact labels in the context menu may vary:

1. Right-click on the **UserManagementClient** project. Then, click **Add** and select **Service Reference…**, as demonstrated in the following screenshot:

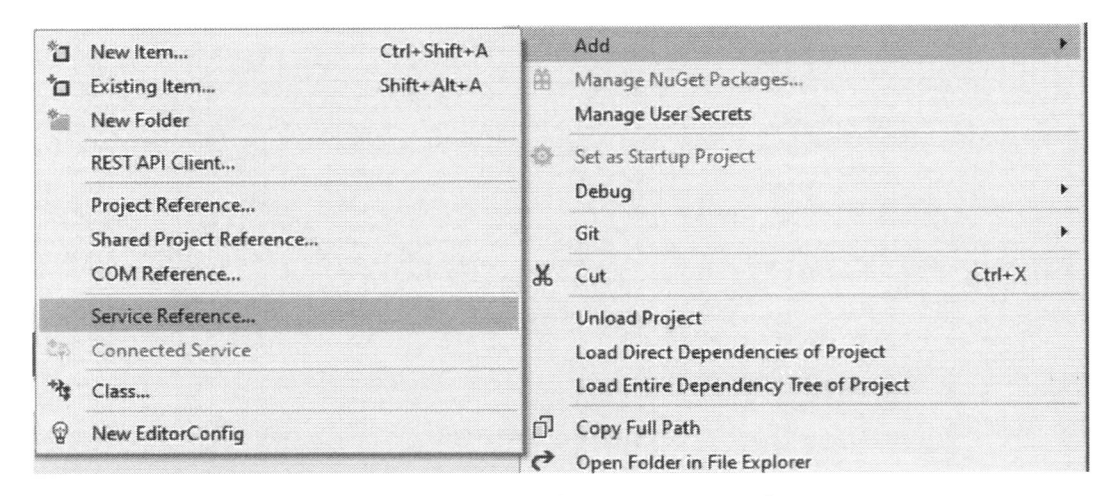

Figure 9.2 – Selecting the Service Reference… option in the context menu

2. Select **gRPC** as the service type, as demonstrated in the following screenshot:

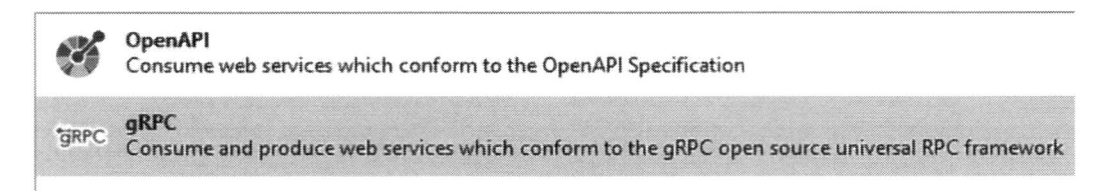

Figure 9.3 – Selecting the gRPC service type

3. Select the **URL** option, enter `http://localhost:5002/protos/users.proto` into the field, and select **Client** as the role, as demonstrated in the following screenshot:

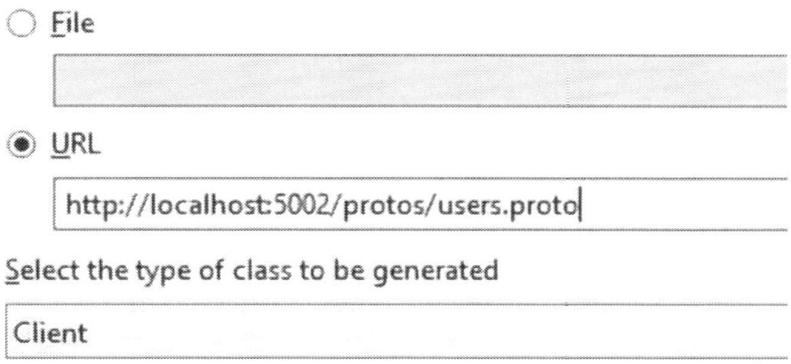

Figure 9.4 – The final setup screen for the service reference

If you then click **Next** and wait for the process to finish, you should expect a copy of the `users.proto` file to be generated inside the `Protos` folder in the `UserManagementClient` project. At this point, all necessary **NuGet** packages will be installed, and the proto file will be automatically registered in your `UserManagementClient.csproj` file.

If your IDE or code editor doesn't have the ability to import gRPC service references, then you will have to go through this process manually. We will describe how to do this in the next section.

Configuring the gRPC client manually

If you can't auto-generate gRPC client bindings based on a published web service definition, you can follow these steps to set up your client:

1. From the `UserManagementClient` project folder, run the following commands to install all of the necessary NuGet packages:

```
dotnet add UserManagementClient.csproj
  package Grpc.Net.ClientFactory
dotnet add UserManagementClient.csproj
  package Google.Protobuf
dotnet add UserManagementClient.csproj
  package Grpc.Tools
```

2. Create a `Protos` folder inside the `UserManagementClient` project folder and copy the `users.proto` file into it from the `Protos` folder of the `UserInfoManager` project.

3. Add the following markup to the `UserManagementClient.csproj` file:

```xml
<ItemGroup>
  <Protobuf Include="Protos\users.proto"
    GrpcServices="Client">

    <SourceUri>http://localhost:5000/protos/users.proto
    </SourceUri>
  </Protobuf>
</ItemGroup>
```

And that's it – our client project now has all of the required dependencies. And our project setup is identical to what it would have been if we had auto-generated the binding from the service reference.

Please note that the Protobuf reference inside the project file contains the `SourceUri` element. This element holds the address of the original service reference. Other than that, it can be ignored.

We are now ready to complete our gRPC client setup and make an unencrypted call from it to our gRPC server.

Adding the remaining client logic

Our client project consists of a single functional class: `Program`. This is the class that we will need to modify:

1. Ensure that the following `using` statements are referenced by our class:

```csharp
using Google.Protobuf.WellKnownTypes;
using Grpc.Core;
using Grpc.Net.Client;
using System;
using System.Threading.Tasks;
using Users;
```

2. Change the `Main` method signature to the following:

   ```
   static async Task Main()
   ```

3. Replace the content of the `Main` method with the following:

   ```
   Console.WriteLine("Please enter the gRPC service
     URL.");
   var url = Console.ReadLine();
   using var channel = GrpcChannel.ForAddress(url);
   var client = new
     UserManager.UserManagerClient(channel);

    using var call = client.GetAllUsers(new Empty());

   while (await call.ResponseStream.MoveNext())
   {
   }

   Console.ReadKey();
   Insert the following code into the while loop:
   var user = call.ResponseStream.Current;

   Console.WriteLine("User details extracted");
   Console.WriteLine($"First name: {user.FirstName}");
   Console.WriteLine($"Surname: {user.Surname}");
    Console.WriteLine($"Gender: {user.Gender}");
   Console.WriteLine($"Date of birth:
     {user.DateOfBirth.ToDateTime():yyyy-MM-dd}");
   Console.WriteLine($"Nationality: {user.Nationality}");
   Console.WriteLine($"Address:
     {user.Address.FirstLine}");
    Console.WriteLine($"Postcode or Zip code:
     {user.Address.PostcodeOrZipCode}");
   Console.WriteLine($"Town: {user.Address.Town}");
   Console.WriteLine($"Country: {user.Address.Country}");
   Console.WriteLine(string.Empty);
   ```

The console application will prompt us to enter the URL of the gRPC server endpoint. And if there is an unencrypted endpoint that we can use, the URL will work even if we use HTTP instead of HTTPS.

Prior to .NET 5, there was an additional configuration that you needed to apply on the gRPC client. Before you initialized the client, you needed to add the following statement:

```
AppContext.SetSwitch( "System.Net.Http.SocketsHttpHandler
    .Http2UnencryptedSupport", true);
```

But .NET 5 has removed the need to do this. On .NET 5 and later, unencrypted URLs will work by default, as long as the server supports them. We can test this by launching our console application and entering `http://localhost:5000` as our URL. If you remember, 5000 is the port number we've assigned to HTTP/2 on the server. And, as can be seen in the following screenshot, it will work without us having to apply any additional parameters:

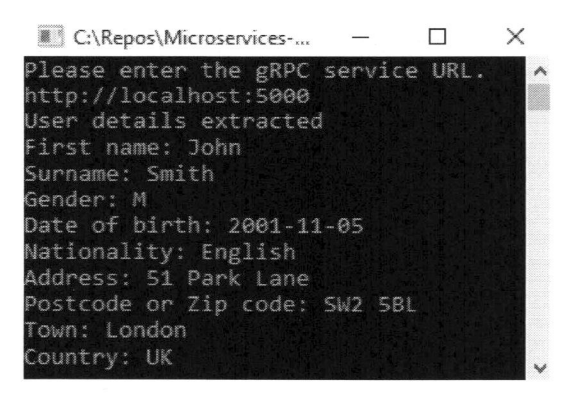

Figure 9.5 – The gRPC client was able to successfully make an unencrypted call

And because we have overridden the default configuration, there is no attempt by the server to apply TLS on any HTTP/2 port. This means that our application is expected to work equally well on any OS, including macOS.

But even though unencrypted communication is perfect for an OS-independent development environment, it is not something you would want to do in most production scenarios. This is why you need to know how to apply digital certificates to your applications. But before you can do this, we need to create a suitable certificate, and this is what we will cover next.

Creating and trusting a self-signed certificate

There are many different ways of creating TLS certificates for your web application. But regardless of the method you use, the principles remain the same.

For gRPC, all the principles of applying a certificate are identical to those for an ordinary web application that is accessible via HTTP/1.1. We even use the same kind of file to encrypt communication between the endpoints.

However, in an ASP.NET application, the application of the certificate differs depending on the kind of server you want to host your application on. Applying a certificate on IIS would be different from applying one on **Kestrel**. But even on the same type of server, there are still different ways to apply a certificate. For example, just like the HTTP port mappings we covered in the previous section, you can reference the certificate directly in the code, or you can reference it in the application settings.

Covering all of the different ways of applying certificates on all types of servers is beyond the scope of this chapter. Here, we will show a limited number of examples, but the general principles will be the same, regardless of how you choose to configure the certificates.

The basics of a TLS certificate

In this chapter, we will not go into the advanced details of how TLS certificates work. However, we will cover enough information for you to be confident applying certificates on your hosted web applications and troubleshooting the most frequent problems with them.

In order for your application to work with a TLS certificate, both the client machine and the server machine need to trust it. In our case, we will probably be running both the client and the server on the same machine, so getting the machine to trust any specific certificate will make the certificate trusted by both applications.

Trusting a certificate is important. By default, if an untrusted certificate is used, the client applications will either warn you when an attempt is made to connect to an endpoint protected by such a certificate, or it will refuse to connect. This is done to make sure that you aren't sharing data with potentially malicious applications.

In general, there are two ways of trusting a certificate. If the certificate is signed by a recognized CA, it will be trusted automatically. However, if you want to use a self-signed certificate that you have created yourself, you can also configure it to be trusted. In this scenario, it needs to be explicitly added to the list of trusted certificates. And this needs to happen for both the client and the server. Usually, this is done at the machine level, but it's also possible to get a specific application to trust a specific certificate.

A certificate doesn't just store the encryption keys and the signature of the relevant CA. It also contains metadata, such as the name of the host that the certificate was assigned to, the certificate's expiry date, a hexadecimal string representing the certificate's identity (known as a *thumbprint*), the certificate's common name (known as a *subject*), and other pieces of information. These metadata fields can be used to confirm that the certificate is still valid and hasn't been revoked.

Usually, your server certificate can be exported into a file with the .pfx extension. This file contains a full certificate chain with all the metadata, but it also contains both the public and private keys. This is why such a file needs to be securely stored on the server and never shared with a client.

There are also other file extensions associated with TLS certificates, for example, the .cer and .crt extensions represent a file that contains a public key and the minimum amount of metadata needed to prove that the certificate is valid. This file can be shared with clients.

You can have many different certificates on the server and choose a specific one to encrypt your web application. Next, we will have a look at how you can create and trust a self-signed certificate.

Trusting a default development certificate

In *Chapter 1, Creating a Basic gRPC Application on ASP.NET Core*, we looked at an example of how to trust a development certificate that comes with the .NET SDK. If you are on either a Windows or Linux machine, all you have to do is run the following command:

```
dotnet dev-certs https --trust
```

On Linux, there are additional steps you will need to apply to trust a development certificate. Those are distribution-specific – that is, the steps you will need to take on **Fedora** would be different from those you would need to follow on **Ubuntu**. And as there are several different Linux distributions available, covering them all would be beyond the scope of this chapter. However, the links to the relevant documentation will be provided in the *Further reading* section.

If you want to configure your application to use a specific certificate file, you can also do this with a development certificate. The `dotnet dev-certs` tool allows you to export the certificate into files of different formats. For example, this is a command you can use to export the certificate into a `.pfx` file that will reside inside the folder that you are running the command from:

```
dotnet dev-certs https -ep UserInfoManager.pfx -p password
```

The `-ep` parameter represents the path to the file. The `-p` parameter represents a certificate password. It is recommended that your `.pfx` file is protected by a strong password so that only approved applications can use it.

But the `dotnet dev-certs` tool abstracts away some important steps of certificate creation. It applies some default settings, such as assigning the certificate to the `localhost` domain. With these settings, the certificate will only be valid if you use the specified domain. For example, it will not work if you try to send an HTTPS request to the `127.0.0.1` IP address directly, which is the IP address that the `localhost` domain represents. There are some other tools you can use to apply even more customizations to a certificate and even create a production-grade certificate.

Creating a self-signed certificate on Windows using PowerShell

If you are a Windows user, the easiest way to create a self-signed certificate is via **PowerShell**. To do so, you will need to run PowerShell as an administrator. Then, we can navigate to the folder that we want to export the certificate into and apply the following steps:

1. Create a new certificate by executing the following command:

```
New-SelfSignedCertificate -DnsName "localhost",
"localhost" -CertStoreLocation "cert:\LocalMachine\My"
-NotAfter (Get-Date).AddYears(20) -FriendlyName
"localhost-client" -KeyUsageProperty All -KeyUsage
CertSign, CRLSign, DigitalSignature
```

2. This will create a certificate in the machine storage and associate it with the localhost domain. The certificate will be known under the name of localhost-client and will be valid for 20 years from today. If the command executes successfully, we will get the certificate thumbprint output on the screen:

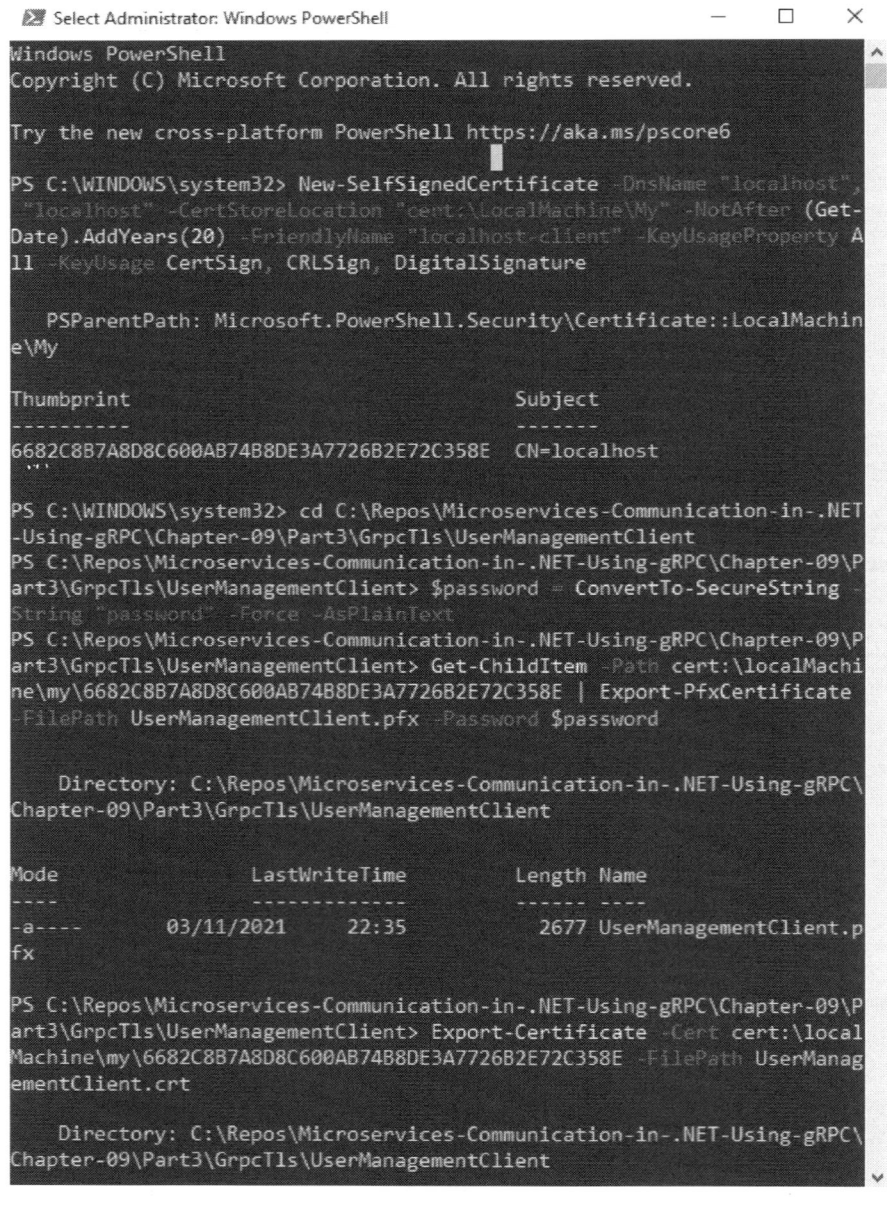

Figure 9.6 – The certificate thumbprint and subject

3. We will need the thumbprint for later. But for now, let's create the certificate password by executing the following command:

```
$password = ConvertTo-SecureString -String "password"
-Force -AsPlainText
```

4. This command will create a `password` object with the value of `password` and store it as plain text. Next, we will export the certificate into a `.pfx` file by executing the following command. Please note that you need to replace the `{thumbprint}` placeholder with the actual thumbprint. With the output we received previously, this would be `6682C8B7A8D8C600AB74B8DE3A7726B2E72C358E`. But your own output will be unique:

```
Get-ChildItem -Path cert:\localMachine\my\{thumbprint}
 | Export-PfxCertificate -FilePath UserInfoManager.pfx
-Password $password
```

5. We will also create a certificate file, which we can then import to our trusted root folder:

```
Export-Certificate -Cert
cert:\localMachine\my\{thumbprint} -FilePath
UserInfoManager.crt
```

6. We will then trust the certificate by importing it into a trusted root. This can be done via the following command:

```
Import-Certificate -FilePath UserInfoManager.pfx -
CertStoreLocation 'Cert:\LocalMachine\Root'
```

We have now created a `.pfx` file with the same name that we previously created by running the `dotnet dev-certs` command. We have also added the certificate to our trusted root. Now, we will briefly go through the process of creating a self-signed certificate on the **Unix** OS, which applies to both macOS and Linux.

Creating a self-signed certificate on Unix using OpenSSL

OpenSSL is a command-line tool that is available on any OS, including Windows. Normally, if you are using **Git** for source control, OpenSSL is already included with it. You can verify its presence by typing the following command in your terminal:

```
openssl help
```

If you don't happen to have it installed, you can obtain the documentation on how to install it from its official GitHub repository, which can be found at https://github.com/openssl/openssl.

Once the tool is available, we can complete the following steps to create a self-signed certificate:

1. Execute the following command to create the certificate and the key. Please note that the .crt and .key filenames should be the same as the name of the domain that you are assigning the certificate to:

    ```
    openssl req -x509 -newkey rsa:4096 -sha256 -days 365
        -nodes
        -keyout localhost.key -out localhost.crt -subj
        "/CN=localhost" -extensions v3_ca -extensions v3_req
    ```

2. You will need to enter the certificate password when prompted. Then, export the certificate chain into a .pfx file by using the following command:

    ```
    openssl pkcs12 -export -out UserInfoManager.pfx -inkey
        localhost.key -in localhost.crt
    ```

If you are on Windows, trusting the certificate can be done by running the same Import-Certificate PowerShell command we described previously. However, instructions for how to trust certificates on Unix-based OSes will be provided in the *Further reading* section.

In the next section, we will go over the process of applying a specific trusted .pfx file to enable TLS on the gRPC server.

Applying a certificate on ASP.NET Core

> **Note**
> The remaining instructions in this chapter cannot be implemented on macOS. Therefore, if you are using a Mac as your development machine, you will need to set up either a Linux or a Windows VM on it to be able to follow the instructions.

We will now modify our gRPC server application so that it will apply a custom self-signed certificate that we have created and subsequently enforce HTTPS. This means that if an attempt is made to connect to an unencrypted HTTP endpoint, it will be redirected to a dedicated HTTPS port. To do this, we will complete the following steps:

1. First, we need to add the following `using` statement to the `Startup` class in our `UserInfoManager` project, or `Program.cs` file if we are using .NET 6 template:

   ```
   using System.Net;
   ```

2. We will then add the following statement anywhere before the `app.UseRouting()` call in the `Configure` method of the `Startup` class (or the main body of `Program.cs` file on .NET 6):

   ```
   app.UseHttpsRedirection();
   ```

3. This statement will ensure that whenever a call is made from a client to an unencrypted HTTP endpoint, it will be redirected to an encrypted HTTPS port. However, it will not currently work, as we don't have an HTTPS endpoint configured. We will need to tell the application which port to redirect the request to. To do this, we add the following snippet to the `ConfigureServices` method of the `Startup` class:

   ```
   services.AddHttpsRedirection(options =>
   {
       options.RedirectStatusCode =
           (int)HttpStatusCode.PermanentRedirect;
       options.HttpsPort = 5001;
   });
   ```

4. However, our redirection logic still will not work because we don't have any listeners configured for port `5001`. To configure one, we will need to move into the `Program` class of the same application. In there, inside the call to the `ConfigureKestrel` method, we will need to add the following statement:

```
options.ListenAnyIP(5001, o => o.UseHttps());
```

5. We will then need to add the following `using` statement to the class:

```
using System.Security.Cryptography.X509Certificates;
```

6. Finally, we need to tell our application to use a specific `.pfx` file as the HTTPS certificate. To do so, we need to insert the following statement at the beginning of the call to the `ConfigureKestrel` method:

```
options.ConfigureHttpsDefaults(o =>
{
    o.ServerCertificate =
        new X509Certificate2("UserInfoManager.pfx",
            "password");
});
```

7. This call assumes that we have a `UserInfoManager.pfx` file inside the folder that has the executable of our application in it. It also assumes that the certificate password is `password`. To make it work, we will need to create the `UserInfoManager.pfx` file by using any method we have previously covered and get our system to trust it. Then, we will need to place the file inside the `UserInfoManager` project folder and apply the following setting to the `UserInfoManager.csproj` file:

```
<ItemGroup>
    <None Update="UserInfoManager.pfx">
        <CopyToOutputDirectory>PreserveNewest
        </CopyToOutputDirectory>
    </None>
</ItemGroup>
```

This setting will ensure that the file is copied into the output folder of our project whenever the code is compiled into the executable assemblies unless an up-to-date version of this file is already present inside the output folder.

There are also other ways we could have applied a certificate in our application. For example, instead of doing it directly in the code, we could have done it inside one of the configuration files. Or we could have done it at even a higher level – that is, in the settings of the server that hosts our application.

For example, we could have inserted the following entry into the `appsettings.json` file to enable the HTTPS port:

```
"https_port": 5001
```

Or, we could have applied the following Kestrel settings in that file:

```
"Kestrel": {
    "Endpoints": {
        "Http": {
            "Url": "http://localhost:5000"
        },
        "Https": {
            "Url": https://localhost:5001,
            "Certificate": {
                "Path": "UserInfoManager.pfx ",
                "Password": "password"
            }
        }
    }
}
```

Also, we have only demonstrated the Kestrel example in this instance, and different server types will have different configurations.

In a nutshell, there are many different ways to configure TLS on ASP.NET Core applications. There is no right or wrong way of doing it. Instead, the way you'll choose to configure it will depend on your needs and/or personal preferences.

But the principles will remain the same, regardless of how you have chosen to configure TLS. When the client application sends a request to your server, it will be able to do so via an encrypted HTTPS channel. And it will be the certificate of your choice that will provide the encryption.

There is no difference between applying TLS to the standard HTTP/1.1 endpoints and applying it to gRPC – the principles are the same. In the preceding example, the same configuration will control both. We can now test both the HTTP/1.1 and HTTP/2 endpoints to make sure that both direct HTTPS requests and requests redirected from HTTP work correctly.

Testing custom certificates and HTTPS redirection

To ensure that our TLS configuration has been applied correctly, we will launch the `UserInfoManager` project in debug mode inside your IDE. Then, open a browser and enter the following URL:

`https://localhost:5001/protos/users.proto`

If the TLS certificates have been configured correctly, you should expect to see an output similar to the following screenshot:

```
syntax = "proto3";

package users;

import "google/protobuf/empty.proto";
import "google/protobuf/timestamp.proto";

service UserManager {
  rpc GetAllUsers (google.protobuf.Empty) returns (stream UserInfo);
}

message UserInfo {
  string first_name = 1;
  string surname = 2;
  string gender = 3;
  google.protobuf.Timestamp date_of_birth = 4;
  string nationality = 5;
  AddressInfo address = 6;
}

message AddressInfo {
    string first_line = 1;
    string town = 2;
    string postcode_or_zip_code = 3;
    string country = 4;
}
```

Figure 9.7 – The Protobuf definition displayed via an HTTPS endpoint

Then, if you replace the URL with `http://localhost:5002/protos/users.proto`, you should expect to see it redirected back to `https://localhost:5001/protos/users.proto`. This will confirm that HTTPS redirection works as expected for HTTP/1.1 communication.

Next, we will verify that the certificate we configured works for gRPC too. To do so, we will need to launch the `UserManagementClient` application by executing the `dotnet run` command inside its project folder. When the application has started and you have been prompted to enter the URL of the gRPC server, enter `https://localhost:5001`. This should give you an output similar to that in the following screenshot:

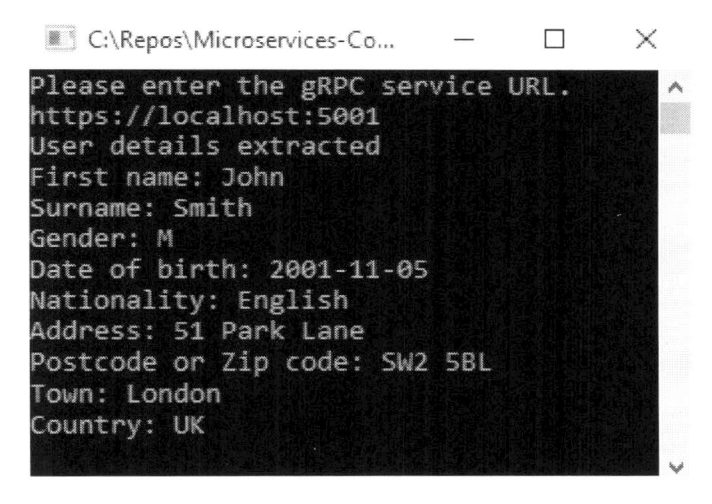

Figure 9.8 – The gRPC client is able to make a call on an HTTPS endpoint

Next, we will test whether HTTPS redirection works with gRPC. To do so, we will launch the client application again. This time, we will input `http://localhost:5000` as the URL. But before we do so, we will place a breakpoint anywhere inside the `GetAllUsers` method from the `UserInfoService` class of the `UserInfoManager` application.

So, if we launch the client application and enter `http://localhost:5000` as the URL when prompted, we will be able to examine the `Host` property of the `context` object to confirm that the request has been redirected to the HTTPS port, which is `5001`. This is how it should look in your IDE:

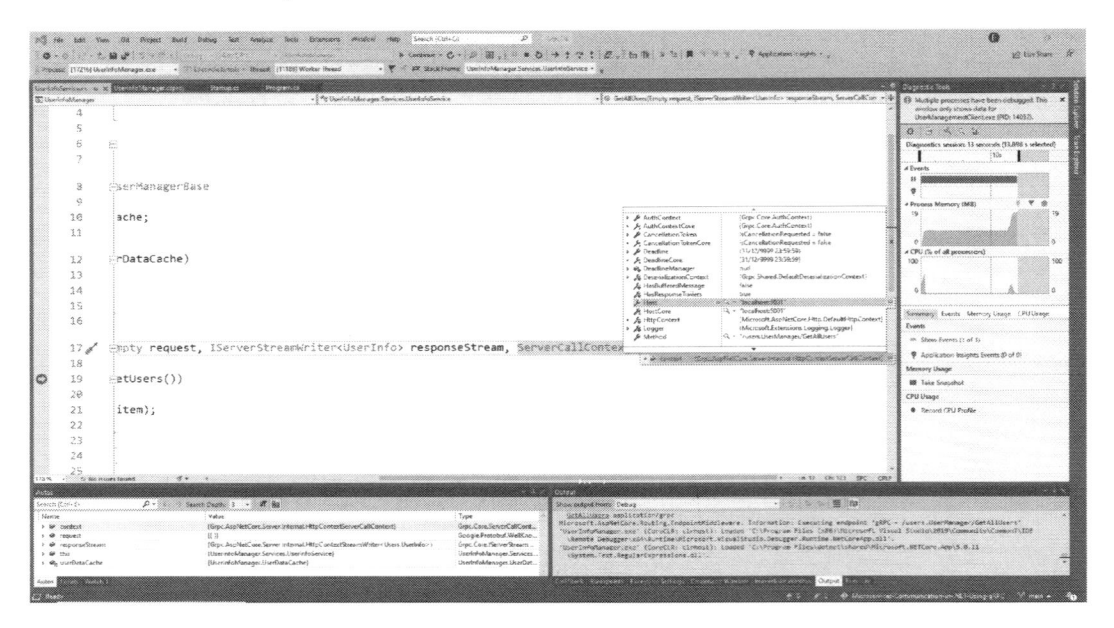

Figure 9.9 – The Host property of the context parameter confirms that HTTPS redirection took place

Then, if we allow the code to continue executing, we will see the standard results in the terminal of the client application, which should be similar to the ones displayed here:

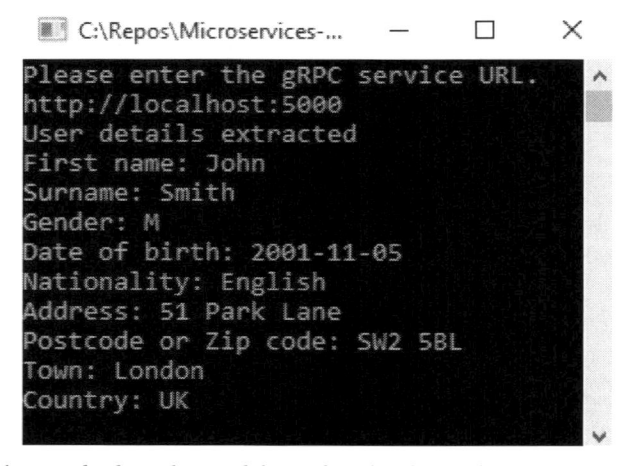

Figure 9.10 – The standard results are delivered to the client when the HTTP URL is entered

This concludes our demonstration of TLS on the server. But the server is not the only place where you can apply for certificates. You can also do this on the client, and this is what we will cover next.

Applying certificate authentication on the gRPC client and server

We have already established that on the server, security certificates are used for enabling TLS. That means a trusted certificate confirms to the client that it is safe to exchange keys with the server. This is how secure communication can be established between the client and the server.

But the same types of certificates can be used by clients too. However, their purpose is different from the server certificates. Client certificates are used for authentication. That means they are there to confirm that the client is allowed to access the server application.

To ensure that the client can be trusted, the certificate that the client shows to the server needs to be trusted by the server too. But this time, it's not necessary to get a CA involved to sign the certificate. For example, it is safe to use a certificate that has been issued by the server as the client certificate. The server will already trust it, and it will then be able to confirm that the data from the certificate matches the other data that the client sends.

Certificate authentication is especially relevant to gRPC because it is primarily used in RPC scenarios. In these scenarios, it will normally be another software application calling the server, rather than a human user. And this is why, instead of getting the client application to authenticate with a username and password in the way a human user would, it might be simpler to use a certificate that stays with the application – either permanently, or until it is revoked.

To enable certificate authentication, we need to apply the relevant configuration to the server. Then, we will need to configure the client to use a certificate.

Configuring the gRPC server for certificate authentication

We will now apply some changes to the `UserInfoManager` application to enable certificate authentication. To do so, we will complete the following steps:

1. Inside the call to the `ConfigureHttpsDefaults` method in the `Program` class, add the following statement:

   ```
   o.ClientCertificateMode =
       ClientCertificateMode.RequireCertificate;
   ```

2. This will ensure that clients will require a certificate. Now, open the `Startup` class (or `Program.cs` file if you are on .NET 6) and ensure that it contains all of the following `using` statements:

   ```
   using Microsoft.AspNetCore.Authentication.Certificate;
   using Microsoft.AspNetCore.Builder;
   using Microsoft.AspNetCore.Hosting;
   using Microsoft.AspNetCore.Http;
   using Microsoft.Extensions.DependencyInjection;
   using Microsoft.Extensions.Hosting;
   using System;
   using System.Net;
   using System.Security.Claims;
   using System.Threading.Tasks;
   using UserInfoManager.Services;
   ```

3. We will now add some event handlers for certificate authentication. To do so, add the following block into the `ConfigureServices` method (or insert the statement into `Program.cs` file if you are on .NET 6, while applying appropriate modifications, as per prior examples):

   ```
   services.AddAuthentication(CertificateAuthentication
       Defaults.AuthenticationScheme)
           .AddCertificate(options =>
           {
           })
           .AddCertificateCache();
   ```

4. We will now add the following option to the `AddCertificate` call to ensure that we accept any type of certificates, including self-signed certificates:

   ```
   options.AllowedCertificateTypes =
       CertificateTypes.All;
   ```

5. Next, we will add the event handlers into the same call, which will be as follows:

   ```
   options.Events = new CertificateAuthenticationEvents
   {
       OnCertificateValidated = context =>
       {
       },
       OnAuthenticationFailed = context =>
       {
       },
   };
   ```

6. The `OnCertificateValidated` event will be triggered when the client certificate has passed validation. We will populate this event handler with the following content, where we will be logging some data extracted from the certificate and using some of its other data as a claim principle, which we will need for authentication:

   ```
   var claims = new[]
   {
       new Claim(ClaimTypes.Name,
           context.ClientCertificate.Subject,
           ClaimValueTypes.String,
           context.Options.ClaimsIssuer)
   };

   context.Principal = new ClaimsPrincipal(
       new ClaimsIdentity(claims, context.Scheme.Name));

   Console.WriteLine($"Client certificate thumbprint
       {context.ClientCertificate.Thumbprint}");
   Console.WriteLine$"Client certificate subject:
       {context.ClientCertificate.Subject}");
   ```

```
context.Success();
return Task.CompletedTask;
```

7. The `OnAuthenticationFailed` event will be fired when the validation of a certificate fails. We will populate its body with the following:

```
context.NoResult();
context.Response.StatusCode = 403;
context.Response.ContentType = "text/plain";
context.Response.WriteAsync(context.Exception.ToString
    ()).Wait();
return Task.CompletedTask;
```

8. To make it work, we will need to add the following call to the `Configure` method. It should go anywhere before the `app.UseRouting();` line:

```
app.UseAuthentication();
```

9. Finally, to see how the information extracted from the certificate has populated the `context` parameter of a gRPC method, we will insert the following block of code at the beginning of the `GetAllUsers` method in the `UserInfoService` class:

```
Console.WriteLine($"Client authenticated:
    {context.AuthContext.IsPeerAuthenticated}");

if (context.AuthContext.IsPeerAuthenticated)
{
    Console.WriteLine($"Auth property name:
        {context.AuthContext.PeerIdentityPropertyName}");
    Console.WriteLine($"Auth property value:
        {context.AuthContext.Properties.FirstOrDefault()
            ?.Value}");
}
```

What we are doing here is confirming whether or not the client has been authenticated. Then we extract and log the properties that the client has been authenticated with.

Of course, we could do much more with certificate authentication on the server side. We could add custom event handlers and extra validation logic. But this example is sufficient to demonstrate its basic principles.

Now, we will go ahead and configure our client for certificate authentication. Then, we will verify that it all works as we expect it to.

Enabling certificate authentication on the gRPC client

Our client project, `UserManagementClient`, will only require a small number of alterations, as per the following steps:

1. Create a self-signed certificate by using either PowerShell or OpenSSL and export the `UserManagementClient.pfx` file. Ensure that the target domain of the certificate (for example, the subject) is `localhost`. Set the certificate as `trusted`. Please note that certificates generated by the `dotnet dev-certs` tool will not work as client authentication certificates.

2. Copy the `.pfx` file into the `UserManagementClient` project folder and add the following snippet to the `UserManagementClient.csproj` file:

   ```
   <ItemGroup>
     <None Update="UserManagementClient.pfx">
       <CopyToOutputDirectory>PreserveNewest</CopyToOutputDirectory>
     </None>
   </ItemGroup>
   ```

3. Add the following `using` statements to the `Program` class inside the project:

   ```
   using System.Net.Http;
   using System.Security.Cryptography.X509Certificates;
   ```

4. Add the following block of code just before the `channel` variable is instantiated:

   ```
   var certificate = new
     X509Certificate2("UserManagementClient.pfx",
       "password");
   var handler = new HttpClientHandler();
   handler.ClientCertificates.Add(certificate);
   ```

5. Replace the instantiation of the `channel` variable with the following:

   ```
   using var channel = GrpcChannel.ForAddress(url, new
     GrpcChannelOptions
     {
   ```

```
            HttpHandler = handler
});
```

And that's it – we can now test our application to see if the certificate authentication works correctly.

Testing certificate authentication

We will first launch the `UserInfoManager` application by executing the `dotnet run` command inside its project folder. Then, we will execute the same command inside the `UserManagementClient` project folder.

When prompted, we will enter `https://localhost:5001` into the console of the gRPC client application. If everything has been configured correctly, we should see results similar to those in the console in the following screenshot:

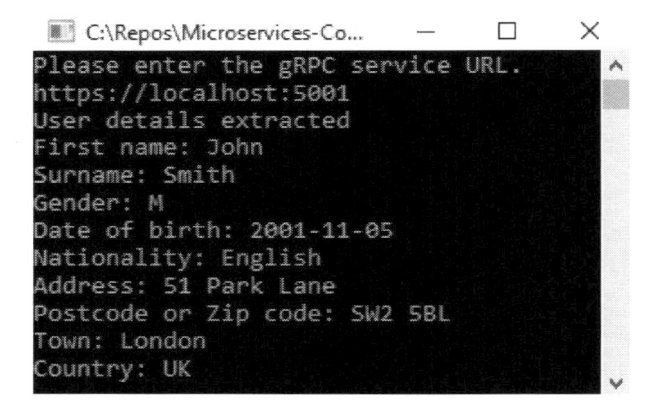

Figure 9.11 – The gRPC call results when a client certificate is applied

Then, to verify that the server has been able to successfully validate the certificate, we will need to look at the server console. There, you should be able to see the information that gets logged when the validation event is fired. This will look similar to the following screenshot:

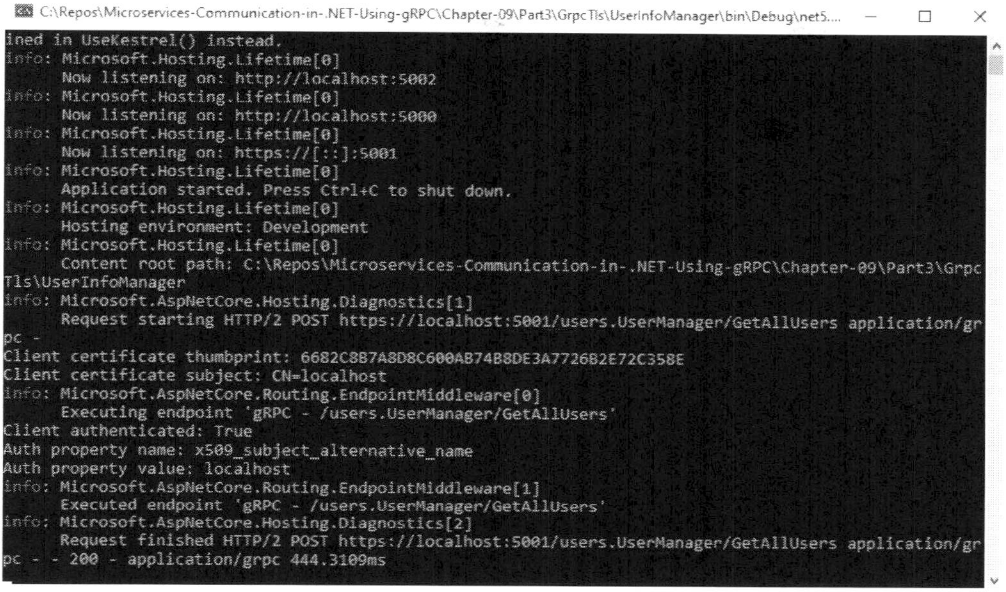

Figure 9.12 – The client certificate information logged by the server-side validation event

Then, we can verify that the gRPC call context has been successfully populated with the information extracted from the client certificate. If so, there will be entries in the console similar to the following:

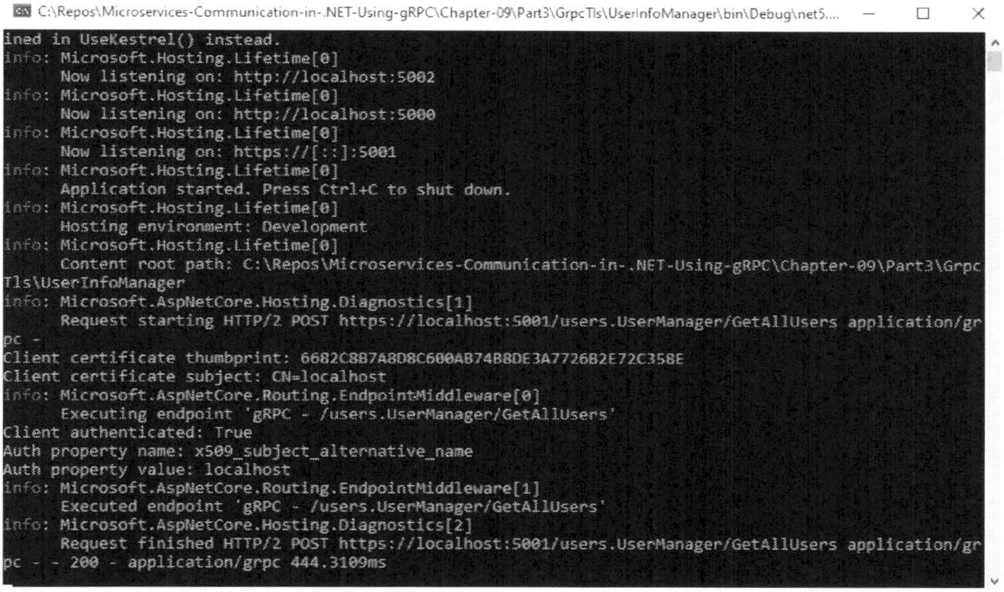

Figure 9.13 – The client certificate information successfully added to the gRPC call context

And this concludes our chapter on using TLS to secure gRPC endpoints. Now, let's summarize what we have learned.

Summary

In this chapter, you have learned that TLS is used for securing HTTP endpoints, including the HTTP/2 endpoints used by gRPC. This is achieved with the use of HTTPS, which is enabled by *digital security certificates*.

You have learned that in order for the certificates to work, they need to be *trusted* by both the server and the client machines. Typically, this will be achieved by getting the certificate signed by a CA. However, it can also be achieved by explicitly marking the certificate as trusted on the machine.

You have learned that there are several *tools* that you can use to generate and trust certificates. These include PowerShell (which is Windows-only) and OpenSSL (which is OS-independent). We also discussed the `dotnet dev-certs` tool, which is available with the dotnet CLI. This is simpler to use than other tools, but it's not suitable for all scenarios.

You have also learned that security certificates aren't used only on the server side – they are used on the client side too. However, clients use them for different purposes, for example, as an authentication tool.

Authentication is something we have briefly touched on in this chapter. In the next chapter, we will cover authentication in more depth, and we will also cover the difference between *authentication* and *authorization*.

Questions

1. What would you use to encrypt HTTP communication between a client and a server?

    A. SSL

    B. TLS

    C. gRPC

    D. Bearer tokens

2. Why can't you use the `Http1AndHttp2` configuration for an unsecure gRPC port?

   A. You can use `Http1AndHttp2` for an unsecure gRPC port.

   B. The port uses either HTTP/1.1 or HTTP/2 and you cannot have both.

   C. With this configuration, unsecure requests are routed to HTTP/1.1.

   D. You cannot use unsecure gRPC ports at all.

3. Which of the following tools can be used to generate a self-signed certificate?

   A. PowerShell

   B. The .NET CLI

   C. OpenSSL

   D. All of the above

4. What is the difference between `.pfx` and `.crt` files?

   A. They are interchangeable.

   B. They belong to different operating systems.

   C. A `.crt` file stores the complete certificate chain, while a `.pfx` file only stores the public key and any related metadata.

   D. A `.pfx` file stores the complete certificate chain, while a `.crt` file only stores the public key and any related metadata.

5. What is a client certificate used for?

   A. For authentication

   B. To store the public key of the server's certificate

   C. To encrypt the server response

   D. To encrypt server-sent events

Further reading

- Enforce HTTPS in ASP.NET Core: https://docs.microsoft.com/en-us/aspnet/core/security/enforcing-ssl
- Configure endpoints for the ASP.NET Core Kestrel web server: https://docs.microsoft.com/en-us/aspnet/core/fundamentals/servers/kestrel/endpoints

- Configure certificate authentication in ASP.NET Core: `https://docs.microsoft.com/en-us/aspnet/core/security/authentication/certauth`
- Generate self-signed certificates with the .NET CLI: `https://docs.microsoft.com/en-us/dotnet/core/additional-tools/self-signed-certificates-guide`
- OpenSSL documentation: `https://www.openssl.org/docs/`
- Making CA certificates available to Linux command-line tools: `https://www.redhat.com/sysadmin/ca-certificates-cli`
- Importing the root CA certificate to Debian and Ubuntu: `https://help.f-secure.com/product.html?business/threatshield/latest/en/task_9B68ADC2A12A4CC591A7B0271B57A499-threatshield-latest-en`

10
Applying Authentication and Authorization to gRPC Endpoints

Authentication and authorization are very important topics in any type of application development. Almost any public-facing application will have at least some of its functionality restricted to only specific users, as you wouldn't want an anonymous user to gain access to sensitive information.

There are many different types of sensitive information that you would want to restrict access to. Personal information of registered users is one example; so is the history of their personal communication with other users; so is any financial information.

There are many examples of this on the public web. No social media platform would allow you to publish content or contact other users until you have logged in with a username and password. Neither would an online banking app grant you access to the account information without verifying who you are.

Because **Google Remote Procedure Call (gRPC)** endpoints are routinely used to provide access to all kinds of sensitive data, it is important to know how to ensure that only known and authorized users can use them, and this is where authentication and authorization come into play.

In the previous chapter, we have already had a look at how to enable gRPC client authentication by using **Transport Layer Security (TLS)** certificates, but this type of authentication would not be suitable in every scenario. The certificate will tell the server that the client is authorized to connect to it, but what if the client is being used by an anonymous user? This is why it is important to know how to restrict access to gRPC endpoints.

We will cover the following topics in this chapter:

- Setting up the authentication backend
- Restricting gRPC endpoints to authenticated users
- Restricting endpoints to authorized users only

By the end of this chapter, you will have learned the difference between authentication and authorization and how to apply both in the context of gRPC on ASP.NET Core. You will also have learned how to set up your own **single sign-on (SSO)** system and use it to share authorization metadata between different applications of your ecosystem so that users don't have to log in separately to access separate applications.

Technical requirements

To follow the instructions in this chapter, you will need the following:

- A computer with either a Windows, Mac, or Linux operating system
- A supported **integrated development environment** (IDE) or code editor (Visual Studio, **Visual Studio Code** (**VS Code**), or JetBrains Rider)
- The .NET 5 **software development kit** (**SDK**)
- A self-signed development **HyperText Transfer Protocol Secure** (**HTTPS**) certificate enabled on the machine

Instructions on how to set all of these up were provided in *Chapter 1, Creating a Basic gRPC Application on ASP.NET Core*. All the code samples used in this chapter can be found at https://github.com/PacktPublishing/Microservices-Communication-in-.NET-Using-gRPC/tree/main/Chapter-10.

Please visit the following link to check the CiA videos: https://bit.ly/3pXmFim

Setting up the authentication backend

There are multiple ways of setting up the authentication backend of your application. It's common to see the user data being stored inside the main application itself. However, this approach is not scalable. The users stored directly inside the application will only be valid within the context of this application. So, if your estate has multiple applications, it will be problematic to authorize all of them with a single login.

An alternative approach is to use a separate authorization provider that all applications will integrate with. This way, when the user logs in, a token is issued to the user that is then stored in the session. Then, this user is free to access any other application until they log out or the token expires due to inactivity. This system is known as SSO.

When you use SSO, your authentication information will not be stored in any of the user-facing applications. Instead, there will be a dedicated application that will act as an authentication provider. All other applications will be registered on it as clients, and every time the user logs in, it will be the SSO application that authenticates the user and returns the token.

There are several ways of enabling an SSO, but the de facto standard for web-based applications is to use a combination of OpenID Connect and **Open Authorization** (**OAuth**). OpenID Connect is used for authentication, while OAuth is used for authorization. The differences between these two concepts are outlined here:

- Authentication verifies that the user is who they claim to be
- Authorization ensures that a specific user is allowed to access a specific resource

The user is authenticated when they are able to prove they are who they say they are. One of the most common ways to do this is to enter a username and password, the latter of which—in theory—is supposed to be known only to the user. So, the user is authenticated if the username matches a record on the system and the user is able to provide secret information that is supposed to be only known to them.

There are also other security procedures, such as **multi-factor authentication** (**MFA**). This is where the user is asked to provide more details about themselves, such as a temporary numeric code that is sent to their device. MFA is beyond the scope of this chapter, however.

Authorization refers to when the user record has specific attributes that allow them to access a specific resource. For example, users may be given roles, such as `User` and `Admin`. There might be some resource that only the user with the `Admin` role is allowed to access. In this case, if an authenticated user without such a role attempts to access the resource, the system would know who the user is but the user would not be granted access.

On the web, it is typical to receive a `401 (Unauthorized)` HTTP response code for an unauthenticated user and `403 (Forbidden)` for an authenticated user that doesn't have permission to access a particular resource.

We will set up an SSO provider, but before we do, let's have a brief look at how OpenID Connect and OAuth work.

OpenID Connect and OAuth flow

OpenID Connect and OAuth are actually related. OAuth is a protocol that was developed to specify a pattern for granting authorization. However, it didn't specify how to authenticate the user, and that is what OpenID Connect was developed for.

OpenID Connect and OAuth work in tandem. There are multiple ways they can be used, but a typical flow looks like this:

1. If the user is not authenticated, the application redirects the user to the login page of the SSO provider, while passing client information in the request.

2. The user enters their credentials. If the login is successful, the SSO provider redirects the client back to the original application with a **one-time access code (OTAC)**.

3. The code is sent back to the SSO provider, which returns a **JavaScript Object Notation (JSON) Web Token (JWT)** to the application.

4. If necessary, the web server uses the token to retrieve additional information about the user. But otherwise, the user is now authenticated and the token can be shared between relevant applications.

The following diagram provides a visualization of this flow:

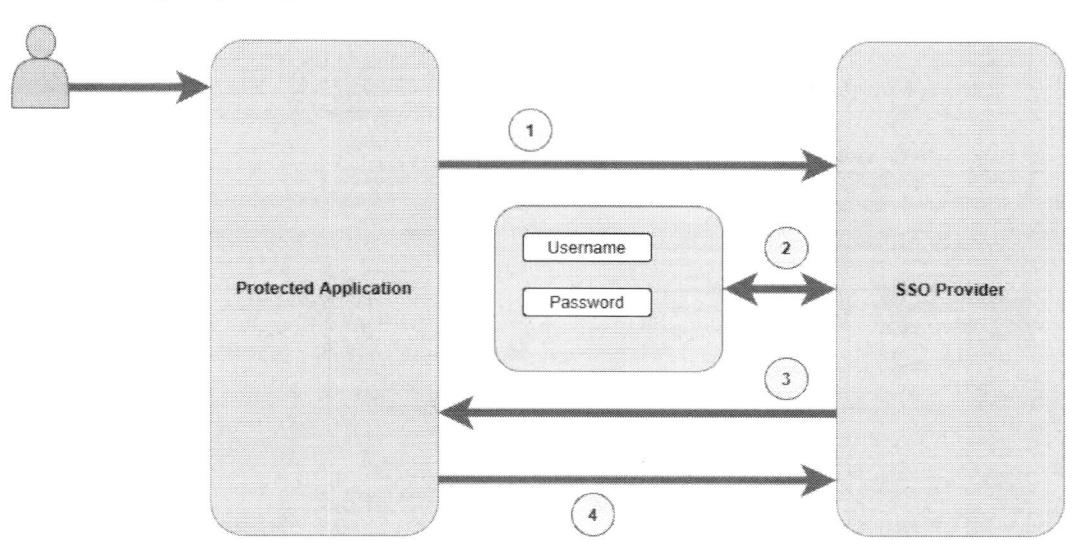

Figure 10.1 – OpenID Connect flow

A JWT is a Base64-encoded string that, when decoded, consists of three JSON parts: a header, a payload, and a signature. Those elements are separated by full stops inside the encoded string.

The header contains an encryption algorithm and the token type, which will typically be HS256 and JWT respectively. Its structure will look similar to this:

```
{
    "alg": "HS256",
    "typ": "JWT"
}
```

The payload contains all relevant information about the user that the system needs to determine whether or not the user is allowed to access any particular resource. The fields inside the JSON payload object are known as **claims**. Some claims are standard, such as aud (audience) or iat (issued at time). However, any custom claims can be used too. It's the claims in the JWT payload that indicate whether or not a user is authorized to use a resource—for example, they may contain roles the users are assigned to.

A payload would look similar to this. However, in a real-life scenario, it will probably contain way more fields than this:

```
{
    "sub": "1234567890",
    "name": "John Smith",
    "iat": 1516239022
}
```

A signature is used for verification of the token. The SSO provider will have a so-called **secret** associated with a client application: an arbitrary string of characters that only the application will know. Without the secret, it will not be possible to obtain a matching signature, which is how the application knows that the token was issued by a valid SSO provider. The formula for calculating the signature is shown here:

```
HMAC_SHA256( secret, base64urlEncoding(header) + '.' +
    base64urlEncoding(payload))
```

The `secret` parameter is the value of the secret string that is used for `SHA256` encoding. The other parameters are a combination of a Base64-encoded header and a payload linked together by a period character.

This concludes our overview of how a JWT works for authorization. We will now build an SSO provider to enable authentication and authorization for the gRPC service we will build later.

Configuring IdentityServer4

There are many SSO providers that we can choose from. Some of them are premium with expensive enterprise-grade licenses, while others are free and open source. In our case, we will be using IdentityServer4, which is free and open source. Moreover, unlike other providers, it's built entirely on .NET, so we won't have to install any additional SDKs.

But the choice of an SSO provider isn't important. OpenID Connect and OAuth are standard protocols that all major SSO solutions use. Different providers will differ in terms of **user interface** (**UI**) and configuration, but they will work in exactly the same way. In fact, you can replace one SSO provider with another and, as long as you have configured it to run on the same domain, have the clients with the same **identifiers** (**IDs**), and make it produce the same claims in the JWT, chances are that your applications will still work the same way as before. Therefore, the principles that we will use to build SSO based on IdentityServer4 will be equally applicable to other providers, such as Keycloak and Okta.

IdentityServer4 is easy to deploy because a number of .NET project templates were already provided for it. All we will have to do is install a relevant template, create a project from it, and reconfigure it to meet our needs, as follows:

1. Install the collection of IdentityServer4 templates by running the following command:

   ```
   dotnet new -i IdentityServer4.Templates
   ```

2. We will need a solution for our projects to make the process easier. To create a solution, first, create a `GrpcAuthentication` folder. Then, open a terminal inside this folder and execute the following command:

   ```
   dotnet new sln
   ```

3. We will need an instance of `IdentityServer4` with a web-based management UI to make it as easy to configure as possible. To create such a project, we will run the following command inside the solution folder:

   ```
   dotnet new is4admin -o AuthProvider
   ```

4. Now, from the solution folder, execute the following command to add the project to the solution:

   ```
   dotnet sln add AuthProvider\AuthProvider.csproj
   ```

5. We will now need to configure our authentication provider to use HTTPS, as it will be then easier for the clients to access it without having to add extra configuration. To do so, open the `launchSettings.json` file in the `Properties` folder of the `AuthProvider` project. Ensure that the `applicationUrl` entry has an HTTP **Uniform Resource Locator** (**URL**) listed and that it comes first in the list. The entry should look like this:

   ```
   "applicationUrl":
      https://localhost:5001;http://localhost:5000
   ```

6. Next, we will need to open the `env.js` file that can be found in the `wwwroot/admin/assets` folder and replace all URLs in there with the HTTP URL we inserted into the `launchSettings.json` file previously. Then, we will launch the application by executing a `dotnet run` command inside its project folder.

7. To verify that the application works, we can navigate to the HTTP URL we set previously, followed by the /admin path. In the preceding example, it would be https://localhost:5001/admin. If everything has been configured correctly, the following page should be displayed and no error messages should be shown:

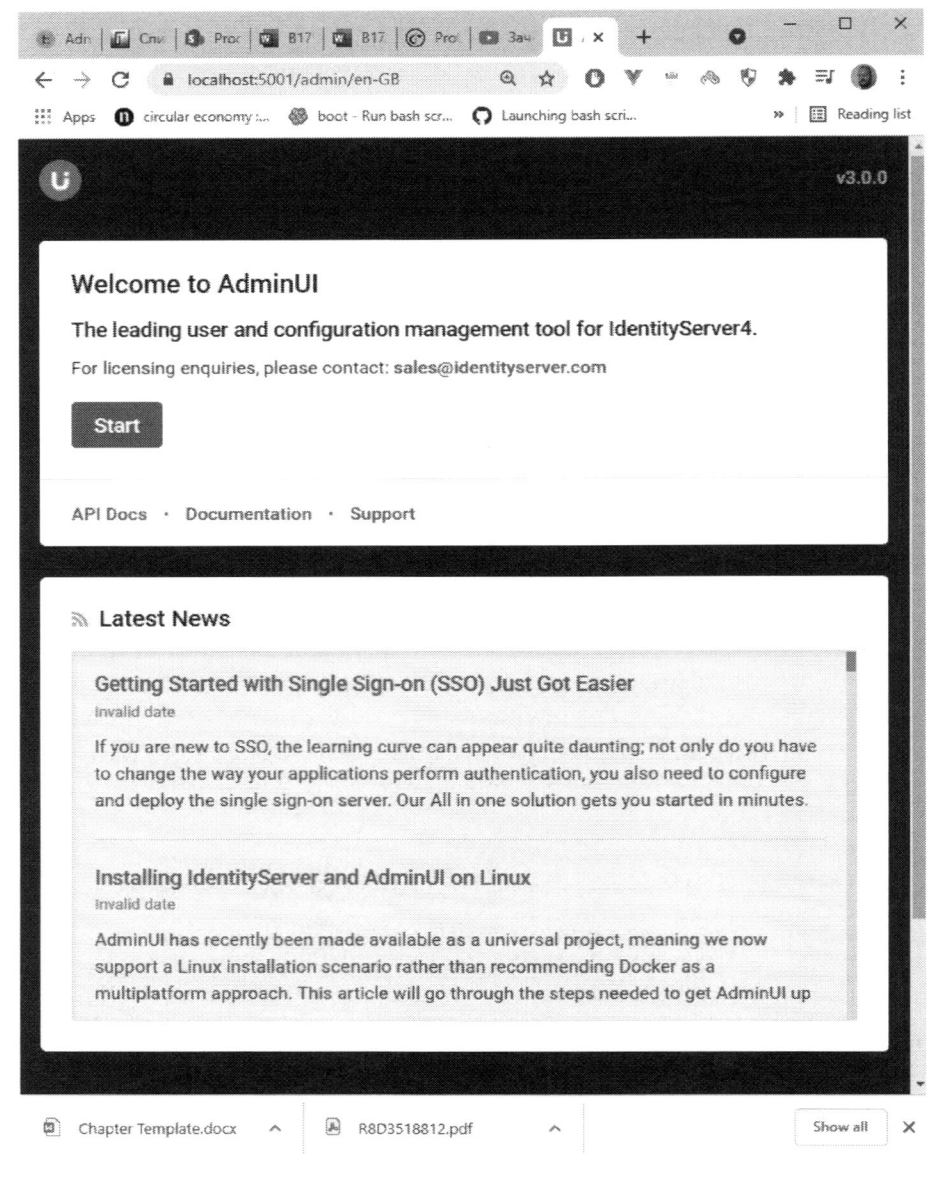

Figure 10.2 – IdentityServer4 admin page

The admin page will attempt to connect to various backend components asynchronously, so it will display errors if anything hasn't been configured correctly. But if there are no errors, all you will need to do is click **Start**. This will take you to the management screen where you can start adding data.

Adding SSO users, roles, and clients

To make our authentication provider work, we will need to add roles, users, and clients. We will start with roles, as follows:

1. In the admin UI, click on the **Roles** tab. Then, click on **Add Role**, enter User as the role name, and click **Save**.
2. Do the same for the Admin role. After you've done that, you should have the following roles listed:

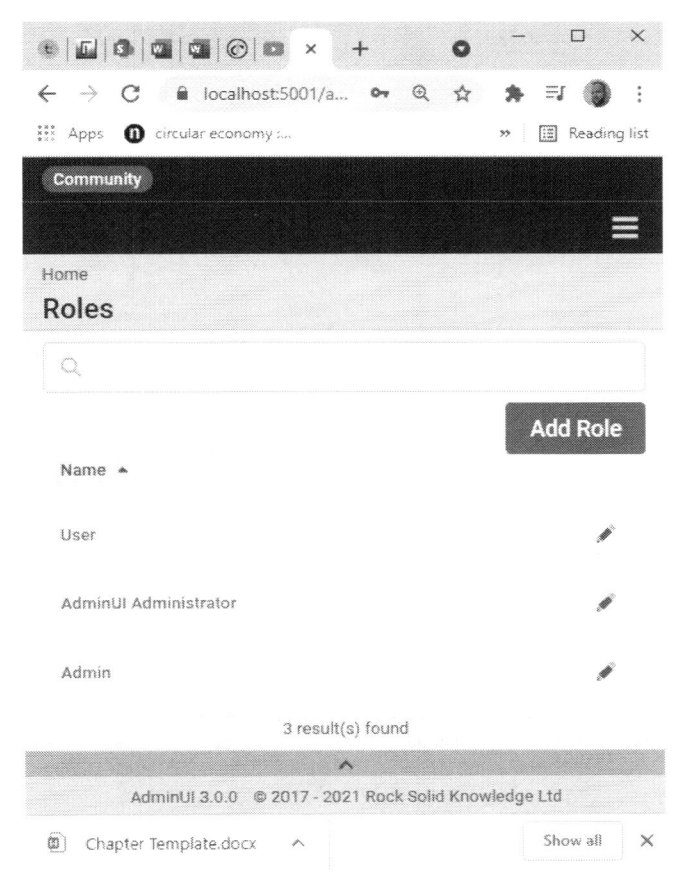

Figure 10.3 – User and Admin roles are listed alongside the default reserved role

370   Applying Authentication and Authorization to gRPC Endpoints

3. Now, navigate to the **Users** tab and click on the **Add User** button. Fill in the form with any details of your choice. Then, click **Save & Configure**.

4. On the screen that appears, navigate to the **Roles** tab (but not the one in the header). You should now be able to see all the roles listed on the left. To assign the user the role of the **User**, select the role from the list and click on the button with the arrow pointing right, as demonstrated in the following screenshot:

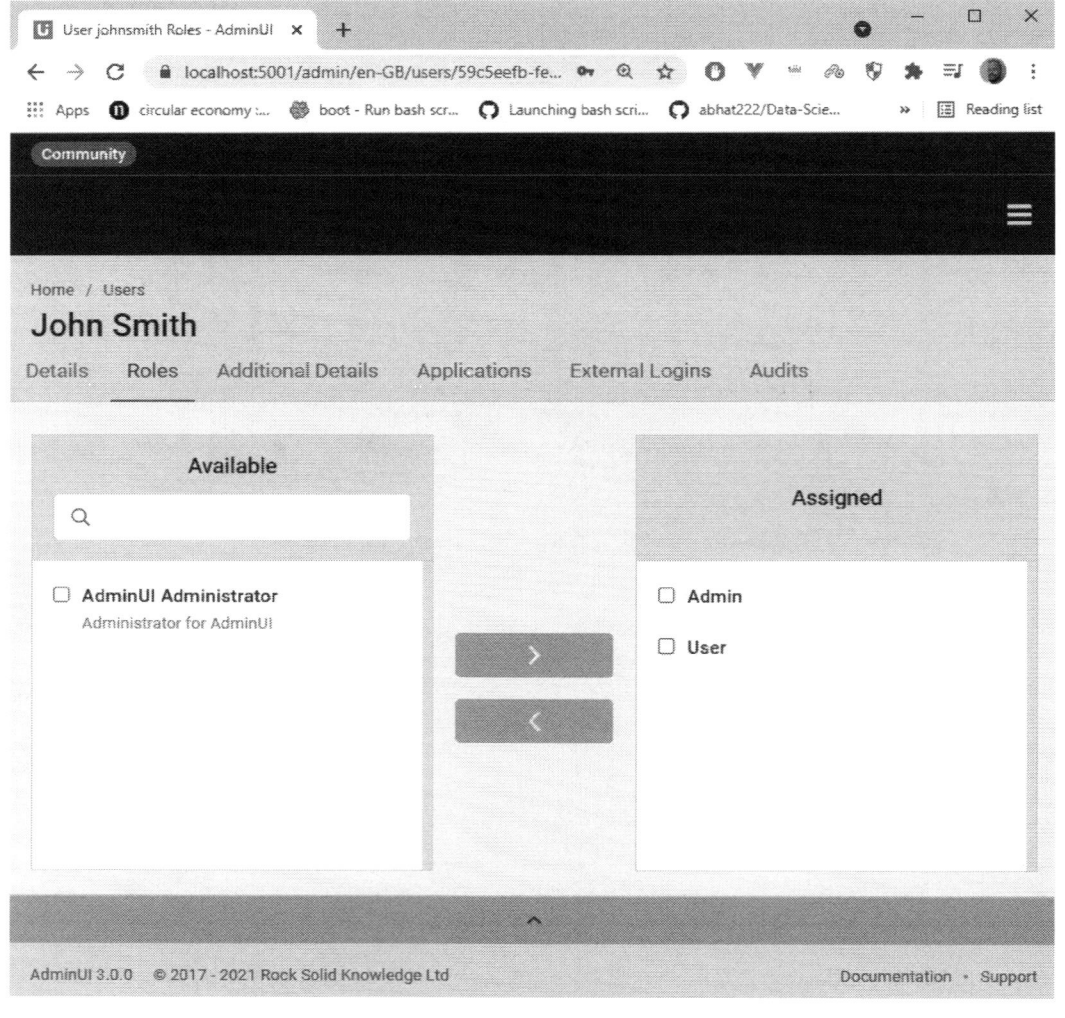

Figure 10.4 – Role assignment screen on IdentityServer4

5. Now, navigate back to the **Users** section by clicking on the **Users** tab on top of the screen. Repeat *Steps 3* and *4* to create a new user, but this time, assign the `Admin` role to the user.
6. Create another user and assign both `Admin` and `User` roles to them.
7. Create another user and assign no roles to them.
8. We will next create a client. To do so, click on the **Clients** tab and then click on **Add Client**. We will first select **Web App** and click **Start**. On the next screen, we will fill in the form with the following details:

- **Client ID**: `userFacingApp`
- **Display Name**: `User Facing App`

9. We will set our callback URL to `https://localhost:44349/signin-oidc` and click **Next**. On the next screen, we will leave the logout URL blank and click **Next**.
10. On the next screen, we will set the **Shared Secret** value to `userFacingAppSecret`. We made this value easy to work with. However, in a real-life scenario, this should be some string that is hard to guess. We will need to click **Add** to get the secret added, and then we'll click **Next**.
11. On the next screen, we will assign `profile` and `openid` to the client and click **Next**. We will leave all other settings as default and keep clicking **Next** until we see a screen with a **Save** button. This is the button we will click to save the profile.

Our SSO provider has now been fully configured, and because it's a stateful application that saves data in a local database, it will keep all the data stored even if we bring the application down. The next time the application is brought up, it will have the same state as before.

Next, we will create a web application that will use the SSO provider. We need an application with a UI, so we will use ASP.NET Core MVC. We will force this application to redirect the user to the SSO provider if the user hasn't been authenticated.

Forcing login redirect on a web application

We will create a new project based on a **Model-View-Controller** (**MVC**) template. Then, we will add all necessary dependencies to it so that it can use an SSO redirection mechanism. Finally, we will modify the application so that it can connect to our SSO provider. Follow these next steps:

1. In the solution folder, run the following command to create a new project from the MVC template:

   ```
   dotnet new mvc -o UserFacingApp
   ```

2. Add the project to the solution by executing the following command:

   ```
   dotnet sln add UserFacingApp\UserFacingApp.csproj
   ```

3. We will now need to add a NuGet package that will allow us to enable OpenID Connect middleware in our application so that we won't have to do the authentication flow manually. To do so, run the following command from the `UserFacingApp` project folder:

   ```
   dotnet add UserFacingApp.csproj package
   Microsoft.AspNetCore.Authentication.OpenIdConnect
   ```

4. We will now open the `Startup.cs` file (or the `Program.cs` file if you are using a .NET Core project template) inside the project and ensure that all of the following `using` statements are present:

   ```
   using System.IdentityModel.Tokens.Jwt;
   using Microsoft.AspNetCore.Builder;
   using Microsoft.AspNetCore.Hosting;
   using Microsoft.Extensions.Configuration;
   using Microsoft.Extensions.DependencyInjection;
   using Microsoft.Extensions.Hosting;
   ```

5. Then, insert the following code into the `ConfigureServices` method. If you are using a .NET 6 project template, you will just need to insert it into the main body anywhere before the `Build` event and replace `services` with `builder.Services`:

   ```
   JwtSecurityTokenHandler.DefaultMapInboundClaims =
       false;
   ```

```
services.AddAuthentication(options =>
{
    options.DefaultScheme = "Cookies";
    options.DefaultChallengeScheme = "oidc";
})
.AddCookie("Cookies")
.AddOpenIdConnect("oidc", options =>
{
    options.Authority = "https://localhost:5001";
    options.ClientId = "userFacingApp";
    options.ClientSecret = "userFacingAppSecret";
    options.ResponseType = "code";
    options.CallbackPath = "/signin-oidc";
    options.SaveTokens = true;
});
```

An important point to remember is that, in a real-life scenario, these values will be in a configuration file rather than hardcoded, but we didn't do that here to make the demonstration of the key concepts simpler.

This code will add middleware for authentication based on OpenID Connect, and this will store the token inside a cookie. The options under `AddOpenIdConnect` represent the configuration we have applied to the SSO application. `Authority` represents the base URL of our SSO application. `ClientId` represents the ID of the client we have configured. `ClientSecret` is the secret we have added to the client. `ResponseType` with the value of `code` tells the middleware to use a **one-time code** (OTC) after the redirection to retrieve the token. `CallbackPath` represents the path in the current application that the SSO application will redirect to after successful authentication. It needs to match one of the redirection URLs defined in the client configuration on IdentityServer4. Finally, we tell the middleware to save the token by setting the `SaveToken` option to `true`.

6. We will now add the middleware to the pipeline. To do so, add the following lines of code in the `Configure` method (or in the main body of the code if you are using .NET 6) after the `app.UseRouting()` call:

```
app.UseAuthentication();
app.UseAuthorization();
```

7. Now, to force our application to redirect to the SSO login screen, we will need to replace the logic inside the `UseEndpoints` call with the following code:

```
endpoints
    .MapDefaultControllerRoute()
    .RequireAuthorization();
```

8. We will now modify our `HomeController` class, which is located inside the `Controllers` folder of the application. First, we will add the following `using` statements to it:

```
using Microsoft.AspNetCore.Authentication;
using Microsoft.AspNetCore.Authentication.Cookies;
```

9. Then, add the following code before the `return` statement inside the `Index` method:

```
var accessToken = await
    HttpContext.GetTokenAsync("access_token");
Console.WriteLine($"Access token: {accessToken}");
```

10. Next, add the following method to the controller:

```
public IActionResult LogOut()
{
    return new SignOutResult(new[]
    {
        CookieAuthenticationDefaults.AuthenticationScheme,
        "oidc"
    });
}
```

This will log the user out by clearing the authentication cookies, but we will need a link to this action method. To do so, we need to open the `_Layout.cshtml` file located in the `Shared` folder inside the `Views` folder. Locate the `ul` element with the `class` attribute set to `navbar-nav flex-grow-1` and add the following **HyperText Markup Language** (**HTML**) to it after the existing `li` items:

```
<li class="nav-item">
    <a class="nav-link text-dark" asp-area="" asp-controller="Home" asp-action="LogOut">Log Out</a>
</li>
```

11. Finally, open the `launchSettings.json` file inside the `Properties` folder and ensure that the HTTPS URL is set to `https://localhost:44349`. This is the base URL of the redirect URL that we have used inside the client configuration of the SSO application. If, for some reason, you can't use this particular port, then change it in both the `launchSettings.json` file of the current application and the client configuration of the SSO application.

We have now set up an SSO along with a user-facing application that can use it. We will now test our setup. If we launch both applications by executing the `dotnet run` command inside the corresponding project folders and then navigate to the URL of the MVC application, we should be redirected to the login screen of the SSO application, which should look like this:

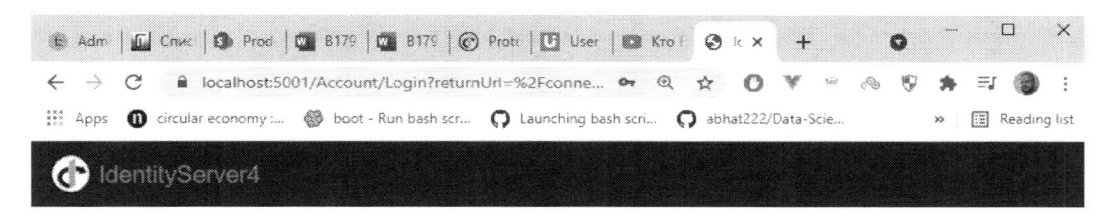

Figure 10.5 – IdentityServer4 login screen

After successful login with any of the registered credentials, you should be redirected to the home page of your MVC application. Also, if you have a look at the console output of the application, you should see an access token similar to this:

Figure 10.6 – Access token in the console of MVC application

We can now decode the token and have a look at its header and payload. To do so, we can visit the `https://jwt.io` site and paste the token into the **Encoded** section. You should then see something similar to this:

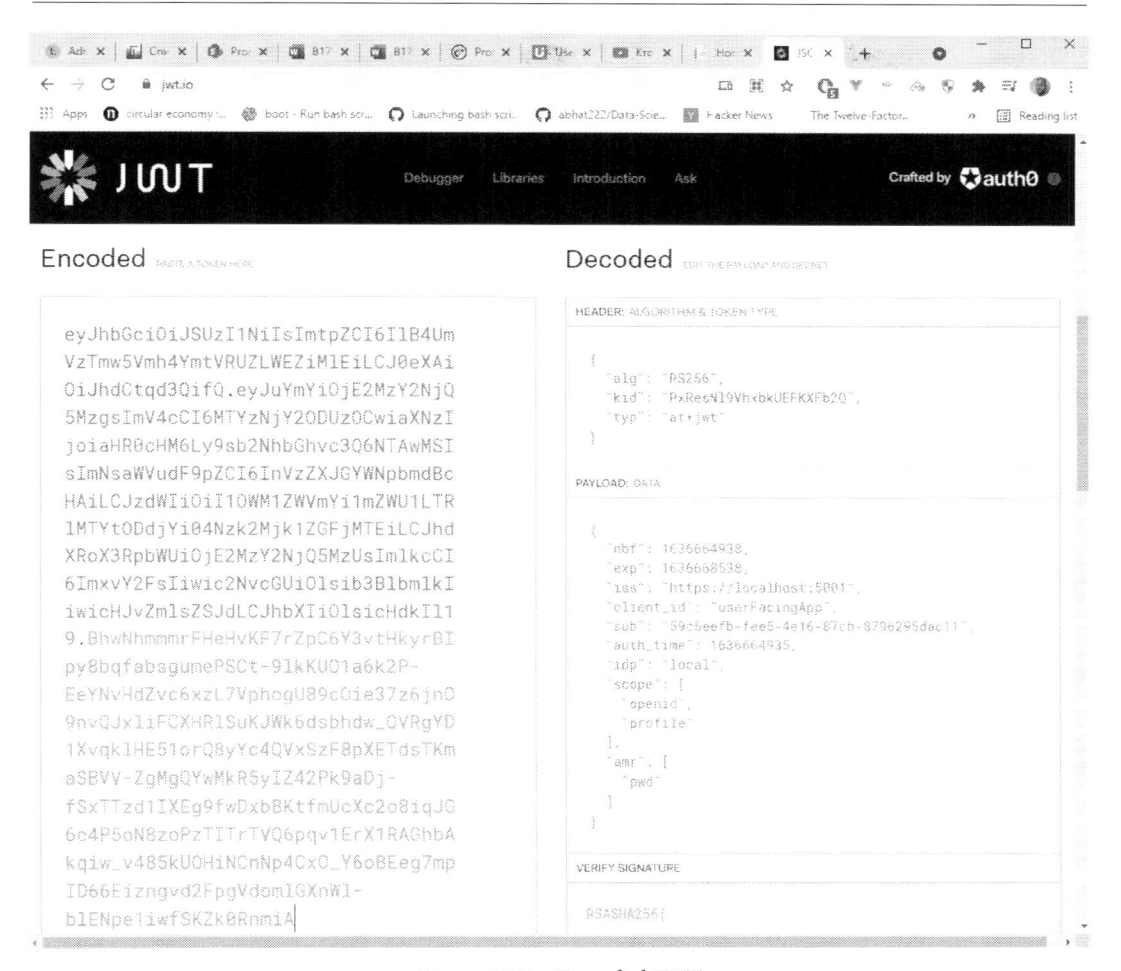

Figure 10.7 – Decoded JWT

We can also test the logout functionality by going back to the home page of the MVC application and clicking the **Log Out** tab. You should be redirected to the logout page of IdentityServer4. Then, entering the base URL of the MVC application will redirect us back to the login screen, and this demonstrates the OpenID Connect flow in action. If we configure our SSO client to connect to the SSO provider and its configuration matches the client configuration in the SSO application, we can force the client application to automatically redirect to the authentication screen provided by the SSO application. If the user has been successfully authenticated, we can then retrieve a JWT, which we can store in a cookie.

The token will be valid until we either log out by clearing the cookie or the token expires. But while it is valid, the user remains authenticated and we don't get redirected to the login screen.

In the preceding examples, we have also demonstrated how we can extract the JWT with our backend code, and this is precisely what will allow us to authenticate into a protected gRPC application, which we will have a look at next.

Restricting gRPC endpoints to authenticated users

gRPC is primarily designed for the backend; therefore, in most cases, it won't be possible to redirect to an SSO login. There simply won't be a UI that we will be able to do it from.

But because the OpenID Connect workflow obtains a token that is then stored in the application, we can simply reuse this token to get the user-facing application to authenticate into the gRPC application that it needs to communicate with. We will now demonstrate how to do this.

Setting up shared gRPC dependencies

We will start by creating a library that both the client and the server will share. As we did in the previous chapters, we will do so to ensure that both the client and the server use identical **Protocol Buffers** (**Protobuf**) definitions. Follow these next steps:

1. Navigate to the `GrpcAuthentication` solution folder and execute the following command to create a class library project:

   ```
   dotnet new classlib -o GrpcDependencies
   ```

2. Add this project to the solution by executing the following command:

   ```
   dotnet sln add
   GrpcDependencies\GrpcDependencies.csproj
   ```

3. Next, navigate to the `GrpcDependencies` project folder and add the relevant NuGet packages by executing the following command:

   ```
   dotnet add GrpcDependencies.csproj package
   Grpc.Net.Client
   dotnet add GrpcDependencies.csproj package
   Google.Protobuf
   ```

```
dotnet add GrpcDependencies.csproj package Grpc.Tools
dotnet add GrpcDependencies.csproj package
Grpc.AspNetCore
```

4. We will then create a `Protos` folder inside the project folder and place a `secrets.proto` file there with the following `package` and `service` definitions:

```
syntax = "proto3";

package secrets;

service SecretStore {
rpc GetSecret(GetSecretRequest) returns
  (GetSecretResponse);
}
```

5. We will then add the relevant `message` definitions, as follows:

```
message GetSecretRequest {
int32 id = 1;
}

message GetSecretResponse {
oneof payload {
SecretData data = 1;
string error_message = 2;
}
}

message SecretData {
int32 id = 1;
string title = 2;
string description = 3;
SecretLevel level = 4;
}

enum SecretLevel {
```

```
RESTRICTED = 0;
SECRET = 1;
TOP_SECRET = 2;
}
```

6. This service will return a payload containing some secret information that only authorized users will be able to access. We will need to register this file inside `GrpcDependencies.csproj` by adding the following code to it:

```
<ItemGroup>
    <Protobuf Include="Protos\secrets.proto" />
</ItemGroup>
```

We have now added a library with shared gRPC dependencies that both the client and the server will use. Now, we are ready to set up the gRPC server application.

Setting up the gRPC server

We will now add a gRPC service project with an endpoint that will only be accessible by authenticated users. Follow these next steps:

1. Navigate back to the `GrpcAuthentication` solution folder and execute the following command to create a new gRPC service project:

   ```
   dotnet new grpc -o SecretsManager
   ```

2. We will then add the project to the solution by executing the following command:

   ```
   dotnet sln add SecretsManager\SecretsManager.csproj
   ```

3. We now need to add a library that will enable us to add JWT middleware to our application. To do so, navigate to the `SecretsManager` project folder and execute the following command:

   ```
   dotnet add SecretsManager.csproj package
   Microsoft.AspNetCore.Authentication.JwtBearer
   ```

4. Now, we will open the `SecretsManager.csproj` file and add the following code to it:

   ```
   <ItemGroup>
       <ProjectReference Include="..\GrpcDependencies
   ```

```
            \GrpcDependencies.csproj" />
        </ItemGroup>
```

5. We can also remove the existing reference to `Grpc.AspNetCore` NuGet package from the project file, as this package will be implicitly referenced via the reference to the `GrpcDependencies` project.

6. We will now add a `SecretsCache.cs` file to the project with the following content:

```
using Secrets;
using System.Collections.Generic;
using System.Linq;

namespace SecretsManager
{
    public class SecretsCache
    {
        private readonly List<SecretData> secrets;

        public SecretsCache()
        {
            secrets = new List<SecretData>();
        }

        public SecretData GetSecret(int id)
        {
            return secrets.FirstOrDefault(s => s.Id ==
                id);
        }
    }
}
```

7. We will then need to populate the `secrets` list with the initial data. To do so, we can add the following code into the constructor:

```
secrets.Add(new SecretData
{
    Id = 1,
```

```
            Title = "Undercover Operative",
            Description = "We have an undercover operative in
              Northern Alaska",
            Level = SecretLevel.Restricted
        });
        secrets.Add(new SecretData
        {
            Id = 2,
            Title = "Ship Position",
            Description = "The current ship's coordinates are
              54.55, 4.9",
            Level = SecretLevel.Secret
        });
        secrets.Add(new SecretData
        {
            Id = 3,
            Title = "Bioweapon",
            Description = "A bioweapon has been in development
              since 2009",
            Level = SecretLevel.TopSecret
        });
```

8. Now, we will add `SecretsManagerService.cs` to the `Secrets` folder of the project. The content of the file will be as follows:

```
using Grpc.Core;
using Microsoft.AspNetCore.Authorization;
using Secrets;
using System;
using System.Threading.Tasks;

namespace SecretsManager
{
    [Authorize]
    public class SecretsManagerService :
      SecretStore.SecretStoreBase
    {
```

```
            private readonly SecretsCache secretsCache;

            public SecretsManagerService(SecretsCache
                secretsCache)
            {
                this.secretsCache = secretsCache;
            }
        }
    }
```

Please note that we have the `Authorize` attribute on top of the class signature. This attribute, if specified without any additional parameters, will restrict access to all endpoints in the class to only those users who have successfully authenticated. We can also place the attribute on an individual endpoint, which will restrict access to only this specific endpoint. It's the same attribute that is used in action methods of the controllers and inside the SignalR hub.

9. We will then add the `GetSecret` RPC implementation method to the class, which will look like this:

```
        public override Task<GetSecretResponse>
          GetSecret(GetSecretRequest request, ServerCall
            Context context)
        {
            var secret = secretsCache.GetSecret(request.Id);

            if (secret is not null)
                return Task.FromResult(new GetSecretResponse
                {
                    Data = secret
                });

            return Task.FromResult(new GetSecretResponse
            {
                ErrorMessage = $"No secret found for id
                  {request.Id}."
            });
        }
```

10. We will then need to apply some changes to the `Startup` class (or the `Program.cs` file if you are using a .NET 6 project template). First, we need to make sure that the class has the following `using` statement:

```
using Microsoft.IdentityModel.Tokens;
```

11. Next, we will add the JWT authentication middleware. To do so, we will insert the following code into the `ConfigureServices` method. If you are using a .NET 6 template, `services` will need to be replaced with `builder.Services` and the code will need to be inserted before the `Build` event:

```
services.AddAuthentication("Bearer")
    .AddJwtBearer("Bearer", options =>
    {
        options.Authority = "https://localhost:5001";
        options.TokenValidationParameters = new
          TokenValidationParameters
          {
              ValidateAudience = false
          };
    });
```

Here, we are specifying the authority, which is the URL of our SSO application. Then, we are switching off audience validation. This is because the intended audience of the token is the user-facing MVC application. So, we need to make sure that the token still works if passed into the current application.

12. After this, we have a choice. Since we already have the `Authorize` attribute on our `SecretsManagerService` class, we can add blank authorization middleware by adding a `services.AddAuthorization();` statement to the `ConfigureServices` method. But to make it clearer, we can also add authorization middleware that explicitly states that only authenticated users are allowed access. To do so, we will add the following statement:

```
services.AddAuthorization(options =>
{
    options.AddPolicy("GrpcAuth", policy =>
    {
        policy.RequireAuthenticatedUser();
    });
});
```

13. Next, we will need to insert the following statements into the `Configure` method (or, for .NET 6, the main body of the file after the `Build` event) after the `app.UseRouting` call:

    ```
    app.UseAuthentication();
    app.UseAuthorization();
    ```

14. We will then need to register our gRPC service implementation by adding the following statement to the `UseEndpoints` call:

    ```
    endpoints.MapGrpcService<SecretsManagerService>();
    ```

15. Optionally, we can force the endpoint to use the authorization policy that we defined earlier by modifying the registration call, as follows:

    ```
    endpoints.MapGrpcService<SecretsManagerService>()
        .RequireAuthorization("GrpcAuth");
    ```

16. Finally, we will need to change the application ports in the project to make sure that they don't clash with other applications. To do so, we will open the `launchSettings.json` file and will replace the `applicationUrl` entry with the following code:

    ```
    "applicationUrl": "",
    ```

> **Note**
> If you are running your server-side application on a Mac, you will need to apply some modifications to it. Instructions on how to do so can be found in the *Running a gRPC service on a Mac* section of *Chapter 1, Creating a Basic gRPC Application on ASP.NET Core*.

We are now ready to enable relevant changes on the `UserFacingApp` project, which will act as our gRPC client.

Enabling gRPC client functionality

We will now open the `UserFacingApp` project and make all the necessary changes to it to make it act as a gRPC client and to make it pass an authorization token to the gRPC server. Follow these next steps:

1. We will first need to add shared gRPC dependencies to the project by adding the following code to the `UserFacingApp.csproj` file:

    ```xml
    <ItemGroup>
        <ProjectReference Include="..\GrpcDependencies
        \GrpcDependencies.csproj" />
    </ItemGroup>
    ```

2. We will then need to create a model for one of our views. To do so, insert a `SecretDetails.cs` file into the `Models` folder with the following content:

    ```csharp
    namespace UserFacingApp.Models
    {
        public class SecretDetails
        {
            public int Id { get; set; }
            public string Title { get; set; }
            public string Description { get; set; }
            public string SecretLevel { get; set; }
        }
    }
    ```

3. Next, we will insert a `GrpcClientWrapper.cs` file into the root of the project and add the following content to it:

    ```csharp
    using Grpc.Core;
    using Secrets;
    using System;
    using System.Threading.Tasks;
    using UserFacingApp.Models;

    namespace UserFacingApp
    {
        public class GrpcClientWrapper
    ```

```
    {
        private readonly SecretStore.SecretStoreClient client;
        public GrpcClientWrapper(SecretStore.SecretStoreClient
           client)
            {
    this.client = client;
            }


        }
}
```

4. Next, we will add a method to the class that makes a call to the gRPC server and applies the authorization token to the header while doing so, as follows:

```
public async Task<SecretDetails> GetSecret(int id,
    string accessToken)
{
    var metadata = new Metadata
        {
            { "Authorization", $"Bearer {accessToken}" }
        };
    var request = new GetSecretRequest
        {
            Id = id
        };

    var response = await
        client.GetSecretAsync(request, metadata);

    if (string.IsNullOrEmpty(response.ErrorMessage))
        return new SecretDetails
            {
                Id = response.Data.Id,
                Title = response.Data.Title,
                Description = response.Data.Description,
                SecretLevel =
                   response.Data.Level.ToString()
```

```
        };

        throw new Exception(response.ErrorMessage);
}
```

This method adds an `Authorization` header. The value of the header consists of the authorization type and the attribute that is used for authorization. In our case, we are using an authorization token, which is also known as a bearer token. In this case, we need to use `Bearer` as the authorization type. Then, we will just add the JWT that we have received from the SSO application.

5. This time, we will inject a gRPC client from an inbuilt factory. To do so, we will need to add the following `using` statement to the `Startup` class of the project (or the `Program.cs` file if you are using .NET 6):

```
using Secrets;
```

6. Then, we will add the following **dependency injection** (**DI**) registration statements to the `ConfigureServices` method. The client address is the address of the `SecretsManager` application we set up previously:

```
services.AddGrpcClient<SecretStore.SecretStoreClient>(
    o =>
    {
        o.Address = new Uri("");
    });
services.AddSingleton<GrpcClientWrapper>();
```

7. We will now insert a gRPC client wrapper into our `HomeController` class. To do so, we will add it as a private field and will replace the class constructor with the following code:

```
private readonly GrpcClientWrapper clientWrapper;

public HomeController(GrpcClientWrapper clientWrapper)
{
    this.clientWrapper = clientWrapper;
}
```

8. We will now add the following action method, where we will use the gRPC client wrapper class:

```csharp
public async Task<IActionResult> Details(int id)
{
    var accessToken = await
        HttpContext.GetTokenAsync("access_token");
    var secretDetails = await
        clientWrapper.GetSecret(id, accessToken);
    return View(secretDetails);
}
```

9. We will now need to add a view for this method. To do so, add a `Details.cshtml` file to the `Home` folder of the `Views` folder with the following content:

```cshtml
@model UserFacingApp.Models.SecretDetails

@{
    ViewData["Title"] = "Secret Details";
}

<h1>@ViewData["Title"]</h1>

<p><b>ID: </b> @Model.Id</p>
<p><b>Title: </b> @Model.Title</p>
<p><b>Description: </b> @Model.Description</p>
<p><b>Secret Level: </b> @Model.SecretLevel</p>
```

10. Then, replace the content of the `Index.cshtml` file with the following code:

```cshtml
@{
    ViewData["Title"] = "Home Page";
}

<div class="text-center">
    <h1 class="display-4">Please enter the id of the
        secret you want to view:</h1>
    <form asp-action="Details" method="get">
```

```html
        <p>
            <input type="text" name="Id" />
            <input type="submit" value="Submit" />
        </p>
    </form>
</div>
```

We are now ready to launch our applications and see how the authorization token is passed through to the gRPC service. After executing the `dotnet run` command inside all project folders except `GrpcDependencies`, we can open the MVC application in the browser and log in by using any of the available credentials. We should then be greeted by the following page:

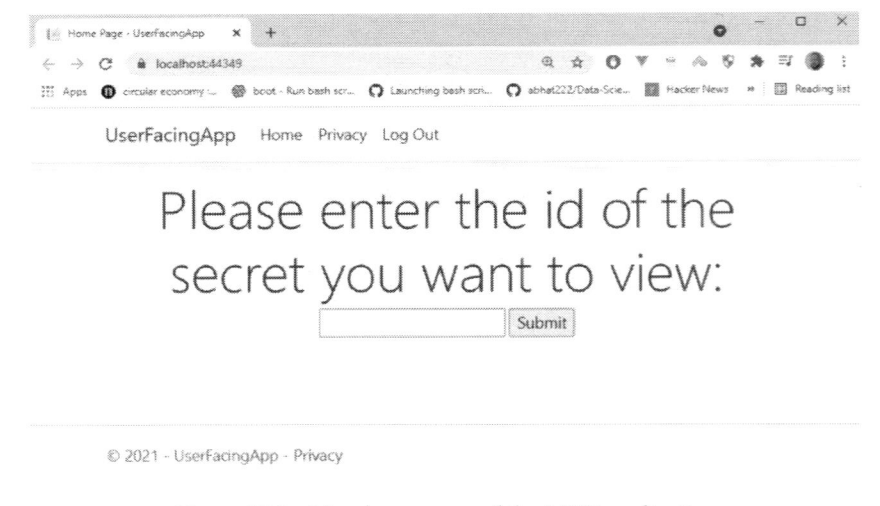

Figure 10.8 – New home page of the MVC application

If we enter the value of 1, the page should change to the following:

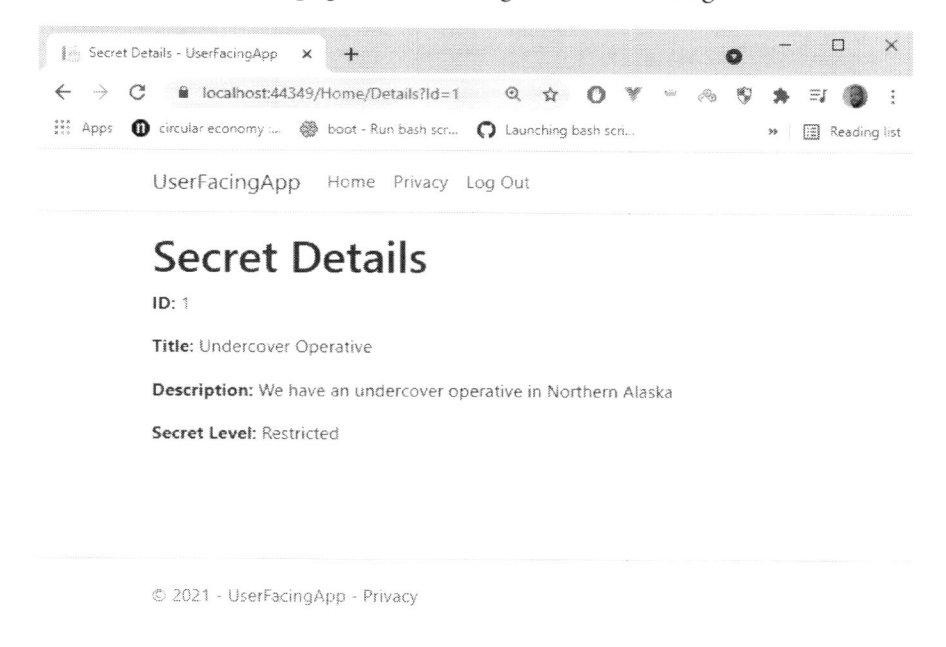

Figure 10.9 – Screen showing successfully obtained data from gRPC

However, if you change your client code and don't pass the authorization token to the gRPC call, you will receive a 401 HTTP error instead of this page.

We have demonstrated how authentication works on gRPC, but now, we will go further and apply authorization to it too.

Restricting endpoints to authorized users only

User authorization is based on claims that are present in the payload of a JWT. We can use any claims for authorization, including any custom ones. For example, we can use a standard `role` claim to restrict endpoints to only those clients that have specific roles defined inside this claim, or we can just create a custom claim based on the combination of various fields in the object that represents the user. For example, we may add a particular claim to the payload of the token if the user has a specific role and also belongs to a specific organization. Then, on the server side, we can configure an authorization policy based on this claim.

There are many ways you can apply authorization in gRPC on ASP.NET Core, so we won't be able to cover them all in this chapter. We will focus on the standard role-based authorization. However, the general principles demonstrated in the following examples will be applicable to different types of authorization.

But before we apply authorization to our gRPC endpoints, we will need to make some changes to our SSO application because, as you may recall from *Figure 10.6*, IdentityServer4 doesn't insert a `role` claim into the JWT payload by default.

Configuring SSO provider to insert role claim into the JWT

In order for our IdentityServer4 implementation to insert user roles into the JWT on successful authentication, we will need to add some custom code to it. So, we will need to stop any running instances of our application and apply the following changes to the `AuthProvider` project:

1. Insert a `UserProfileService.cs` file into the root of the project folder and add the following `using` statements to it:

    ```
    using AuthProvider.Models;
    using IdentityModel;
    using IdentityServer4.Extensions;
    using IdentityServer4.Models;
    using IdentityServer4.Services;
    using Microsoft.AspNetCore.Identity;
    using System;
    using System.Linq;
    using System.Security.Claims;
    using System.Threading.Tasks;
    ```

2. Then, we will add the following class body:

    ```
    namespace AuthProvider
    {
        public class UserProfileService : IProfileService
        {
            private readonly
                IUserClaimsPrincipalFactory<ApplicationUser>
                    claimsFactory;
    ```

```
            private readonly UserManager<ApplicationUser>
               usersManager;

            public UserProfileService(
               UserManager<ApplicationUser> usersManager,
               IUserClaimsPrincipalFactory<ApplicationUser>
                  claimsFactory)
            {
               this.usersManager = usersManager;
               this.claimsFactory = claimsFactory;
            }


      }
}
```

3. Next, we will implement the interface by first adding the following method to it:

```
public async Task
 GetProfileDataAsync(ProfileDataRequestContext context)
{
     var subject = context.Subject.GetSubjectId();
     var user = await
        usersManager.FindByIdAsync(subject);
     var claimsPrincipal = await
        claimsFactory.CreateAsync(user);
     var claimsList = claimsPrincipal.Claims.ToList();
     claimsList = claimsList.Where(c => context
        .RequestedClaimTypes.Contains(c.Type)).ToList();

     if (usersManager.SupportsUserRole)
     {
         foreach (var roleName in await
            usersManager.GetRolesAsync(user))
         {
             claimsList.Add(new
                Claim(JwtClaimTypes.Role, roleName));
         }
```

```
            }
            context.IssuedClaims = claimsList;
}
```

4. This method contains the logic to add a `role` claim to the token, but we will also need to add the following method as it's also defined in the interface:

```
public async Task IsActiveAsync(IsActiveContext
    context)
{
    var subject = context.Subject.GetSubjectId();
    var user = await
        usersManager.FindByIdAsync(subject);
    context.IsActive = user != null;
}
```

5. Next, we will need to register this class in the DI container of the `Startup` class (or the `Program.cs` file if we are using .NET 6). To do so, we will first add the following `using` statement to the class:

```
using IdentityServer4.Services;
```

6. Then, we will add the following line at the end of the `ConfigureServices` method (or just before the `Build` event if you are using .NET 6):

```
services.AddScoped<IProfileService,
    UserProfileService>();
```

It is important that we add this registration at the very end of the method; otherwise, it will be overwritten by the default implementation.

Next, we will add `rpc` definitions to our Protobuf. This will be needed so that we can apply different authorization rules to different endpoints.

Applying different authorization rules to different gRPC endpoints

We will first make some changes to the `secrets.proto` file. Then, we will add the new endpoints to the server-side code and apply authorization to them. Follow these next steps:

1. Add the following `import` statement to the `secrets.proto` file in the `GrpcDependencies` project:

   ```
   import "google/protobuf/empty.proto";
   ```

2. Add the following `rpc` definitions to the `SecretStore` service:

   ```
   rpc GetSecretsCount (google.protobuf.Empty) returns
     (SecretsCount);
   rpc InsertSecret (SecretData) returns
     (google.protobuf.Empty);
   ```

3. Now, add the following `message` definition:

   ```
   message SecretsCount {
       int32 count = 1;
   }
   ```

4. We are now ready to add the implementations of these new RPCs to our `SecretsManagerService` class of the `SecretsManager` application project. But first, we will need to add the following methods to the `SecretsCache` class:

   ```
   public int GetCount()
   {
       return secrets.Count;
   }

   public void InsertSecret(SecretData data)
   {
       data.Id = secrets.Max(s => s.Id);
       secrets.Add(data);
   }
   ```

5. Then, add the following using statement to it:

```
using Google.Protobuf.WellKnownTypes;
```

6. Then, add the following method to the class:

```
[AllowAnonymous]
public override Task<SecretsCount>
  GetSecretsCount(Empty request, ServerCallContext
    context)
{
    return Task.FromResult(new SecretsCount
    {
        Count = secretsCache.GetCount()
    });
}
```

The AllowAnonymous attribute allows clients to access this endpoint without any authorization token even if class-wide authorization was enabled. In our case, the endpoint is merely returning the count of secrets, which we don't deem to be sensitive information.

7. Next, we will add the following method to the class:

```
[Authorize(Roles = "Admin")]
public override Task<Empty> InsertSecret(SecretData
  request, ServerCallContext context)
{
    secretsCache.InsertSecret(request);
    return Task.FromResult(new Empty());
}
```

We are restricting access to this endpoint to only those users that have the role of Admin. We could also specify multiple roles by separating them with commas. Also, we could restrict access by Policy (as with GrpcAuth, which we have specified in the Startup class) or AuthenticationScheme (as with Bearer, Cookie, oidc, and so on). We could, for example, define a custom policy that requires specific claims by calling the RequireClaim method on the AuthorizationPolicyBuilder object while registering the policy in the Startup class.

8. We will finish off by adding the following attribute to the `GetSecret` method:

```
[Authorize(Roles = "User")]
```

So, we now have three gRPC endpoints. The endpoint that returns secret information is restricted to those who have been assigned the role of `User`. The endpoint that allows you to insert a new secret is restricted to only those who have the role of `Admin`. And there is an unrestricted endpoint that can be accessed by absolutely anyone, even if they aren't authenticated at all.

The roles of `Admin` and `User` are independent of each other, so if the JWT contains only one of those roles, only one of these endpoints will be accessible. We will shortly see this principle in action. Let's make the necessary changes to the client to do so.

Applying gRPC client changes

We will now open the `UserFacingApp` project. We will first modify the gRPC client wrapper class. Then, we will add all necessary action methods to the controller and the corresponding views. Follow these next steps:

1. We will need to add the following `using` statement to the `GrpcClientWrapper` class:

    ```
    using Google.Protobuf.WellKnownTypes;
    ```

2. Then, add the following method to it:

    ```
    public async Task<int> GetSecretsCount()
    {
        var response = await
            client.GetSecretsCountAsync(new Empty());
        return response.Count;
    }
    ```

3. Please note that we aren't passing the authorization token to the gRPC call, but we will pass one in the following method that we will add next:

    ```
    public async Task InsertSecret(SecretDetails details,
        string accessToken)
    {
        var metadata = new Metadata
        {
            { "Authorization", $"Bearer {accessToken}" }
    ```

```
    };
    var secret = new SecretData
    {
        Title = details.Title,
        Description = details.Description,
        Level = (SecretLevel)System.Enum.Parse
           (typeof(SecretLevel), details.SecretLevel)
    };
    await client.InsertSecretAsync(secret, metadata);
}
```

4. We will then add the following methods to the `HomeController` class:

```
public IActionResult Add()
{
    return View();
}

[HttpPost]
public async Task<IActionResult> Add(SecretDetails
   details)
{
    var accessToken = await
       HttpContext.GetTokenAsync("access_token");
    await clientWrapper.InsertSecret(details,
       accessToken);
    return RedirectToAction("Index");
}
```

5. These methods will correspond with the view that will allow us to insert a new secret and the POST action that gets triggered when we submit the form. We will also have the action method for getting the secret count, as illustrated in the following code snippet:

```
public async Task<IActionResult> Count()
{
```

```
        ViewData["Count"] = await
            clientWrapper.GetSecretsCount();
        return View();
    }
```

6. We will then add the corresponding views. First, we will add an Add.cshtml file to the Home folder inside the Views folder. Its content will be as follows:

```
@model UserFacingApp.Models.SecretDetails

@{
    ViewData["Title"] = "Add New Secret";
}

<h1>@ViewData["Title"]</h1>

<form asp-controller="Home" asp-action="Add"
  method="post">
    Title: <input asp-for="Title" /> <br />
    Description: <input asp-for="Description" /><br />
    Description: <select data-val="true"
      id="SecretLevel" name="SecretLevel">
        <option value="Restricted">Restricted</option>
        <option value="Secret">Secret</option>
        <option value="TopSecret">Top Secret</option>
    </select><br />
    <button type="submit">Submit</button>
</form>
```

7. Then, we will add a Count.cshtml file with the following content:

```
@model UserFacingApp.Models.SecretDetails
@{
    ViewData["Title"] = "Secret Count";
}

<h1>@ViewData["Title"]</h1>
<p><b>@ViewData["Count"]</b></p>
```

8. Finally, we will insert the following markup into the `Index.cshtml` file immediately after the closing `form` tag:

```
<br />
<a class="nav-link text-dark" asp-area="" asp-
   controller="Home" asp-action="Count">Get secrets
    count</a>
<br />
<a class="nav-link text-dark" asp-area="" asp-
   controller="Home" asp-action="Add">Add a new
    secret</a>
```

We can now launch all of our applications by executing the `dotnet run` command inside all three of our ASP.NET Core project folders. By then using different logins, we can check whether we can access various gRPC endpoints. If we just want to navigate to the `Count` view, we should be able to do so with absolutely any user. We should be able to see content on the page similar to this, regardless of which login we use:

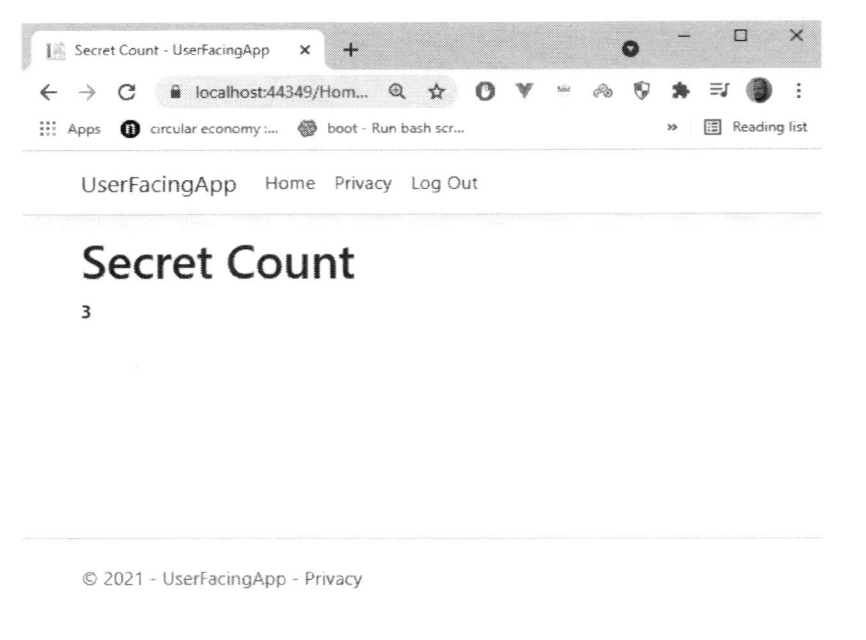

Figure 10.10 – AllowAnonymous endpoint will return data to any user

On the other hand, if you try to either access secret details with a login that doesn't have a `User` role or insert a secret with a login that doesn't have an `Admin` role, you will get a `403` HTTP code returned.

This concludes our summary of applying authentication and authorization to gRPC endpoints. Let's summarize what we have learned.

Summary

In this chapter, you have learned the fundamental principles of authentication and authorization and how to apply both to gRPC endpoints. You now know that authentication is when the user proves that they are who they claim to be, while authorization is making sure that the user has the necessary permissions to access a resource.

You have learned how a separate application can act as an SSO provider to allow you to authenticate a user into all applications inside your ecosystem. You have learned how the OpenID Connect protocol is used to authenticate the user into a relevant application, while OAuth is used for user authorization.

You have learned that a JWT contains a JSON payload object that describes the user so that the protected application can tell whether the user is who they claim to be and whether they have the necessary permissions. A JWT is validated by a signature to protect it from forgery.

And this concludes the chapter on applying authentication and authorization on gRPC endpoints. In the next and final chapter, we will have a look at how to trace events in your gRPC application by applying logs and metrics to it.

Questions

1. What is authentication used for?

    A. To ensure that only users with specific permissions can access the application

    B. To ensure that a user is who they claim to be

    C. To ensure that only users that have specific roles are allowed to access the application

    D. To ensure that only users that have an email address can access the system

2. What is authorization used for?

    A. To ensure that only users with specific permissions can access the application

    B. To ensure that a user is who they claim to be

    C. To ensure that only users that have specific roles are allowed to access the application

    D. To ensure that only users that have an email address can access the system

3. Which of the following statements is true?

    A. OpenID Connect is used for authorization

    B. OAuth is used for authentication

    C. OpenID Connect is used for authentication

    D. All of the above

4. Which parts does a JWT consist of?

    A. Header, body, and footer

    B. Header, payload, and footer

    C. Header, payload, and signature

    D. Payload and signature

5. What is a claim in a JWT payload?

    A. An encrypted signature

    B. Any JSON field in the payload

    C. Any field in a JSON payload with a singular value

    D. Specific reserved JSON fields

Further reading

- IdentityServer4 documentation: `https://identityserver4.readthedocs.io/en/latest/`
- OpenID Connect documentation: `https://openid.net/connect/`
- OAuth documentation
- *Understanding OAuth 2.0 and OpenID Connect*: `https://blog.runscope.com/posts/understanding-oauth-2-and-openid-connect`
- *Overview of ASP.NET Core authentication*: `https://docs.microsoft.com/en-us/aspnet/core/security/authentication`
- *What is multifactor authentication and how does it work?*: `https://searchsecurity.techtarget.com/definition/multifactor-authentication-MFA`

11
Using Logging, Metrics, and Debugging in gRPC on .NET

We have reached the final chapter of the book, and it covers a very important topic that will help you to identify problems easily if something in your **gRPC** application isn't working as expected when you are writing it. Also, you will learn how to monitor your application once it's up and running. This will allow you to identify any issues early and respond to them *proactively* rather than *reactively*.

We will start by going through various debugging techniques you can use on both the gRPC client and server. Of course, to debug your own code, all you have to do is place breakpoints in it. However, during the development of gRPC applications, you may encounter situations where it's not your own code that is generating an issue. Therefore, we will need to be able to extract as much information from the gRPC middleware as we can.

But once your application is up and running, you would want to know what it's doing. Otherwise, you wouldn't be able to diagnose any problems that may arise with it. This is why you need to capture various pieces of information in the logs, especially details of any errors that happen inside your application's logic.

Finally, you might want to collect other data to use for various types of analytics. For example, you might want to know how many requests your application receives, how many errors occur inside of it, and how long it takes for the requests to get processed. This is where the concept of **metrics** comes in.

In this chapter, we will cover all of these concepts. We will go through the following topics:

- Debugging gRPC client components inside a .NET application
- Debugging gRPC server components inside a .NET application
- Applying logs to gRPC
- Applying metrics to gRPC

By the end of this chapter, you will have learned how to diagnose unexpected behavior and any other problems when developing your gRPC application. You will also have learned how to monitor your application once it's up and running by getting it to write data into logs and by getting it to generate metrics.

Technical requirements

To follow the instructions in this chapter, you will need the following:

- A computer with a **Windows, Mac,** or **Linux operating system** (**OS**)
- A supported **integrated development environment** (**IDE**) or code editor (for example, **Visual Studio, Visual Studio Code,** or **JetBrains Rider**)
- The **.NET 5 software development kit** (**SDK**)
- A self-signed development HTTPS certificate enabled on your machine

The instructions on how to set all of these up were provided in *Chapter 1, Creating a Basic gRPC Application on ASP.NET Core*. All of the code samples used in this chapter can be found at https://github.com/PacktPublishing/Microservices-Communication-in-.NET-Using-gRPC/tree/main/Chapter-11.

Please visit the following link to check the CiA videos: https://bit.ly/3m3Wkht

Debugging gRPC client components inside a .NET application

We all know how to debug our own code. We can place breakpoints on the line we want to see the behavior of. We can get the code to output to the console. We can get it to output to a file.

But what if we need to debug a third-party library? What if it's not our own code that doesn't behave as expected and we need to know why? After all, unless you try to decompile the library or try to get hold of its source code, its internal code is inaccessible to us. But even if we could get hold of the source code, it would be cumbersome to apply it to our own solution.

Luckily, gRPC libraries on .NET allow you to debug their internal middleware. If you are getting some unexpected behavior from them, you will be able to capture their actions and see what they are trying to do.

We will now go through the techniques you can apply to obtain as much debugging information from gRPC components as possible. We will start with the gRPC client side. To debug gRPC from the client side, we will need to configure the server application to return detailed errors from it. This will allow us to identify the source of the problem down to the individual line. Then, we will apply interceptors to our client, which will allow us to intercept any type of communication event, log any relevant information from it, and handle any exceptions that may be thrown by the gRPC middleware.

Setting up shared gRPC dependencies

As we've done in the previous chapters, we will add a class library that will contain all of the gRPC dependencies we will need, and we will do this both on the server and the client side. This class library will then be used by both of the applications:

1. Create a folder called `GrpcAnalytics` anywhere on your machine and initiate a *solution* by running the following command inside of it:

    ```
    dotnet new sln
    ```

2. In the solution folder, execute the following command to create a class library project:

    ```
    dotnet new classlib -o GrpcDependencies
    ```

3. Then, execute the following command to add the project to the solution:

   ```
   dotnet sln add
   GrpcDependencies/GrpcDependencies.csproj
   ```

4. Now, navigate to the `GrpcDependencies` project folder. Execute the following command to add the necessary NuGet package. This will be the only package that we will need, as it already references all of the other gRPC libraries that we will be using:

   ```
   dotnet add GrpcDependencies.csproj package
   Grpc.AspNetCore
   ```

5. Create a `Protos` folder inside the project folder and add a `iot_analytics.proto` file to it with the following content:

   ```
   syntax = "proto3";

   import "google/protobuf/empty.proto";
   package iot_analytics;

   service IotStatusManager {
   rpc GetAllStatuses (google.protobuf.Empty) returns
       (stream LocationStatusResponse);
   rpc GetLocationStatus (LocationStatusRequest) returns
       (LocationStatusResponse);
   }

   message LocationStatusRequest {
   int32 location_id = 1;
   }

   message LocationStatusResponse {
   int32 location_id = 1;
   string location_name = 2;
   string device_serial_number = 3;
   int64 total_requests = 4;
   int64 total_errors = 5;
   }
   ```

6. To finish off our class library, we will add the following block to the `GrpcDependencies.csproj` file:

   ```
   <ItemGroup>
       <Protobuf Include="Protos\iot_analytics.proto" />
   </ItemGroup>
   ```

So, as the name of our **Protobuf** suggests, we will pretend that we are monitoring the status of **Internet of Things** (**IoT**) devices. Next, we will build our gRPC service application and configure it so that the client will receive as much debugging information from it as possible.

Adding a gRPC service application and getting it to display detailed errors

In this example, we will intentionally make one of the **remote procedure calls** (**RPCs**) throw an error to see what information the client will receive. We will be able to see how this information changes depending on whether detailed errors have been enabled on the server. Here's how it's done:

1. We will navigate back to our `GrpcAnalytics` solution folder and execute the following command to create a new gRPC service project:

   ```
   dotnet new grpc -o IotDeviceManager
   ```

2. We will then add this project to the solution by running the following command:

   ```
   dotnet sln add
   IotDeviceManager/IotDeviceManager.csproj
   ```

3. Then, we will navigate to our project folder and add the reference to the class library we created earlier by inserting the following section into the `IotDeviceManager.csproj` file:

   ```
   <ItemGroup>
      <ProjectReference Include="..\GrpcDependencies\
         GrpcDependencies.csproj" />
   </ItemGroup>
   ```

4. Also, because the class library already has a reference to the gRPC library that we need, we can remove any direct NuGet references from the `IotDeviceManager.csproj` file.

5. We will then add a `LocationDataCache.cs` file to our project. The initial content of the file will be as follows:

```csharp
using IotAnalytics;
using System;
using System.Collections.Generic;
using System.Linq;

namespace IotDeviceManager
{
    public class LocationDataCache
    {
        private readonly List<LocationStatusResponse>
            statuses;

        public LocationDataCache()
        {
            statuses = new
                List<LocationStatusResponse>();
        }
```

6. We will then add the following public methods to the class:

```csharp
        public IEnumerable<LocationStatusResponse>
            GetAllStatuses()
        {
            return statuses;
        }

        public LocationStatusResponse GetStatus(int
            locationId)
        {
            return statuses.FirstOrDefault(s =>
                s.LocationId == locationId);
        }
    }
}
```

7. We can pre-populate the `statuses` collection by inserting the following code into the constructor:

```
var random = new Random();

for (var i = 0; i < 100; i++)
{
    statuses.Add(new LocationStatusResponse
    {
        LocationId = i + 1,
        LocationName = $"Location {i}",
        DeviceSerialNumber = $"{i}{i}{i}-DEMO-{i *
            20}",
        TotalRequests = random.Next(1000, 1000000),
        TotalErrors = random.Next(1000)
    });
}
```

8. Next, we will add the gRPC service implementation to the `Services` folder of the project. The file we will insert into the folder will be called `IotStatusManagerService.cs` and it will have the following content:

```
using Google.Protobuf.WellKnownTypes;
using Grpc.Core;
using IotAnalytics;
using System.Threading.Tasks;

namespace IotDeviceManager.Services
{
    public class IotStatusManagerService :
        IotStatusManager.IotStatusManagerBase
    {
        private readonly LocationDataCache dataCache;

        public IotStatusManagerService
            (LocationDataCache dataCache)
        {
```

```csharp
            this.dataCache = dataCache;
        }
    }
}
```

9. Then, we will add `rpc` implementations as follows:

```csharp
public override async Task GetAllStatuses(Empty
    request, IServerStreamWriter<LocationStatusResponse>
    responseStream, ServerCallContext context)
{
    foreach (var status in dataCache.GetAllStatuses())
    {
        await responseStream.WriteAsync(status);
    }
}

public override Task<LocationStatusResponse>
    GetLocationStatus(LocationStatusRequest request,
    ServerCallContext context)
{
    throw new Exception("This call is not ready
        yet.");
}
```

10. So, this is where we have deliberately made one of the `rpc` implementations throw an error to see what will happen if the client tries to call it. Next, we will open the `Startup` class (or the `Program.cs` file if you are using **.NET 6** project templates). In this file, we will add the following variable to indicate whether we are using the development environment:

```csharp
private readonly bool isDevelopment =
    Environment.GetEnvironmentVariable(
        "ASPNETCORE_ENVIRONMENT") == "Development";
```

11. Then, replace the content of the `ConfigureServices` method with the following. If you are using .NET 6, you will need to apply this code to the `builder.Services` property inside the main body of the code, and you will need to delete the existing `builder.Services.AddGrpc` call:

    ```
    services.AddGrpc(options =>
    {
        options.EnableDetailedErrors = isDevelopment;
    });
    services.AddSingleton<LocationDataCache>();
    services.AddSingleton<TracingInterceptor>();
    ```

    So, we have enabled detailed errors if the code is running on the development environment. Otherwise, the server would be expected to produce only the standard error information, without revealing too many details.

12. We will then need to register our newly added gRPC service implementation by adding the following statement to the `UseEndpoints` call:

    ```
    endpoints.MapGrpcService<IotStatusManagerService>();
    ```

> **Note**
> If you are running your server-side application on a Mac, you will need to apply some modifications to it. The instruction on how to do so can be found in the *Running a gRPC Service on a Mac* section in *Chapter 1, Creating a Basic gRPC Application on ASP.NET Core*.

And now we have everything we need on the server side. Let's now build the client and add some extra debugging capabilities to it.

Adding a gRPC client with additional debugging capabilities

When an error comes from gRPC middleware on **ASP.NET Core**, it will throw an exception of the `RpcException` type. Of course, such an exception doesn't necessarily come from the internal components of gRPC libraries. We are free to throw this type of exception ourselves. But unless we throw an exception of this type manually, the only place it will be generated is in the internal gRPC middleware. And this is why – in order to diagnose the problem that originates inside the middleware – we need to catch an exception of this type.

We will now add a gRPC client and apply global exception handling to it. This means we won't have to catch it for every individual gRPC call. We will do this by applying the so-called *interceptors*. Also, once the client is completed, we will be able to see what happens with and without the `EnableDetailedErrors` option being set to `true` on the server:

1. First, we will navigate back to our `GrpcAnalytics` solution folder and run the following command to create a new **ASP.NET Core** Web API project:

   ```
   dotnet new webapi -o IotApiGateway
   ```

2. We will then add the project to the solution by executing the following command:

   ```
   dotnet sln add IotApiGateway/IotApiGateway.csproj
   ```

3. Then, we will open our project folder and insert the following markup into the `IotApiGateway.csproj` file:

   ```
   <ItemGroup>
       <ProjectReference Include="..\GrpcDependencies\
           GrpcDependencies.csproj" />
   </ItemGroup>
   ```

4. These are all of the dependencies we need. We will leave any existing NuGet dependencies as they are. Next, we will add a gRPC interceptor to the project. The interceptor will reside in the `TracingInterceptor.cs` file that will be placed into the root of the project folder. Its content will be as follows:

   ```
   using Grpc.Core;
   using Grpc.Core.Interceptors;
   using System;
   using System.Threading.Tasks;

   namespace IotApiGateway
   {
       public class TracingInterceptor : Interceptor
       {
       }
   }
   ```

5. This is a custom class that will override the logic inside the standard gRPC interceptor that is run by the middleware. This class will allow us to trigger custom logic whenever a gRPC call of a particular type is made. We will add examples of interceptor methods for all call types. The first one is a *blocking unary call*, which will be as follows:

    ```
    public override TResponse BlockingUnaryCall<TRequest,
      TResponse>(TRequest request, ClientInterceptor
        Context<TRequest, TResponse> context,
          BlockingUnaryCallContinuation<TRequest,
            TResponse> continuation)
    {
        try
        {
            return continuation(request, context);
        }
        catch (RpcException ex)
        {
            Console.WriteLine(ex);
            throw;
        }
    }
    ```

6. The `continuation` parameter allows us to call the next step in the middleware. And because the call is blocking, we can just return the result of the `continuation` call. It will throw an exception if there is a problem with the connection. Next, we will add a method for an *async unary call*:

    ```
    public override AsyncUnaryCall<TResponse>
      AsyncUnaryCall<TRequest, TResponse>(Trequest
        request, ClientInterceptorContext<TRequest,
          TResponse> context, AsyncUnaryCallContinuation
            <TRequest, TResponse> continuation)
    {
        var call = continuation(request, context);
        return new
    ```

```
            AsyncUnaryCall<TResponse>(HandleCallResponse
        (call.ResponseAsync), call.ResponseHeadersAsync,
        call.GetStatus, call.GetTrailers,call.Dispose);
}
```

7. In this case, because the call is asynchronous, we won't be able to just catch the exception by calling the `continuation` parameter. Instead, we can attach a custom handler to some of the actions. We have done this by attaching a call to `HandleCallResponse` to the `ResponseAsync` action. Whenever this method is called by the code that uses the client, this handler will be called. So, we can place all of our exception-handling logic there. We will add this method later. But for now, we will add a *client-streaming call*:

```
public override AsyncClientStreamingCall<TRequest,
    TResponse> AsyncClientStreamingCall<TRequest,
    TResponse>(ClientInterceptorContext<TRequest,
    TResponse> context, AsyncClientStreamingCall
        Continuation<TRequest, TResponse> continuation)
{
    var call = continuation(context);
    return new AsyncClientStreamingCall<TRequest,
      TResponse>(
        call.RequestStream,
        HandleCallResponse(call.ResponseAsync),
        call.ResponseHeadersAsync,
        call.GetStatus,
        call.GetTrailers,
        call.Dispose);
}
```

8. Because this type of call returns the same kind of response as a blocking unary call, we can apply the same handler to the method that returns its response. Next, we will add an interceptor method for a *server-streaming call*:

```
public override AsyncServerStreamingCall<TResponse>
    AsyncServerStreamingCall<TRequest, TResponse>
        (TRequest request, ClientInterceptorContext
            <TRequest, TResponse> context, AsyncServer
                StreamingCallContinuation<TRequest, TResponse>
                    continuation)
{
    try
    {
        return continuation(request, context);
    }
    catch (RpcException ex)
    {
        Console.WriteLine(ex);
        throw;
    }
}
```

9. In here, we can also associate handlers with various actions. But we will need to write a different type of handler – one that is appropriate to the action. After this, we will add an interceptor method for a *bi-directional call*:

```
public override AsyncDuplexStreamingCall<TRequest,
    TResponse> AsyncDuplexStreamingCall<TRequest,
        TResponse>(ClientInterceptorContext<TRequest,
            TResponse> context, AsyncDuplexStreamingCall
                Continuation<TRequest, TResponse> continuation)
{
    try
    {
        return continuation(context);
    }
    catch (RpcException ex)
    {
```

```
            Console.WriteLine(ex);
            throw;
        }
    }
```

10. Once again, we haven't added any handlers to any of the actions. But you can experiment with this method and add your own. Finally, we will need to add the method for the actual handler that we referenced previously:

```
private async Task<TResponse> HandleCallResponse
    <TResponse>(Task<TResponse> responseTask)
{
    try
    {
        var response = await responseTask;
        return response;
    }
    catch (RpcException ex)
    {
        Console.WriteLine(ex);
        throw;
    }
}
```

11. And all we have to do now is add this interceptor to our client. To do so, we will modify our `Startup` class (or the `Program.cs` file if you are using .NET 6 project templates). Whichever file we are using, we need to make sure that we have the following `using` statement in it:

```
using IotAnalytics;
```

12. Then, we will need to add the following code to the `ConfigureServices` method. If you are using a .NET 6 template, replace `services` with `builder.Services`, and insert this code anywhere before the `Build` action. If you are running your gRPC server on macOS, the `Address` option should be `HTTP` with the relevant port number added:

```
services.AddGrpcClient<IotStatusManager.IotStatus
    ManagerClient>(options =>
    {
```

```
            options.Address = new
               Uri("https://localhost:5001");
        })
        .AddInterceptor<TracingInterceptor>();
```

13. The gRPC client has now been added to the dependency injection container and our custom interceptor has been added to it. We will now add a controller where we will be able to use the client. We will do this by adding a `DevicesController.cs` file to the `Controllers` folder with the following content:

```
using Google.Protobuf.WellKnownTypes;
using IotAnalytics;
using Microsoft.AspNetCore.Mvc;
using System.Collections.Generic;
using System.Threading;
using System.Threading.Tasks;

namespace IotApiGateway.Controllers
{
    [ApiController]
    public class DevicesController : ControllerBase
    {
        private readonly IotStatusManager
            .IotStatusManagerClient client;

        public DevicesController(IotStatusManager
            .IotStatusManagerClient client)
        {
            this.client = client;
        }
    }
}
```

14. We will then add endpoint methods that correspond with both of the `rpc` definitions in Protobuf:

```csharp
[HttpGet("")]
public async Task<IEnumerable<LocationStatusResponse>>
    GetAllStatuses()
{
    var response = new List<LocationStatusResponse>();
    using var call = client.GetAllStatuses(new
        Empty());
    while (await call.ResponseStream.MoveNext
        (CancellationToken.None))
    {
        response.Add(call.ResponseStream.Current);
    }

    return response;
}

[HttpGet("{id}")]
public async Task<LocationStatusResponse>
    GetStatus(int id)
{
    return await client.GetLocationStatusAsync(new
        LocationStatusRequest
        {
            LocationId = id
        });
}
```

We are now ready to launch our application and see what error information will be logged from it. After all, it will be easy to trigger an error, as we haven't implemented one of the `rpc` definitions on the server. Nonetheless, we have the code that will attempt to call it.

Viewing gRPC error information on the client

Make sure that the `launchSettings.json` files in the `IotApiGateway` and `IotDeviceManager` projects have different ports specified in the `applicationUrl` field. Otherwise, one application will prevent the other from running. Once this is done, launch the applications by executing the `dotnet run` command in each of the project folders.

We can now navigate to the `Swagger` page of the `IotApiGateway` application, which will be available at the following address:

```
{base URL as defined in launchSettings.json file}/swagger
```

This page will allow us to execute both of our `DeviceController` endpoints. The first endpoint calls a gRPC method that has been fully implemented, so you will be able to see some data returned. The second endpoint, however, will encounter an error that is being deliberately thrown by the server. If you try to execute the `Devices/{id}` endpoint, you would expect to see the following error logged in the console of the `IotApiGateway` application:

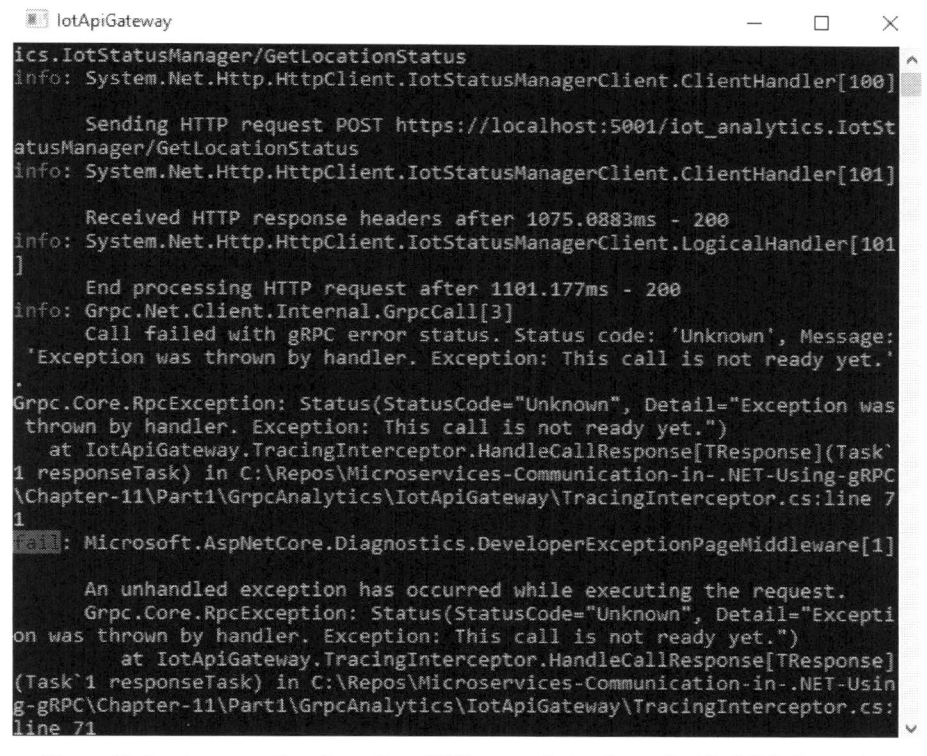

Figure 11.1 – An exception from the gRPC server being logged with full information

We can see the inner message of the exception that we have deliberately thrown. However, if we now stop both of our applications and set the `EnableDetailedErrors` option on the gRPC server to `false`, we will see a different outcome in our client console after re-launching the applications. The exception would still be caught and logged, but this time, there will be no original error message present, as this image demonstrates:

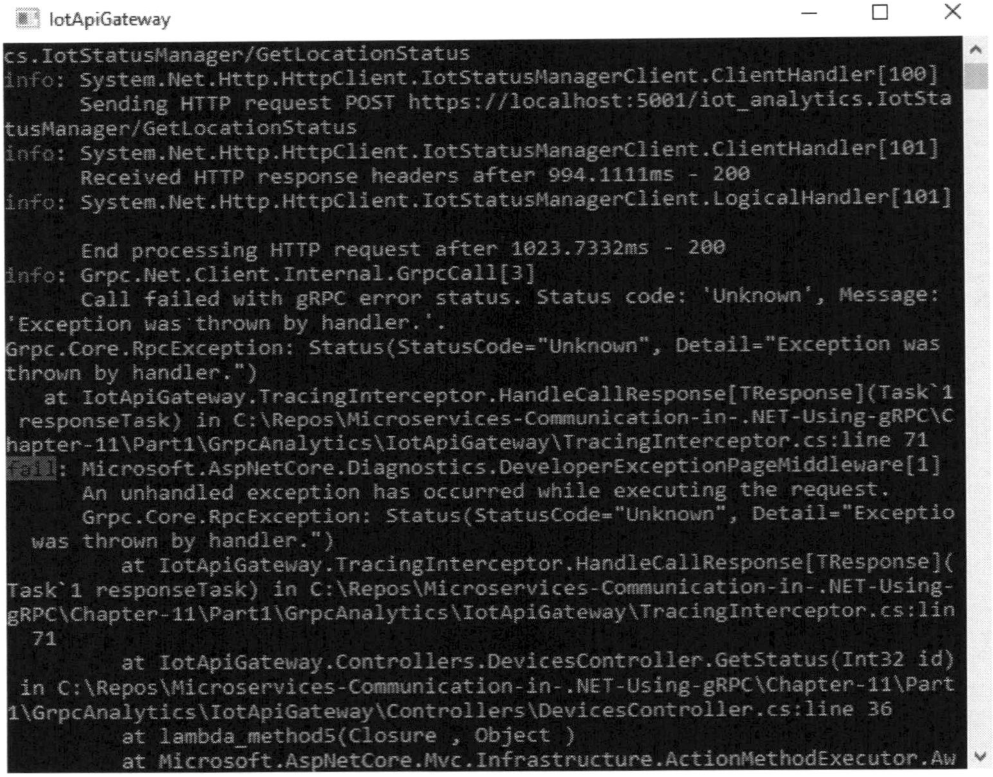

Figure 11.2 – An exception from the gRPC server being logged without the inner error message

In short, if we enable the `EnableDetailedErrors` option, the error message would be `Exception was thrown by handler. This call is not ready yet.` But if we disable this option, it would just be `Exception was thrown by handler.` This is how you can get detailed error information on the development environment while hiding it from the users in production.

But it's not only the client that allows you to use interceptors and extract inner error information from gRPC middleware – you can do this on the server too. And this is what we will do now.

Debugging gRPC server components inside a .NET application

An ASP.NET Core application with gRPC capabilities allows you to get gRPC middleware to output internal debugging information to the application console. It is switched off by default, but we can turn it on by applying a simple change to the application settings.

Likewise, the gRPC server application allows you to use interceptors, just like we did on the client. The server-side interceptor would inherit from the same base class as the client-side one, but it will have different methods defined in it that are only applicable to the server-side events:

1. To enable the debug log from the gRPC middleware to be printed in the console, you would need to open the `appsettings.json` file (and `appsettings.Development.json`, if you have it) in the `IotDeviceManager` project folder, locate the `LogLevel` section, and insert the following entry within it:

   ```
   "Grpc": "Debug"
   ```

2. Now, we will add our server-side interceptor. To do this, we will add the `ServerTracingInterceptor.cs` file to the root of the project and add the following content to it:

   ```
   using Grpc.Core;
   using Grpc.Core.Interceptors;
   using System;
   using System.Threading.Tasks;

   namespace IotDeviceManager
   {
       public class ServerTracingInterceptor :
           Interceptor
       {
       }
   }
   ```

3. We will then add the call handling methods to it one by one. First, we would add the following handler for a unary call:

```
public override async Task<TResponse> Unary
    ServerHandler<TRequest, TResponse>(TRequest request,
        ServerCallContext context, UnaryServerMethod
            <TRequest, TResponse> continuation)
{
    try
    {
        return await continuation(request, context);
    }
    catch (Exception ex)
    {
        Console.WriteLine(ex);
        throw;
    }
}
```

4. Then, we will add a handler for a *client-streaming call*:

```
public override async Task<TResponse> Client
    StreamingServerHandler<TRequest, TResponse>
        (IAsyncStreamReader<TRequest> requestStream,
            ServerCallContext context, ClientStreaming
                ServerMethod<TRequest, TResponse> continuation)
{
    try
    {
        return await continuation(requestStream,
            context);
    }
```

```
            catch (Exception ex)
            {
                Console.WriteLine(ex);
                throw;
            }
        }
```

5. Next, we will apply a handler for a *server-streaming call*:

```
        public override async Task ServerStreamingServer
          Handler<TRequest, TResponse>(TRequest request,
            IServerStreamWriter<TResponse> responseStream,
              ServerCallContext context, ServerStreaming
                ServerMethod<TRequest, TResponse>
                  continuation)
        {
            try
            {
                await continuation(request, responseStream,
                  context);
            }
            catch (Exception ex)
            {
                Console.WriteLine(ex);
                throw;
            }
        }
```

6. And finally, we will add a handler for a *bi-directional streaming call*:

   ```
   public override async Task DuplexStreamingServer
       Handler<TRequest, TResponse>(IAsyncStreamReader
           <TRequest> requestStream, IServerStreamWriter
               <TResponse> responseStream, ServerCallContext
                   context, DuplexStreamingServerMethod
                       <TRequest, TResponse> continuation)
   {
       try
       {
           await continuation(requestStream,
               responseStream, context);
       }
       catch (Exception ex)
       {
           Console.WriteLine(ex);
           throw;
       }
   }
   ```

7. We will now need to register our handler. To do this, navigate to either the Startup.cs file (for .NET 5) or the Program.cs file (for .NET 6) and then place the following statement inside of the AddGrpc call:

   ```
   options.Interceptors.Add<ServerTracingInterceptor>();
   ```

8. And we will also need to register the interceptor in our dependency injection container by adding the following statement, replacing services with builder.Services if you are on .NET 6:

   ```
   services.AddSingleton<ServerTracingInterceptor>();
   ```

Viewing the debug output on the gRPC server console

Now, if we launch both of our applications and call the working gRPC method from the **REST API** via the `Swagger` page, we will be able to see debugging information in our gRPC server console. For example, the following figure demonstrates that each message on the stream is being read individually. Those entries are clearly marked as `debug`:

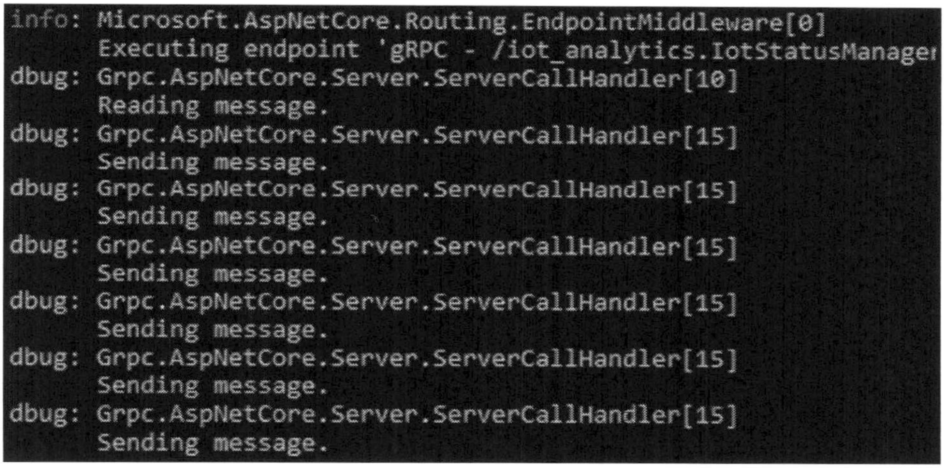

These are all of the changes we wanted to make on the server side. Let's now launch the applications and have a look at the changes in their behavior.

Figure 11.3 – The debug output from gRPC in the server-side log

As for the gRPC call that was deliberately designed to fail, we can see that we have been able to intercept the exception and print it to the console even before the default logger has picked it up, as can be seen in the following figure:

Figure 11.4 – The server-side interceptor intercepting the exception

And this is how you can use interceptors to handle all of your exceptions globally, instead of adding a `try/catch` block to every individual RPC implementation. If you have a handler for a specific RPC type, any exception that originates in any of the RPCs of that type would be caught in it.

So far, we have been logging our exceptions as plain messages directly in the console. This is acceptable for debugging, but if you want to release an application, you would need to use a proper logger. And this is what we will have a look at next.

Applying logs to gRPC

In software development, logging is a very important concept. Not only will it allow you to identify problems while you are developing your application, but it will also allow you to monitor an application that has been released into production. If anything happens to the application, you would be able to have a look in the logs to see what the application was doing and whether it produced any errors.

There are many different types of logs. You can write the log messages to the console, as we did. You can write them to a file. You can write them to **Azure Blob Storage** somewhere in the cloud. You can select whichever method suits you best.

In ASP.NET Core applications, it's good practice to use dependency injection for logging, just as you would for other service types. The places in your code that write messages to the log would call relevant methods on the logger interface. And it's up to you to configure what exact implementation of that interface those objects would receive. This is how you can swap loggers of different types depending on the environment. For example, in the development environment, logging to the console may be all you need. But in the production environment, you will need to send your logs where it would be easy to query them.

When you use configurable loggers, it's not only the output type that you can configure but also the log level. You can get the logger to only output messages if they are of a specific severity. We saw this when we configured an inbuilt gRPC logger to output debug messages to the console of the server application. Typically, the severity levels of a logger would be as follows; however, some variations may exist depending on what logger you are using:

- **Debug**: This is for detailed information on internal functionality that is only useful for debugging purposes.
- **Info**: This is for information about important events happening inside the application.
- **Warning**: This means some unexpected behavior was detected but it is not classed as an error.
- **Error**: This means an error occurred inside the application.
- **Critical/Failure**: This means a critical error has occurred, which prevented an important functionality from working.

These severity levels are shown from the lowest to the highest. If you set a log severity level in your application, it will log everything from that severity level and above, but it will ignore anything below it. For example, if you set it to **Debug**, everything will be logged. However, if you set it to **Warning**, the **Debug** and **Info** messages will be ignored. In other words, only the **Warning**, **Error**, and **Critical** messages will be logged.

With a custom logger, you can get gRPC middleware to write to your own log. But with interceptors in place, you can also associate custom log messages with gRPC calls. Now, we will go ahead and demonstrate how logging works both on the client and on the server.

Configuring a logger on the gRPC client

We will now configure a logging provider for the gRPC client application and will replace all console logs with proper logging:

1. In the `Program.cs` file of the `IotApiGateway` application, add the following block immediately after the call to `CreateDefaultBuilder`. If you are using a .NET 6 template, there will be no `ConfigureLogging` method, and the statements inside of it will be added to `builder.Logging`:

    ```
    .ConfigureLogging(logging =>
    {
        logging.ClearProviders();
        logging.AddConsole();
    })
    ```

2. We have now added a default console logger to our application. We are still logging into the console, but our output will now be annotated with a color-coded severity level. We will now be able to insert the logger into the places that need it via dependency injection. We will start with the `TracingInterceptor` class. To enable us to inject the logger, we will add the following `using` statement to it:

    ```
    using Microsoft.Extensions.Logging;
    ```

3. Then, we will replace the class constructor, while also adding the logger as a `private readonly` field:

   ```
   private readonly ILogger<TracingInterceptor> logger;
   
   public TracingInterceptor(ILogger<TracingInterceptor>
      logger)
   {
       this.logger = logger;
   }
   ```

4. Next, we will replace the content of the `LogException` method with the following:

   ```
   logger.LogError(ex, "gRPC error occured");
   ```

5. And we will add the following `private` method to the class:

   ```
   private void LogException(RpcException ex)
   {
       logger.LogError(ex, "gRPC error occured");
   }
   ```

6. Then, at the beginning of every call interceptor method, we will call this method like this:

   ```
   LogCall(context.Method);
   ```

7. We can also inject our custom logger directly into a gRPC client. I will demonstrate this by creating another standalone instance of the client inside the `DevicesController` class. First, we will need to add the following `using` statements to the class:

   ```
   using Grpc.Net.Client;
   using Microsoft.Extensions.Logging;
   ```

8. Then, we will add the following `private readonly` field:

   ```
   private readonly ILoggerFactory loggerFactory;
   ```

9. Then, we will replace the class controller with the following:

   ```
   public DevicesController(IotStatusManager.
     IotStatusManager Client client, ILoggerFactory
       loggerFactory)
   {
       this.client = client;
       this.loggerFactory = loggerFactory;
   }
   ```

10. Next, we will add the following method to use a single-use client. Please note how we are inserting our own logger into the gRPC channel:

    ```
    [HttpGet("single-use-client")]
    public async Task<IEnumerable<LocationStatusResponse>>
      GetAllStatusesSingleUseClient()
    {
        var option = new GrpcChannelOptions
        {
            LoggerFactory = loggerFactory
        };

        var channel = GrpcChannel.ForAddress
          ("https://localhost:5001", option);
        var localClient = new IotStatusManager.
          IotStatusManagerClient(channel);

        var response = new List<LocationStatusResponse>();
        using var call = localClient.GetAllStatuses(new
          Empty());
        while (await call.ResponseStream.MoveNext
          (CancellationToken.None))
        {
    ```

```
            response.Add(call.ResponseStream.Current);
    }

        return response;
}
```

11. Finally, to actually see the debug output in our console, we need to open the `appsetting.Development.json` file (or `appsettings.json`, if you don't have it) and set the `Default LogLevel` entry to `Debug`. We can also remove any other entries in that section.

Now, the internal middleware of the gRPC client will log its events into whichever place our logger has been configured to log them to. And we will be able to query those event messages the same way as we can query our own log entries.

Next, we will apply a logger to the server.

Applying a logger on the gRPC server

We will apply the same type of logger on the server as we did on the client. After that, we will look at the console output to see how it's different from what we had before:

1. We will first append the following call to the `CreateDefaultBuilder` call in the `Program.cs` file. We will need to modify these statements for .NET 6 implementations, as has been described previously:

    ```
    .ConfigureLogging(logging =>
    {
        logging.ClearProviders();
        logging.AddConsole();
    })
    ```

2. Next, we will open the `ServerTracingInterceptor.cs` file and add the following `using` statement to it:

    ```
    using Microsoft.Extensions.Logging;
    ```

3. We will then add the following `private readonly` field and constructor:

   ```
   private readonly ILogger<ServerTracingInterceptor>
       logger;

   public ServerTracingInterceptor(Ilogger
       <ServerTracingInterceptor> logger)
   {
       this.logger = logger;
   }
   ```

4. Next, we will replace the content of the `LogException` method with the following:

   ```
   logger.LogError(ex, "gRPC error occurred");
   ```

5. We will then add the following method:

   ```
   private void LogCall(ServerCallContext context)
   {
       logger.LogDebug($"gRPC call request:
           {context.GetHttpContext().Request.Path}");
   }
   ```

6. And we will also add a call to this method at the beginning of every handler method, like so:

   ```
   LogCall(context);
   ```

7. We will now need to open the `appsetting.Development.json` file (or `appsettings.json`, if you don't have it) and set the `Default LogLevel` entry to `Debug`. We can also remove any other entries in that section.

So, we are now ready to launch our applications and see what kind of output will be produced.

Testing our log output

We will launch both of our applications and the `Devices/single-use-client` endpoint from the `Swagger` page in the browser. If you then observe what happens in the console, you will see the full debug output coming from the gRPC client library, along with the custom debug message that we have added, as the following figure demonstrates:

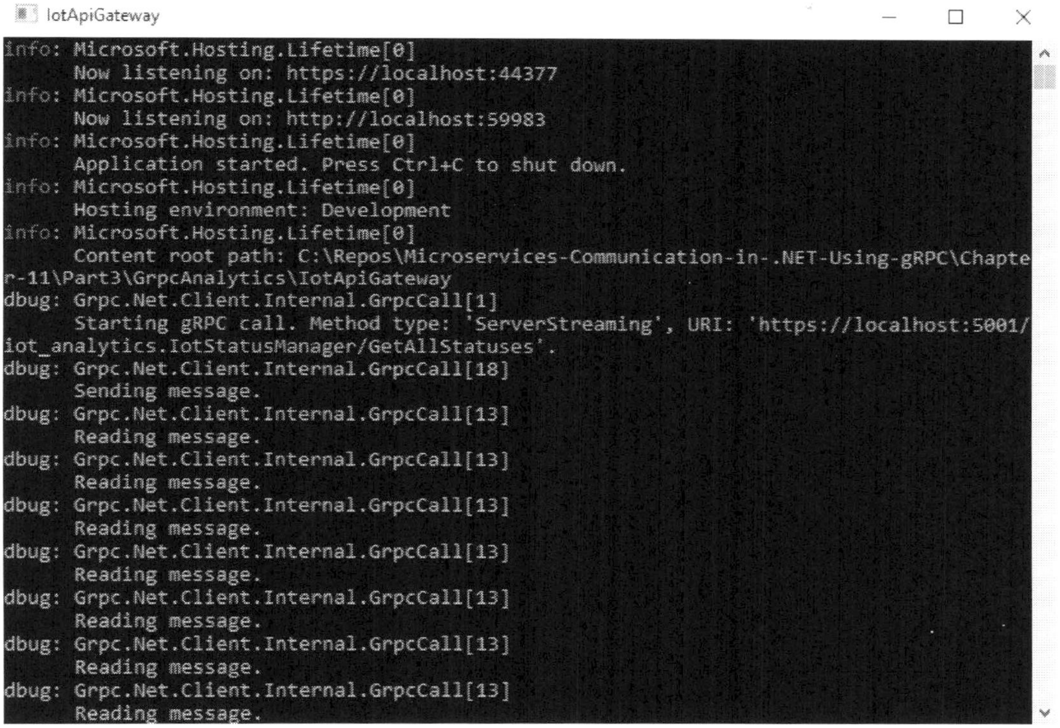

Figure 11.5 – The debug output in the console of the client application

You will see all of the debugging information in the server console too, as can be seen in the following figure:

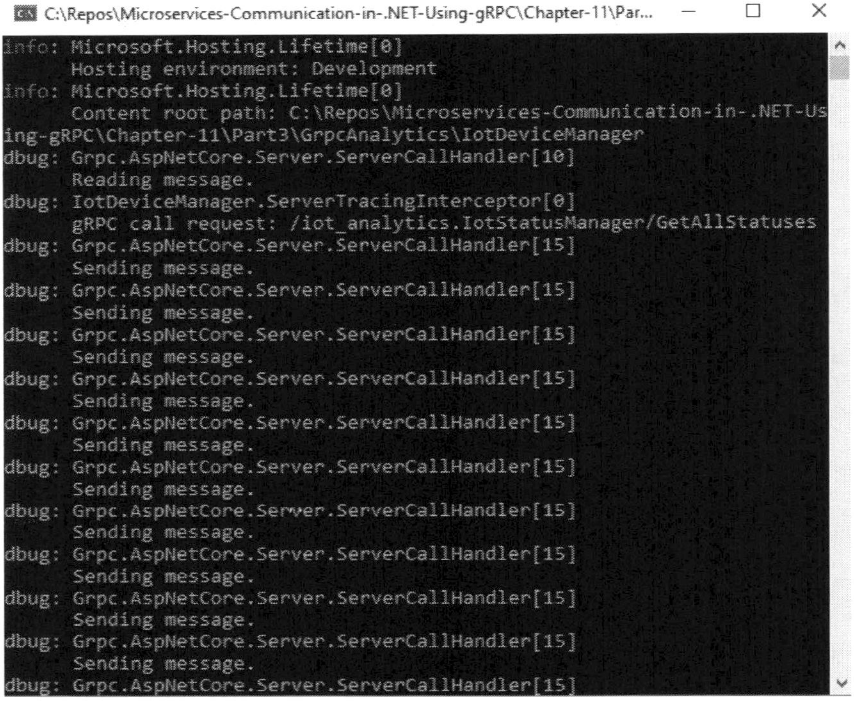

Figure 11.6 – The debug output in the gRPC server console

This logging is very useful to find out the exact point at which interceptor methods are being called. For example, it is apparent from the server console that gRPC reads the incoming message first, and only then calls the interceptor. And, of course, if you set the default log level to something other than Debug in your application's settings, you will not see any of this output in the console.

Now, we will call our `Devices/{id}` endpoint from the `Swagger` page to see how the exception is being logged. And, as can be seen in the following figure, our custom log message is now annotated with a color-coded severity level:

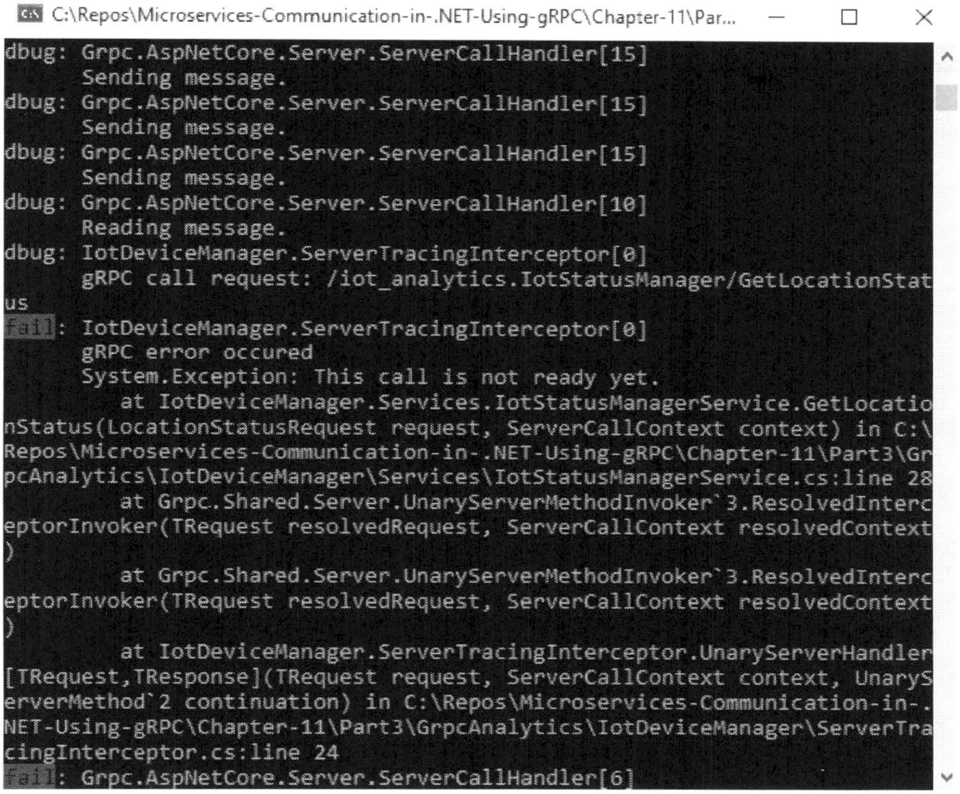

Figure 11.7 – The logged exception, annotated with a color-coded log severity level

This concludes our overview of applying logging to the gRPC functionality in an ASP.NET Core application. But logging individual messages is not the only way you can monitor your applications – you can also apply *metrics* to them. This is what we will have a look at next.

Applying metrics to gRPC

Metrics are fundamentally different from log messages. Typically, metrics would represent fairly basic measurements, such as counters, durations, and so on. But they can work nicely alongside logging. For example, if you are counting errors, you can see when they occur, and you can then query the logs for this specific period of time. Likewise, if you measure request latency, you can see when it goes above the acceptable threshold. And then you can query the logs produced within the same period to find out exactly what was happening inside your application.

Metrics are typically stored in a time series database, such as **Prometheus**, **InfluxDB**, or **TimescaleDB**. Because metrics represent simple data, they can be easily aggregated and plotted on a time series graph. For example, **Grafana** software was specifically designed to visualize metrics information. It can plot metrics on graphs similar to that in the following figure:

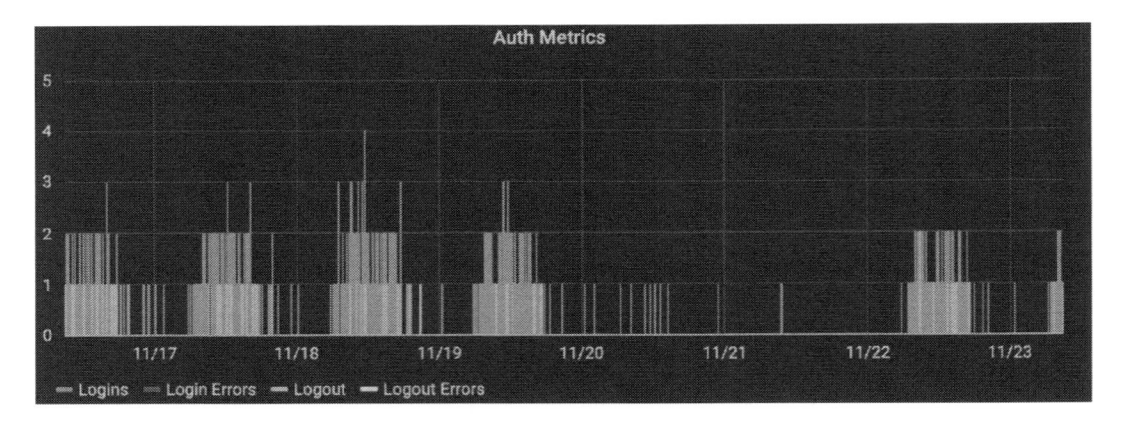

Figure 11.8 – An example of a Grafana metrics graph

There are several different metrics technologies available, but they usually follow either of the following principles:

- Collect the metrics and push them to a database endpoint at set intervals.
- Publish metrics via a URL endpoint and let a third-party probe collect them.

Typically, if you have a URL endpoint, it will be hidden behind a firewall, so only the specific piece of software that collects the metrics will be able to access it. This is done because some of the metric types get reset during every collection.

The metrics types that get reset during every collection include counters. These metrics typically just increment the number of actions within a specific period of time. And in the next cycle, we will only be concerned with how many actions occurred within the current cycle. So, none of the previously incremented values get passed into the next collection cycle. Some examples of counters may include the number of requests, the number of errors, and more.

A *gauge* is an example of a metric type that doesn't get reset. These metrics get incremented and decremented when various events occur. And we are always interested in their real-time value. A gauge can be used, for example, to indicate how many user sessions are currently active.

In our example, we will generate Prometheus-style metrics that will be collectible via a URL endpoint.

Configuring metrics on the gRPC server

We will need to add some NuGet packages to the class library that is shared between the client and the server. Then, we will need to add some relevant configurations to our gRPC server application:

1. First, open the `GrpcDependencies` project folder and execute the following commands to add the relevant NuGet dependencies:

   ```
   dotnet add GrpcDependencies.csproj package prometheus-net.AspNetCore
   dotnet add GrpcDependencies.csproj package prometheus-net.AspNetCore.Grpc
   ```

2. Next, we will open the `Startup.cs` file (or the `Program.cs` file if you are on .NET 6) of the `IotDeviceManager` project and add this `using` statement to it:

   ```
   using Prometheus;
   ```

3. Next, we will add the following statement immediately after `app.UseRouting`:

   ```
   app.UseGrpcMetrics();
   ```

   This will enable the automatic collection of metrics associated with gRPC.

4. Then, we will add the following statement inside the call to `app.UseEndpoints`:

   ```
   endpoints.MapMetrics();
   ```

This will add the default metrics collection endpoint to our application, which will be accessible via {base URL}/metrics.

With this setup, we are able to collect the default metrics from gRPC. But what if we wanted to apply some custom metrics too? Well, on our client, we will do exactly this.

Enabling metric collection on the gRPC client

On the gRPC client, we will do exactly the same metrics registration that we have done on the server. But this time, we will also apply some custom metrics:

1. In the `IotApiGateway` project, open the `Startup.cs` file (or `Program.cs` if you are on .NET 6) and add the following using statement to it:

   ```
   using Prometheus;
   ```

2. Then, add the following statement immediately after `app.UseRouting`:

   ```
   app.UseGrpcMetrics();
   ```

3. Next, add the following statement inside the call to `app.UseEndpoints`:

   ```
   endpoints.MapMetrics();
   ```

4. Now, let's open the `TracingInterceptor` class and add the following using statement on top of it:

   ```
   using Prometheus;
   ```

5. Then, add the following private fields to the class:

   ```
   private static readonly Counter
     BlockingUnaryCallsCount = Metrics.
       CreateCounter("blocking_unary_calls_count", "Count of
         blocking unary calls.");
   private static readonly Counter AsyncUnaryCallsCount =
     Metrics.CreateCounter("async_unary_calls_count",
       "Count of async unary calls.");
   private static readonly Counter
     ClientStreamingCallsCount = Metrics.
   CreateCounter("client_streaming_calls_count", "Count of
     client streaming calls.");
   private static readonly Counter
   ```

```
    ServerStreamingCallsCount = Metrics.
      CreateCounter("server_streaming_calls_count", "Count
        of server streaming calls.");
private static readonly Counter
  DuplexStreamingCallsCount = Metrics.
    CreateCounter("duplex_streaming_calls_count", "Count
      of bi-directional streaming calls.");
private static readonly Counter FailedGrpcCallsCount =
  Metrics.CreateCounter("failed_grpc_calls_count",
    "Count of failed gRPC calls.");
private static readonly Histogram GrpcCallDuration =
  Metrics.CreateHistogram("grpc_call_duration",
    "Durations of gRPC calls.");
```

6. We will then add the following line just before the `return` statement of every interceptor method. This will measure the duration of the call:

   ```
   using GrpcCallDuration.NewTimer();
   ```

7. And now we will increment our counters. First, insert the following line at the beginning of the `BlockingUnaryCall` method:

   ```
   BlockingUnaryCallsCount.Inc();
   ```

8. After this, insert the following line at the beginning of the `AsyncUnaryCall` method:

   ```
   AsyncUnaryCallsCount.Inc();
   ```

9. Then, insert the following line into the `AsyncClientStreamingCall` method:

   ```
   ClientStreamingCallsCount.Inc();
   ```

10. Afterward, insert the following line into the `AsyncServerStreamingCall` method:

    ```
    ServerStreamingCallsCount.Inc();
    ```

11. Finally, insert this line at the beginning of the `AsyncDuplexStreamingCall` method:

    ```
    DuplexStreamingCallsCount.Inc();
    ```

We have now enabled custom metrics in our gRPC client application. Now, we will launch our applications and see how the metrics get produced.

Viewing gRPC metrics

After launching both applications and triggering a number of gRPC calls via the `Swagger` page, we can evaluate what metrics get collected by our applications. If you then navigate to the `metrics` endpoint of the client application, which is accessible via the base URL from the `launchConfig.json` file followed by the `/metrics` path, you will see a combination of core metrics produced by the gRPC middleware alongside the custom metrics that we added. This can be seen in the following figure:

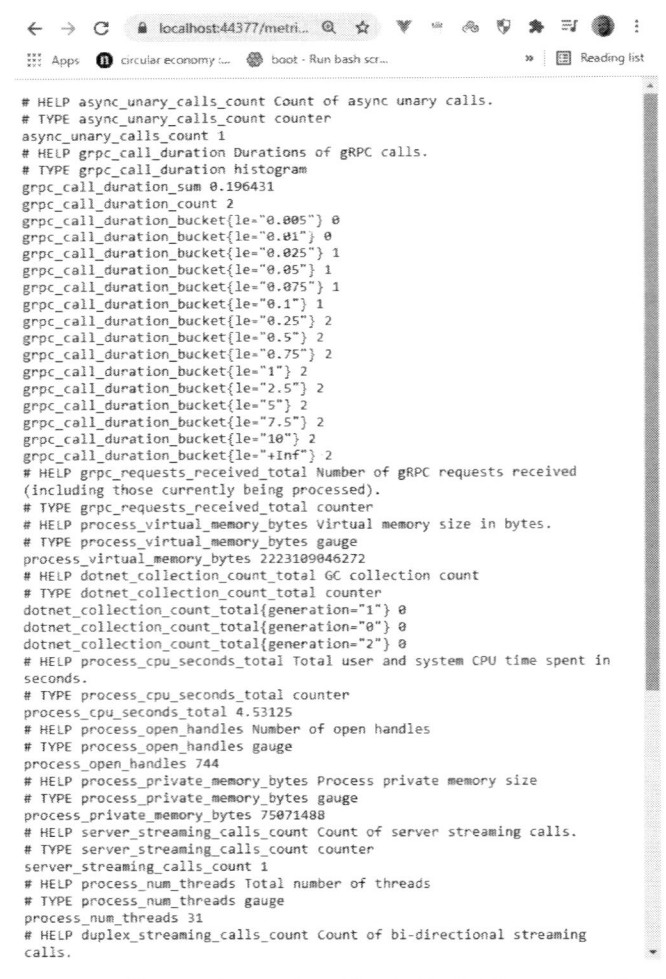

Figure 11.9 – The metrics produced by the IotApiGateway application

If you navigate to the `metrics` endpoint of the `IotDeviceManager` application, you will see a combination of metrics produced by ASP.NET Core system processes and gRPC middleware, as the following figure demonstrates:

```
# HELP process_num_threads Total number of threads
# TYPE process_num_threads gauge
process_num_threads 30
# HELP dotnet_total_memory_bytes Total known allocated memory
# TYPE dotnet_total_memory_bytes gauge
dotnet_total_memory_bytes 3240608
# HELP process_cpu_seconds_total Total user and system CPU
time spent in seconds.
# TYPE process_cpu_seconds_total counter
process_cpu_seconds_total 2.40625
# HELP process_working_set_bytes Process working set
# TYPE process_working_set_bytes gauge
process_working_set_bytes 63070208
# HELP dotnet_collection_count_total GC collection count
# TYPE dotnet_collection_count_total counter
dotnet_collection_count_total{generation="1"} 0
dotnet_collection_count_total{generation="2"} 0
dotnet_collection_count_total{generation="0"} 0
# HELP grpc_requests_received_total Number of gRPC requests
received (including those currently being processed).
# TYPE grpc_requests_received_total counter
grpc_requests_received_total{service="iot_analytics.IotStatus
Manager",method="GetLocationStatus"} 1
grpc_requests_received_total{service="iot_analytics.IotStatus
Manager",method="GetAllStatuses"} 2
# HELP process_virtual_memory_bytes Virtual memory size in
bytes.
# TYPE process_virtual_memory_bytes gauge
process_virtual_memory_bytes 2223084826624
# HELP process_private_memory_bytes Process private memory
size
# TYPE process_private_memory_bytes gauge
process_private_memory_bytes 64032768
# HELP process_open_handles Number of open handles
# TYPE process_open_handles gauge
process_open_handles 671
# HELP process_start_time_seconds Start time of the process
since unix epoch in seconds.
# TYPE process_start_time_seconds gauge
process_start_time_seconds 1637338017.166932
```

Figure 11.10 – The metrics generated by the IotDeviceManager application

Out of the box, the gRPC middleware generates only the most basic metrics. This is why it makes sense to generate your own to make application monitoring more targeted. The following metrics get produced by the gRPC client library:

- `total-calls`: Total calls
- `current-calls`: Current calls
- `calls-failed`: Total calls failed
- `calls-deadline-exceeded`: Total calls deadlines exceeded
- `messages-sent`: Total messages sent
- `messages-received`: Total messages received

The gRPC server library will generate the same metrics, but there is one additional metric that the server generates:

- `calls-unimplemented`: Total calls unimplemented

And this concludes the overview of gRPC metrics. Let's now summarize what we have learned in this chapter.

Summary

Congratulations! You have now reached the end of this book.

In this chapter, you have learned how to debug both client and server implementations of gRPC on .NET. You now know how to configure the server to return detailed errors to the client. Likewise, you have learned how to apply interceptors to both the client and the server to enable global error reporting and event logging.

You have also learned how to use loggers in gRPC on .NET. We have covered the fundamentals of configuring logging on ASP.NET Core, and you have learned how to insert these logs both into gRPC interceptors and internal gRPC processes.

We have also gone through the concept of applying metrics to your application. You now know that metrics consist of data that can be easily plotted on time series graphs to help you identify trends, and we explored counters and durations as an example of this.

You have been shown how to extract built-in metrics emitted by gRPC libraries on .NET. Also, we have gone over some examples of how to apply custom metrics where necessary.

We have now concluded this book on using gRPC on .NET to enable effective communication between microservices. We have covered all the fundamental topics of using gRPC on .NET, so you should now be fully equipped to use it in your own solutions. I hope you have enjoyed the journey and found the information in this book useful.

Questions

1. How do you get the gRPC server to send detailed error diagnostics to the client?

    A. You have to add your custom logic to the gRPC service implementation.

    B. You have to use interceptors.

    C. You can set the `EnableDetailedErrors` option on the server.

    D. You have to throw `RpcException`.

2. How do you enable the middleware of the gRPC service on ASP.NET Core to output debugging information?

    A. Set the `Grpc` entry in the logging settings to `Debug`.

    B. Attach event listeners to the gRPC assembly.

    C. Insert a custom logger into the gRPC channel.

    D. This is not possible.

3. What is the easiest way to determine if an error came from the inner gRPC middleware on ASP.NET Core?

    A. You can do this by looking up special keywords in the exception message.

    B. You can do this by checking if the exception is of the `RpcException` type.

    C. You can do this by checking if the exception is of the `HttpException` type.

    D. You can do this by looking up special numeric codes in the exception message.

4. How can you pass a shared application logger to the inner middleware of the gRPC client?

    A. You can do this by adding it to the interceptor.

    B. You can do this by adding an `ILoggerFactory` implementation to the `GrpcChannel` options.

    C. This is not possible.

    D. It's only possible when catching exceptions that originated from the inner middleware.

5. What is the difference between *logs* and *metrics*?

   A. Metrics provide detailed information, while logs only contain basic messages.

   B. Metrics consist of data that can be easily aggregated (for example, counters, gauges, histograms, and so on), while logs provide detailed information of each event.

   C. Metrics represent the metadata behind the log entries.

   D. Metrics are used strictly for measuring performance, while logs contain detailed event information.

Further reading

- *Logging and diagnostics in gRPC on .NET*: https://docs.microsoft.com/en-us/aspnet/core/grpc/diagnostics
- *Logging in .NET Core and ASP.NET Core*: https://docs.microsoft.com/en-us/aspnet/core/fundamentals/logging/
- An overview of Prometheus: https://prometheus.io/docs/introduction/overview/
- The Prometheus-net library documentation: https://github.com/prometheus-net/prometheus-net
- *30 best practices for logging at scale*: https://www.loggly.com/blog/30-best-practices-logging-scale/

Assessments

You'll find the answers to the questions in all chapters of the book in this section.

Chapter 1, Creating a Basic gRPC Application on ASP.NET Core

1. **B**. "You cannot have a Protobuf message definition without any fields" is an incorrect statement. You can have empty message definitions in Protobuf.

2. **A**. ASP.NET Core is a cross-platform framework that works on Windows, Linux, and macOS, so gRPC can be implemented on them.

3. **C**. You need to register each proto file by adding a Proto element to your project file. Then, you can specify the `GrpcServices` attribute inside it, which can be set to `Server`, `Client`, or `Both`. It's set to `Both` by default, so if you don't specify this attribute, both client and the server code will be generated. If you specify `Server`, only the server code will be generated. So, either `Both` or `Server` is a valid option for generating server code.

4. **C**. To get gRPC to work inside an ASP.NET Core server app, you need to add all the required references to the project. Then, for each gRPC service definition, you need to create a C# class that overrides from a class that was auto-generated from a proto file, representing one of its service definitions. Then, you need to register gRPC capabilities inside the `Startup` class. Finally, you need to register your custom C# implementation of a gRPC service as an endpoint in your middleware.

5. **C**. The client-side code that's generated with both the synchronous and asynchronous versions of each RPC is defined in a proto file. The name of the synchronous function is the same as the one defined in the proto file. The asynchronous version has the same name but with `Async` at the end.

Chapter 2, When gRPC Is the Best Tool and When It Isn't

1. **B.** Yes, by utilizing streaming
2. **C.** Yes, but only by using async/await on the client
3. **A.** Server-streaming calls
4. **B.** Yes, both on the server and the client
5. **D.** Calls from the server to the client without a request from the client

Chapter 3, Protobuf – the Communication Protocol of gRPC

1. **A.** `long`.
2. **A.** The `int32` data type will have only as many bytes allocated as necessary, while `fixed32` always occupies 4 bytes.
3. **C.** Create a repeated field of a message that itself has a repeated field.
4. **B.** The original field gets unset, and the new field gets set.
5. **D.** You can keep the original Proto file that is specified in the `import` directive but get it to import the new proto file via the `import public` directive.

Chapter 4, Performance Best Practices for Using gRPC on .NET

1. **B.** Channel.
2. **C.** 100.
3. **A.** Apply the `stream` keyword before the `rpc` keyword.
4. **D.** Apply the `stream` keyword before both the input and output parameters.
5. **A.** When you intend to modify the original byte array after this call.

Chapter 5, Applying Versioning to the gRPC API

1. **C.** It will not affect the functionality.
2. **B.** `sfixed32` and `int32`.
3. **A.** It will be populated with the default value on the client.

4. **D.** Use the `reserved` keyword, followed by the sequence numbers of the removed fields.
5. **C.** Using separate Protobuf definitions for separate API versions.

Chapter 6, Scaling a gRPC Application

1. **C.** To split a large number of requests between multiple instances of the application.
2. **C.** By getting the list of individual endpoint addresses and calling them directly.
3. **D.** All of the above.
4. **A.** The client connects to the proxy endpoint and the proxy redirects it to individual application instances.
5. **C.** Support for HTTP/2.

Chapter 7, Using Different Call Types Supported by gRPC

1. **B.** Yes
2. **C.** Only when you make asynchronous calls
3. **A.** Unknown
4. **C.** To set a strict timeout on the call's completion time
5. **D.** By using the `stream` keyword between the request and response message definitions

Chapter 8, Using Well-Known Types to Make Protobuf More Handy

1. **C.** `google/protobuf/wrappers.proto`.
2. **C.** `Fixed64Value`.
3. **A.** `Duration` is equivalent to `DateTimeOffset`.
4. **D.** All of the above.
5. **C.** The `Any` data type cannot store strings.

Chapter 9, Securing gRPC Endpoints in Your ASP.NET Core Application with SSL/TLS

1. **B.** TLS.
2. **C.** With this configuration, insecure requests are routed to HTTP/1.1.
3. **D.** All of the above.
4. **D.** A `.pfx` file stores the complete certificate chain, while a `.crt` file only stores the public key and any related metadata.
5. **A.** For authentication.

Chapter 10, Applying Authentication and Authorization to gRPC Endpoints

1. **B.** To ensure that the user is who they claim to be.
2. **A.** To ensure that only users with specific permissions can access the application.
3. **C.** OpenID Connect is used for authentication.
4. **C.** Header, payload, and signature.
5. **B.** Any JSON field in the payload.

Chapter 11, Using Logging, Metrics, and Debugging in gRPC on .NET

1. **C.** You can set the `EnableDetailedErrors` option on the server.
2. **A.** Set the `Grpc` entry in the logging settings to `Debug`.
3. **B.** By checking if the exception is of the `RpcException` type.
4. **B.** By adding the `IloggerFactory` implementation to the `GrpcChannel` options.
5. **B.** Metrics consist of data that can be easily aggregated (counters, gauges, histograms, and so on), while logs provide detailed information about each event.

Index

Symbols

.NET application
  gRPC client components, debugging 407
  gRPC server components,
    debugging 423-426
.NET CLI
  used, for initializing ASP.NET
    Core project 15, 16
.NET SDK
  downloading 11
  reference link 11

A

Any and Value data types
  adding, to gRPC server 308-312
Any and Value fields
  populating, from gRPC client 313-316
Any data type 122
API versioning
  factoring, at design stage 190, 191
API versioning strategy
  need for 168
API versioning strategy demonstration
  client communication to server,
    verifying 174-176
  gRPC client application,
    creating 172, 173
  gRPC client logic,
    implementing 173, 174
  server application, creating 169, 170
  server-side gRPC components,
    implementing 170, 171
application
  launching 83-88, 301, 302
  running 298
Application Layer Protocol
  Negotiation (ALPN) 39
application programming
  interface (API) 44
ASP.NET Core
  about 413
  self-signed certificate,
    applying on 345-348
ASP.NET Core project
  gRPC server, component
    adding to 16-19
  initializing, via IDE 12-15
  initializing, via .NET CLI 15, 16
asynchronous gRPC endpoints
  testing 72-74

authenticated users
  gRPC endpoints, restricting to 378
authentication backend
  IdentityServer4, configuring 366-369
  login redirect, forcing on web
    application 372-378
  OAuth flow 364-366
  OpenID Connect 364-366
  setting up 363, 364
  SSO clients, adding 369-371
  SSO roles, adding 369-371
  SSO users, adding 369-371
auto-generated code
  examining, for wrapper fields 287-292
Azure Blob Storage 429

B

bi-directional streaming
  enabling 274
  server-side components,
    enabling for 275, 276
bi-directional streaming call
  about 94
  client-side implementation,
    adding of 276-278
  performance, monitoring 158, 159
bi-directional streaming RPC
  setting up 155-158
binary fields
  adding, to Protobuf 160-163
binary payloads
  using, to decrease data's size 160
Blazor WebAssembly 74

C

C# code
  generating, with proto file 29
certificate authentication
  applying, on gRPC client 351
  applying, on gRPC server 351
  enabling, on gRPC client 355
  gRPC server, configuring 352-354
  testing 356-358
certification authority (CA) 324
claims 365
client
  building, for gRPC communication 333
  communication to server,
    verifying 174-176
  data, streaming from 265
  Protobuf definitions,
    exposing to 330-333
client and server application
  gRPC dependencies, sharing
    between 37, 38
  proto file, sharing between 34
  shared class library, creating 34, 35
  shared gRPC component, adding
    to class library 35-37
client application
  backend components, adding 206-210
  controller, adding 210-212
  creating 205
  dependencies, registering 212, 213
  gRPC dependencies, using in 260-262
  Protobuf definition, modifying 178, 179
  setting up 137-146
client certificates 324, 325

Index 453

client logic
  adding 336-338
client-side call implementations
  applying 255-260
client-side implementation
  adding, of bi-directional
    streaming call 276-278
client-side load balancing, with gRPC
  about 216
  components, enabling 217, 218
  custom load balancers, creating 224-230
  DNS resolver, enabling for
    load balancer 219-221
  NuGet package, updating 216, 217
  resolvers, creating 224-230
  static resolver, using for load
    balancer 221-223
client-streaming call
  about 94
  adding, to server application 266, 267
client-streaming gRPC call
  client logic, adding for 267, 268
client types
  performance, comparing 146-149
collections
  using, in Protobuf 109
collections types
  map fields 111-113
  repeated fields 109-111
command-line interface (CLI) 45
Command Prompt (CMD) 62
comments
  creating, in Protobuf 95
connection concurrency
  configuring, on gRPC client 149-152
cross-origin resource sharing (CORS) 74
cryptographic keys 324

custom certificates
  testing 348-350

D

data
  streaming, from client 265
dates
  using, in Protobuf 299, 300
debug output
  viewing, on gRPC server
    console 427, 428
default development certificate
  trusting 340, 341
dependency injection (DI) 54, 388
dependency inversion principle (DIP) 57
digital certificate 324
dotnet CLI 323
duration
  adding, to server 300, 301

E

Empty data type
  adding, to server-side
    application 303-305
empty messages
  exchanging 303
Empty object
  applying, on client 305-307
enum data type 104, 105
external enum definition 105

F

Fedora 340

454   Index

G

Google Remote Procedure Calls (gRPC)
  about 4, 5
  application, testing 189
  benefits 5
  for asynchronous communication 64
  for microservices 44, 45
  logs, applying to 429
  metrics, applying to 438, 439
  not best for browser 74
  old and unused fields, deprecating 187
  on ASP.NET Core 6
  supporting, RPC types 92
  unary calls, making on 242
  using, in ASP.NET Core application 6
Grafana software 438
gRPC call
  making, to versioned endpoint 195, 196
  streaming procedure, testing 278, 279
gRPC channels
  using, reasons 132, 133
gRPC client
  adding, with additional debugging
    capabilities 413-420
  Any and Value fields, populating
    from 313-316
  building 251-254
  certificate authentication, applying 351
  certificate authentication, enabling 355
  changes, applying 397-401
  changes, applying to 301, 302
  component, adding to 24-27
  component, applying to code 27-29
  configuring, for asynchronous
    communication 68-71
  configuring, for unencrypted
    communication 323

  configuring, via service
    reference 334, 335
  connection concurrency,
    configuring on 149-152
  functionality, enabling 386-391
  keep-alive pings, setting up on 153, 154
  logs, configuring 430-433
  manually, configuring 335, 336
  metrics collection, enabling 440-442
  project, initializing 23
  server-streaming call, making
    from 273, 274
  setting up 22, 296, 297
gRPC client application
  creating 172, 173
gRPC client components
  debugging, in .NET application 407
  gRPC client, adding with additional
    debugging capabilities 413-420
  gRPC error information,
    viewing 421, 422
  gRPC service application,
    adding 409-413
  gRPC service application, adding to
    display detailed errors 409-413
  shared gRPC dependencies,
    setting up 407-409
gRPC client implementation
    version-specific
  creating 194
gRPC client logic
  implementing 173, 174
gRPC communication
  client, building 333
gRPC component
  code, adding to 20-22
gRPC dependencies
  using, in client application 260-262

gRPC endpoints
  authorization rules, applying
      to different 395, 396
  restricting, to authenticated users 378
  restricting, to authorized users 391, 392
gRPC, for asynchronous communication
  client-streaming gRPC
      endpoints, adding 64-67
  server-streaming gRPC
      endpoints, adding 64-67
gRPC, for microservices
  distributed application, launching 62, 63
  REST API gateway service,
      setting up 55-62
  shared dependencies, setting up 45-48
  solution, setting up 45-48
  status manager microservice,
      setting up 49-54
gRPC metrics
  viewing 442-444
gRPC, not best for browser
  Blazor WebAssembly gRPC
      client, setting up 74-78
  gRPC server, modifying to
      enable gRPC-Web 79, 80
  gRPC-Web application, launching 80
gRPC server
  Any and Value data types,
      adding to 308-312
  ASP.NET Core project,
      initializing via IDE 12-15
  certificate authentication, applying 351
  client-side configuration, modifying 39
  component, adding to ASP.
      NET Core project 16-19
  configuring, for certificate
      authentication 352-354

  configuring, for unencrypted
      communication 323
  logs, applying 433, 434
  metrics, configuring 439, 440
  running, on Mac 39
  server-side component, configuring 39
  setting up 11, 380-385
gRPC server application
  logic, adding to 292-294
  setting up 286, 287
gRPC server components
  debugging, in .NET application 423-426
gRPC service application
  adding, to display detailed
      errors 409-413
  setting up 325-329

H

HTTPS redirection
  testing 348-350
HyperText Markup Language
    (HTML) 55, 374
Hypertext Transfer Protocol
    Secure (HTTPS) 323

I

IdentityServer4
  configuring 366-369
InfluxDB 438
integer data types
  fixed32 and fixed64 data types 100
  int32 and int64 data types 97
  sfixed32 and sfixed64 data types 101
  sint32 and sint64 data types 99
  uint32 and uint64 data types 98

integrated development
    environment (IDE)
  about 6
  setting up 6
  setting up, on Linux 10, 11
  setting up, on Mac 9, 10
  setting up, on Windows 7-9
  used, for initializing ASP.NET
    Core project 12-15
interceptors 414
internal enum definition 105
Internet of Things (IoT) 409

J

JavaScript Object Notation (JSON) 45
JWT
  SSO provider, configuring to insert
    role claim into 392-394

K

keep-alive pings
  setting up, on gRPC client 153, 154
Kestrel 339

L

library
  adding, with Protobuf
    dependencies 133-135
Linux
  IDE, setting up 10, 11
load balancing 200
load balancing, fundamental principles
  application, running 214-216
  client application, creating 205

multiple instances, creating of
    server-side application 204, 205
  shared gRPC dependencies,
    adding 201, 202
  shared library, creating for server-side
    application instances 202, 203
logger level
  critical/failure 429
  debug 429
  error 429
  info 429
  warning 429
logic
  adding, to gRPC server
    application 292-294
logs
  applying, on gRPC server 433, 434
  applying, to gRPC 429
  configuring, on gRPC client 430-433
  output, testing 435-437
loosely typed fields
  using, in Protobuf message 308

M

Mac
  gRPC server, running 39
  IDE, setting up 9, 10
map field collections 111-113
metrics
  applying, to gRPC 438, 439
  collection, enabling on gRPC
    client 440-442
  configuring, on gRPC server 439, 440
Model-View-Controller (MVC) 372
multi-factor authentication (MFA) 363

Index 457

multiple instances
  creating, of server-side
    application 204, 205
multiple Protobuf versions
  adding, to server application 191, 192
  server application, allowing
    to use 192, 193

N

native Protobuf data types
  enum 104, 105
  integer data types 97
  non-integer numeric data types 101
  non-numeric data types 102
  reviewing 95, 96
nested messages 106-108
non-integer numeric types
  double data types 102
  float data type 102
non-numeric data types
  bool 103
  bytes 103
  string 103
NuGet package 121
nullable data types
  using, in Protobuf 285, 286

O

OAuth flow 364-366
oneof keyword
  making, communication
    efficient 114-117
one-time access code (OTAC) 364
OpenID Connect 364-366

OpenSSL
  used, for creating self-signed
    certificate on Unix 344
option keyword
  field-level options 119, 120
  global-level options 117
  message-level options 118
  used, for customizing behavior 117

P

PowerShell
  used, for creating self-signed
    certificate on Windows 341-343
Prometheus 438
Protobuf
  about 409
  binary fields, adding to 160-163
  collections, using 109
  comments, creating 95
  dates, using 299, 300
  nullable data types, using 285, 286
  server-streaming RPC, adding to 269
  special keywords, using 113
  supporting, RPC types 93, 94
Protobuf definitions
  exposing, to clients 330-333
  modified applications,
    launching 179-181
  modifying, in client application 178, 179
  modifying, in server
    application 177, 178
  modifying, on client side 183
  server-side implementations,
    creating of 245-250
Protobuf dependencies
  used, for adding library 133-135

Protobuf message
　loosely typed fields, using 308
Protobuf versions
　existing fields, modification
　　avoidance 181, 182
Protobuf versions modification
　avoiding, demonstration
　applications, launching 183, 184
　applications, re-launching 186, 187
　changes, making to client
　　application 185
　Protobuf definitions, modifying
　　on client side 183
Protocol Buffer (Protobuf) 5, 44, 378
proto files
　auto-generated code, storing 30, 31
　external proto packages,
　　importing 121, 122
　internal proto files, referencing 122-124
　Protobuf namespaces, modifying 31-34
　referencing 121
　representing, sequence
　　numbers 176, 177
　sharing, between client and
　　server application 34
　used, for generating C# code 29
　using, as relays 124, 125
Proxy load balancing, with gRPC
　about 230
　HTTP/2 proxy, launching 233, 234
　web application, building 230-233
public key certificate 324

R

real-time communication (RTC) 44
remote procedure calls
　(RPCs) 47, 52, 324, 409

repeated field collections 109-111
REpresentational State Transfer (REST) 44
reserved keyword
　applying, to server-side Protobuf
　　interface 187, 188
Rider
　download link 7
RPC types
　Protobuf, supporting 93, 94
　supported, by gRPC 92

S

self-signed certificate
　applying, on ASP.NET Core 345-348
　creating 339
　creating, on Unix with OpenSSL 344
　creating, on Windows with
　　PowerShell 341-343
　trusting 339
sequence numbers
　in proto file 176, 177
server
　duration, adding to 300, 301
　timestamp, adding to 300, 301
server application
　client-streaming call, adding to 266, 267
　creating 169, 170
　Protobuf definition, modifying 177, 178
　setting up 133
server certificates 323, 324
server project
　shared Protobuf library, adding to 135
server-side application
　Empty data type, adding to 303-305
　multiple instances, creating 204, 205
server-side application instances
　shared library, creating 202, 203

server-side components
  enabling, for bi-directional streaming 275, 276
server-side gRPC components
  implementing 136, 137, 170, 171
server-side implementations
  creating, of Protobuf definitions 245-250
server-side Protobuf interface
  reserved keyword, applying to 187, 188
server-streaming call
  making, from gRPC client 273, 274
  setting up, on server side 270-273
server-streaming RPC
  adding, to Protobuf 269
service reference
  gRPC client, configuring via 334, 335
shared dependencies
  setting up 294, 295
shared gRPC dependencies
  adding 201, 202
  setting up 243-245, 378-380, 407-409
shared library
  creating, for server-side application instances 202, 203
shared Protobuf library
  adding, to server project 135
SignalR 81
SignalR application
  setting up 81-83
SignalR client
  adding 83-88
single connection and multiple connections
  performance, comparing 152, 153
software development kit (SDK) 6
special keywords
  oneof keyword 114-117

option keyword, used for customizing behavior 117
  using, in Protobuf 113
SSO clients
  adding 369-371
SSO provider
  configuring, to insert role claim into JWT 392-394
SSO roles
  adding 369-371
SSO users
  adding 369-371
streams
  reading, from server 269
subject 340

T

thumbprint 340
TimescaleDB 438
timestamp
  adding, to server 300, 301
TLS certificates
  basics 339
  client certificates 324, 325
  role 323
  server certificates 323, 324
Transport Layer Security (TLS) 132
  removing, on HTTP/1.1 329, 330
  removing, on HTTP/2 329, 330

U

Ubuntu 340
unary call endpoints
  testing 262-265
unary calls
  making, on gRPC 242

Uniform Resource Locator (URL) 58, 367
Unix
　self-signed certificate, creating
　　with OpenSSL 344
user interface (UI) 55

V

Visual Studio 2019
　download link 8
Visual Studio Code
　reference link 9

W

web application
　login redirect, forcing on 372-378
Windows
　IDE, setting up 7-9
　self-signed certificate, creating
　　with PowerShell 341-343
wrapper fields
　auto-generated code, examining
　　for 287-292

Packt>

Packt.com

Subscribe to our online digital library for full access to over 7,000 books and videos, as well as industry leading tools to help you plan your personal development and advance your career. For more information, please visit our website.

Why subscribe?

- Spend less time learning and more time coding with practical eBooks and Videos from over 4,000 industry professionals
- Improve your learning with Skill Plans built especially for you
- Get a free eBook or video every month
- Fully searchable for easy access to vital information
- Copy and paste, print, and bookmark content

Did you know that Packt offers eBook versions of every book published, with PDF and ePub files available? You can upgrade to the eBook version at packt.com and as a print book customer, you are entitled to a discount on the eBook copy. Get in touch with us at customercare@packtpub.com for more details.

At www.packt.com, you can also read a collection of free technical articles, sign up for a range of free newsletters, and receive exclusive discounts and offers on Packt books and eBooks.

Other Books You May Enjoy

If you enjoyed this book, you may be interested in these other books by Packt:

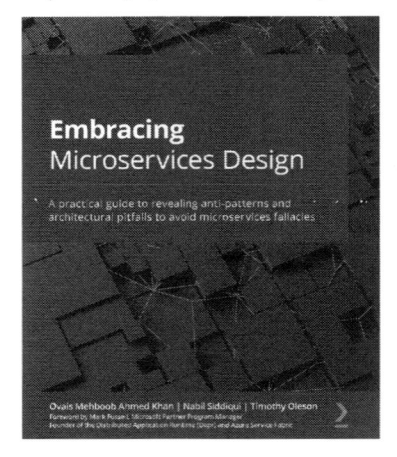

Embracing Microservices Design
Ovais Mehboob Ahmed Khan, Nabil Siddiqui, Timothy Oleson
ISBN: 978-1-80181-838-4

- Discover the responsibilities of different individuals involved in a microservices initiative
- Avoid the common mistakes in architecting microservices for scalability and resiliency
- Understand the importance of domain-driven design when developing microservices
- Identify the common pitfalls involved in migrating monolithic applications to microservices
- Explore communication strategies, along with their potential drawbacks and alternatives
- Discover the importance of adopting governance, security, and monitoring
- Understand the role of CI/CD and testing

Practical Microservices with Dapr and .NET

Davide Bedin

ISBN: 978-1-80056-837-2

- Use Dapr to create services, invoking them directly and via pub/sub
- Discover best practices for working with microservice architectures
- Leverage the actor model to orchestrate data and behavior
- Use Azure Kubernetes Service to deploy a sample application
- Monitor Dapr applications using Zipkin, Prometheus, and Grafana
- Scale and load test Dapr applications on Kubernetes

Packt is searching for authors like you

If you're interested in becoming an author for Packt, please visit `authors.packtpub.com` and apply today. We have worked with thousands of developers and tech professionals, just like you, to help them share their insight with the global tech community. You can make a general application, apply for a specific hot topic that we are recruiting an author for, or submit your own idea.

Share Your Thoughts

Now you've finished *Microservices Communication in .NET Using gRPC*, we'd love to hear your thoughts! Scan the QR code below to go straight to the Amazon review page for this book and share your feedback or leave a review on the site that you purchased it from.

https://packt.link/r/1-803-23643-4

Your review is important to us and the tech community and will help us make sure we're delivering excellent quality content.

Made in the USA
Las Vegas, NV
09 February 2022